The

A Guide ...
John Bi...

Published in Scotland by Andes
4th Edition, 2015

THE ANDES - A GUIDE FOR CLIMBERS

4th Edition, 2015
3rd Edition, 2005
2nd Edition, 1999
1st Edition published as 'The High Andes', 1996

PUBLISHER

Published by Andes, 37a St Andrew Street, Castle Douglas, Kirkcudbrightshire, DG7 1EN, SCOTLAND. Phone 00 44 1556 503929. Email john@andes.org.uk

Printed by Alba Printers, Dumfries, SCOTLAND
Trade distribution by Cordee, Leicester, ENGLAND

BRITISH LIBRARY CATALOGUING IN PUBLICATION DATA

A catalogue record for this book is available from the British Library
ISBN (paperback) 978-0-9536087-4-4
ISBN (E-book) 978-0-9536087-5-1

DISCLAIMER

Mountaineering is an inherently dangerous activity. The author accepts no liability whatsoever for any loss, injury or inconvenience resulting from the use of this guide. Mountain conditions, especially routes on glaciers, can vary dramatically from one season to the next; always seek local advice on current conditions.

Front cover photo: **Volcan Llaima from the peak of Sierra Nevada, Lakes District, Chile.**
Front cover inset photos, L to R: **Climbing the S face of Palomani, Bolivia. The summit of Cazadero, Argentina. Skiing Volcan Lanin, Argentina.**
Rear cover photo: **The author on Mururata, Cordillera Real, Bolivia.**
Rear cover inset photo: **The central peaks of the Cordillera Huayhuash, Peru.**
Title page photo: **Espeletia flowers on Pan de Azucar, Sierra Nevada del Cocuy, Colombia.**
Opposite photo: **Parinacota and Pomerape from high on Volcan Guallatiri, Cordillera Occidental, Chile.**

CONTENTS

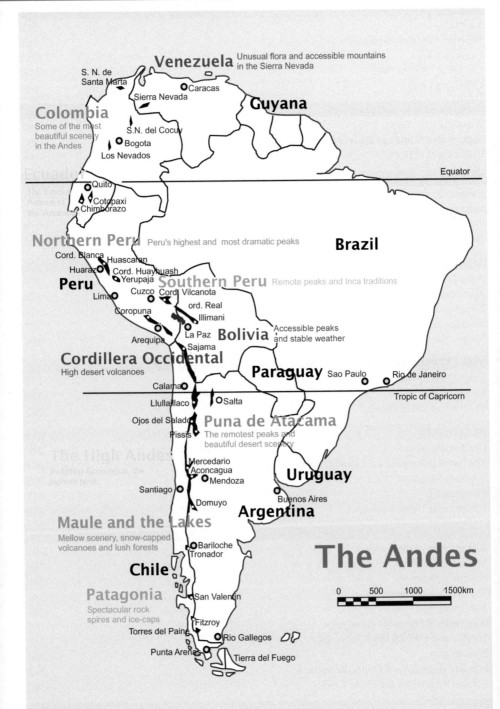

Venezuela Unusual flora and accessible mountains in the Sierra Nevada

S. N. de Santa Marta

Caracas

Sierra Nevada

Guyana

Colombia
Some of the most beautiful scenery in the Andes

S.N. del Cocuy

Bogota

Los Nevados

Equator

Ecuador
The famous Avenue of the Volcanoes

Quito

Cotopaxi
Chimborazo

Northern Peru Peru's highest and most dramatic peaks

Cord. Blanca

Huascaran

Huaraz

Cord. Huayhuash

Brazil

Yerupaja

Peru

Cuzco

Southern Peru Remote peaks and Inca traditions

Cord. Vilcanota

Lima

ord. Real

Coropuna

Illimani

Arequipa

La Paz

Bolivia

Accessible peaks and stable weather

Sajama

Cordillera Occidental
High desert volcanoes

Paraguay Sao Paulo

Rio de Janeiro

Calama

Llullaillaco

Salta

Tropic of Capricorn

Ojos del Salado

Pissis

Puna de Atacama
The remotest peaks and beautiful desert scenery

The High Andes
Including Aconcagua, the highest peak

Mercedario
Aconcagua

Uruguay

Mendoza

Santiago

Domuyo

Buenos Aires

Argentina

Maule and the Lakes
Mellow scenery, snow-capped volcanoes and lush forests

Bariloche
Tronador

The Andes

Chile

Patagonia
Spectacular rock spires and ice-caps

San Valentin

0   500   1000   1500km

Fitzroy

Torres del Paine

Rio Gallegos

Punta Arenas

Tierra del Fuego

INTRODUCTION

The Andes are one of the world's greatest mountain ranges, second in height to only the Himalaya. The range extends the full length of the west coast of South America, often rising straight from the Pacific. Much of the range consists of an upland plateau from 3000-4500m high with scattered mountain ranges and isolated volcanoes rising to over 6000m.

The Andes offer mountaineers an experience that is in many ways half way between the European Alps and the Himalaya. In terms of height, difficulty and access the Andes fall somewhere between the relatively civilised mountains of Europe or North America and the wild peaks of Asia. They are an ideal destination for experienced mountaineers aspiring to greater heights or remoter peaks without the bureaucratic problems of a Himalayan expedition.

Within the Andes you can choose from a complete range of mountaineering experiences. There is something for everyone, from easily ascended volcanoes to desperate ice faces. Peru and Bolivia are countries still steeped in the culture of the Incas, but Chile and Argentina are modern nations very much like a part of Europe. The Andes of Venezuela and Ecuador rise from tropical forests, those of northern Chile rise above the driest desert in the world, those of Patagonia from some of the wettest temperate forest and largest temperate ice-caps in the world.

SCOPE OF THIS GUIDEBOOK

This fourth edition of this guidebook covers the whole of the Andes range. Included are details of how to climb all the major 6000m peaks and the most accessible and popular 5000m peaks, plus information on a selection of the most popular and prominent of the mountains of Patagonia. This edition has extended coverage of the ski-mountaineering opportunities in the range.

This guidebook is intended for the average mountaineer who wants to climb some prominent peaks by moderately interesting routes. In most cases only the easiest ascent route for any peak is described in detail, with other harder routes being described where they are climbed relatively often. The majority of more technically difficult routes are not detailed, but references to where this information can be obtained are given.

This guidebook assumes a basic ability to route find in high mountain terrain and as a consequence fairly brief descriptions are given. A mixture of maps, photos and sketches are used to illustrate the routes as appropriate.

Information is as reliable and accurate as possible. But because this guidebook is a compilation of information from many hundreds of sources and contains over ten thousand items of information complete reliability cannot be guaranteed. Personal experience or the knowledge of close friends was used for the vast majority of the routes described. Other reliable sources have been used for most of the other routes. However to produce a comprehensive guidebook some peaks have been included for which information is scanty or even non-existent; in these cases the best guess at routes and access has been made from visual inspection of the peak and/or maps. One such route description from our second edition was used successfully to make the first ascent of an unclimbed 6000m peak! Hopefully this edition will also inspire further exploration - please let me know what you find out there.

This guidebook is intended to be used along with a good travel guide to the countries concerned which will provide more general information about public transport, hotels, etc.

USING THIS GUIDEBOOK

The mountains of the Andes are described from North to South, split as logically as possible into ranges and areas. Where necessary a secondary West to East order has been used. There is an introduction for each chapter detailing general conditions. The facilities (particularly those useful to climbers) in base towns and cities are described where appropriate.

TIMES

Timings (in days) given in the peak heading bars are for a return trip to climb the one named peak approaching from the base camp or town listed in the access section. Climbing several summits in one area will obviously save on approach times. All these times assume climbers are already acclimatised to the height of the normal base camp/area and are reasonably fit. Because acclimatisation is so crucial at altitude and varies so much between individuals it is difficult to please everyone. For example high but easy and accessible peaks like Pissis and Ojos del Salado, which are both given 4 days in this guidebook, have been climbed from sea level in 24 hours by exceptionally acclimatised people, but each could take a week or more for slower acclimatisers.

The compromise times used in this book should be seen as **'reasonable minimums'** for fit people with a week or more acclimatisation. These allow for no delays in travelling to the mountain and as much use of 4x4 vehicles as possible. They allow for no route finding problems and no spare days for bad weather, but do allow for further days of acclimatisation high on the mountains if these are thought to be necessary for the average climber. To be sure of a successful ascent it would be wise to plan an extra day or more to allow for bad weather, route finding problems or other unforeseen circumstances. Extra days will almost certainly be needed if relying on public transport.

Times given within the text descriptions (usually in hours) are for ascent only.

NAMES

Names used in the descriptions are normally those used on the recommended map, however there are several spelling systems for translating Quechua and Aymará names via Spanish into English. The system used is the one (consistent with the Spanish alphabet) where HU is used for W and either C, QU or Q is used for K. Alternative names and spellings are given if they are in common use. Translations are given where these are available but many mountain names are not translatable.

HEIGHTS

When possible the height used by the relevant national military mapping agency (IGM) is given. In the case of border peaks on the Chile-Argentina frontier precedence has normally been given to the Chilean heights as their surveys are more recent, more extensive and probably more accurate.

Other sources include Neate's reference book and the 2000 SRTM (Shuttle Radar Topography Mission) data. The SRTM data has been used to improve the heights of some previously poorly surveyed peaks. The accuracy of any given SRTM height measurement is about 10m. However the data cannot give accurate peak heights since it is based on a 3 second (c.100m) grid. Although the data is fairly useful in areas of low relief (e.g. Puna de Atacama) it is of limited use in areas of high relief like Peru and Bolivia and in areas of extreme relief there is usually no data. In general the SRTM data has only been used in two circumstances 1. When it gives a higher height than accepted surveys (this gives at least a new minimum value for the height) or 2. When it indicates a height that is at least 50m lower than the IGM or previously accepted height. I have received much help over the years on interpreting this data from both Jonathan de Ferranti and Eberhard Jurgalski.

GRADES

For each peak standard UIAA alpine grades (F, PD, AD, D, TD, ED, ED+) are given for the easiest ascent route in 'normal' conditions. These alpine grades should be found consistent in any one range but because of the variety of information sources used there may be some variation between ranges. Split grades denote either some uncertainty or mountains where conditions are variable. The AD+, PD-, PD+ etc. grades are not used in the main headings as it is felt they give an impression of a precise grade which does not reflect the very variable conditions in the Andes. N/K denotes that the grade is not known - an estimate of the difficulty will be found in the text.

There is a wide range in the overall physical effort needed to climb the different peaks, (e.g. Huayna Potosi is for this reason an 'easier' peak than Aconcagua). No attempt has been made to grade for this, but a glance at the height and number of days needed to climb a peak will give an indication of the effort needed to reach the summit.

An indication will be given in the text whether a route is mainly on rock, snow, glacier or on mixed ground. Pitch grades are occasionally given using the standard UIAA system (I, II, III, IV for rock and 40°, 50° etc. for snow or ice). For a few of the harder rock routes in Patagonia, French grades F6b, F7a etc., are given. A rough comparison table for the lower rock grades is given here.

UIAA	British	USA	French	Australian
I	Mod	5.2	1	-
II	Diff	5.3	2	11
III	V. Diff	5.4	3	12
IV	4a-4b	5.5	4	13
V	4b-4c	5.6	5	14-15
VI-	5a	5.7	5	16-17
VI	5a/b	5.8	6a	18
VI+	5b	5.9	6a+	19

GRADE VARIATION

The grades given in this guidebook are for good normal conditions and any variation is likely to make routes harder. These effects are particularly severe in El Niño - La Niña cycles; e.g. in summer 1997 the Peruvian ranges were swamped by large quantities of snow and many routes became dangerous, then in summer 1998 there was virtually no snow and many peaks in Peru and Bolivia were bare and icy (and therefore harder). The single biggest factor in these variations is probably the quantity of off-season (winter) snowfall, but the weather patterns of the last month or two will also have an effect. The climatic disturbances of El Niño may also have been to blame for the irregularities experienced in 2002-03 and again in 2010. The simple and sensible solution is to obtain recent local reports on the condition of a peak before attempting it.

PHOTO-DIAGRAMS AND SKETCHES

Arrows indicate the approximate line of a route. Where a route is not shown on a mountain it is for one of two reasons. Either it is because the mountain is climbable with the same degree of difficulty pretty much anywhere, or because the route is on the other side of the peak and a photo of the route was unavailable.

GPS CO-ORDINATES

At altitude, when skiing and particularly on the Patagonina ice-caps the use of a GPS is highly recommended. With a record of vehicle and camp locations and other major route finding waypoints a safe descent should be possible even in bad weather.

Whenever possible GPS co-ordinates have been given for base camps, road-ends, higher camps and summits. These have been given to the nearest arc-second, i.e. about 30m on the ground. As with the sketch maps these are intended to help with general orientation only and are not intended to be a complete set of navigational waypoints. Some peaks may require as many as twenty waypoints.

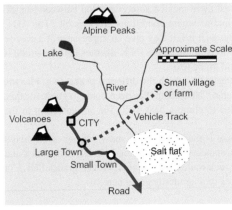

**AREA & COUNTRY
MAPS**

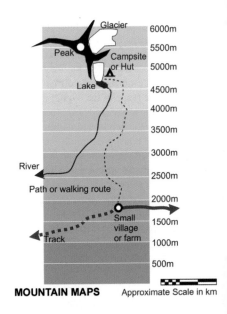

MOUNTAIN MAPS   Approximate Scale in km

MAPS

The sketch maps are intended to help with general orientation only and are of very limited use for navigation. Not all mountains, rivers, glaciers etc. are shown. A vehicle track may only be passable to a high wheel base 4x4, a walking route does not imply that there is actually a path and a campsite sign does not imply that there is any water (there certainly won't be any hot showers!). Please refer to the text for more specific information about route conditions and facilities. All maps have north at the top.

WHERE TO GO AND WHEN TO CLIMB

Please refer to the table on the following page which contains a quick reference summary of the different areas including the best times to travel, reliability of weather and conditions in the best season, type of peaks and accessibility. Unfortunately, at the best times of year peaks will be busiest.

When choosing where and when to climb in the Andes one of the main considerations is the climate. Two main factors determine the best climbing seasons in South America. South of the Tropic of Capricorn (the Puna de Atacama and anywhere further south) the best time to climb is the southern hemisphere summer. In the tropical areas covering the remainder of the Andes the best time to climb is in the dry season. This occurs in the hemisphere winter for the area concerned - i.e. around July for Peru and Bolivia and around January for Colombia and Venezuela. There are two transition zones with less well defined seasons - Ecuador is wet most of the year and the Atacama area is dry all year.

There is quite a wide variation in the reliability of weather and climbing conditions in the different areas of the Andes and the areas have been given a star rating * to *****, in the table to give a general indication of the reliability of climate and conditions.

Two other main considerations are whether you wish to climb easier volcanic peaks or harder 'alpine' peaks (see table on opposite page), and what sort of cultural experience you want. If you want to see llamas, traditional costumes and bustling markets then go to either Peru, Bolivia or Ecuador. If you want a modern country and infrastructure with big air conditioned buses and supermarkets go to Chile or Argentina. Venezuela and Colombia are about half way between these two extremes. This advice should be treated only as a useful generalisation as all the Andean countries are a bit of a mixture between the old and the modern.

AREA	BEST SEASON	RELIABILITY in season	TYPE OF PEAKS	HEIGHT OF PEAKS	ACCESS
VENEZUELA	NDJFM				
Sierra Nevada		***	Alpine	4500-5000m	Easy
COLOMBIA	DJFM				
Santa Marta & Cocuy		***	Alpine	4500-5700m	Medium-Diff.
Los Nevados		****	Volcanic	4500-5500m	Easy
ECUADOR	JJASONDJF				
Volcanoes		**	Volcanic	4500-6300m	Easy
NORTHERN PERU	MJJAS				
Cordillera Blanca		***	Alpine	5000-6800m	Easy-Medium
Cordillera Huayhuash		***	Alpine	5000-6700m	Easy-Medium
Cordillera Central		****	Alpine	5000-5900m	
SOUTHERN PERU	AMJJAS				
Cordillera Urubamba		**	Alpine	5000-6300m	Medium-Diff.
Cordillera Vilcanota		***	Alpine	5000-6400m	Medium
BOLIVIA	MJJAS				
Cordillera Apolobamba		****	Alpine	5000-6100m	Medium
Cordillera Real		*****	Alpine	5000-6500m	Easy-Medium
Cordillera Lipez		*****	Volcanic	5500-6000m	Medium-Diff.
PERU.BOLIVIA.CHILE	AMJJASON				
Cordillera Occidental		*****	Volcanic	5500-6600m	Easy-Medium
ARGENTINA	SONDJF				
Chañi and Cachi		***	Alpine & Volcanic	5500-6400m	Medium-Diff.
ARGENTINA/CHILE	NDJFMA				
Puna de Atacama		****	Volcanic	5500-6900m	Medium-Diff.
ARGENTINA/CHILE	DJFM				
Agua Negra		****	Alpine &	5000-6400m	Easy-Medium
Aconcagua and area		***	Volcanic	5000-7000m	Easy-Medium
ARGENTINA/CHILE	NDJFMA				
Maule		****	Alpine &	3000-4700m	Easy-Medium
Lakes District		***	Volcanic	2000-3500m	Easy
ARGENTINA/CHILE	NDJFM				
Chaiten and Aisen		**	Alpine,	2000-4000m	Medium-Diff.
Southern Patagonia		*	Volcanic	2000-3500m	Easy-Difficult
Tierra del Fuego		*	& Icecap	1500-2500m	Very Difficult

GENERAL ADVICE FOR TRAVEL TO THE ANDES

VISAS

At present visas are not needed by most US, Canadian and EU citizens for short stays (up to 60-90 days) in any of the Andean nations. French, Spanish and Portuguese citizens need visas for some countries and Australian, New Zealand and South African citizens will need visas for most countries. Other nationalities may need visas for some or all of the countries. The requirements are sure to change so it is best to check with the embassy in your country.

FLYING TO SOUTH AMERICA

Further details of how to get to each area of the Andes are given in each chapter. There are only a few direct flights from London to South America, e.g. Bogota, Buenos Aires and Sao Paulo.

From Europe and the UK there are three main options. 1. Fly with a European airline via a European capital e.g. Air France via Paris, KLM via Amsterdam, Iberia via Madrid or Lufthansa via Frankfurt. This is often the best option in terms of service and economy. 2. Fly with either United, Delta or American Airlines, via the USA. This is usually a bit more expensive and a bit more time consuming, but there are daily schedules to almost all big South American cities. 3. Fly with a South American airline, either direct or via some other South American city. These flights are usually cheap but the service (with the exception of LAN) is not always reliable. However, you may get a very good deal with a South American airline if you also need an internal flight in the country concerned. In Europe, the cities of Madrid, Paris, Milan and Frankfurt are well served by LAN and Avianca.

From North America the cheapest option is often to fly via Miami or Atlanta which are served daily by all the major national South American airlines and United, Delta and American Airlines. These three also have daily services from New York, LA and Houston to many South American capital cities. There are also some direct flights from Toronto on Air Canada.

From Australasia there are LAN and Qantas flights direct across the Pacific from Australia and NZ to Santiago, or flights often on US airlines, via Los Angeles and/or Miami.

Arequipa airport and El Misti

BUDGET AND MONEY

South America is not particularly cheap. On the whole it is not expensive either, but expect to pay prices similar to those in the US or Europe for many services, particularly in the more expensive countries like Chile and Argentina. Public transport everywhere is usually a bargain. If you need to save money you can use budget hotels and eat from street stalls, but on an expedition with specific mountaineering objectives these measures may be counterproductive if you end up ill or have all your equipment stolen.

An average expedition staying in clean and secure hotels, eating in reasonable restaurants and using some hired transport and mule services will work out at about $40-50 per person per day, noticeably more for ascents of Aconcagua, trips to Patagonia or very remote Puna mountains, slightly less in Ecuador and Bolivia. Budgeting carefully and always using public transport you could easily half this figure to under $20 per day and still have a great time. Money should be taken in a mixture of US$ cash and credit or ATM cards (VISA and MasterCard are good, AMEX is not). Cash dollars can be used readily in some countries and may get you a better exchange rate in countries like Argentina and Venezuela with poor financial systems. They can almost always be used if you're stuck for local currency. Credit cards are accepted widely by larger businesses in all cities. ATM's are now widely available in all the main cities.

SPANISH

The more Spanish you speak the easier your trip to South America will be. Some knowledge is **essential**. Only in Cuzco and a few other tourist centres is much English spoken. Out in the mountains there is **no chance** of finding anyone who speaks English. It is a fact that people with poor Spanish are more likely to be charged inflated prices by muleteers, drivers etc. and if things go wrong you could have real trouble getting help. You have to be able to negotiate and make yourself understood to get good prices, good service and to make friends. Make the effort.

ACCOMMODATION

This guidebook does not list recommended hotels in the access towns and cities, for which a regular travel guide will be necessary. Hotel accommodation varies enormously in price and you don't always get what you pay for, but in most cities you'll get a comfortable bed, with private bathroom for about $30-40 for a double room. Accommodation down to about $10 per couple can still be very reasonable, but budget accommodation tends to be shabby, insecure and with poor service. Camping is not a safe or practical option in South American cities.

Hosteria ACA, Cachi, Argentina

SECURITY

The author has witnessed only one theft in twenty years of travelling in South America. The overwhelming majority of Andean people are friendly and honest. You should not be paranoid about rip-offs, just sensible. Don't get drunk, wander into poor parts of towns, walk down quiet alleys or walk alone at night. If you do any of these things you may get ripped off - if you do more than one you are almost sure to be ripped off.

Be especially careful in markets and at bus stations and anywhere that there are lots of tourists. Take taxis round town if arriving late or leaving early or if you've lots of luggage. Never put a bag down in the street. Keep your camera hidden.

Armed robbery and banditry, often linked to the drug trade, does occur occasionally in Colombia, Peru, Ecuador and Bolivia but is extremely rare in Chile and Argentina. This is not a problem that should stop you going to South America but take local advice about the current situation and avoid any dangerous areas.

In the mountains there are occasional problems with organised theft of large amounts of climbing kit. The Ecuador peaks, the Q. Ishinca and Alpamayo base camps in the Cordillera Blanca, and the Zongo pass in Bolivia are the areas which have been troubled in the past. In these areas you should consider hiring someone locally to watch your tent. This will only cost a few $ per day and can be better than an insurance policy. In Chile and Argentina and all quieter valleys in Peru and Bolivia, or above the snow-line anywhere, there is virtually no problem.

A more minor problem in some areas is petty theft and pilfering, so never leave any belongings outside your tent when it is unattended during the day or at any time overnight.

The South American Explorers Club is a good source of up to date information on security issues. Visit their offices in Quito, Cuzco or Lima or their website at www.saexplorers.org

ACCLIMATISATION AND ALTITUDE

Anyone travelling to the Andes must make themselves aware of the symptoms of altitude sickness, both mild and severe. Read and absorb a good textbook such as 'Medicine for Mountaineering' by Wilkerson, or better still read one specifically on Altitude Illness such as 'Altitude Illness' by Bezruchka
Generally speaking at least a week should be spent over 4000m before contemplating an ascent to over 6000m. A good idea is to first spend three or four nights at 3000m - many towns and base camp areas in the Andes are at this height. Then spend three or four nights at 4000m, then think about moving to 5000m for two nights and only then attempt a 6000m peak. Spend the first day at each new camp resting. If anyone in the group is ill at any time stop ascending and if the illness persists for more than 24 hours, descend to your last camp. While your body gets used to the altitude you can climb lower peaks, trek, or enjoy the cultural and archaeological sites that are numerous in the Andean nations.
After camping for an extended time at 5000m or higher it is a very good idea to descend (e.g. to 3000m) to allow your body time to rest and recover.
Fitness, particularly heart and lung fitness, certainly helps at high altitude. However, fit people are just as susceptible to altitude illness because they can do so much more. Experience suggests that the best method to avoid altitude illness and acclimatisation problems is to be fit before arrival then 'underexercise' (i.e. do considerably less climbing than you would on a trip to the Alps or Rockies). This means some time sitting around in camps, so bring a good book, a pack of cards, or a pair of binoculars.

HEALTH

For most of the countries concerned the following immunisations are advisable: Tetanus, Typhoid, Polio and Hepatitis. The vaccine for Cholera is generally not very effective. Yellow fever and Malaria precautions are only needed if you will be below 2500m in forest areas i.e. Venezuela, Colombia, Ecuador and the Amazon side of the Andes in Peru and Bolivia.
Remember the problems of cold injury, both frostbite and hypothermia. Above 6000m it is difficult for the body to generate enough heat to keep warm, so good insulating layers are necessary. Peripheral circulation is impaired at altitude so good gloves and warm boots and socks are essential.
Biting insects are very rare in the mountains, but there are very occasionally problems in Peru with black flies or Patagonia with mosquitos. Dogs can be a nuisance, particularly in Peru and Bolivia - to chase them away throw a stone towards them or pretend to throw a stone - some dogs will even back off if you just pretend to pick up a stone!
Water will need to be purified at all busier camps and in all villages and settlements. Boiling for two minutes is by far the best, cheapest and safest method. Iodine or Chlorine Dioxide tablets or drops are probably the next best method for mountaineers. Specially designed water filters may clog up rapidly in silty glacial water, are hard work to pump at altitude and are heavier to carry.

A basic medical kit should be carried with plasters, blister kit, needle and thread, spare lip-salve, scissors, strong safety pins and drugs for diarrhoea, headaches, coughs and perhaps altitude sickness. On more remote trips consider antibiotics, antihistamine, strong painkillers, eye-drops and an anti-inflammatory. Carry some bits and pieces for general repairs to non-body parts, e.g. strong cord, plastic zip-ties, wire, strong tape and superglue.

Use sunglasses!

PLANNING A MOUNTAINEERING EXPEDITION

PEAK FEES AND PERMITS

Peak fees are currently only required for Aconcagua in Argentina, costing up to $1000 per person for foreigners to climb in high season (but they do provide helicopter evacuation from base-camps and keep the mountain tidy!). There are national park fees in many other areas, but these are usually only a few $ per person per day at most.

Several areas of the Andes now require you to hire a local guide, including all big peaks in Ecuador, some areas of Colombia and (intermittently) the Cordillera Blanca in Peru. These kind of regulations are often rescinded after a few years because of the damage they do to the local tourist economy.

BORDER PEAKS

Problems climbing border peaks are very rare. Officially you need permission to climb a border peak in Chile, but this only ever seems to be enforced around Ojos del Salado and Parinacota. For details of how to obtain permission see under that mountain. In all border areas you should obviously travel with your passport at all times. If approaching by road you may need to officially leave the country at the last border post and/or you may need to leave your passport with the border guards.

MAPS

Alpenvereinskarte of Austria publish a few maps of the Cordillera Blanca and Cordillera Real. Otherwise the best maps are generally those published by the Instituto Geografico Militar (IGM) of the country concerned. These are usually only available from the head office in the capital city, but some are now available from www.omnimap.com Although they are useful, these maps are generally poor. Rivers, roads and snowfields are often incorrectly marked and such features should not be relied on.

In the UK it's worth trying The Map Shop (01684 593146) or Stanford's (0207 836 1321) to obtain these and other maps.

The addresses for the national IGM's are as follows. Opening hours vary - it is best to go in the morning. Take local currency and your passport.

Colombia	Agustin Codazzi, Carrera 30 # 48-51, Bogota
Ecuador	Seniergues E4-676 y Gral. T. Paz y Miño, El Dorado, Quito
Peru	Av. Aramburu 1190, San Isidro, Lima (best to take a taxi)
Bolivia	"Catastro Rural" - a small door on Calle Juan XXIII, near the junction of Calle Rodriguez and Calle Murillo, or the main office at Estado Mayor General, Av. Saavedra 2303, La Paz.
Chile	Dieciocho 369, Santiago (Metro station Los Heroes)
Argentina	Cabildo 381, Casilla 1426, (Subte D to Ministero Carranza), Buenos Aires

OTHER GUIDEBOOKS & ONLINE SOURCES

As already stated, this guidebook does not include general travel information which can be obtained in many other guidebooks and online. Other climbing and walking guidebooks and online resources which might be useful are mentioned in each area introduction and in the bibliography. Although a bit dated 'Mountaineering in the Andes' by Jill Neate is a very useful book for tracking down journal references to obscure peaks and routes.

OBTAINING LOCAL INFORMATION

In Huaraz, La Paz, Mendoza and a few other major mountaineering centres it will be fairly easy to obtain up to date information on the peaks you wish to climb and any access problems. Just ask in the many agencies, the better ones are listed in this book. In places like Cuzco you may be able to get some useful information from the numerous trekking agencies. In most other areas of the Andes there is very little known about the mountains and mountaineering. However even in the smallest and most remote village the locals will know the surrounding area very well and asking around can often produce valuable information on access routes and conditions as well as valuable help in organising transport, accommodation and mules. The author has never been stuck for long in South America; if you speak Spanish and are not in too much of a hurry the people in out of the way areas are invariably very friendly and helpful. When arriving in an unknown village and needing help with transport or accommodation try asking in shops or cafes, in the town hall or at the police station.

PUBLIC TRANSPORT

Most peaks in this guidebook can be reached reasonably well using public transport. Exceptions are mainly in the Cordillera Occidental of Chile and Bolivia and the Puna de Atacama as well as some of the more remote Peruvian and Bolivian ranges. Good areas to go to if you'll only be using public transport are the Cordillera Blanca, the Cordillera Real, the Sajama area of the Cordillera Occidental, the Mendoza and Santiago area and the Chilean Lake District.

The abbreviation (PT) in the text denotes the last place on the way to a mountain which can be reached easily and regularly using public transport. Specific details of transport connections are not given as they change so frequently and are available in general travel guidebooks.

HIRED TRANSPORT

In many areas the best way to reach the mountain is by hiring a jeep or similar vehicle with or without a driver. This is relatively expensive but very convenient. Expect to pay about $100 for a driver to drop you off 100km away (and another $100 to get picked up). Some spoken Spanish and prior knowledge of the condition of your road are very useful to help negotiate a good price. With a brief written contract and a written record of collection dates and times most drivers are very reliable. To find a driver in an unfamiliar town try either tourist agencies, car hire companies or mountaineering organisations. For short journeys on good roads just use local taxi drivers.

CAR AND 4x4 RENTAL

If climbing many peaks in a few days in one area, e.g. the Andean Lake District, the Puna de Atacama or Cordillera Occidental, then a self drive vehicle rental may be the most economical and practical option. This is particularly the case in Chile and Argentina where driving standards and road standards are relatively high and wages to pay a driver are also higher. While an ordinary car is adequate for the Lake District a 4x4 camioneta (pick-up truck) will be more useful for the Puna and Occidental.

On the way back from Licancabur

MOUNTAIN RESCUE

With the exception of Aconcagua there is little reliable and well organised mountain rescue in South America and on most of the higher peaks rescue from an outside agency before you die is extremely unlikely, if not impossible. Expeditions should be self sufficient and able to effect their own rescues. In a few areas where mountaineering is better developed e.g. Cordillera Blanca, Cordillera Real, Ecuador, there is an informal system in place where the local 'guides' will assist any mountaineers in trouble but this is likely to take several days at least.

PACK ANIMALS

In many parts of the Andes llamas, donkeys, mules or horses are available to assist with establishing a base camp. They will always come with an arriero (muleteer) to look after them. They are particularly useful for approaching more technical or more remote peaks, where the weight of kit is much higher, but be sure that you can speak a little Spanish to the arriero. Try to get a written contract (though the arriero may not be able to write) and agreed price in writing. Booking through an agency in a town or city will put up the price but eliminate some of the hassles.

Llamas can carry about 20kg, donkeys can carry 40kg, mules and horses up to 60kg. One arriero can look after 3 or 4 animals. Prices are extremely variable. Normal rates in Peru and Bolivia are about $10-15 per day per animal and about $20 per day per arriero, but in Argentina and particularly on Aconcagua expect to pay $30-50 per animal per day and $50 or more per day for an arriero. In Peru and Bolivia you will be expected to feed and shelter your arriero, or at least to pay for his food.

In popular areas you can often just turn up and leave with your donkeys and arriero, sometimes within ½h! In less popular areas you may need to wait one or two days for animals to be gathered and locals to organise themselves to help you. In these kind of places it may be worth trying to organise animals in advance.

PORTERS

Porters are readily available in only a few parts of the Andes, such as on the busier peaks of Peru and Bolivia. In many places either the standard of living is too high for this to be attractive work or there is not the mountaineering infrastructure to support these jobs. Rates in Peru and Bolivia are about $20 per man per day, up to $50 for porters with glacier skills in the Cordillera Blanca. On Aconcagua and around Chalten in Patagonia porters are also available but will cost over $100 per man per day.

Do not use children as porters - giving a 20kg sack to a child to carry is not something any civilised person should attempt to justify as fair labour.

MOUNTAIN GUIDES

There are mountain guides available in a few of the main mountaineering centres in South America, particularly Quito, Huaraz, La Paz, Mendoza and Bariloche. They don't always have the same level of training and experience as a European or North American guide, even the IFMGA approved guides in Peru. In some areas some 'qualified' guides are genuinely dangerous. Try to get good reports from someone who knows the guide well and don't expect to get a cheap guide without compromising your safety.

However there are some good guides, and they can be well worth hiring as they have extensive knowledge of the local mountains and conditions, are good at organising arrieros, porters etc. and are very fit at altitude. Rates are from about $100 per day in Peru and Bolivia, depending on the size of the group and the technical difficulty of the climb. In Argentina expect to pay $200 or more per day.

CAMPING FOOD

Most cities have a reasonably good supermarket somewhere - see individual city information entries. The quality and variety of food is very good in Chile and Colombia. Supermarkets are less good in Argentina, Peru, Ecuador and Bolivia, except in the bigger cities. They are often harder to find, tucked away in an affluent suburb. For these countries it's a good idea to bring some dried or high altitude food from home. In smaller cities, notably Huaraz, there are no good supermarkets but most supplies can be found eventually.

Useful camping food always available in the larger towns in South America includes :- bread, flour, sugar, dried milk, tea and coffee, dried soups, porridge oats, dried potato mix and pasta. Also available are chocolate bars, biscuits, boiled sweets, powdered fruit drinks.

Items not usually available include :- freeze dried food, dehydrated meals, good quality dried fruit and nuts, instant puddings.

In some areas such as Huaraz, Cuzco and La Paz, local cooks can be employed for base camp.

FUEL

The recommended fuel to use in South America is white gas (bencina blanca) which is similar to Coleman fuel. It is now quite easy to find at chemists (farmacias) or hardware stores (ferreterias) in most popular trekking and climbing areas. It ignites easily, burns powerfully and is very clean. Petrol is more dangerous and more likely to cause problems with blocked stoves, but of course is readily and almost universally available. The best alternative to a white gas or petrol based stove is a camping gas stove. The style with a flexible hose are probably the best at altitude because you can (carefully) pre-heat the cylinder in the warming water. However gas cylinders are expensive and they can be hard to find outside the most popular climbing destinations such as Huaraz, Quito, Cuzco and La Paz. Screw on style cylinders are generally only available in towns like these where there are many climbers or trekkers, but piercing style cylinders are often available from hardware stores (ferreterias). Remember that you can't carry any fuel on an aeroplane.

RENTING AND BUYING EQUIPMENT IN SOUTH AMERICA

If you can possibly avoid it do so. There is some equipment for purchase and rental in major centres like Huaraz, Quito, Cuzco and La Paz where you may even get half decent equipment, but the choice is usually limited and climbing equipment is of dubious origin. In many areas finding any camping equipment to rent will be a long job and finding climbing equipment will be impossible.

CLIMBING CONDITIONS AND HAZARDS

Only conditions and hazards particular to the Andes are mentioned here. All areas suffer to some extent from the usual mountain hazards of bad weather, loose rock, avalanches etc.

SUN
The sun is much stronger at high altitude in the Andes than it is in Europe and the USA. It is higher in the sky, the air is thinner, there are fewer clouds and there is generally more snow cover. UV radiation levels rise very rapidly with altitude, and with snow cover, with levels at 6000m possibly 5 or 6 times those normally encountered at sea level. A hat with a brim and neck flap, glacier goggles and high factor sun cream and lip salve are essential for a safe expedition.

ELECTRICAL STORMS
These are extremely rare compared with the European Alps but do occur from time to time, most frequently in Peru, Bolivia and NW Argentina in the wet season.

GLACIERS
True valley glaciers are common only in the Patagonian Andes where there are some enormous 100km long glaciers. In the high Andes glaciers are normally only found on the steeper upper parts of mountains though there are a few small valley glaciers in the Cord. Blanca and Vilcanota in Peru and in the Santiago area of the High Andes. No glacier in the Cordillera Blanca is even 5km long and the longest glacier in the Santiago area is 15km. Glaciers are receding everywhere. Treat all descriptions of glacier routes in this guidebook with some caution as glacier retreat means many routes are becoming steeper and/or more dangerous and/or significantly harder.
Seracs and crevasses on glaciers in the tropical areas should be treated with at least the same caution as anywhere else. There is some evidence that seracs may be more unstable due to the large daily temperature variations and very strong sun. Crevasses tend to be larger than they are in the temperate Alps or Rockies.

SNOW AND ICE
In the tropical areas, from Colombia to Bolivia, all but the very steepest parts of the mountains are glaciated. Steep serac covered slopes are a feature of this area and make the mountains look very different to the bare rock faces of the summertime Alps or Rockies. In some parts of the Andes snow lies on faces up to 70° and forms unconsolidated snow flutings which give rise to very precarious climbing. The Peruvian Cordilleras (Blanca, Huayhuash, Vilcabamba and Vilcanota) are particularly notorious for these beautiful but dangerous features. In much of Peru there is generally good quality hard ice on north facing slopes while the shaded south facing slopes have the worst of the unconsolidated powder snow. East and west slopes are a bit of a mixture.
Further south, the Cordillera Real of Bolivia has very stable conditions and some of the best hard snow and ice on all faces during the very cold months of June and July. In the Puna and Cordillera Occidental the small glaciers and snowfields also generally remain firm all day.
Conditions around Mendoza and Santiago tend to be more like the Alps or Rockies in summer. Snow does not lie on such steep faces, so there are generally more exposed rock faces in this part of the Andes. The snowpack will usually soften considerably during the day and freeze again overnight.

AVALANCHES
Snow and ice slopes tend to be stable in the Andes in the regular climbing seasons. Long spells without precipitation, very cold nights and penitente formations probably account for this. Avalanches undoubtedly happen but seem to be relatively rare in the climbing seasons. Ecuador with its stormy

climate has the worst reputation, with some well documented, large and fatal slab avalanches. Fresh snow avalanches have also been seen by the author in the Cordillera Blanca and on Aconcagua. In the driest parts of the Andes, such as the Puna, Cordillera Occidental and Bolivia, avalanches are very rare.

PENITENTES

Penitentes are vertical spikes of snow or ice common in parts of the Andes. At 20cm they are a mild nuisance but at 5m they can make a climb virtually impossible. Formed due to vapour transport properties in very dry air and/or accumulations of dust they are at their worst in the driest areas such as the Puna de Atacama and Cordillera Occidental, but are common also around Aconcagua and in parts of southern Peru and Bolivia. They tend to line up in rows; climbing with the grain is much easier than going across it. Penitentes can often be seen with binoculars or a sharp eye and avoided. In the Puna and Santiago-Mendoza area they grow during the summer and will be at their worst in February.

On the good side penitentes are probably responsible for the low avalanche risk in parts of the Andes. In some areas they can also form nice little walls along the edges of crevasses, preventing snowblind mountaineers from plunging to their deaths!

Penitentes in the Cordon de los Pioneros, Puna de Atacama

ROCK QUALITY

With the obvious exception of Patagonia there are few areas of the Andes renowned for good quality rock. Volcanic areas such as the Puna, Cord. Occidental and Ecuador tend to have only extremely poor rock. Much of the Cord. Blanca, Cord. Real and the High Andes of Chile and Argentina are composed of poor shale type rock, though in all three regions there are small areas of granite which give much better climbing. Patagonia, particularly Fitzroy and the Torres del Paine has some superb granite big walls of generally good rock.

MINEFIELDS

These are signalled in Spanish by 'Zona de minas' or 'Campo de minas'. They are a potential hazard in passes on or near the Chile-Bolivia and Chile-Argentina borders. These are probably anti-vehicle mines but they should be presumed dangerous to pedestrians too. Though usually fenced the minefields are not always well marked (and certainly not on maps). Any fence, upright or not, in any remote border area should be treated with some suspicion as it may indicate the edge of a minefield.

LACK OF WATER

On many peaks in the Cordillera Occidental and Puna de Atacama lack of water is a serious problem. The following notes give some tactics for dealing with this logistical problem but the seriousness of running out of water on a remote desert mountain should never be underestimated. Allow up to 5 litres per day per person and don't put all your supply in one big water barrel!

A recent snowfall will make water logistics much easier. In some cases a fit and well acclimatised party can reach the snow line in only one day from the nearest road. The dry climate and easy nature of the mountains mean a fast and lightweight bivvy expedition can help offset having to carry more water. Another tactic is to climb high and carry snow back down to a lower camp - this is easier than carrying water up hill but should only be attempted if easily achievable.

If nothing else is going to work you may just have to load carry water uphill separately from the other equipment.

EQUIPMENT

CAMPING EQUIPMENT

Tents used at altitude need to be lightweight and strong enough to survive the occasional storm force winds. There are many such tents available these days e.g. Those from North Face, Mountain Hardwear and Terra Nova. Don't try to use a cheap tent; it won't survive the high winds common in many parts of the Andes. Add loops of cord to the main pegging points so that you can use rocks to pitch your tent. Practice pitching and maintaining your tent in extreme weather conditions before you go to the Andes.

Stoves must be robust, able to melt snow quickly and easy to repair in the field. Again it is very worthwhile testing your stove and cooking system in bad weather before your expedition. At altitude a cigarette lighter may be easier to use than matches - flames don't burn well without oxygen!

Very low temperatures (-20°C) at night mean a 5 season sleeping bag is more or less essential for camps above 5000m, particularly in southern Peru, Bolivia and the Puna in the coldest months of June and July. See also the following 'tips' section for more details on camping equipment.

MOUNTAINEERING EQUIPMENT

One ice-axe and crampons are needed for almost every ascent in this guide. Many routes are also on glaciers and full precautions against a crevasse fall must be taken. This will require a rope, harness, prussik loops and snow and ice belay equipment - and, of course, at least one companion. The knowledge of how to use this equipment to prevent a serious crevasse fall is also crucial. A chest harness (improvised) should be used on glaciers when carrying a heavy rucksack.

Routes of AD or above will obviously require a second ice tool and more belay and climbing equipment. Snow stakes and ice-screws are the most commonly used protection on the harder routes in Peru and Bolivia, with rock protection obviously useful on the mixed routes.

Trekking poles are strongly recommended because they save energy on loose ground (like snow or scree) and at altitude and when carrying heavy packs. Energy savings of c.20-30% easily make two poles worth the extra weight. Poles are also useful for improvised navigation markers, river crossings, fending off dogs, making washing lines and walking with bad blisters. If the worst happens they make a great improvised stretcher!

Snowshoes may be a good idea if attempting some of the less frequently climbed peaks with large snowy plateaux in the Cordillera Blanca and other Peruvian ranges. Hualcan, Copa and Ausangate are all peaks where they could be very useful.

CLOTHING

In most areas clothing suitable for a summer trip to the highest peaks of the European Alps will be suitable for climbing most 6000m peaks, though an extra layer (e.g. Down jacket) will be required to climb peaks over 6500m. It can feel extremely hot on a glacier at 6000m in the sunshine, but in bad weather hypothermia and frostbite are very real dangers. A modern flexible clothing system should be used. Essential items for all peaks are several fleece layers and a complete windproof shell, a warm hat and mountain gloves.

Temperatures at altitude at night drop a lot lower than they do in the Alps so a very good sleeping bag should be used. An extra layer of clothes or a down jacket will be very useful for colder early morning starts. Wind chill is a particular hazard in the Puna de Atacama and on Aconcagua.

NAVIGATION EQUIPMENT

A GPS is a highly recommended piece of navigation equipment for many peaks in this guidebook. None of the published IGM maps are adequate for fine navigation in bad weather or at night and most are difficult to use with a compass. In order to safely retrace your steps from a summit take waypoints as necessary, paying particular attention to avoid hazardous areas such as cliffs and crevasses.

SOME TIPS FOR HIGH ALTITUDE EXPEDITIONS

This section contains some notes for novices to high altitude which will hopefully make your first expedition run more smoothly. Many climbers fail on their first expedition to high altitude due to poor expedition skills rather than a lack of climbing skills. High altitude is not the place to learn any new skill. This problem is particularly prevalent on Aconcagua. Here are a few tips to help make things go more smoothly, but the best advice of all is to go out and practice camping in some foul winter weather at home first.

EXPECTATIONS

Don't travel to South America expecting to achieve as much as you would in the Alps or Rockies. Most Andean peaks are more remote, travel is generally more complicated and altitude will certainly cut down the number of routes you can do in a given time. A typical 3 week expedition might only achieve two or three 5000m peaks followed by two 6000m peaks. Fitness, particularly heart and lung fitness helps with acclimatisation to altitude (though its no guarantee you won't get altitude illness) so get fit before you go to South America.

REST AND RECOVERY

Remember your body will not recover and repair itself above 5000m. If possible descend to a lower altitude (e.g. 3000m) and better living conditions (e.g. hotels and restaurants) for a rest between peaks. Any acclimatisation you lose will be nothing to what you gain in general fitness.

PITCHING TENTS

You'll probably need to pitch your tent with rocks, so either buy one with valances or add on 2m loops of cord (rock guys) to the main pegging points. If you're leaving the tent unattended in very stormy weather weight the internal groundsheet with some well protected rocks - modern geodesic tents rely on this internal weight for stability. When pitching on snow and glaciers use either 15cm snow-pegs, (which often bend because they are not strong enough), or fill plastic bags with snow and bury them. Overnight and in storms you can reinforce these with your ice-axes and snow-stakes and/or skis. Never leave anything outside the tent overnight as it may get buried in the snow. Practice pitching your tent in high winds before you travel.

STOVES

If using a petrol stove bring a small wooden board to sit your stove on to prevent it melting down into the snow - this can also help protect vegetation. Melt snow the night before a climb and store it (insulated) in a water carrier (e.g. those by Ortlieb) overnight so that you can get away quickly in the morning. Ice melts faster than snow and both melt faster when immersed in water. Practice using your stove in extreme conditions before you reach 5000m! Work out how much fuel you will use before leaving home. Generally a litre of white gas or petrol will last two people about five days, but perhaps only half this time if you are melting snow every day. A small 190/250g gas cylinder will generally be enough for two people overnight.

SKI STICKS - TREKKING POLES

Use them. They save a lot of energy at high altitude, when carrying a big pack and on loose scree or deep snow.

VEHICLES

Diesel vehicles don't perform well at altitude due to the cold and low air pressure (which results in poor compression). Unfortunately it is very difficult to get a petrol 4x4, but this is definitely the best solution if it is possible. Otherwise try to rent a 4x4 with as low a mileage as possible so that the engine compression is better, and also make sure the battery is good. Park the vehicle at night so that the engine will be in the sun first thing in the morning (i.e. facing east). Consider using some sort of insulating tarpaulin or blanket over the engine. It may also help to heat the engine compartment by placing a gas stove underneath, or push hot air from a stove into the air intake... but take care!

ENVIRONMENTAL IMPACT & RESPONSIBLE TOURISM

There is no excuse for the poor attitude of previous generations and previous expeditions. People will follow in your footsteps and have to suffer the consequences of your actions.

1. Travel as a small lightweight group. Four to six climbers is probably the best size. This is guaranteed to improve your chance of success and reduce your impact.
2. Carry as little as possible into the mountains and all your refuse back out.
3. Be careful where you defecate. Use a toilet if there is one. In busy areas try to go during the day when away from camps if at all possible, or walk a long way (downhill) from the camp and dig a pit to bury your faeces. In very low use areas leave your faeces exposed to the wind and sun. Do not foul water or snow supplies.
4. Never give unearned gifts. This only encourages begging, which will probably become aggressive. If you give a present in return for a favour or good service try to make it a useful or educational item, e.g. a pen for a child, a pocket knife for an arriero.
5. Never give children sweets - they don't have dentists.
6. Respect privacy when taking photos.
7. Treat local staff (guides, porters, arrieros) with respect and consideration. Look after them if they are ill.

Tinqui, Cordillera Vilcanota, Peru

SKI MOUNTAINEERING

Some brief notes follow on the best ski-mountaineering opportunities in the Andes.

The only area to receive significant winter snowfall is from latitude 35° southwards. This is therefore the only area which produces similar conditions to the Alps or North America (but in the Southern Hemisphere spring months of August-October). It is also the only area where the snow-line ever extends significantly below the glaciers and longer ski tours from valley to valley are possible.

In all other areas skiing is almost exclusively on individual mountains and glaciers. In these tropical and sub-tropical areas crevasses are never as well bridged as they are in the Alps during the spring touring season, making the skiing significantly more dangerous. The best snow conditions in these areas are generally found towards the end of the wet season (i.e. March-May in Peru and Bolivia).

Ski resorts of a reasonable standard exist in several places in the southern Andes. The best of these are the large linked resorts of La Parva, El Colorado and Valle Nevado near the Chilean capital Santiago. Portillo further north in Chile and the small resort of Penitentes near Mendoza are interesting and quirky. Further south in the Chilean Lake District the new resort at Corralco on Volcan Lonquimay, and Pucon-Villarrica on the slopes of the same volcano are good. Chapelco at San Martin and Catedral on the outskirts of Bariloche in Argentina are also both good. Further south are a scattering of small but intriguing resorts and ski-fields. Typically resorts are open from early July to late September.

Volcan Lanin, Chile

COLOMBIA

In the Los Nevados range, Nevado El Ruiz is a good, if short, ski peak with few crevasses and nice slopes. In the north of the country, in the Sierra Nevada del Cocuy the peak of Ritacuba Blanco can also be skiied, generally with good snow conditions. The final summit pyramid is often 45°. Best season is probably November-March.

ECUADOR

Only the big four peaks, Chimborazo, Cotopaxi, Cayambe and Antisana can sensibly be skied and all have some potentially dangerous crevasses and relatively high avalanche risk. However access to all the peaks is very easy, with roads almost to the snow-line.

CORDILLERA BLANCA

Several areas provide good ski-mountaineering opportunities. The Copa and Hualcan massif is reputed to make a good ski traverse, although it is a long climb to the snow-line. Huascaran has been skied and snowboarded and steep peaks like Tocllaraju and Artesonraju have been skiied by the brave. Several areas further south with lower peaks, such as the Raria group, are more limited but often much less crevassed. Best season is the end of the wet season, about April-June.

Skiing Culin Thojo, Bolivia

BOLIVIA

The most extensive glaciated area is the Sorata massif and Ancohuma probably provides the best opportunity to ski a really big peak in the Cordillera Real. The Khara Khota valley makes a great base from which to do multiple smaller peaks of about 5000m, see page 165-167. At the southern end of the Cordillera Real the peak of Mururata is an ideal ski peak. Parts of the Apolobamba, e.g. Huellancalloc and around Ascarani, could also offer good skiing. Chacaltaya, at over 5000m, used to have the worlds highest drag tow but the skiing is now very limited. The best season is the end of the wet season, about April-June.

CORDILLERA OCCIDENTAL

Sajama and Parinacota have both been skied, and are both very good under good snow conditions. In Peru the massive plateau of Coropuna (12km continuously above 5900m) would make a fine traverse. A common problem in this range are the penitentes which can easily make skiing impossible - recent wet season snow or significant recent wind packed snow will be required.

PUNA DE ATACAMA

There is normally too little snow to make this area worth exploring on skis, although after a recent heavy snowstorm almost all peaks would give fine ski ascents over good terrain. Of the big peaks the best opportunity for skiing is definitely Monte Pissis, which has a large northern glacier often with reasonable snow conditions. As in the Cordillera Occidental the presence of penitentes could be a major problem and snow can also often be very wind blown and crusty. One area that receives more reliable snow cover is the Nevados de Cachi in Argentina, with the same wet season as Bolivia and best conditions in March to May, but access from road ends is very long.

THE HIGH ANDES

More ski mountaineering has probably been done in this area than anywhere else in the Andes, with local Mendoza and Santiago climbers regularly going skiing. Unfortunately the highest peaks (Aconcagua etc.) do not always have good cover due to the almost continuous high winds but many worthwhile tours and ascents can be done in the 2500-4000m range. Several parties have made E-W traverses through the mountains in this area. The best season is August-October, when the snowline is as low as 2000-2500m.

Except for a few areas near Santiago and the Cordon del Plata near Mendoza the access to the mountains can be very long and difficult. Good areas to try on the Argentine side of the Andes include the Agua Negra valley, the Vallecitos valley in the Cordon del Plata, the Atuel valley above Sosneado and the Quebrada Matienzo by Puente del Inca. On the Chilean side there are fewer access roads but the Maipo valley above Baños Morales can be very good. The author has skied successfully in all these areas.

Skiing on the peak of Sierra Nevada, Chilean Lakes District

MAULE AND THE LAKES DISTRICT

This region is one of the best areas for ski-mountaineering in the Andes, with ascents of volcanic peaks and traverses of forested ranges possible. Winter snowfall is usually reliable with the average winter snowline varying from 2000m in the north to 1000m in the Lakes District. The best season is August-October, though skiing into November can also be good. Access to many of the mountains is relatively easy as this is a well populated area. Most peaks can be done in one long day from access roads that reach ski resorts and small ski fields near the tree line, making this area the best in the Andes for an amenable ski-mountaineering "holiday".

In Chile the volcanoes Chillan, Antuco, Lonquimay, Llaima, Villarrica, Lanin and Osorno all make for fine ascents and descents. In Argentina the bigger peaks of Tromen and Domuyo have been skiied. Further south there are good day trips and short tours in the Cordillera Catedral and other peaks near Bariloche.

Skiing towards Fitzroy and Cerro Torre on the South Patagonian Icecap

PATAGONIA

The northern and southern Patagonian ice-caps provide one of the best opportunities for serious ski-mountaineering in the Andes. Indeed skis are generally necessary to reach the more remote peaks and have been used on all traverses of the ice-caps. In winter the snowline can reach sea level.

However this part of the Andes really entails some tough, expedition style skiing. There can be serious navigational problems and there are some truly enormous crevasses. Steep descents are few and far between, generally speaking very large loads will need to be carried or pulled on a sledge and the weather can be truly appalling, often resulting in stormbound days in the tent.

In the north the author has skiied San Lorenzo and made an attempt on San Valentin, the highest point on the northern ice-cap. Good peaks to ski from the southern ice-cap include the (relatively) accessible Gorra Blanca and the more remote pairing of Volcan Lautaro and Cerro Moreno.

UPDATES

Users of this guidebook should be aware that while the author has done everything to ensure it is as accurate as possible, it would be impossible for every description in this guidebook to be completely up to date. Though every care has been taken in compiling this information, climbing routes (particularly those on glaciers) are subject to continual change and new roads are always opening up new possibilities for access.

Users are requested to send any updated or improved information on climbing routes, access etc. to the publisher so that we can improve future editions of this guide. All major contributions will receive a free copy of the next edition. Please send any information to:

John Biggar, 37a St Andrew Street, Castle Douglas, DG7 1EN, SCOTLAND.

Phone 00 44 1556 503929

Email john@andes.com   john@andes.org.uk

Web www.andes.org.uk   www.johnbiggar.com

Further copies of our guidebooks can be obtained from this address by mail order if you have trouble finding them in your local shops.

THE AUTHOR

The author John Biggar is based in Castle Douglas, Kirkcudbrightshire, Scotland. His first publication was an internal report for the nuclear physics department at Edinburgh University, entitled "Anisotropies in the Sequential Break-up of Li6".

Since those days John has done little nuclear physics but has been climbing and ski-mountaineering in the Andes a lot. He has climbed many of the highest peaks, including 19 of the 20 highest, made over 100 ascents of 6000m peaks, plus 180 ascents of Andean 5000m peaks. He has made first ascents of six 6000m peaks and also made the first ski descent of Domuyo, the highest peak in Patagonia. A professional mountaineering instructor, he runs a business which specialises in mountaineering, skiing and ski-mountaineering expeditions to South America.

John is pictured here on his first ever sand-boarding expedition to the dunes of Taton near the famous wee town of Fiambala in Argentina in 2012.

VENEZUELA

INTRODUCTION

The Andes of Venezuela are restricted to one small area around the city of Merida, and are lower than the great ranges of the Andes further south. However the mountains rise directly from the tropical lowlands, and the changes in vegetation zones as you climb from the forest to the rocky summits are a fascinating feature of this range. Most ascents will start in tropical forest at 1500-2000m, cross mist shrouded moorland (known as páramo) at 3000-4000m and finish on snow and ice. Particularly attractive are the frailejone plants which grow on the páramo. The mountains are also particularly easy to get to, utilising the worlds highest cable car station, although this was closed in 2008 and after a re-build is due to re-open in 2015.

GETTING THERE

From Europe the cheapest flights are from major European cities to the capital city of Caracas with Air France, Lufthansa or Iberia. From North America there are many daily flights to Caracas from Miami, Houston and New York with Delta, American and United. For the Sierra Nevada in Venezuela an internal flight to Merida from Caracas is recommended.

SEASON AND WEATHER CONDITIONS

The weather is generally wet and tropical. The driest season and certainly the best time to climb is from December to March with January usually the best month. A shorter less pronounced dry spell is also possible in July. However there can be mist, rain and storms at any time in these ranges. Temperatures fall just a few degrees below freezing at night above about 4000m in the January dry season.

CLIMBING CONDITIONS

There are only tiny glaciers left and crevasses present no problems. The snow is usually soft for most of the day in the dry season and icy conditions are rarely encountered. Many routes involve a fair amount of rock scrambling and overnight falls of snow can make these routes tricky. The weather can be poor, even in the dry season and many summits will cloud over early every day e.g. 11a.m.so an early start is recommended. In the wet season fresh snow and very poor weather can make ascents difficult.

OTHER GUIDE BOOKS

Expediciones a la Sierra Nevada de Merida, Chalbaud, Ediciones Paraguacocha, 1959, now very dated!
Hiking/Backpacking in the Venezuelan Andes, Leighty, ISBN 0-9632950-0-4.

MERIDA The principal city of the Venezuelan Andes   1550m

Merida is a small city lying at the foot of the Sierra Nevada, the highest part of the Venezuelan Andes and the only range with permanent snow. A cable car (teleferico) connects the city centre with the top of Pico Espejo at 4768m. This closed in 2008 and at the time of writing was being completely re-built, due to re-open in 2015. The Sierra Nevada are a dramatic and rocky range with good potential for rock-climbing, though little seems to have been done. To the N of the city lie the lower Sierra de la Culata (Cordillera del Norte) with many easy peaks up to 4700m high.

SIGHTS The trip on the teleferico is worth doing even if you are not climbing or hiking.

FOOD There are plenty of supermarkets in the central area. The most convenient is the Chinese run one on Av. Las Americas opposite the viaduct.

FUEL Gas canisters and white gas (bencina blanca) from the climbing and trekking agencies at the end of C24 near the teleferico.

MOUNTAIN TRANSPORT The cable car will again be the best and easiest option when it re-opens. It leaves from the centre of town (S end of Calle 24) in the mornings. Booking is recommended at weekends and on holidays if you don't want to queue. For Mucuy and other nearby roadheads just use a city taxi.

MOUNTAIN EQUIPMENT AND INFORMATION From the Inparques office at the bottom station of the teleferico (cable car) in Merida or from several agencies nearby. 'Expedicion Andina' seems to be the best of these. Several shops here sell a little climbing equipment including ropes, krabs and rock shoes. Mountaineers must register their plans and prove they have adequate equipment at the Inparques office by the teleferico station before going into the mountains (minimal charge, takes 10 minutes).

PAN DE AZUCAR 4620m   2 days   F
PIEDRAS BLANCAS 4712m   2 days   F

These are the two highest peaks in the Sierra de la Culata (also known as the Cordillera del Norte) which lie N of Merida and provide excellent views of the Sierra Nevada. These two ascents can be combined in a trek of three or four days.

ACCESS Permission from the Inparques office in Merida is officially required but there are no checkpoints on the route. For Piedras Blancas start in La Toma (PT) and walk up the 4x4 track on the LHS of the Q. La Toma taking the L fork (Q. El Banco) at the major junction. A camp can be made S of Piedras Blancas, near the end of the track at 3900m, 3h from La Toma. This track could be driven if you knew how to get permission. From this camp a signposted trail leads via the Lag. Carbonera to the Barro Negro camp (4300m) SE of Pan de Azucar, 4h. The Barro Negro camp can also be reached more directly by walking up the Rio Mucujun on good trails from La Culata (PT), 5-6h.

Piedras Blancas from the S

PIEDRAS BLANCAS CLIMB The peak can be climbed easily from the camp at 3900m in the Q. El Banco by the SE slopes approx. 4h.

PAN DE AZUCAR CLIMB The peak can be climbed very easily from the Barro Negro camp by either the S or E ridges, 2h.

BEST MAP Parque Nacional Sierra de la Culata - approx.1:50,000 available in Merida from the Inparques office on C-19 and occasionally from the outdoor shops by the teleferico.

The Sierra Nevada from Pan de Azucar

Pico BOLIVAR 4979m   2 days   AD

Bolivar is the highest peak in the Sierra Nevada and in Venezuela, perhaps rather optimistically given a height of 5007m in some sources. Pico Bolivar is named after the liberator of South America, Simon Bolivar, who was born in Venezuela. A giant bust of him sits on the small summit of the peak.

ACCESS Easiest using the cable car from central Merida to **Pico Espejo 4768m**. From the Pico Espejo station descend onto the shoulder to the S then scramble NE along the flank of Bolivar to a high camp at Lag. Timoncitos (4750m), 1½h. This is a very easy but very exposed rock scramble. The route is well marked. This exposed route can be avoided by dropping about 200m lower down the S shoulder of Pico Espejo and traversing on screes, 2½h.

Going high on the cable car allows no time for acclimatisation and it may be better to walk at least some of the way. There are two main possibilities for walking. **1.** Walk all or part of the route of the cable car, 1-2d. An easily followed path leaves from La Pueblita across the river from the cable car station or from the road at Los Cochinos, or take the cable car to one of the lower stations and walk from there. **2.** A longer approach starts from the ranger station at Mucuy (2300m). Follow the path through forest up the valley to the SE - a good trail is normally cut and signposted. This leads past the Lag. Coromoto (3300m - nice camps) and the Lag. Verde (4000m) to the rocky col known as La Ventana (4500m). From here a traverse with a slight drop, (called La Travesia) can be made along the SE flank of Bolivar to reach Lag. Timoncitos, 3d.

CLIMB The normal route is known as Ruta Weiss after the first ascensionist. This is a rock scramble mostly II but with a short section of IV and a very exposed traverse near the summit. This route follows the prominent gully sometimes containing snow or ice on the L of the face above Lag. Timoncitos. There are bolt belays where necessary. Ice-axe and crampons are not normally needed but sections can be icy. A pitch of II known as Las Escaleras is followed by some easy ground then an icy pitch in the gully of III or IV. More easy ground leads to a col in the SW ridge 50m below the summit. From here move onto the NW face along an exposed ledge and finally climb up III chimneys to the summit. There can be a lot of snow on this last section. 3h. Beware of rockfall danger in the gully if there are other parties.

route goes behind

Bolivar from the S

Summit

From Timoncitos

OTHER ROUTES There are several other routes on Bolivar. **1. Ruta Bourgoin**. From Lag. Timoncitos go up to the snowfields in the wide couloir R of the Ruta Weiss, known as the Garganta Bourgoin (there was a glacier here that has all but disappeared). Climb this couloir and follow the ridge W to the summit. Exact grade n/k but slightly harder than Ruta Weiss. **2.** N face, **Ruta Vinci**. Make a rising traverse under the N face of Pico Espejo from Loma Redonda to gain the W glacier. Climb this to join the final part of the Ruta Weiss on the NW face.

OTHER PEAKS The rocky **Pico La Concha, 4922m PD/AD** can be climbed from a camp halfway across La Travesia by the SW ridge. This is joined from the S at a prominent notch.

KEY WAYPOINTS Shoulder S of Espejo 08°31'45" 71°03'10" End of Traverse 08°32'06" 71°02'58" Timoncitos camp 08°32'16" 71°02'52" Bolivar summit 08°32'30" 71°02'45"

BEST MAP Parque Nacional Sierra Nevada - Mapa para Excursionistas, 1:50,000 available in Merida from the Inparques office on C-19 or from several of the agencies near the teleferico.

The summit of Pico Bolivar

Climbing Pico Bolivar

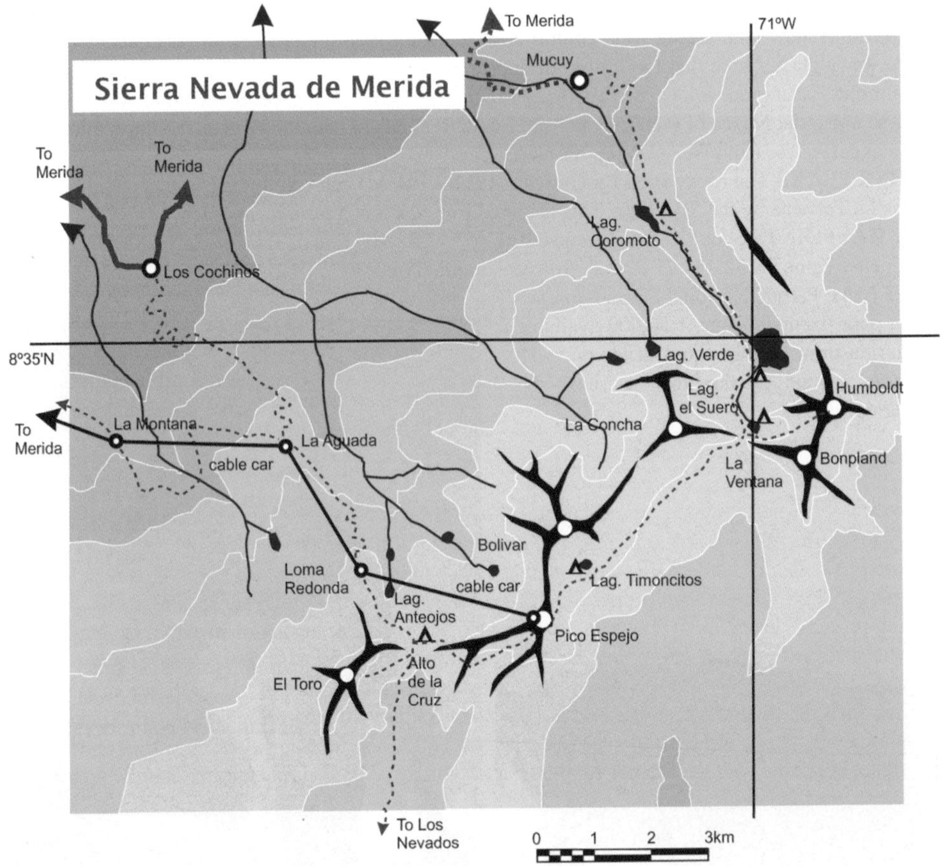

Sierra Nevada de Merida

To Merida

71°W

Mucuy

To Merida

To Merida

Lag. Coromoto

Los Cochinos

8°35'N

Lag. Verde

Humboldt

Lag. el Suero

To Merida

La Montana

La Aguada

La Concha

Bonpland

cable car

La Ventana

Bolivar

Loma Redonda

cable car

Lag. Timoncitos

Lag. Anteojos

Pico Espejo

El Toro

Alto de la Cruz

To Los Nevados

0   1   2   3km

Pico EL TORO 4758m   1 day   F

A fine rock scramble, Pico El Toro can be climbed in a few hours from the third cable car station or combined with Pico Leon to give a longer day.

ACCESS From Merida to the Loma Redonda cable car station (4000m).

CLIMB From Loma Redonda follow the wide path to the Alto de la Cruz pass. At the pass turn R over broken ground towards the W and make a rising traverse under the S slopes of Toro. There is a faint path and cairns and a possible camp at a small lagoon at 4300m. Just below the summit of Toro scramble easily up a steep 20m gully (II) on the R, then go L along the ridge to the top, 3h.

OTHER PEAKS The traverse from Toro SW to **Pico Leon 4746m**, is a classic exposed rock scramble grade n/k.

KEY WAYPOINTS Alto de la Cruz pass 08°32'00" 71°04'44" Bottom of 20m gully 08°31'45" 71°05'26"

BEST MAP As for Pico Bolivar.

Pico HUMBOLDT 4942m

4 days   PD

The second highest peak in the Sierra Nevada de Merida, about 6km E of Bolivar. Humboldt is the northern of two peaks known as La Corona, after the glacier on their NW slopes. Humboldt is named after the famous naturalist. The normal camp is by the beautiful blue Lag. El Suero.

ACCESS By either of the routes described above for Bolivar to a camp below La Ventana at Lag. El Suero (4200m). One long day via Espejo by the teleferico, "La Travesia" and La Ventana (4500m) or two short uphill days from Mucuy.

CLIMB Go round the RHS of Lag. Suero on a path, cross the stream and follow the LHS of the stream up over rock slabs (cairns) to a higher lagoon at 4400m. Scrambling to grade III in places but not exposed. Climb rubble slopes on the L of the glacier until reaching a saddle at 4800m between the glacier and a small rock peak. Go on to the glacier here and cross it directly towards the summit pyramid of Humboldt, one very small crevasse. Follow the final rocky crest easily to the summit.

OTHER PEAKS Humboldt's twin peak **Pico Bonpland 4885m**, can be climbed the same day as Humboldt. Follow the route for Humboldt onto the Corona glacier but then bear R to join the NE ridge of Bonpland. Some further rock climbing, quite exposed, grade n/k but probably about AD.

KEY WAYPOINTS La Ventana 08°32'56" 71°00'51" Lag. El Suero 08°33'06" 71°00'40" Glacier Edge 08°32'55" 71°00'02" Summit 08°32'58" 70°59'47"

BEST MAP As for Pico Bolivar.

Pico MUCUÑUQUE 4672m   2 days   F

A fine easy scramble. Pico Mucuñuque is also known as Pico Santo Domingo. It is about 25km E of the main peaks of the Sierra Nevada on the S side of the main valley.

ACCESS From Merida a 2h. drive to the Laguna Mucubaji recreation area at 3600m.

CLIMB Follow the path up the valley to the SE to good campsites at 4000m before a steep wall split by a gully. Continue up the gully and then S to a saddle at about 4500m from where the summit is about 1km away to the left. Mucuñuque could be climbed in one long day from Mucubaji.

BEST MAP VIGM, sheet not known.

Pico Mucuñuque from the N

COLOMBIA

INTRODUCTION

The Andes of Colombia are divided into three distinct chains, with the capital Bogota lying in the eastern chain. However only small areas of each of these chains rise above the snowline and are of interest to mountaineers, the majority of each range being a rolling plateau at 3500-4000m known as the paramo. The Colombian mountains are surrounded by extensive tropical lowlands, and this partly explains the bad weather common in this part of the Andes. Some of the mountains are very accessible, e.g. the Los Nevados range, but others, particularly the Sierra Nevada de Santa Marta, are very difficult (and indeed dangerous) to get to.

Colombia is a very warm and friendly country, with some magnificent scenery, which is well worth visiting if you take care. However in the past the country has not always been a safe destination due to guerrilla violence and kidnappings. Although the situation has improved in recent years travel to some of the mountain areas of Colombia is still not advisable. Lack of safe access means descriptions for some of the peaks in this chapter have not been checked in recent years.

GETTING THERE

From Europe the cheapest flights are from London and other major European cities to the capital city of Bogotá with the Colombian carrier Avianca, Air France, Lufthansa and Iberia. From North America there are many daily flights to Bogotá from Miami, Atlanta, Houston and New York as well as direct services from Miami and New York to Cali and Barranquilla.

For many of the Colombian ranges it is probably best to acclimatise and buy some supplies in Bogotá before flying on to your chosen area. Fly to Bucaramanga for the S. N. del Cocuy, Cali for Nevado del Huila, Manizales for Los Nevados, Popayan for Purace, and Pasto for Galeras and Cumbal. Fly to Valledupar or the city of Santa Marta for the S. N. de Santa Marta.

The Los Nevados and Cocuy ranges are near enough to Bogotá to be reached by bus. For other areas this is also an option for those short of funds. Buses are generally comfortable, but are often dangerously driven and the roads in Colombia are tortuously slow. Crime can also be a problem, particularly on night buses. The most reliable companies are Bolivariano in the S and their partners Brasilia in the N.

SEASON AND WEATHER CONDITIONS

The weather is generally wet and tropical. There can be mist, rain and storms at any time in all these ranges. Weather patterns are very complex with each different range having slightly different wet and dry seasons. See individual peak entries for more specific details. However the driest season generally and probably the best time to climb in Colombia is from November to March, with January usually the best month. Temperatures fall below freezing at night above about 4500m in the January dry season.

CLIMBING CONDITIONS

Glaciers are generally very small and crevasses present few major problems. The snow is usually soft for most of the day in the dry season. The weather can be poor, even in the dry season, and many summits will cloud over early every day e.g. by 9am.

SECURITY & ACCESS

Colombia has had an ongoing civil war for many decades, in general with left wing guerillas fighting the army and rightwing paramilitaries, and all mixed up with the illegal drugs trade. The situation began to improve noticeably in the 2000's and by 2015 most cities and many areas of the country were reasonably safe to travel through. The only mountains considered reasonably safe at present are the

Los Nevados and Cocuy ranges. The areas around Nevado del Huila and a few areas in the rural SW have seen recent guerrilla activity, and the S. N. de Santa Marta have a complex range of access issues. Volcanic hazards can also often close peaks and areas to climbers.

OTHER GUIDE BOOKS
Alta Colombia by Cristobal von Rothkirch. In Spanish or English, mostly a photographic record but with some useful maps, Villegas 1998.

BOGOTÁ The capital city of Colombia   2650m

The capital of Colombia is a huge city in a pleasant setting. Because of its height it has a fairly cool climate. It is a city of both marked prosperity in the northern suburbs and terrible poverty in the southern barrios. Like many South American cities the centre can be roughly divided into old and new districts. Few streets in Bogotá have names, instead numbers are used to identify the Calles (C) and Carreras (Cra). This is also true of many other Colombian cities.

SIGHTS There are plenty of cultural sights to see - the usual mix of museums, churches and cathedrals surrounding Plaza de Bolivar. **Co. de Monserrate 3200m** to the E can be ascended by funicular, cable car or on foot for a good view of Bogotá.

ROCK CLIMBING AND BOULDERING There is very good rock climbing and some bouldering at Suesca 1½h. by bus N of the city. There is a campsite and cafes by the crag and it is very popular at weekends with climbers and picknickers. The crag is on the RHS of the road about 1km before the town and is accessed by an old railway line. There are single pitch and multipitch routes up to 100m, mostly bolted.

MOUNTAIN INFORMATION Try the Central Nacional de Montaña, at at Diagonal 108, number 9A-11, Bogotá. There's a nice cafe here too. Or try the 'Cafes y Crepes' cafe at Carrera 16, No. 82-17

MOUNTAIN EQUIPMENT As above or try the shop 'Almacen Aventura' at Carrera 13, No. 67-26, or Carrera 7, No. 121-53.

Antique coffee machine in a Bogota cafe

Pico COLON c.5710m 　　　　　　　　　7 days 　 F/PD
Pico BOLIVAR c.5710m 　　　　　　　　7 days 　 N/K

These neighbouring peaks in the Sierra Nevada de Santa Marta are the two highest peaks in Colombia. They are sometimes quoted with identical heights but in fact the author has been assured that Bolivar is slightly higher. The Sierra Nevada de Santa Marta is a range which rises directly from the Caribbean and is technically not part of the Andean chain. Cristobal Colon is the Spanish name for Christopher Columbus, Simon Bolivar was the liberator of South America.

This range is driest in January to March, but there is also a short dry season in June and July.

Reports are that all access to the mountains has been forbidden since 1996 and since then there have been few, if any, ascents. Details are given below from an ascent in the early 1990's, in the hope that these beautiful mountains may re-open in future.

The local Arhuaco Indians are hostile to outsiders travelling in what they consider a sacred area – even when access was allowed a local guide was often essential for safe passage. There are also problems with left wing guerillas, the army and drug cultivation.

ACCESS A permit to access the mountains used to be necessary and was obtained from the Casa Indigena just outside Valledupar. From the city of Valledupar get to either San Sebastian or (probably better) Donachui. A 4x4 may be needed. From either of these villages use local Indian guides and mules to reach the Lag. Nabobo base camp (4450m) which lies SE of the two peaks, 2-3d. All food and fuel should be brought from Valledupar.

COLON CLIMB From the Nabobo camp go N past two smaller lakes then head direct for the SE side of Colon, to a high camp at the edge of the snowline (5000m). Climb the glacier keeping close to the E face of Bolivar then climb up to the col between the peaks called La Horqueta (5550m). Then easily to the top of Colon, 5h. from the high camp.

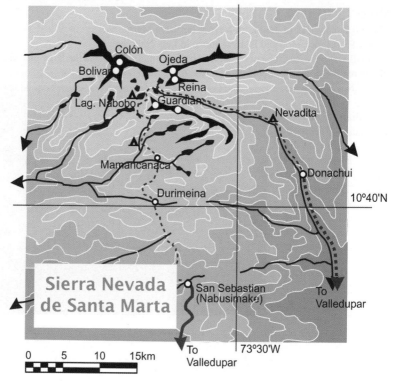

BOLIVAR CLIMB Bolivar is normally climbed from La Horqueta too. It is reputedly harder than Colon, probably about AD and mostly on snow.

KEY WAYPOINTS Colon summit 10°50'19" 73°41'12" Bolivar summit 10°50'04" 73°41'29"

BEST MAP CIGM sheets 19, 20, 26, 27 at 1:100,000 cover the range and will be needed for access. These two peaks are on sheet 19.

Bolivar

Colon from the E

Pico la REINA 5536m   7 days   N/K

The third main peak of the Sierra Nevada de Santa Marta.

ACCESS As for Colon and Bolivar above to Lag. Nabobo.

CLIMB From the Lag. Nabobo base camp the normal route is via the large glacier on the NW slopes. Grade n/k but probably about PD/AD. About 5h. from the lake.

OTHER PEAKS SE of Lag. Nabobo is **El Guardián 5285m**, the most difficult of the big peaks in the Santa Marta range. The easier **Pico Ojeda 5490m**, just to the N of La Reina, is normally climbed from the S. Grade n/k but probably about PD.

BEST MAP CIGM sheets as for Bolivar.

Ojeda

Reina

Ojeda and Reina from the W

RITACUBA BLANCO 5410m 　　　　　　2 days　　　PD

Ritacuba Blanco is the highest point of the Sierra Nevada del Cocuy, a beautiful mist enshrouded range with a reputation for bad weather. The range consists of two parallel chains running N-S. The W chain is higher and much more accessible. Both chains rise gently on the W side and drop very steeply on the E. A beautiful trek circles the mountains in 6-7 days.

The best time to climb in the Sierra Nevada del Cocuy range, according to the locals, is in November and December. January is also alright, but this range gets very wet by March.

ACCESS From Bogotá go direct by bus to El Cocuy (2700m) or the higher village of Guicán (PT) (2900m). Both are beautiful little villages with a few shops and small hotels. These villages can also be reached from the city of Bucaramanga. From these villages a jeep can easily be hired to get to the Cabañas Kanwara at the foot of Ritacuba Blanco, where there is camping and accomodation.

CLIMB Horses can be hired at Kanwara. From Kanwara traverse along an aqueduct then follow a good path up the Q. Playitas to a camp on rock slabs beneath the glacier at 4600m, 2h. This is as far as horses can go. From here climb upwards and leftwards to the glacier edge (4800m). Ascend the easy angled glacier slopes before finally an exposed and sometimes steep climb up the summit pyramid, 4h. from Playitas.

OTHER PEAKS From the same high camp at 4600m **Ritacuba Negro, c.5350m,** can be climbed. It is a more complex ascent usually with some ice pitches to about 50°, grade about AD. Traverse onto the mountain from about 5200m on the Ritacuba Blanco route and climb the steep SW ridge.

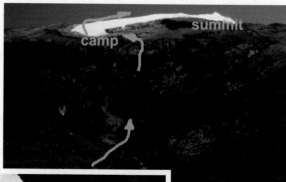

KEY WAYPOINTS Cabañas Kanwara 06°28'20" 72°21'15" Playitas Camp 06°29'16" 72°19'25" Glacier Edge 06°29'40" 72°19'06" Base of summit pyramid 06°29'40" 72°17'48"

BEST MAP CIGM sheet 137 'El Cocuy', 1:100,000.

Cocuy Hotel

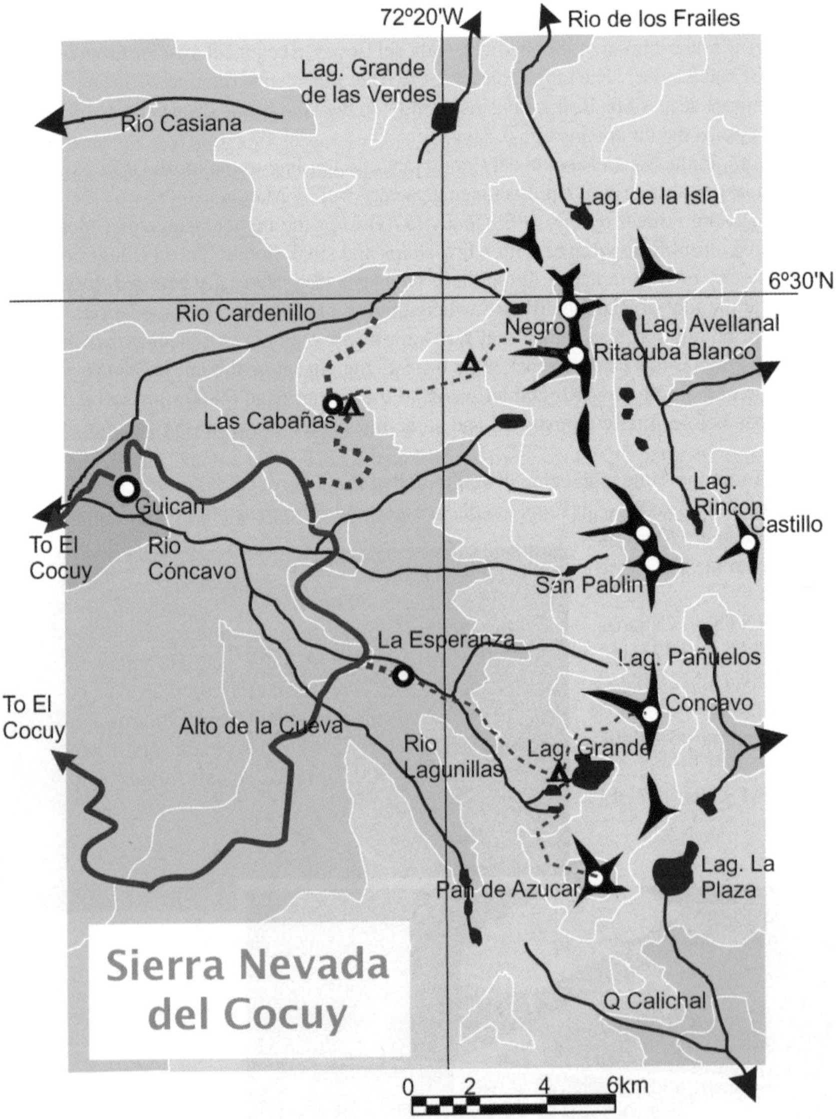

72°20'W

Rio de los Frailes

Lag. Grande de las Verdes

Rio Casiana

Lag. de la Isla

6°30'N

Rio Cardenillo

Negro

Lag. Avellanal

Ritacuba Blanco

Las Cabañas

Guican

To El Cocuy

Rio Cóncavo

Lag. Rincon

Castillo

San Pablin

La Esperanza

Lag. Pañuelos

To El Cocuy

Alto de la Cueva

Rio Lagunillas

Lag. Grande

Concavo

Pan de Azucar

Lag. La Plaza

Q Calichal

Sierra Nevada del Cocuy

0   2   4   6km

Pico del CASTILLO 5123m   7 days   N/K

Castillo is a remote peak, the highest point of the E range. It is also known as Punta Helvetia.

ACCESS The northern and southern routes are about equally long, both will take about 3 days to reach a base camp at 4400m at Lag. Rincon, but the scenery is fantastic. For the northern route trek in around the N end of the main range, with camps at Lag. Grande de las Verdes and Lag de la Isla. For the southern route walk from La Esperanza with intermediate camps at Lag. Grande de la Plaza and Lag. Pañuelos.

CLIMB Castillo is easiest by the W ridge, partly on glacier and partly on good quality rock. Grade n/k but about AD.

BEST MAP CIGM sheet 137 'El Cocuy', 1:100,000.

Ritacuba Blanco summit panorama

San Pablin

Castillo

W ridge   Lag. Rincon

Nevado el CONCAVO c.5180m
PAN de AZUCAR c.5140m

2 days   F
2 days   F

These two southern peaks in the Sierra Nevada del Cocuy are easy but interesting ascents, which can be done from a single high camp near the very scenic Laguna Grande.

ACCESS From Guican or Cocuy take a hired jeep to the Hacienda La Esperanza. From here follow the well marked trail up the valley to the southeast to camps at 4500m by the Laguna Grande, 5-6h.

CONCAVO CLIMB Concavo is an easy ascent by the SW glacier directly from Lag. Grande, finishing on the W ridge, 3h.

PAN DE AZUCAR CLIMB Pan de Azucar can be climbed easily by the W ridge, passing the foot of the obvious rock tower of the Pulpito del Diablo. Reach the W ridge either directly from the col at the head of the valley above La Esperanza, or by traversing SW over moraines for 2h. from Lag. Grande then climbing up through easy rock terraces, 5h.

OTHER PEAKS The 70m high flat-topped **Pulpito del Diablo** is about a grade V or VI rock climb by the easiest route, which lies on the E face. The route climbs the RH crack in the large gully/scoop at the N end of the E face, starting just L of the rubble pile. The top pitch up a corner crack (fingers) is the hardest.

Between Concavo and Pan de Azucar, the peak of **Toti c.5050m** can also be climbed from the Lag. Grande by the W glacier then rock terraces in 3-4h.

North of these two peaks lie the twin peaks of **San Pablin.** The S peak is the highest at about c.5200m. It can be climbed easily from the Laguna San Pablin by the W ridge and slopes at about F/PD.

KEY WAYPOINTS
Concavo summit 06°24'37" 72°16'53"
Pan de Azucar summit 06°22'10" 72°17'45"
BEST MAP CIGM sheet 137 'El Cocuy', 1:100,000.

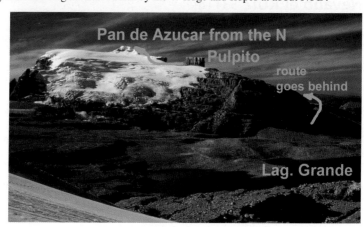

Pan de Azucar from the N

Pulpito

route goes behind

Lag. Grande

Concavo from the SW

Lag. Grande

Pulpito del Diablo

Nevado el RUIZ 5311m   1 day   F
Nevado SANTA ISABEL c.4950m   2 days   F

These are the two most northerly peaks of a group of volcanoes commonly called Los Nevados. El Ruiz erupted in 1985 and a mudslide killed thousands in the town of Armero, over 50km away. There were also minor eruptions in 2012. It is possible to combine climbing these two mountains with an ascent of Nevado Tolima by traversing the high páramo between them. Higher altitudes are often quoted for all the mountains in this range.

The Los Nevados range are generally driest in December and January, but also have a short drier spell in July and August.

ACCESS From the stunning city of Manizales (2150m) transport can be arranged to the park entrance at 4050m, just S of the Manizales to Murillo road. Check at the Inderena office, C 20A, No 21-45 or at the tourist office in Manizales about access and transport to the national park. There is accommodation just inside the park at the small Arenales hut (4150m). With good conditions and a 4x4 it is possible to continue further S up the road to within 2km of the summit at a car park and another small refugio, snacks but no accommodation (4750m). Otherwise this refugio is a 2h. walk from Arenales.

For Santa Isabel turn R at the junction at the col just below the higher refugio and drive a further 1h., past the El Cisne refugio to a valley known as Conejeras. There is a tiny path on the L leading up the valley, difficult to see from the road, but it is about 6km beyond El Cisne and about 200m S of a road cutting.

EL RUIZ CLIMB The authorities sometimes prohibit climbing due to volcanic activity. From the refugio at 4750m climb the steep boulder slopes on the LHS of a gully for 200m to the glacier edge. Turn left (eastwards) and climb to the highest visible point (5100m) then E over a fairly flat glacier to the highest summit on the crater edge. There are only a few very small crevasses on the glacier, 3-4h.

SANTA ISABEL CLIMB From the road at Conejeras follow the path easily for 1h. through grass and quenoa trees to beautiful campsites in the bottom of the hanging valley at 4250m. From the camp follow the path up the RH valley heading for a low point between two rock outcrops. Continue over moraines and slabs on a good path to the glacier edge, 4550m. Climb onto the glacier and up the initial steep slope, then turn L to reach the highest N summit, 3h. from camp. The Central and S summits can also be climbed easily, or a complete traverse done.

OTHER PEAKS The peak of **El Cisne, c.4700m, F** can be climbed easily in 2-3h. from the El Cisne refugio (4050m) on the road between Ruiz and Santa Isabel. A faint trail starts from the E side of the track about 100m S of the hut. Follow this trail up the LHS of the valley to a basin below the peak at 4350m, then up scree to the N ridge and easily to the summit.

The sandy volcanic cone of **La Olleta c.4800m, F** can be climbed in just ½h. from the road a short way S of Arenales.

EL RUIZ KEY WAYPOINTS Refugio 04°53'51" 75°20'21" Signpost 04°53'27" 75°19'58" Near summit 04°53'35" 75°19'24"

SANTA ISABEL NORTE KEY WAYPOINTS Conejeras 04°49'54" 75°22'32" Santa Isabel, glacier edge 04°49'00" 75°22'23" Near the summit 04°49'00" 75°22'02"

BEST MAP A locally produced map at 1:12,500 could be very useful, but otherwise CIGM sheet 225 'Nevado El Ruiz', at 1:100,000 is a good sheet to have for the entire Los Nevados range.

Ruiz from the N

Santa Isabel peaks from the N

La Olleta from Ruiz

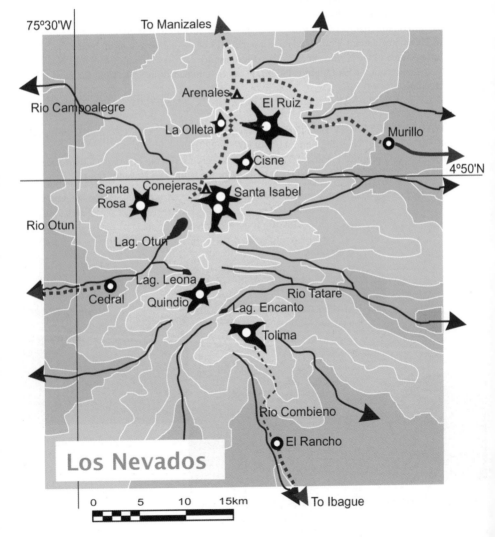

75°30'W

To Manizales

Rio Campoalegre

Arenales △

El Ruiz

La Olleta ○

Cisne

Murillo ○

4°50'N

Santa Rosa ○

Conejeras △

Santa Isabel

Rio Otun

Lag. Otun

Lag. Leona

Cedral ○

Quindio ○

Rio Tatare

Lag. Encanto

Tolima ○

Rio Combieno

El Rancho ○

Los Nevados

0   5   10   15km

To Ibague

Nevado del TOLIMA 5274m

3 days   F

Tolima is the second highest peak in the Los Nevados range. It is an active volcano which last erupted in 1943.

ACCESS The easiest access is from the town of Ibagué (1250m) via the villages of Las Juntas and El Silencio (small shop). Then walk up the valley to the El Rancho hot spring on the S side of the mountain at 2700m - a beautiful spot with some food and accommodation.

CLIMB From El Rancho climb the steep and muddy trail up the valley to get to La Cueva just above the treeline (3800m) (poor refugio, water), 4h. Continue on up NW over páramo to the large cross at Latas (4500m), 3h. Camping and water here. Head direct to the summit, with the snowline at 4800m. The snow is steep at first then easier, 4h. Some small crevasses.

NORTHWEST ROUTE From Armenia via the town of Salento (shops, hotels, guides, etc.), then take a jeep to Cocora. From here it is a 2d. walk through dense forest which will get you to a high camp known as the "helipuerto" at about 4500m on the NW slopes of Tolima. A guide is recommended to find this trail. From the "helipuerto" camp go easily over broad snow slopes to the summit.

OTHER PEAKS The peak of **No. El Quindio 4798m, F** is best climbed starting from Cedral to the W, via the pass at 4410m then by the N ridge.

KEY WAYPOINTS Summit 04°39'31" 75°19'46"

BEST MAP CIGM sheet 225 'Nevado El Ruiz', at 1:100,000.

Tolima from the S

Tolima from the W

Balconies, Salento

Nevado del HUILA 5375m

6 days   N/K

This peak is the highest point of the Cordillera Central. It consists of four summits in a roughly N-S line. The highest point is known as Mayor. The often quoted height of 5750m is almost certainly an exaggeration, the above height is taken from the SRTM data. After many years of lying dormant this volcanic peak erupted in 2006 and continues to erupt. The historic route as described below will have been seriously affected by these recent eruptions which have caused some major mudslides and melted a large proportion of the glaciers.

Huila is likely to be driest in June, July and August, with a short less dry spell in January, but this is a mountain that attracts a lot of rainfall even for Colombia!

ACCESS Get reliable up-to-date advice about the security situation before venturing into this area as there have been long term problems with guerilla activity around Huila. From the city of Cali to Toez (PT) where there are some shops. The trail starts at an altitude of 3000m about 25km N of Toez. Leave the road approx. 2km N of the Inderena hut (2910m) and climb up the Q. Verdun to the NE through forest (a guide and a few machetes will be useful) for about 2½km then turn S and head up steeply at first onto the páramo. Then head generally SE towards the mountain to the snowline at about 4400m. Make a high camp on the glacier at 4600m, 2d.

CLIMB The ordinary route is on the W face over glaciers. Grade is now n/k, but it was about PD/AD in the 1990's. A new volcanic cone has begun to develop in the general area of this route, so expect major changes once Nevado del Huila becomes safe enough to climb again.

OTHER PEAKS The high peak at the N end of the chain, **Pico La Cresta 5100,** is a difficult mixed climb by the S ridge. Probably AD or harder.

BEST MAP In the book Alta Colombia. CIGM sheet 321, 1:100,000, shows the approach but has no detail for the summit.

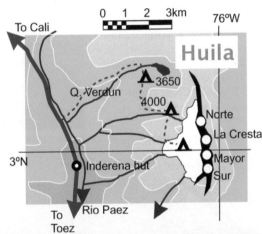

Nevado del Huila from the NE

Volcan PURACE 4646m   1 day   F
Cerro PAN de AZUCAR 4670m   3 days   F

These peaks are the highest two in the chain of volcanic summits known as the Sierra Nevada de los Coconucos. There is a chain of four summits in a roughly NW-SE line. Snow is not very common in this range. With other peaks in the extreme SW of Colombia, these two mountains are best climbed in a dry season during June, July and August. There have been problems in the past with access to these mountains due to FARC guerilla activity.

ACCESS From the beautiful colonial city of Popayan to the village of Purace (PT) and La Cruz on the NW slopes of the mountain, and then on up a very rough track to the small settlement of Pilimbala at 3500m. This track now continues on to radio masts at 4050m, but may not be driveable or accessible.

PURACE CLIMB Purace is an easy ascent from the radio masts, 2-3h. by the NW slopes.

PAN DE AZUCAR CLIMB Pan de Azucar lies approximately 5km SE of Purace. The easiest option is to continue onwards from the summit of Purace, with a high camp as necessary. There are a number of intermediate peaks, mainly volcanic craters.

OTHER PEAKS 25km SW of these two peaks is another high volcano, **Volcan Sotara 4580m**. No details known of the easiest access.

KEY WAYPOINTS End of road 02°20'06"N 76°23'45" Purace summit 02°18'50"N 76°23'51"

BEST MAP CIGM sheet 365, "Coconuco" at 1:100,000, has good topographic detail but does not show roads and tracks well. There is also a good sketch map in the book Alta Colombia.

Volcan Purace from the NW

Pan de Azucar from Purace

Popayan city centre

Volcan GALERAS 4276m

1 day   F

Galeras is a highly active volcano near the city of Pasto. Its summit is a crater blown out to the W, with a new ash and cinder dome growing inside the crater. The highest point is on the crater rim. The peak was the location of a disastrous scientific expedition in 1993 when six vulcanologists were killed by a sudden eruption. Access to the peak is often barred because of the danger of a repeat accident.

Volcan Galeras from Pasto

ACCESS AND CLIMB From the city of Pasto a dirt road leads up to the crater. Stroll easily to the summit

BEST MAP Not known

Volcan CUMBAL 4764m

2 days   F

Cumbal is a high peak near the border with Ecuador.

ACCESS From the city of Ipiales to the wee town of Cumbal, which lies at 3000m on the SE flanks of the volcano. From here follow a track upwards, passing close to the Laguna Cumbal, to reach a col at 3450m that is immediately E of the peak.

CLIMB From the end of the track it is about 5km over generally easy terrain to the summit.

OTHER PEAKS About 20km further south, **Volcan Chiles 4723m F,** lies on the border with Ecuador. In recent years it has been very active volcanically and there have also been problems with FARC guerilla activity in the area. No recent ascents are known.

BEST MAP There is a good sketch map in the book Alta Colombia.

ECUADOR

INTRODUCTION
Ecuador has been a popular destination for mountaineers travelling to South America ever since Whymper climbed in the famous 'Avenue of the Volcanoes' at the end of the 19th century. The fame of mountains such as Chimborazo and Cotopaxi surpasses the importance of the mountains of Ecuador in the Andes as a whole; in reality the Andes of Ecuador are a small fraction of the what the continent has to offer.

The volcanoes of Ecuador are generally busy mountains and the climate in Ecuador can best be described as variable and not ideal for mountaineering. On all the big peaks in Ecuador conditions have been getting worse over the years, with more crevasse problems and more rockfall danger. The mountains will be something of a disappointment to more experienced mountaineers and recently it has become mandatory to hire an Ecuadorian guide, making them even less attractive. However for novices the mountains are some of the most accessible in the Andes. They provide relatively easy ascents to high altitude, the logistics are easy and there are huts on all the high peaks.

MANDATORY GUIDE POLICY
Since 2012 Ecuador has had a policy that all climbs in protected areas such as national parks must be done with an Ecuadorian guide. This unfortunately includes almost all of the peaks of interest to independent climbers. Unlike in other parts of the Andes, where experienced and/or qualified mountaineers can usually climb without a guide, in Ecuador this rule seems to be strictly enforced. Until this law is revoked Ecuador is not a good destination for independent climbers.

GETTING THERE
From Europe there are direct flights to Quito from only Amsterdam (KLM) and Madrid (Iberia). From London and other cities you will need to change planes either in Europe or in Panama or Bogotá. From North America there are direct flights to Quito from Miami, New York, Atlanta and Houston.

SEASON AND WEATHER CONDITIONS
The weather patterns are very complicated and very localised but with two dry(ish) seasons; June to July and November to January. Neither of these seasons is perfectly dry and climbs can be successful at other times of the year. The only period to avoid completely is the very wet March to May. Expect on average only 2-3 good days in a week even in the dry seasons.

The eastern peaks are particularly affected by the proximity of the Amazon basin and Antisana, El Altar and Sangay suffer from very wet climates. These peaks are best in December to February. The western peaks are driest from June to August but also have a short dry season around December. These western peaks are very wet from February to April. Cotopaxi, surrounded by the other peaks, is noticeably drier than most.

CLIMBING CONDITIONS
Ecuador gets lots of fresh snow so climbs are often in heavy or windblown snow, however the popularity of the normal climbing routes means there will almost always be a good trail. Whenever you climb the weather is likely to be unreliable and a very early start should be made to reach the summit soon after first light. Cloud often builds on the summits as early as 8am.

The refuges can be very busy at weekends due to the easy access and the popularity of climbing in Ecuador. Most have basic facilities i.e. water, WC, cooking facilities and bunks, but you'll usually need your own sleeping bag and food.

OTHER CLIMBING GUIDEBOOKS
Ecuador: Climbing and Hiking guide, Rachowiecki and Thurber, Viva Travel Guides, 2009.
Ecuador: A Climbing Guide, Brain, Cordee, 2000.

QUITO The capital of Ecuador and an excellent base 2800m

The capital of Ecuador is a beautifully situated city with views to the snow capped volcanoes Cotopaxi
and Cayambe. It was the northern capital of the Inca Empire at the time of the Spanish conquest.
Although no trace of the Incas remain, many beautiful Spanish colonial buildings can be seen in the
old town, parts of which have been designated as a world heritage site. At an altitude of 2800m the
city makes a good base for climbing the volcanoes of Ecuador. The nearby peaks of Pasochoa, Rucu
Pichincha and Fuya Fuya, all described below, are good for day walks to acclimatise.

SIGHTS There are the usual mixture of museums in the city and a few kilometres N the Equator
itself can be visited in a half day trip. The spectacular crater at Pululagua is also worth seeing while
acclimatising.

FOOD There is a good choice of supermarkets, called 'Supermaxi' in the new town, e.g. in the
Multicentro on 6 de Diciembre or in the Iñaquito and Jardin shopping malls near Parque Carolina.

FUEL Most of the mountain refuges have gas stoves. Bencina blanca (white gas) can be bought from
'Los Alpes' on Reina Victoria, on the corner with Wilson. Gas canisters from here or various other
sports and mountain equipment retailers around the new town (see below).

MOUNTAIN INFO Try the South American Explorers Club at Jorge Washington 311 or the Nuevos
Horizontes Club at Colon 2038 or the agencies listed below.

MOUNTAIN TRANSPORT For private transport to the mountains try one of the following agencies:
Javier Herrera can be particularly recommended, contact him online through his agency Andean Face.
Safari (online) and Alta Montaña on Jorge Washington have also been in the business for a long time
and have been reliable.

MOUNTAIN EQUIPMENT There are several shops on Mera that sell gear, including Tatoo and
'Andes 6000' which are almost next door to each other. Or try Los Alpes on Reina Victoria, address as
above. Some of the agencies will rent gear, especially if you are climbing with them.

Quito rooftops

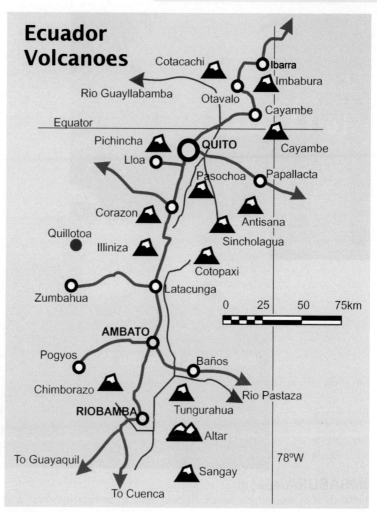

Ecuador Volcanoes

COTACACHI 4944m — 2 days — AD

Cotacachi is a rock peak lying NW of the tourist town of Otavalo and near the spectacular Lag. Cuicocha. The rock is not very good quality and rockfall is a big danger.

ACCESS From Quito via Otavalo, Cotacachi town and then Quiroga to the Lag. Cuicocha park entrance station at 3100m. From here a road on the R (normally gated) leads up the S side of the mountain to a number of radio antennae at 4100m. This is a 4x4 drive or a 4-5h. walk.

CLIMB At a hairpin bend at 4050m, just before the end of the road at the antennae, take a trail heading R up a grassy ridge. At the first rocks start a rising traverse L over the S slopes (rockfall) to reach a prominent notch on the SW ridge. Cross the notch then traverse under the S peak until reaching a short couloir (rock to grade IV) which is climbed with a deviation to the R at about 15m, then followed up to the summit ridge, 4-5h. Descend by abseil.

KEY WAYPOINTS Cuicocha park entrance 00°17'34"N 78°21'15" End of track 00°20'11"N 78°20'24" Summit 00°21'39"N 78°20'57"

BEST MAP EIGM 1:50,000 sheet 3995-III 'Imantag'

Cotacachi from Otavalo

Imbabura from the S

summit

IMBABURA 4621m
1 day   PD

Imbabura is an impressively steep and grassy volcano, particularly when viewed from the start of the S route. It lies just north of the scenic Lago San Pablo. The summit is on the W side of a partial crater rim, which is blown out to the E.

ACCESS The normal route is from the N and the little village of La Esperanza. A 4x4 track reaches about 3000m on the NE slopes Access is also possible to the S side of the mountain through the village of San Pablo del Lago. Turn R when you reach the plaza, then 1km out of town turn L onto a cobbled road. Follow this steeply up through eucalyptus and farmsteads for 3km (4x4 not necessary), to park at about 3100m.

NORTHERN CLIMB Climb steeply up the NE slopes on a good path to the N summit. The final section along the crater rim to the main summit includes some scrambling on poor quality rock.

SOUTHERN CLIMB The S route is steeper and slightly more difficult than the N route. It is also reported to be harder to follow. Several starts are possible, but climb the grassy slope R of the big gully until below the summit cone. Traverse R here to reach the RH end of the crater ridge, and then climb steeply back W to the true summit.

KEY WA YPOINTS S start 00°13'21"N 78°10'38" Summit 00°15'39"N 78°10'51"

BEST MAP EIGM sheet 3994-I 'San Pablo del Lago' 1:50,000.

CAYAMBE 5790m   2 days   PD/AD

Cayambe is the highest mountain in the world actually on the equator. The grade can vary from F to AD depending on the difficulties at the last big crevasse. Like many peaks in Ecuador conditions have been getting steadily worse for many years, with more crevasse problems and more rockfall danger.

ACCESS From Quito to Cayambe town. 1km S of Cayambe town take a cobbled road which reaches the Hacienda Piemonte Bajo just after a tunnel. Turn L here and continue past the Hacienda Piemonte Alto (3600m) to the refuge on the SW slopes of Cayambe (4650m), good facilities but no food. The last part of this road (about 1h. walk) requires 4x4 and some of it may have to be walked if it is in poor condition or if your driver is timid.

CLIMB Climb the rocky peak behind the refuge, pass a small lagoon and then go directly on to the glacier at 4900m. Climb N past small rock outcrops at 5200m towards the vague W ridge of Cayambe. Just before reaching this ridge turn E towards the summit. There can be large and difficult crevasses here in some years, and a long traverse R or L may be needed, 7h.

OTHER ROUTES The old route from the N joins the normal route at the W ridge.

OTHER PEAKS 20km SE of Cayambe is **Sara Urcu, 4670m** reached by taking the R turn at Hac.

Piemonte Bajo. Drive a few km then walk about 30km to the W side of the peak. A local guide and mules are recommended. No details of the climb but reported to be easy. There is a small glacier, 6d.

KEY WAYPOINTS Hut 00°00'28"N   78°00'46"
Summit   00°01'30"N 77°59'21"

BEST   MAP   EIGM sheet 3994-II 'Cayambe' and 4094-III 'Nevado Cayambe' both 1:50,000. Sheet 4093-IV 'Sara Urcu' for Sara Urcu.

Cayambe from the hut

hut

ANTISANA 5758m   3 days   PD/AD

Antisana is an active but no longer conical volcano. The central summit is the highest. It is usually the hardest of the four big summits in Ecuador. It gets fewer ascents than the other big peaks because there is no hut.

ACCESS Permission needs to be obtained from the owners of the Hacienda Antisana in Quito. Phone 02 455697. From Quito to Pintag (2850m) (PT). Just beyond the town is a locked gate. Go L and follow the good new road towards the Hac. Antisana (4100m). Turn L towards the mountain just before reaching the hacienda then after 2-3 km take a very faint grassy track on the L (4x4 necessary from here) which leads NE to the Lag. Santa Lucia. Just before reaching the lagoon a faint 4x4 track on the R climbs the W side of the mountain to a base camp below the moraines (4600m). Antisana can also be approached from Lag. Papallacta to the N.

CLIMB Climb the moraines and cross a stream to gain the glacier on the R. Climb steep slopes directly towards the summit. The best route across the glacier changes frequently. In particular the summit is surrounded by a big crevasse and a long traverse (R or L depending on the year) may be needed to cross it, 7h.

OTHER ROUTES The old route began further S and climbed towards the lowest point of the ridge joining the central and S summit (known as Antisanilla). Just before the ridge turn L and follow the glacier slope N avoiding crevasses. The **S peak**, sometimes called Antisanilla, can be climbed from a high glacier camp on the old normal route. Mixed rock and ice.

SUMMIT WAYPOINT 00°29'04"S 78°08'29"

BEST MAP EIGM sheet 3992-I 'Papallacta' 1:50,000.

Antisana from the W

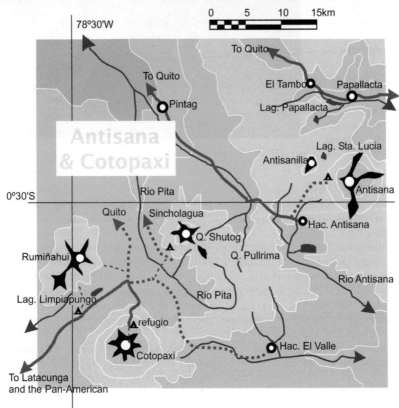

GUAGUA PICHINCHA 4784m
RUCU PICHINCHA 4627m

1 day   F
1 day   F

The Pichinchas are two rock peaks lying immediately above Quito. Guagua is an active volcano which erupted in 1999. Rucu Pichincha has a short but attractive scramble on its SE ridge as well as an easy N ridge. The peaks can be climbed indivdaully from either access route, or combined into a traverse in one long day or with a high camp.

RUCU PICHINCHA ACCESS The best access to Rucu Pichincha is directly from Quito via the Teleferiqo cable car, which runs to Cruz Loma (3980m) above the city.

GUAGUA PICHINCHA ACCESS For vehicle access to the peaks, and the shortest approach for Guagua, drive from Quito to the village of Lloa (PT). In Lloa take the cobbled Calle Pichincha which leads past the Hac. Concepcion de Monjas and continues to the 'Refugio Volcan' at 4600m on Guagua Pichincha. (workers hut - no accommodation).

Guagua

Rucu

The Pichinchas from Cruz Loma

RUCU CLIMB From the top of the cable car head along the long grassy ridge to below the SE ridge of Rucu. From here follow a good path R that makes a rising traverse across sandy slopes to reach the N (or NW) ridge. This ridge gives enjoyable grade I scrambling. The SE ridge gives more sustained scrambling at about grade III, the best descent is by the normal route.

GUAGUA CLIMB From the hut at 4600m go up a diagonal path L to the crater rim then walk back R (N) along the rim to the first summit and then the highest summit, some easy scrambling, ½h.

RUCU FROM GUAGUA At about 4100m on the road to the Refugio Volcan there is a large car park. From here follow the valley N to a broad col at 4300m then climb the hill to the E. From this hill (Co. La Plazuela) follow the ridge N and then E over another summit to the summit of Rucu Pichincha, 2-3h. To reach Guagua from Cruz Loma follow the obvious valley up and E of Rucu.

RUCU PICHINCHA WAYPOINTS Cruz Loma 00°11'12"S 78°32'14" Below SE ridge 00°09'56"S 78°33'36" Col in NW ridge 00°09'41"S 78°34'00".

GUAGUA SUMMIT WAYPOINT 00°10'40"S 78°35'57".

BEST MAPS EIGM sheets 3893-I 'Nono' and 3893-II 'Quito' both at 1:50,000

summit   SE ridge

normal route goes around back

Rucu Pichincha

FUYA FUYA 4279m
Cerro PASOCHOA 4199m

1 day   PD
1 day   PD

These two peaks make good acclimatisation days from Quito. Both can be climbed in long day trips from the city. Pasochoa is a climb through forests 30km south of the city, Fuya Fuya is the highest point of the huge, lake filled, Mojanda crater to the north.

PASOCHOA Drive from Quito via Sangolqui to the park. The turn off is well signposted, 2km S of Amaguaña on the main road to Aloag. Entry to the park is expensive. Follow signed trails up through interesting tropical forest then up a grassy ridge with a tricky rock step at 3900m and on to the summit, 5h.

FUYA FUYA From Quito or Otavalo get a hired vehicle to take you to the Mojanda crater. From the NW corner of the lagoon follow trails across the hillside then make a rising traverse of the grassy S slopes to a col behind the E peak. Continue along the ridge to the higher W peak, with short sections of climbing to grade III.

BEST MAPS For Pasochoa EIGM sheets 3892-I 'Amaguaña' and 3992-IV 'Pintag'. For Fuya Fuya EIGM sheet 3994-III 'Mojanda'.

CORAZON 4782m

1 day   PD

An easy and accessible rock peak. Corazon means heart in Spanish. Permission (possibly with payment) may be required from the Hacienda San Juan.

ACCESS From Quito to the town of Machachi (PT) then by taxi or colectivo through Aloasi to the disused station at 3100m, 4km W of Machachi. From the station go N for 150m then turn L across the railway and uphill. Follow this cobbled road for 300m then turn L again and follow this dirt track up the hill through several gates, ignoring any R or L turns. This track becomes increasingly difficult, but with a 4x4 it may be possible to reach 3800m.

CLIMB When it is no longer possible to drive continue walking up the track, taking the L fork at 4100m, until it finally ends at 4300m in a basin beneath the prominent col immediately N of Corazon. Climb to the col (4460m) then climb the LHS of the NE ridge including an easy 5m rock step (II).

CORAZON WAYPOINTS Turn onto dirt track 00°30'55"S 78°36'08" 3400m 00°31'06"S 78°36'43" End of track 00°31'40"S 78°39'00" Below ridge 00°31'39"S 78°33'23" .

BEST MAP EIGM 1:50,000 sheet 3892-II 'Machachi'.

Corazon from the NE

NE ridge

ILLINIZA Sur 5245m   3 days   AD/D
ILLINIZA Norte 5105m   2 days   F/PD

The S peak of the twin Illiniza peaks is a steep and glaciated summit, often quite difficult. Snow and ice conditions on this peak are highly variable from season to season but there is much less than there used to be! The N peak is a relatively straightforward rock scramble. Both peaks can be climbed from a staffed refuge in the col which separates them.

ACCESS From Quito to the town of Machachi then to the small village of El Chaupi (3350m)(PT) then on a cobbled road to the park entrance station at 3500m. A deteriorating 4x4 track continues from here via the Hac. El Refugio. It goes W for about 3km then turns L and goes SW up the ridge on the S side of the Q. Pilongo to a car park at 4000m, known as La Virgen, where there is a small campground (water but no toilet). From here follow the track up the ridge to join a path up the sandy ridge which leads to the refuge (15 beds, toilet and gas) at 4750m beneath the col which separates the peaks, 3h from car park.

ILLINIZA SUR CLIMB From the refuge head W towards the col then climb up onto a flattish moraine hill. From here the normal route crosses the lower glacier on the R then climbs back leftwards up a ramp passing large seracs at half height and finishing up a snow gully below the N summit, 6h, ice to 60°. The direct route can be easier or more difficult depending on the year. It climbs the icy couloir directly under the N summit of Illiniza Sur, usually exiting on the L.

ILLINIZA NORTE CLIMB Illiniza Norte can also be climbed from the refuge. From the col climb up easy slopes to gain the SE ridge of the N peak which is an interesting rock scramble blocked by a steep wall two thirds of the way up. To reach the summit skirt this wall on the R, make a rising traverse under the buttresses beneath the summit then climb L up a gully to the summit with the cross, 2h. To continue on to the second summit raises the grade to PD. Normally the route does not require an ice-axe or crampons.

KEY WAYPOINTS Park entrance 00°35'58"S 78°40'09" Car Park 00°37'46"S 78°41'18" Refugio 00°39'19"S 78°42'46" Illiniza Sur summit 00°39'48"S 78°42'57" Illiniza Norte summit 00°38'58"S 78°43'13"

BEST MAP EIGM sheet 3892-II, 'Machachi' 1:50,000.

The Illinizas from El Chaupi

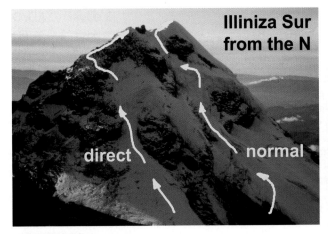

Illiniza Sur
from the N

direct   normal

route goes
behind

Illiniza Norte
from the hut

COTOPAXI 5897m   2 days   PD

Cotopaxi is a spectacular heavily glaciated volcanic cone, seen on the skyline from Quito. The name means 'collar of the moon'. The mountain is often wrongly claimed to be the world's highest active volcano, but several peaks in northern Chile and southern Peru are higher and (at least currently) more active. Cotopaxi was very active from the 1850's to 1870's. The volcano now forms the centrepiece to one of Ecuador's most famous national parks. The normal route is on the N side, in recent years it has been getting steadily more difficult and dangerous.

ACCESS See map on page 58. The nearest PT is at the park entrance station near the Pan American highway about 20km due W of the volcano. In the nearest towns of Lasso and Latacunga jeeps or pickups can be hired for the drive up to a parking area at 4600m. The refuge is ½h directly up hill from here. The refuge was being renovated in 2015. There were about 100 beds and cooking facilities. It can be extremely busy at times.

Cotopaxi from the N

hut

CLIMB Overall, the route now climbs further R than it previously did. From the refuge climb diagonally R across the triangular scree slope and then onto the glacier on the RHS. Move up and around large crevasses passing the huge rockband (known as Yanasacha) on the R. Once past Yanasacha move back L and up steeper snow slopes to the summit crater, 6h. There are now usually at least one or two pitches of steep snow or ice on this route.

OTHER ROUTES It is also possible to climb Cotopaxi from the south, and there is now a hut at Rasularca (4000m). Horses can be rented here. From the hut climb sandy slopes for 3h to reach a sandy high camp at 4700m, just L of the low glacier tongue. Go onto the glacier at 5000m and climb up and L to 5200m to avoid a serac zone, then more directly up to the crater, 5-6h. There are usually a few short sections of steeper climbing (to 40°).

OTHER PEAKS To the SE of Cotopaxi, **Quilindaña, 4878m, about AD** can be climbed from a high camp at the small lake on the NW slopes (4350m). From the lake climb the couloir to the NW ridge. Climb the ridge direct on good rock, grade IV-V. 2d.

KEY WAYPOINTS Refuge 00°39'50"S 78°26'17" Summit 00°40'51"S 78°26'17"

BEST MAP EIGM sheet 3991-IV 'Cotopaxi' 1:50,000. There is also a good 1:40,000 map published by Climbing-map titled "Cotopaxi".

SINCHOLAGUA 4873m 2 days AD
RUMIÑAHUI 4722m 1 day AD

These two rock peaks lie NE and NW of Cotopaxi. Rumiñahui is in the national park.

ACCESS See map on page 58. For Rumiñahui drive as for Cotopaxi to the organised campsite at 3800m near Limpiopungo (toilets and water). For Sincholagua continue through the park to the N entrance station. Turn R just before it and follow the track across the Rio Pita then another track uphill to a base camp at 4000m on a moraine ridge beneath the SW side of the peak (no water).

SINCHOLAGUA CLIMB The normal route is on the NW ridge. From camp follow a long grassy moraine ridge NE, that leads to near the foot of the NW ridge at 4300m. Once on the ridge there is a fair amount of scrambling, often on the LHS, and a short but loose section of grade IV near the top, 4-5h. from the camp at 4000m. Descent by abseil.

route behind summit
NW ridge
Sincholagua from the SW

RUMIÑAHUI CLIMB The highest peak, at the N end of the ridge is the hardest summit to climb. From either the campsite or Limpiopungo head NW over grassy slopes and hills to get beneath the E face of the central summit. From about 4300m make a rising traverse R across the E face on grass and scree until past the lowest point of the ridge above, then climb up to the S ridge of the N summit. Once on the ridge there are several difficulties, mainly turned on the LH side (W side). This S ridge can also be reached by a long grassy ridge more directly from the E, passing a nice campsite in the trees at 4000m. The central and S summits can both be climbed relatively easily by their S or E slopes at grades of F/PD.

SINCHOLAGUA WAYPOINTS Camp at 4000m 00°33'13"S 78°24'04"

RUMIÑAHUI WAYPOINTS National park campsite at 3800m 00°38'04"S 78°28'58"

BEST MAP EIGM sheets 3992-III 'Sincholagua' and 3991-IV 'Cotopaxi' both 1:50,000. Sheet 3892-II, 'Machachi' 1:50,000 for the summit of Rumiñahui.

Central summit

route lies behind

N summit

From Limpiopungo

Rumiñahui from the E

CHIMBORAZO 6270m   2 days   PD/AD

Chimborazo is the highest peak in Ecuador and it was for a time in the 1700's thought to be the highest peak in the world. Due to the earth's equatorial bulge, Chimborazo does in fact have the distinction that its summit is further from the centre of the earth than any other point on the earth's surface. The normal route was from the Whymper refuge on the SW face and W ridge, but this has become very problematical in recent years due to icy conditions and frequent rockfall.

ACCESS For the normal route drive from Riobamba all the way to the Carrel refuge (4850m) at the road end. There is another refuge, called the Whymper refuge, at 5000m, ½h walk from the Carrel hut. It has gas, toilets and 40 bunks and was being renovated in 2015.

CLIMB For the normal route climb from the Whymper refuge NW up scree to gain the glacier by a large ramp below the prominent rock known as El Castillo (rockfall danger). Gaining the glacier can be very difficult in some years (50° ice). Climb R along this ramp then more steeply up and L to the ridge above El Castillo at 5500m. It is possible to camp here on the N side of the ridge, to shorten the summit day considerably. From El Castillo climb the broad glacier W ridge to the Veintimilla summit, a long tedious ascent, total 8h. The main summit is due E and 1km away across the plateau, just ½h more in good conditions. It is possible, and probably safer, to gain the ridge earlier and traverse high up, just underneath the Castillo rock.

Chimborazo from the SW

Veintimilla

Castillo

high approach

old route

OTHER ROUTES Due to the hazards of the old normal route a new route has been developed on the **W face** using the Stubel glacier. This route starts from the Carrel hut by making a long rising traverse N, then NE on scree and sand to a high camp just below the glacier edge at 5000m, 3h. From here climb the glacier with one or two snow/ice pitches, to 50°, then climb snow to gain the W ridge above El Castillo. Continue to the main summit as above, 8h.

From camps on the E side of Chimborazo the E summit of Chimborazo (called Martinez 5570m) can be climbed by the Moreno glacier on the E flank, turning a rock outcrop high up by the SE. The integral traverse (E-W) was first done in 1980 and will require 3-4d.

KEY WAYPOINTS Carrel refuge 01°28'31"S 78°50'45" Whymper refuge 01°28'22"S 78°50'20" Ridge above Castillo 01°27'58"S 78°49'57" Summit 01°28'09"S 78°49'13"

BEST MAP EIGM, sheet 3889-IV 'Chimborazo' 1:50,000.

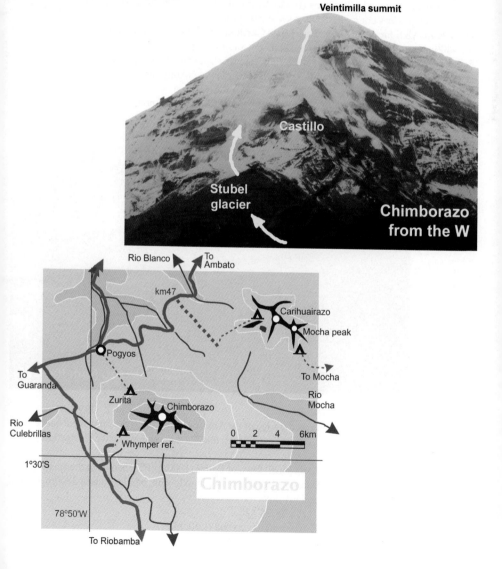

CARIHUAIRAZO 5018m

2 days   AD

Carihuairazo is a small glaciated peak about 10km NE of Chimborazo. The normal route to the highest summit is on the W flank.

ACCESS Approach from the Ambato-Guaranda road (PT) turning off S at km47. Follow this 4x4 track, turning L then immediately R after 1km, to the Abraspungo col at about 4350m. From here make a 2-3h. walk past Lag. Negra and around the N side of a hill called Piedra Negra to gain a camp in the head of the Rio Blanco valley at 4600m. It is also possible to approach the mountain and join the same route via the Mocha and Tigre Saltana valleys which lie to the S of the peak, but this is a longer, steeper walk.

CLIMB Make a rising traverse from the 4600m camp to reach the SW glacier. Traverse the glacier to a ridge which leads upwards to the summit ridge. Once on the summit ridge turn L and climb to the first ridge top, then climb an icy chimney (III) to the foresummit, 3h. The final 10m summit block will be very difficult, grade VI or higher, poor rock and no protection.

OTHER PEAKS From the same camp **Little Carihuairazo, F** (4698m on the map but actually more like 4800m), can be climbed easily as far as the summit pinnacle. The lower east peak, known as **Mocha, c.4980m** can be climbed by the S ridge, approached from the village of Mocha to the E.

KEY WAYPOINTS km47 turn-off 01°23'01"S 78°50'04" Abraspungo col parking 01°24'41"S 78°47'28" Camp 01°24'25"S 78°45'54"

BEST MAP EIGM sheets 3889-I 'Quero' and 3889-IV 'Chimborazo' both at 1:50,000.

Carihuairazo from the SW

TUNGURAHUA 5023m

2 days   F

Tungurahua is a very active volcano on the edge of the Amazon basin. In recent years there has been so much activity, including fresh lava, ash and mud-flows, that the mountain will have changed radically. The old huts have certainly gone!

ACCESS & CLIMB From Quito to the small town of Baños (1800m)(PT) then on to the small village of Pondoa at 2400m. The normal route was from here on a muddy path, passing huts at 3800m, but the mountain will have changed substantially now.

KEY WAYPOINT Summit 01°28'12"S 78°26'42"

BEST MAP EIGM, sheet 3989-IV, 'Volcan Tungurahua' 1:50,000

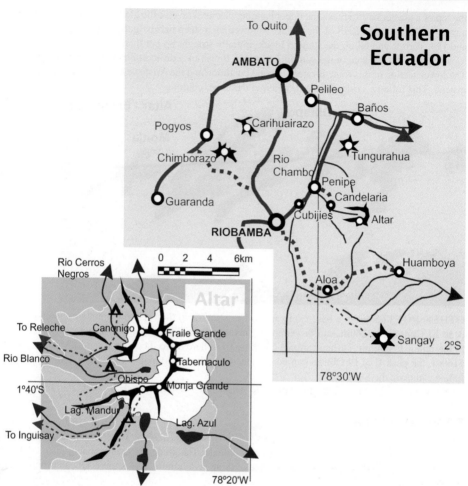

ALTAR 5319m

4 days   D/TD

Altar is the only big peak in Ecuador whose ascent is technically difficult and indeed the first ascent of the highest point was not until 1963. The mountain is a massive blown out crater with steep walls on three sides and a number of pinnacles around the crater rim, the highest of which is known as El Obispo. The rock has a reputation for being very poor, loose and scary. The climate is very wet. The native Quechua name for the mountain is Capac Urcu.

ACCESS From Quito by Riobamba to the village of Cubijies (PT) then by taxi or truck to Vaqueria Inguisay. Mules can be hired here for the walk up the Rio Paila Cajas and Rio Tiaco Chico to the base of the mountain and are strongly recommended. From the head of the Tiaco Chico valley climb steeply up E onto the ridge known as the Cordillera de Mandur and follow this ridge N to the Italian camp located on a level area of the ridge between the Lagunas Azul and Mandur (4600m), 6h from Vaqueria Inguisay using mules.

OBISPO CLIMB Known as the Italian route. From the Italian camp go N along the ridge, then make a short descent to scree slopes which lead up to the lower glacier above Lag. Azul (known as Lag. Negra Paccha on IGM map). Cross the lower glacier and climb a snow gully (50-60°) which cuts out R from the top of a glacier bay, to reach the upper hanging glacier. Traverse the glacier to the R and then climb a ramp on the extreme RHS of the glacier followed by a steep narrow gully to the summit ridge (65° and IV). Turn R and climb the summit block, initially straight up but then make a long traverse on a loose ledge to the far side of the summit block, III. Finish by a difficult 3m wall on better rock, V. 7h. The lower section of this route is rarely in good condition and the Arista de Calvario route is often used instead. This follows a ridge further E to avoid the lower couloir.

Obispo

Altar - El Obispo

Monja

enter gully

Arista de Calvario

OTHER ROUTES From a base camp at Rio Cos. Negros to the N of the mountain the 2nd highest peak **El Canonigo 5260m,** can be climbed. Traverse the NE glacier to reach a small ridge leading to the minor E summit. Difficult mixed climbing from here up to the main summit. **Monja Grande 5160m**, the peak E of El Obispo can be climbed from the col joining it to Obispo, gained from the Italian camp via the S glacier.

BEST MAP EIGM sheets 3988-IV 'Volcan El Altar' and 3989-III 'Palitahua', both 1:50,000.

SANGAY 5230m   8 days   PD

About 40km S of El Altar is the dangerously active volcano, Sangay. It lies in an isolated area of country SW of Riobamba and suffers a very wet climate. The grade of PD is probably justified due to the extreme objective danger from the barrage of large lava bombs. The name is Quechua and means 'the frightener'.

ACCESS From Quito via Riobamba to the village of Alao (3100m)(PT). Guides and mules can be hired here to get through difficult forest terrain to a camp at La Playa SW of the peak. Allow 3-4d. and expect a difficult and wet hike. There is now a small refugio at La Playa (no facilities).

CLIMB Climbing is reputedly safest by the S slopes but active volcanoes change fast! Crampons and ice-axe may be necessary depending on the state of the snow but there are no crevasses. The volcano spits out big boulders so watch out! 8h. from La Playa to the summit.

BEST MAP EIGM sheets 3987-IV 'Volcan Sangay' and 3988-III 'Llactapamba de Alao', both 1:50,000.

Sangay from the N

NORTHERN PERU

INTRODUCTION

The two main ranges of Northern Peru, the Cordillera Blanca and the nearby Cordillera Huayhuash are undoubtedly the most spectacular and challenging of the Andean ranges. There are 15 major 6000m summits, many of them amongst the hardest peaks to climb in the Andes. The twin summits of Huascarán dominate the northern end of the Cord. Blanca and are the 6th and 10th highest peaks in the Andes. Yerupajá towers over the other peaks of the Cord. Huayhuash and is the 13th highest peak in the Andes, and by far the most difficult and dangerous of the high peaks to climb..

For mountaineers the Cord. Blanca have the added bonus of relatively easy access. Most base camps can be reached in a day from the large valley, called the Callejón de Huaylas, which lies to the W of the mountains. The main town in this valley is Huaraz. Access to the Cord. Huayhuash takes a little longer, with most base camps taking at least 2-3 days of trekking to reach from the main roadhead in the village of Llamac.

Also included in this chapter are the Cordillera Raura immediately south of the Cord. Huayhuash with peaks up to 5700m and several ranges inland from Lima with peaks of up to 5900m high, collectively known as the Central Cordilleras.

GETTING THERE

All areas are easiest to approach by flying to Lima, the capital of Peru. From Europe there are direct flights from Madrid (Iberia), Amsterdam (KLM), Paris (Air France) and Frankfurt (Lufthansa) to Lima. There are no direct flights from London so a change in Europe or a flight via the USA, Bogotá or Caracas will be necessary. From the USA there are many direct flights from Miami to Lima and a few from LA, Atlanta, New York and Houston, with LAN or with United, Delta or American.

From Lima there are now regular flights to the Huaraz airport at Anta, currently with LC Peru. However baggage may be limited. There are also regular buses making the spectacular 8h journey. Most buses are reasonably comfortable and the road is now surfaced all the way - the best and safest companies are Cruz del Sur and Movil Tours.

For the Cord. Huayhuash there are direct buses from Lima to Chiquian but it may be easier to go via Huaraz, particularly if you have food, mules etc. to arrange. A few peaks of the Huayhuash are more accessible from Cajatambo to the SW, with direct buses from Lima.

For the Central Cordilleras see individual entries for the best access. This will normally involve a bus journey direct from Lima, though there may be an advantage to basing yourself in one of the highland towns of La Oroya, Cerro de Pasco or Huancayo for the altitude advantage.

Landing at Anta airport, Huaraz

SEASON AND WEATHER CONDITIONS

The climbing season extends from May to September, with June and July reckoned to be the best months. Although this is winter, it is the dry season in the mountains. The weather is generally stable with normally only one or two bad days in a week. Freezing level is about 5000m during the day, but strong sun can make it feel much warmer. Wind is rarely a major problem in the dry season although individual days can be bad. Bad weather comes from the Amazon side of the mountains, from the E or the N. There is a tendency for the weather to cloud over earlier in the day than in the Alps, often from about 8 a.m. to noon, then sometimes clear again by early afternoon.

The Central Cordilleras (Tunshu and Ticlla) have a noticeably drier and more settled climate because they are sheltered from the worst of the Amazon weather. The two ranges providing the shelter, the Cord. Huaytapallana and Cord. Huagaruncho have a noticeably wetter climate.

CLIMBING CONDITIONS

Ascents of the highest peaks are mostly snow and ice routes. In general the N faces are more likely to have good ice or neve, but suffer from the worst soft snow in the afternoons. S and SW faces often have soft unconsolidated powder and E and W faces tend to have mixed conditions. Penitentes are present on some N faces but are neither very common nor very large. Deep soft snow can be a problem above 5500m, but on many of the more popular peaks someone will already have made a trail for you.

Ridges in this part of Peru are famous for being unstable, often doubly corniced, and therefore very difficult. Many, including those on such popular peaks as Alpamayo, are unjustifiably dangerous for the average expedition and most climbers are satisfied with an ascent to the ridge.

Snow avalanches are relatively rare in the climbing season but do occur at the start of the season and after heavy recent snowfall. Serac collapses can be a danger on many of the normal routes, particularly Huascaran - watch where you camp.

Many of the routes change considerably from year to year as the glaciers move. In some years even popular peaks can be impassable to all but the most determined and well equipped expeditions. Good examples are the popular peaks of Tocllaraju and Chopicalqui, both of which have wide 'blocking' crevasses, which if not adequately bridged will make an ascent very problematical. The most stable routes from one season to another are those on SE through to SW faces, such as the normal routes on Alpamayo and Artesonraju. For a successful trip it is really essential to be flexible about your plans and enquire locally when you get to Huaraz about current conditions. It is also wise not to be too fixed on doing a 6000m peak - many of the 5500-5999m peaks are simpler, safer and quieter, in many years!

OTHER CLIMBING GUIDEBOOKS

This is one of the few areas of the Andes with a fair number of guidebooks published.
Classic Climbs of the Cordillera Blanca, **Johnson**, Western Reflections 2003.
Climbs of the Cordillera Blanca of Peru, **Sharman**, 1995.
Yuraq Janka, **Ricker**, American Alpine Club, 1977, now very dated, but still available.
Escaladas en los Andes - Guia de la Cordillera Blanca, **Juanjo Tome**, Spanish Language, Ediciones Desnivel, 2000.
Climbs & Treks in the Cordillera Huayhuash of Peru, **Frimer**, Elaho 2005.

MAPS

Names have mainly been taken from Felipe Diaz's map 'Cordilleras Blanca and Huayhuash' at approx. 1:200,000. This is a very useful map which is available cheaply in Huaraz. The new Alpenvereins (AV) maps (published in 2000 & 2005) are easily the best maps for the Cord. Blanca, and the 2004 Alpine Mapping Guild map is best for the Cord. Huayhuash. The PIGM maps are less detailed and use some unusual names that are often not understood locally.

PEAK HEIGHTS

Heights used in this chapter have mainly been taken from the PIGM maps, with the AV map used when no height is given on the PIGM map. The AV heights are based on an older survey and are generally 20-30m higher. Digital mapping data has cast considerable doubt on the accuracy of accepted heights of many Cord. Blanca peaks. While many peaks do not have good digital elevation data, some of those that do show considerable discrepancies. For this reason Tocllaraju is now believed to be a sub-6000m peak. Photographic analysis has also revealed height and position discrepancies, as well as strong indications that Artesonraju is more likely to be 5999m than 6025m and that Caraz is also probably a sub-6000m peak.

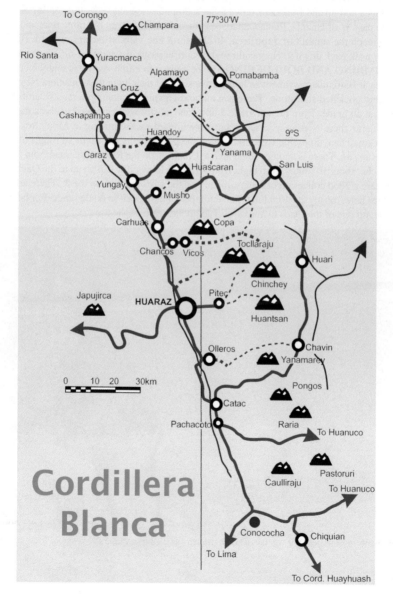

HUARAZ The main town of the Cordillera Blanca　　3100m

Huaraz sits at 3100m in the southern half of the Callejon de Huaylas and makes an ideal base for the Cord. Blanca. It is a cheerful and relatively prosperous town. For mountaineers it has as many facilities as you'll need in Peru and easy onward access to the mountains. Most valley roadheads can be reached in a couple of hours drive by private transport or less than a day by public transport. The town is a very active climbing centre in season with lots of gear shops, plenty of cafes and good but cheap hotels full of climbers looking for partners.

SIGHTS The fascinating underground temple complex at Chavin is well worth a visit (take a torch) although this involves a 4h journey. Immediately above Huaraz are the ruins of Wilkawain, torch also necessary. Get a taxi up and walk back down as an acclimatisation day. For a longer day out take a taxi or bus to the pass W of Huaraz, Punta Callan, 4225m and walk N on an old mine road and the RHS of the ridge to reach the summit of **Japujirca, 4622m** for a fine view of the entire Cord. Blanca. From here you can walk back down to Huaraz through beautiful pastoral scenery, 4-6h. for the return trip.

ROCK CLIMBING AND BOULDERING The best place to climb nearby is undoubtedly the sport climbing area at Hatunmachay, about an hours drive south of the city in the Cordillera Negra. The rock is great quality pocketed sandstone. There is a hut and organised camping here, a beautiful view, and many routes at all grades from French grade 5 upwards, mostly well equipped in about the year 2010. Nearer to Huaraz there is some accessible but very limited rock-climbing at Monterrey, 7km N. of Huaraz. In a small canyon by the river and behind the public baths are ten or so routes of up to 20m, with old pegs in situ. There is another small area at Chancos, on the RHS of the road from Marcara just before Chancos, about 10 routes, 15m high, III to VI. For a longer day trip go up to the Quebrada Llaca, where there are a good collection of routes, mainly on the LHS but also on the R. There are now more than 50 routes here, mostly 20-40m long, bolt equipped and in the 5-6a grade range. For bouldering go to Huanchac, on one of the roads to Wilkawain about 3km, NE of the town.

Climbing at Hatunmachay in the Cordillera Negra

FOOD There are no great one-stop shops in Huaraz. The supermarket on the corner of the main street (Luzuriaga) and Raymondi has the best choice and there are a number of others in this area. The indoor market and surrounding area W of Luzuriaga has a reasonable choice of fresh fruit and vegetables. It is also a good place to look for better quality imported food such as biscuits, chocolate, muesli and dried foods.

FUEL The petrol station ('Grifo' - in Peru) on Raymondi just W of Luzuriaga sells petrol and kerosene and the hardware shops nearby sell bencina blanca. Bencina blanca can also be found on Cruz Romero near the market. Camping gas is available from several of the climbing shops around the Casa de Guias.

MOUNTAIN INFO The best place to go for information on conditions is the Casa de Guias (guides office) in a quiet square just E of Luzuriaga behind the banks. Many of the guides are very competent and well informed, particularly about the current state of popular routes; Damian Aurelio Vargas can be particularly recommended. The PIGM and AV maps can usually be bought here. Some of the tour and trekking agencies along the main street (Luzuriaga) are quite good for information, particularly if you're buying something from them.

If you want a partner try leaving a note at the Casa de Guias.

MOUNTAIN EQUIPMENT Several shops along the main street (Luzuriaga) and around the Casa de Guias in Plaza Ginebra sell and rent equipment. They generally have everything you would need for a high altitude climb but as most of this is second-hand or dumped equipment don't expect great quality. Rock shoes can also be hired if you want to chill out and do some sport routes at Hatunmachay.

MOUNTAIN TRANSPORT Many tour agencies up and down Luzuriaga will provide private transport and arrange donkey or porter services. Also try at the Casa de Guias on Plaza Ginebra. On Lucar y Torre by the river you can hire a rusty old pick-up truck for shorter journeys up to the mountains immediately above Huaraz.

Sunrise on Huascaran and Huandoy Sur, seen from Pisco

Nevado CHAMPARÁ 5735m   5 days   N/K

A small isolated massif lying N of the main range. Very rarely visited.
ACCESS From Huaraz to Yuracmarca then to Hac. Mirasanta (2600m) lying W of the peaks. From here gain access to the steep Q. Coronguillo through a tunnel, then walk up this quebrada keeping very high on the N side, to reach the Lag. Qollurcocha (Coillorcocha) (4000m) NW of the main peak.
CLIMB From Lag. Qollurcocha ascend to a col (c.4900m) on W ridge then traverse the steep N face on snow and ice to reach the summit.
OTHER PEAKS Further N lie the Cord. Rosco, access to this range is via Corongo. The highest peak is called **Rosco Grande 5188m**, climbed from the NW. This area is very rarely visited.
BEST MAP As for Santa Cruz below.

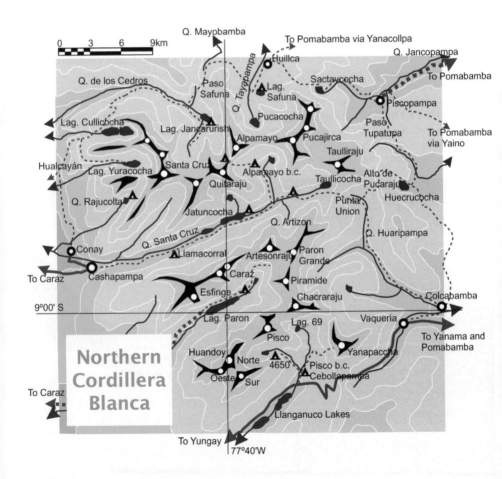

Nevado SANTA CRUZ 6241m   6 days   TD

A superb ice and granite pyramid also known as Pucaraju. A difficult peak by any route, the most frequently climbed line is the W ridge. The name is Spanish for holy cross.

ACCESS From Huaraz via Caraz to the village of Cashapampa (3000m) (PT). This is the start of many routes into the mountains and it is easy to arrange donkeys, find somewhere to sleep, etc. For the W ridge walk N via the village of Hualcayan then steeply up the slopes above to an aqueduct at 4500m. From here traverse R into the Q. Ragranco and up to Lag. Yuraccocha (4600m), 1½d. For SW face and ridge routes, approach via Q. Rajucolta, (Q. de los Baños on PIGM) by a path on the S side to a camp at a lagoon by the moraine (4600m), 1d.

CLIMB W ridge TD. From Yuraccocha climb S to the col, 5300m, overlooking Q. Rajucolta, camp possible. Ascend the W ridge on steep snow and ice slopes, often in runnels on either the LHS or RHS (55-60°), 2-3d from Yuraccocha.

OTHER ROUTES Other 'popular' routes include the **SW ridge, TD** joined from the RHS of the SW face (55-60°) at an altitude of 5600m. The ridge is mixed ground at about 40° with a possible bivouac at 6100m. Also the **N ridge, TD** climbed from Lag. Jancarurish (see Quitaraju for access). For the **NE face, TD** start near the centre of the face, take a steep right sloping ramp on mixed ground then finish up the N ridge.

BEST MAP AV sheet 0/3a 'Cordillera Blanca Nord' 1:100,000 or PIGM sheet 18-h 'Corongo' 1:100,000.

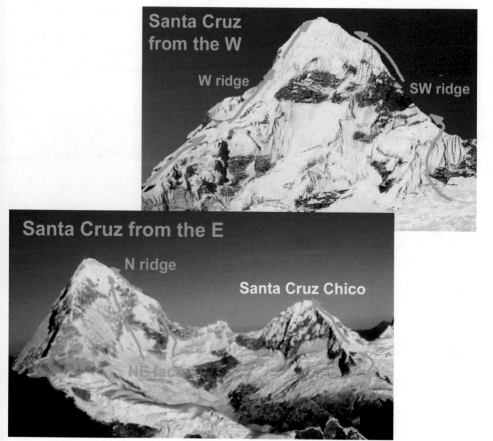

Santa Cruz from the W

W ridge   SW ridge

Santa Cruz from the E

N ridge

Santa Cruz Chico

NE face

Nevado QUITARAJU 6036m

6 days   AD/D

Also spelt Kitaraju. Climbed quite frequently due to the proximity of the more famous Alpamayo. The two peaks can be climbed from a high camp (5500m) in the col which separates them. Allow at least 8-9 days to climb both.

ACCESS From Huaraz to Cashapampa (3000m) (PT) then up the S side of the Q. Santa Cruz and then the Q. Arhuaycocha to the scenic but slightly squalid Alpamayo base camp at 4300m just below Lag. Arhuaycocha, 8-10h. This is normally done in 2 days with an intermediate camp at Llamacorral or Jatuncocha. At the LHS of the base camp is a semi-ruined hut. From behind this hut follow a cairned path steeply up the moraine slopes then over rock slabs (cairns) W to the glacier edge, 2-3h (moraine camp, 5000m). Continue up the glacier to below the Alpamayo-Quitaraju col, 3h. The final 100m section to the col has become much harder and steeper (up to 70°) in the last few years. Camp below the col on the other (north) side (5500m). This is the usual approach for both the W ridge and the N face of Quitaraju as well as for Alpamayo.

KEY WAYPOINTS Alpamayo base camp 08°53'35" 77°38'05" Glacier edge 08°53'24" 77°38'55" 5500m Col 08°53'09" 77°39'21" High Camp 08°53'01" 77°39'19" Summit 08°53'40" 77°39'50"

ACCESS FROM THE NORTH The Alpamayo-Quitaraju col can also be reached from the N and in some years this route may now be easier, if longer, than the S approach. From Cashapampa up the Q. de Los Cedros to the Lag. Jancarurish (c.4500m). Good camping, 3d. Climb the crevassed glacier, keeping close to the W side then traverse L to the col camp at 5500m, ½d.

Quitaraju from the NE

W ridge

N face

col

E ridge

moraine camp

Alpamayo from the S

base camp

CLIMBS W ridge, AD. From the 5500m camp traverse the glacier under the N slopes of Quitaraju and gain the Quitaraju-Loyacjirca col. Choose a route through the seracs of the N flank (to 60°). Climb the narrow ridge more easily to the summit, exposed and enjoyable, 5-8h.

N face, AD/D, Follow the traverse above until under the N face then cross the bergschrund (5600m) just R of a rock rib (45-50°). Climb directly up to reach the summit ridge about 80m W of summit, 6h. Anchors are often in place. Lines further R are more prone to avalanche.

BEST MAP As for Santa Cruz above.

Nevado ALPAMAYO 5947m   6 days   AD/D

One of the world's most impressive and memorable mountains, Alpamayo is a steep fluted wedge of snow and ice. Many parties content themselves with a climb to the summit ridge because traversing to the true S summit is often both difficult and serious. The Ferrari route on the SW face is very popular and there are usually belay/abseil points in place. In July and August there can be long queues of people in both ascent and descent and in recent years there have been several accidents and deaths on the mountain. The mountains name is Quechua and means muddy river.

ACCESS Follow the access to the 5500m camp on the Alpamayo-Quitaraju col detailed for Quitaraju above, 3d. See photo above, waypoints as for Quitaraju and map on page 74.

CLIMB Ferrari route AD+. From the 5500m camp cross easy snow slopes and climb towards the bergschrund at its highest point. Cross the bergschrund and follow flutings slanting up R (45-60°, 350m) to reach the lowest point of the summit ridge, 5-6h. Traversing the ridge to the main summit in most years will increases the grade to D/TD.

OTHER ROUTES Also on the SW face is the **French direct, D/TD** which climbs the 50-65° runnel which leads directly to the S summit. All the other runnels on the SW face have been climbed at grades to TD. All these routes can be severely affected by a massive collapse of the lower RHS of the SW face, which appears to happen every 5-8 years or so.

Alpamayo SW face

Ferrari route

Alpamayo can also be climbed from the N by the **N ridge, D/TD** which was the route of the first ascent. From Lag. Jancarurish (4500m) climb towards the ridge through the ice fall to easy snow slopes at the foot of the ridge. Skirt a bergschrund and start up the ridge 45-50° which steepens with some mixed sections. The summit cornice may be very difficult. Traversing to the main S summit increases the grade to TD. This route can also be started by traversing from the 5500m col camp.

KEY WAYPOINTS High Camp 08°53'01"   77°39'19"   Alpamayo summit 08°52'47" 77°39'09"

BEST MAP As for Santa Cruz above.

PUCAJIRCA Norte 6046m   8 days   TD/ED

Pucajirca (or Pucahirca) is a long chain of peaks lying E of Alpamayo. The highest point is at the N end. These peaks are very rarely climbed. The name means red mountain. The height is given as only 5943m on the PIGM map, and Pucajirca may be under 6000m.

ACCESS From Huaraz to the remote village of Pomabamba (3000m) on the E side of the range (PT). Walk up the Q. Jancapampa to the W, turn N at the head of this and climb the steeper Q. Yanajanca (Q. Laurel on PIGM) to a base camp at c.4000m by Lag. Sactaycocha.

CLIMB The first ascent was by the N ridge from Lag. Sactaycocha. Climb slopes S of the lake, then traverse S and cross over the base of the E ridge (c.5000m) of the subsidiary summit immediately N of Pucajirca Norte. Climb the curving glacier which descends from the col between the main and subsidiary summits, first NW then SW up a chaotic icefall, to reach the col. Climb the short N ridge. The final ascent was made from a camp at 5400m in 9h. Grade probably about TD or ED.

OTHER ROUTES The central and southern peaks are climbed from Q. Santa Cruz at grades of D or TD.

BEST MAP As for Santa Cruz and PIGM sheet 18-i useful for access.

Pucajirca from the S

Pucajirca from the W

Nevado TAULLIRAJU 5830m   6 days   TD/ED

Lying about 7km E of Alpamayo is the spectacular and beautiful Taulliraju. Although the first ascent and probably the easiest lines are on the N side of the mountain, Taulliraju is now more often climbed from the Q. Santa Cruz to the S.

ACCESS See map on page 74. As for Quitaraju above but continue straight up the main Santa Cruz valley to a base camp at Taullipampa (4200m) near the head of the valley, 2d.

ROUTES There are a profusion of difficult (TD or ED) mixed routes on the SW face, the easiest lines are the Fowler and Canadian routes which exit left from the prominent central bay at about TD+ and the SSE ridge from Punta Union at about TD. All these and more are summarised in Sharman's and Juanjo Tomés guidebooks.

BEST MAP As for Santa Cruz above.

Taulliraju
SW face

Nevado CARAZ Oeste c.5980m   4 days   AD/D

Caraz Oeste, also known as Caraz de Paron is the highest of a group of peaks on the N side of Lag. Paron. The route is very variable depending on the state of the glacier and has become more dangerous in recent years. Approaches are normally made from the S by Lag. Paron. Climbing from Q. Santa Cruz to the N is possible but not recommended.

ACCESS See map on page 74. From Huaraz to the village of Caraz (PT) then by hired vehicle to the power station at the outflow from Lag. Paron (4185m). Walk along the N shore of the lake on a good path, then continue up the valley on the N side of a stream to a basecamp below the much smaller Artesoncocha (Lag. Paron Chico) (4250m), 2h.

CLIMB The normal route is on the SE and E slopes. From the basecamp climb moraines to the foot of the SE glacier. There is a small campsite here, (5200m) 2-3h. Climb the LHS of the glacier and then choose a route through the chaotic and dangerous ice fall to reach the plateau between the peaks at 5700m. From this plateau climb the W peak by the E slopes then steeper snow (60°) to the airy summit, 6-8h.

OTHER ROUTES
The **S face** has some very difficult lines on ice to 80° and rock to grade V.

OTHER PEAKS
The neighbouring peak, **Caraz Este 6020m, D** can also be climbed from the plateau by the central ice runnel in the 200m SW face (60°)

BEST MAP As for Santa Cruz. Sheet 19-h 'Carhuas' is useful for the approaches.

Caraz from the S

Torre de PARON (ESFINGE) 5325m   2 days   F-ED+

Also known as the Sphinx (La Esfinge), the Torre de Paron is now a very popular venue for long rock routes on its excellent granite 800m E face. There are now at least a dozen routes at grades from ED (5.10a/A1) up to F7c or 5.13a.

ACCESS Approach from near the road end at Paron. Start about 80-100m before the end of the road at a concrete aqueduct. From here follow a trail up the hillside that soon narrows and enters a gully. Climb the LHS of the gully then move further L, and follow cairns to reach campsites and water below the tower. Descent can be made easily by the **NE ridge, F** or by 3 fixed abseils down from the first col in the ridge.

CLIMBS There are good topos and overall descriptions in the British "High" magazine #238 and #257 from the early 2000's. Check out climbing journals and the web or the Casa de Guias in Huaraz for individual route topos.

BEST MAP As for Santa Cruz. Sheet 19-h 'Carhuas' is useful for the approaches.

ARTESONRAJU 5999m   3 days   D
PIRAMIDE DE GARCILASO 5885m   5 days   D/TD

Artesonraju is a steep smooth sided snow pyramid which should have been voted the most beautiful peak in the world, but unfortunately lost out to neighbouring Alpamayo! Spectacular from all sides, the most commonly climbed route is now the steep and snowy SE face from the Paron valley although the first ascent was by the N ridge from the Q. Santa Cruz. The SE face has also been skied and boarded. The height according to the AV map is 6025m, but photographic surveys indicate that the PIGM height of 5999m is more likely.

The beautiful fluted peak of Piramide de Garcilaso lies in a very dominant position at the head of the Paron valley.

ACCESS As for Caraz to Artesoncocha then up the obvious moraine crest on the LHS to gain the Paron glacier (possible camps at glacier edge). Cross the glacier easily, trending L to a high camp at 5100m S of Artesonraju from which Artesonraju, Piramide and Paron Grande can all be climbed, 3h. from Artesoncocha. See Taulliraju above for details of access to Taullipampa basecamp on the N side of the peak.

ARTESONRAJU CLIMB The most frequently climbed route is the aesthetically pleasing **SE face, D**. From the high camp on the Paron glacier at 5100m climb to the R of a triangular rock area and serac zones to gain the bottom of the face via the bergschrund (60°). Climb the 50-60° snow face usually best towards the LHS and finishing just L of the summit. Anchors are often in place, 5-7h.

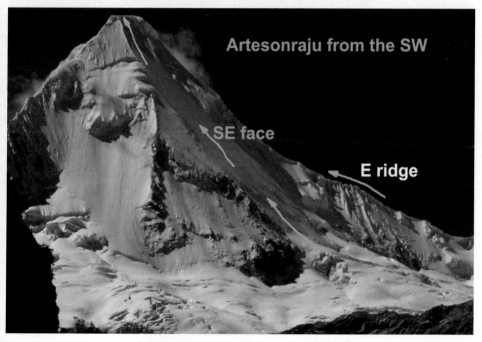

Artesonraju from the SW

SE face

E ridge

ARTESONRAJU OTHER ROUTES The **N ridge** by the NE spur, D/TD can be climbed from Taullipampa in the Q. Santa Cruz. Approach up moraines on the RHS of the Q. Artison then up the RHS of the crevassed glacier leading towards the N shoulder. Climb steep slopes on the LHS of the ridge, making many detours around seracs and crevasses. The **E ridge** can be climbed from either the N at Taullipampa or the S above Artesoncocha.

PIRAMIDE CLIMB Piramide can be climbed from the 5100m camp by its 500m **NW face, D/TD**. There are several lines on the flutings, all more or less 60°.

OTHER PEAKS Paron Grande 5600m, can also be climbed from the camp by its S ridge from the S col. Finish up the W face.

BEST MAP As for Caraz Oeste.

N ridge

E ridge

Artesonraju
from the NE

On Artesonraju

CHACRARAJU Oeste 6108m   5 days   ED+

Probably the hardest 6000'er in the Cord. Blanca and perhaps even in the whole of the Andes. Chacraraju is a narrow and steep sided ridge with summits at either end. The W summit is higher. Chacraraju is most often climbed by the S face although routes from the N may be slightly easier. Few parties reach the true summit because of the serious and difficult ridge. The name is Quechua and comes from the resemblance of the snow flutings to a ploughed field or 'chacra'. Also known as Mataraju, 'twin mountain'.

ACCESS See map on page 74. From the Pisco base camp at Cebollapampa (see Huandoy description) follow the E side of the Q. Demanda up to the NE on a good path, then the side stream up to the simple hut at Lag. 69 (4550m), 3h.

CLIMB The easiest routes to the main W summit appear to be the Bouchard or similar nearby routes such as the Slovenian or French at about ED1 or ED2. Taking 2-3d., and with snow and ice to 90° and hanging bivouacs these are serious routes.

BEST MAP Alpenvereinskarte sheet 0/3a 'Cordillera Blanca Nord' 1:100,000 or PIGM sheet 18-h 'Corongo' 1:100,000. Sheet 19-h 'Carhuas' is useful for the approaches.

Nevado PISCO Oeste 5752m   3 days   F/PD

One of the easiest and most frequently climbed peaks in the Cord. Blanca. There are however some potentially serious crevasse crossings on the SW ridge. Pisco is the Peruvian liquor, large quantities of which were drunk after the first ascent in 1951. Called Matarrojo on the PIGM map.

ACCESS Follow the access for Huandoy detailed below to the refugio and camp at 4600m beneath the huge moraine. Pisco can be climbed from here in a day but many parties camp higher. Climb the huge moraine and descend the very loose inside wall. Cross a boulder covered glacier heading generally L and pass above one circular lagoon (marked on PIGM map) to camp at a higher, smaller lagoon (4900m - not seen until there), 2-3h. from the refugio.

CLIMB From the 4900m camp climb over rock slabs then directly up the glacier to the col (5350m). Turn R at the col and climb the N side of the broad SW ridge, usually one or two large crevasses and with a final short steep section of 50°.

OTHER ROUTES The normal route can also be joined at the col by coming up from the N (Lag. Paron) at about PD. There are a number of steep ice routes on the fluted **S face**. The easiest of these is a fairly direct route exiting just L of the summit, AD/D.

KEY WAYPOINTS Cebollapampa 09°02'46" 77°36'32" Near Refugio 09°01'51" 77°37'47" Crossing moraine 09°01'33" 77°38'11" High camp 09°01'23" 77°38'32" Near col 09°00'49" 77°38'32" Summit 09°00'35" 77°37'57"

BEST MAP As for Huandoy.

Climbing Pisco

Pisco from the S
SW ridge

Nevado HUANDOY Norte 6395m   6 days   AD/D

A beautiful massif of three main summits (N, S and W) rising like the points of a crown from the glacier filled basin (5800m) between them. The safest line to the highest peak, Huandoy Norte, is the NE face route. The easiest route is by the E icefall and central basin, but this suffers from serac and rockfall danger. The S and W peaks are normally climbed via the E icefall and central basin. The native name for the mountain is Tullparaju.

ACCESS From Huaraz drive past the Llanganuco lakes to the first hairpin bend about 2km beyond the second lake (PT). Buses run from Yungay to Yanama and Pomabamba along this route. Just below the road is the meadow known as Cebollapampa or 'Pisco base camp' at the entrance to the Q. Demanda, 5min. Donkeys can normally be hired here. Cross to the N side of the river and follow signposts to gain a path rising steeply up the hill, L of the stream coming down between Huandoy and Pisco. The path is easy to follow. It goes over a flatter area, up a moraine crest, moves R, climbs two substantial rises, passing L of a rock outcrop on the second, to the refugio and camping area at 4600m beneath a huge

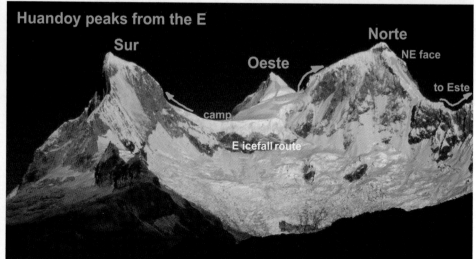

Huandoy peaks from the E
Sur
Oeste
Norte
NE face
to Este
camp
E icefall route

moraine (100m high), 4h. This refugio (80 beds, full service) and campsite are very busy as they are also used for the very popular peak of Pisco.

CLIMB The easiest line to Huandoy Norte is by the **E icefall, AD/D**. From the refugio at 4600m gain the icefall either by climbing up the LHS of the lower glacier or (better) by circling under Huandoy Este from the 4900m high camp on Pisco. Climb the couloir at the extreme R (N) end of the ice-cliff, 200m, 45° (serious serac danger) to reach the upper basin and campsites at 5800m, 8-10h. To climb Huandoy Norte from this camp skirt seracs to the W and then climb a couloir in the SW flank to the summit, 5h.

OTHER ROUTES The highest peak, Huandoy Norte can be climbed more safely by the **NE face, D/TD**. From the 4900m camp on Pisco traverse the glacier under Huandoy Este then climb the snow couloir to the LH of two cols, 400m, 50-70°, 8h. Camp on the small plateau below the N side of the ridge. Climb either the NE ridge or face 500m, 50°. The band of loose rock at the top can be climbed in the centre, III. Then easy snow to the summit, 1-2d. Huandoy Norte can also be climbed from the Paron valley to the N in several days by the **NW slopes, D/TD**. 600m of 50° ice leads to the saddle with the W peak

OTHER PEAKS From the camp at 5800m the second highest peak **Huandoy Oeste 6342m, AD/D** can be climbed by the E slopes and knife edge NE ridge in 5h. **Huandoy Sur, 6160m, D** can be climbed by the NW slopes in 5h. Huandoy Sur has some desperate ED routes up the overhanging S face and can also be climbed from Llanganuco by the SW buttress.

The outlying summit **Huandoy Este 5900, D/TD** is easiest to climb by the W ridge gained by climbing the 400m couloir as for the NE face route on Huandoy Norte, then traverse the W ridge.

BEST MAP Alpenvereinskarte sheet 0/3a 'Cordillera Blanca Nord' 1:100,000 or PIGM sheet 19-h 'Carhuas' 1:100,000.

Huandoy Sur from Huaytapallana

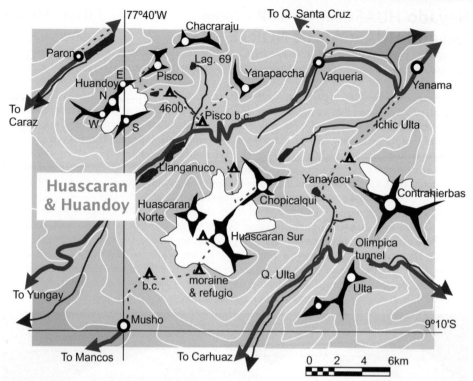

Nevado YANAPACCHA 5460m   2 days   AD

Yanapaccha, the small peak seen at the head of the Llanganuco valley is another good easy ascent and is a much quieter peak than the nearby Pisco.

ACCESS From Huaraz follow the access for Huandoy and Pisco to the Cebollapampa camp and continue up towards the Portachuelo Llanganuco (PT). From the biggest hairpin bend on the L (at about 4500m) traverse slighlty up and round the nose to reach camps by the glacier.

Yanapaccha can also be accessed from Cebollapampa by the Q. Demanda. Follow the path on the RHS of the Q. Demanda then up the zig-zags. At the last bend (where the path goes L to Lag. 69) take a small path down R over two stream beds, then climb steeply up a moraine crest on a deteriorating path. Camps are possible further R at 4200m and by a small lake at 4400m, 2-3h.

CLIMB Climb through a rock band at 4500m then up R over slabs to reach the glacier at 4900m, R of the very prominent rock rib, higher camps possible near here. Climb the glacier to reach the basin below the W side of the summit. From here either reach the NW ridge by a couloir (40-45°) and continue to the summit, often with a steeper finish (to 60°). Or climb direct by the W face, 6-8h.

BEST MAP As for Huandoy.

NW ridge   Yanapaccha from the W

W face

Nevado HUASCARAN SUR 6746m   5 days   PD/AD
Nevado HUASCARAN NORTE 6655m   5 days   AD

The massive peaks of Huascaran dominate the Cord. Blanca. The S peak is the highest mountain in Peru and curiously enough one of the easiest 6000m peaks in Peru. The native name for the peak is Matararaju.

The difficulties are normally in passing through the large ice fall to reach the col, known as the Garganta (6010m), which separates the two peaks. These difficulties vary widely from year to year depending on the number and size of the crevasses but in favourable years the climb can be little more than a walk. Both peaks are then relatively easy ascents from a high camp in the Garganta. In some years recently there have been dangerous conditions on the peak and a number of deaths.

In 1970 an earthquake triggered a huge fall of ice from the N peak, which rapidly melted and formed a devastating mudslide that wiped out the town of Yungay. All but a few people in the town of 18,000 inhabitants died. The quake caused devastation in the entire Callejón de Huaylas.

ACCESS See map on page 87. For the normal routes the start point is the village of Musho, which can be reached from Huaraz by public transport via the village of Mancos. Musho has a couple of small shops and a cafe. Donkeys can be obtained very easily for the one day walk up to the base camp (4150m). The route is fairly direct to the base camp which lies below and slightly L of the ice tongue coming down from the Garganta. The route starts through fields, enters a large eucalyptus plantation and then zigzags on a good path up a moraine above. There is also now a more direct route to the refugio at 4750m near the glacier edge, but you may have trouble persuading arrieros to go this way.

Huascaran from the NW

GARGANTA CLIMB From the base camp go up the short rock groove on the RHS of the stream and then follow the cairns up and R over the slabs (several variations) to reach a larger stream and possible camp (4450m). Some short sections of rock to grade II but never exposed. From 4450m the route goes on over glaciated slabs directly towards the S peak to gain the glacier at the highest slabs immediately R of the lowest glacier tongue (4750m - refugio, full service, 60 beds). From here go up over the easy angled glacier heading for the RHS of the big icefall (camps at 5250m). Follow a route through the icefall up a ramp R of the big cliff and directly under the mitre shaped snowfield known as El Escudo (ice to 60° in some years). There is usually a very big crevasse at the top of the icefall. Once across this crevasse go L (northwards) and rise gradually to reach the Garganta. There is some serac danger on this last section. The usual high camp is under an ice wall at about 5900m below the W side of the Garganta col - great sunsets.

The route to the Garganta col used to go up the LHS of the icefall and if conditions change this may become the normal way again. The Garganta can also be reached from the E by the **E icefall**, grade n/k, but certainly more dangerous.

NORTH PEAK From the camp gain the Garganta proper by crossing or turning several large crevasses. Climb to the shoulder on the S ridge of Huascaran Norte from the Garganta, avoiding crevasses as necessary. Follow the S ridge to the summit (30-40°).

Huascaran Norte and Sur from the SW

SOUTH PEAK Gain the Garganta proper and go NE across this to a steep snow slope that leads up towards some big seracs. Climb this slope (40°) and cross the crevasse above usually by making a long traverse R (but sometimes taken directly and sometimes impassable). Go on up more or less direct over easier slopes to the summit.

Huascaran Sur from Huascaran Norte

OTHER ROUTES NORTH PEAK There are some very impressive routes on the N face of Huascaran Norte all at ED or above. The most famous and frequently climbed appear to be the **Paragot route, ED1** up the RHS of the face (60-80°, V+, 1600m) and the **NE ridge ED1** gained from the NW side (60°, mostly on ice but with some rock, III-V). Both routes will need 3-4 days. See Sharman's guidebook for further information.

OTHER ROUTES SOUTH PEAK The **W face, D/TD** can be climbed from the Garganta camp. The line follows the LHS of the prominent mitre shaped snowfield known as the **Shield (El Escudo)** (400m, 50-60°) above the ice fall, joining the poorly defined W ridge high up, 10h. There are a large number of hard TD and ED lines on the NE and E faces of Huascaran Sur. The SE ridge from the Q. Matara is also TD.

KEY WAYPOINTS Musho village 09°10'10" 77°40'21" Base Camp 09°08'02" 77°38'48" Refugio 09°08'19" 77°38'07" Glacier Edge 09°08'42" 77°37'47" Camp One 09°07'48" 77°37'25" Garganta High Camp 09°06'57" 77°37'04" Summit Huascaran Sur 09°07'14" 77°36'15" Summit Huascaran Norte 09°06'11" 77°37'09" Note that camps and glacier edge may change year to year.

BEST MAP AV sheet 0/3a 'Cordillera Blanca Nord' 1:100,000 or PIGM sheet 1:100,000.

The north face of Huascaran Norte

Nevado CHOPICALQUI 6345m   4 days   AD

Although dwarfed by the neighbouring Huascarán, Chopicalqui is actually one of the highest peaks in the Cord. Blanca. Climbed relatively frequently by the normal route on the SW ridge. In many seasons there is an impassable crevasse high up on this route, but when it is well bridged (or there is a ladder!) the route is relatively easy. There are good views of the E faces of the Huascaran peaks.

ACCESS See map on page 87. From Huaraz via Yungay and the Llanganuco lakes to the big hairpin bend above Cebollapampa at c.4200m (PT). Walk up through trees to a meadow (4300m) where the normal base camp is situated, ½h.

CLIMB SW Ridge, AD. Gain the moraine on the W side of the meadow as soon as possible and follow the crest of it until cairns lead across the rubble covered glacier to the foot of the steeper moraine on the far side. This steeper moraine rises southwards from the inside corner of the junction of the glaciers coming from Chopicalqui and Huascarán. Climb the crest of it on a good path then loose boulders to camps at the edge of the glacier (moraine camp - 4900m), 4h. Go up the glacier above just L of the rock rib then start to move L under a big (and loose) rock wall, bypassing several big crevasses. Cross the basin (poss. camps) then climb a steeper slope to the normal site of the high camp (5700m), 4-5h. From here find a route around some big crevasses to gain the ridge proper. Cross a big crevasse on the extreme L and pass seracs on the L then follow the narrow and exposed ridge to the summit, 5-6h.

OTHER ROUTES The **NW ridge, TD** can be climbed from the normal base camp. Climb ESE over grass and slabs to gain the glacier. Climb via a rocky peak to the foot of the NW ridge, 6h. Climb to the col then the 60° wall and serac to gain the ridge. Climb on the S side of ridge to Chopicalqui N (6050m) then abseil to the ridge beyond. Climb this on the NE side to the summit (55°), 2-3d. There are also several hard routes on the NW and W faces. The E and SE ridges have both been climbed from the Q. Ulta at about TD with bad cornices and snow mushrooms.

KEY WAYPOINTS Moraine camp 09°05'30" 77°35'38" High camp 09°05'46" 77°35'06" Summit 09°05'17" 77°34'26"

BEST MAP AV sheet 0/3a 'Cordillera Blanca Nord' 1:100,000 or PIGM sheet 19-h 'Carhuas' 1:100,000.

Chopicalqui from the W

Chopicalqui at sunset

Nevado CONTRAHIERBAS 5954m   4 days   AD

An extensive mountain which is rarely visited. Not a very difficult climb but bad crevasses can make an ascent time consuming. The native name is Ruricocha 'corner lake'. It is called Yanaraju on the PIGM map. The height is given as 6036m on the AV map.

ACCESS See map on page 87. From Huaraz via Carhuaz then up the Q. Ulta on the road to Chacas. From the point where the road starts to climb out the E side of the valley (4000m) (PT) continue up the main valley on foot on a good mule trail to the Paso Yanayacu 2-3h. Descend the other side to a base camp by the scenic lagoon at 4100m in the Q. Ichic Ulta, 1h. This camp can also be reached from Yanama in 3-4h.

CLIMB From the lagoon follow the stream up to the head of the valley and the first screes. Climb a long straight gully on the L to rock platforms below the glacier at about 5000m (camp). This point could also be reached by climbing steep slopes on the S side of Punta Yanayacu or by a short but difficult traverse from the col itself. From the camp climb onto the glacier and follow the ridge over a small summit. Descend the other side to the NW slopes of Contrahierbas then climb more easily to the summit, passing some large crevasses, 6-8h.

OTHER ROUTES The glacier can also be gained more directly from the lagoon in Q. Ichic Ulta, by scrambling up a gully on the RHS to reach the glacier at about 5200m, but this route has considerable danger from seracs at present. The mountains NE ridge is also a fairly straightforward climb.

OTHER PEAKS On the S side of the Q. Ulta road is the steep mixed peak, **Ulta 5782m, TD/ED**, a difficult mixed climb by either the NW or NE faces.

BEST MAP AV sheet 0/3a 'Cordillera Blanca Nord' 1:100,000 or PIGM sheet 19-i 'Huari' 1:100,000. Sheet 19-h 'Carhuas' is useful for the approaches.

NE ridge

camp

Contrahierbas from the NW

Nevado HUALCAN 6160m   4 days   AD/D

Between them Hualcan and Copa form a vast high plateau, reported to be the best place in the Cordillera Blanca for ski-mountaineering. Deep snow and long marches above 5500m can make these peaks difficult on foot.

ACCESS From Huaraz via Carhuaz to the abandoned hot spring at Hualcan (3100m). Go up the Q. Hualcan to reach Lag. Cochca (4550m) under the SW slopes of the mountain, 5h.

CLIMB The easiest route is now on the snowy **S ridge** gained from the badly crevassed W glacier about 1km N of point 5850 (5808 on PIGM). The summit is usually climbed in two days from Lag. Cochca with a high camp on the glacier plateau at c.5200m.

OTHER ROUTES The **SW ridge, D** can be climbed directly from the same glacier camp at 5200m although the top section has become threatened by a huge serac in recent years.

OTHER PEAKS On the S side of the Q. Ulta road is the very easy peak of **Chequiaraju, 5286m F** climbed from Shilla via a camp at the outflow of Lag. Auquiscocha (4300m) in 2d.

BEST MAP AV sheet 0/3a 'Cordillera Blanca Nord' 1:100,000 or PIGM sheet 19-h 'Carhuas' 1:100,000

SW ridge — summit — S ridge

Hualcan from the SW

Chequiaraju from the S

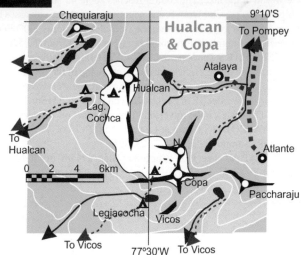

Map: Hualcan & Copa

Chequiaraju · 9°10'S · To Pompey · Atalaya · Hualcan · Lag. Cochca · To Hualcan · Atlante · Paccharaju · Copa · Legiacocha · Vicos · To Vicos · 77°30'W · To Vicos

0 2 4 6km

Nevado de COPA 6188m   3 days   PD

Copa is one of the easier 6000m peaks in the Cordillera Blanca. Named after a local style of hat.
ACCESS From Huaraz via Marcará to the village of Vicos (PT) (3100m). From here walk slightly E
of N through fields and forestry to reach distinct moraines flanking the river coming from Legiacocha.
A good path then climbs the steep hillside S of this river in numerous zigzags. Finally traverse L
towards Lag. Legiacocha, a beautiful blue green lake which makes a good base camp (4700m), 6-7h
from Vicos. The W slopes of Copa can also be gained and climbed from Hac. Copa, although the lower
section of the glacier is very badly crevassed and it will be difficult to find a way through.

Copa from the SW

CLIMB From Legiacocha go around the W side of the lake and climb the wide couloir which lies N of
the W end of the lake. The couloir reaches about 45° and can be icy. Once on the large plateau (5200m
- high camps possible) turn R and negotiate some large crevasses heading straight towards the summit.
From c.5600m traverse L, climb the steeper snow slopes (30°) in the centre of the face then go back R
to reach the summit, 8-10h from Legiacocha, 5-6h from the 5200m camp.
OTHER PEAKS The **N peak 6173m, PD/AD** is usually less severely crevassed. To climb this make a
rising traverse of the glacier plateau from the top of the couloir to a point roughly due W of the summit.
Then go straight to the summit, going around a few crevasses.
The short snow ridge SE of Legiacocha called **Vicos, 5315m, F** makes a good short day or acclimatisation
ascent. The ridge can be traversed in either direction very easily.
KEY WAYPOINTS Camp at Legiacocha 09°17'06" 77°30'30" Camp near top of couloir 09°16'26"
77°30'08" Summit 09°16'13" 77°28'49"
BEST MAP AV sheet 0/3a 'Cordillera Blanca Nord' or PIGM sheets 19-i 'Huari' and 19-h 'Carhuas',
both 1:100,000

Base camp in the Cordillera Blanca

Nevado URUS 5423m
Nevado ISHINCA 5530m

2 days   F/PD
2 days   F/PD

These two easy peaks are popular acclimatisation ascents for mountaineers going on to do harder or bigger things. Both can be climbed from a camp in the upper reaches of Q. Ishinca. Urus, a chain of four peaks is shown as Yanaraju on the PIGM map. Ishinca nestles in the col between the giants Palcaraju and Ranrapalca. The base camp is a very popular area that also has a refugio.

ACCESS See map on page 98. From Huaraz to the village of Paltay (PT) then up the track to Collon to Pashpa (3500m). Animals can be obtained from the arrieros office in Collon, or in Pashpa. From either village follow the N side of the quebrada then the obvious path up the Q. Ishinca valley to the base camp (4300m) in a broad flat valley below a huge moraine, 4-5h from Collon. There is a refugio at this base camp, 60 beds, meals and beers.

URUS CLIMB From the base camp climb the steep moraine crest just W of the refugio to below the glacier. Traverse R across boulder slopes below a rock buttress then back L above the buttress to gain the glacier. Also possible to gain the glacier on the other side of this buttress depending on the year. Climb the glacier (up to 40°) then finish on the rocky E ridge (II), 5h.

ISHINCA CLIMB Cross the stream at the camping area. A path climbs out of the main valley, becoming a good path in the hanging valley. This leads to the Lag. Ishinca, 5000m where there is a small refugio (no facilities). Go up over moraines to a possible high camp at the NW edge of glacier, 3h. Climb the glacier towards the SW ridge and climb this to the summit tower, which sometimes has a difficult bergschrund and short steep section (50-60°), 4h.

OTHER ROUTES Ishinca can also be climbed by the NW slopes, finishing on the **NE ridge, PD** from the Ishinca base camp.

KEY WAYPOINTS Refugio 09°22'04" 77°25'37"
BEST MAP As for Tocllaraju.

Ishinca from the N

SW ridge
route lies behind

NE ridge

Urus
from Ishinca B.C.

High on
Tocllaraju

TOCLLARAJU c.5980m   4 days   AD/D

A popular peak which is usually climbed from the Q. Ishinca but can also be climbed from the Q. Aquilpo to the N. Digital elevation data strongly indicate that Tocllaraju is not a 6000m peak, the accepted height of 6034m is unlikely to be true. The NW ridge is the easiest line but it is often blocked high on the ridge by a big crevasse in which case the steeper W face may be more likely to succeed. The name means trap mountain.

ACCESS As for Urus and Ishinca from Collon to the Ishinca base camp (4300m), 4-5h. From the refugio at Ishinca base camp follow a trail E on the N side of the valley that enters a little valley L of a huge moraine. At 4550m, after ½h, turn L and climb steep slopes, traversing R across a boulder field to reach the glacier at about 5000m. Climb the easy glacier slopes to a camp above and behind two rock pinnacles at 5200m, 4h. The same camp can be gained from Q. Aquilpo to the N.

CLIMB The normal route from the 5200m camp climbs the **NW ridge, AD/D**. From the 5200m camp climb up the glacier to a shoulder at 5300m. Cross the bowl through complex crevasses heading towards the summit. Then move L under the NW ridge until it is possible to climb steeply onto it (40-50°). Follow the NW ridge and slopes on the L to join the N ridge by a couple of steep pitches (50-60°). Follow this easily back to the summit, 5-6h. In some years there is an impassable crevasse high on the mountain.

OTHER ROUTES The **W face D** is also regularly climbed from the 5200m camp. Traverse R under the W face and climb a line at the S end of this face which gains the S ridge 100m from the summit. Pass the upper serac barrier on the R, 6h.

KEY WAYPOINTS Refugio 09°22'04" 77°25'37" Start of ascent 09°21'48" 77°25'04" High camp 09°21'10" 77°24'39" Summit 09°20'52" 77°23'43"

BEST MAP AV sheet 0/3b 'Cordillera Blanca Süd' 1:100,000 or PIGM sheet 19-i 'Huari' 1:100,000

route goes onto N face

NW ridge

W face

Tocllaraju from the W

PALCARAJU c.6200m   4 days   D

Palcaraju means branching mountain and the peak produces several long ridges. The normal route is up the N side of the W ridge, reached from Q. Cojup. The mountain is also known as Cuchilla.

ACCESS See map on page 98. Hire a truck in Huaraz to take you to the entrance of Q. Cojup at 3950m. Walk up the valley on a good trail, first on the S side then on the N side to below Lag. Palcacocha (4500m), 4-5h. Climb the small valley formed by the moraine on the NW side of Palcacocha then up L to camp at the edge of the glacier (c.5000m), 3h.

CLIMB From the high camp cross the glacier using a series of platforms beneath the W ridge to reach the glacier basin under the summit. Turn L and climb steep snow slopes to the col in the W ridge. Climb to the summit on the N face (LHS) of the W ridge, possibly finishing on the NE ridge.

OTHER ROUTES The upper section of this climb can also be reached from the Q. Honda. From Huaraz to the village of Vicos (PT) (3100m) at the entrance to the Q. Honda. There is a rough road up this valley which leads towards Pucaranracocha. Before reaching this large lake climb up the steep W slopes of the valley by a small stream to reach Pacllascocha (4600m), 1d from Huaraz. From Pacllascocha ascend the NW glacier between Palcaraju and Tocllaraju to join the W ridge route near the col. Grade n/k.

BEST MAP As for Tocllaraju

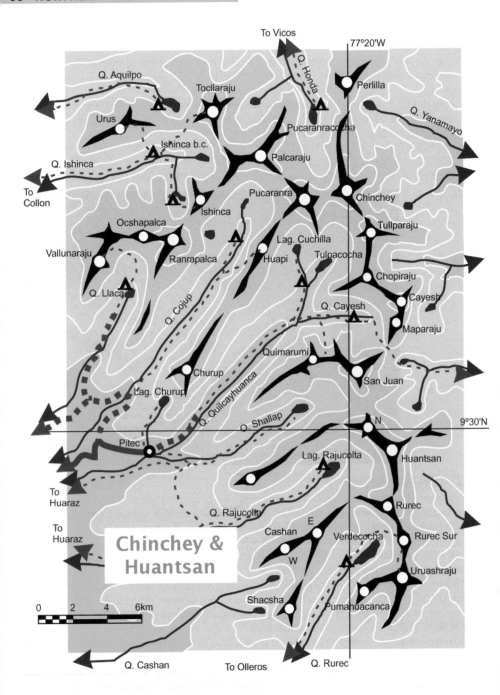

To Vicos

77°20'W

Q. Honda

Q. Aquilpo

Tocllaraju

Perlilla

Urus

Ishinca b.c.

Pucaranracocha

Q. Yanamayo

Palcaraju

Q. Ishinca

To Collon

Ishinca

Pucaranra

Chinchey

Tullparaju

Ocshapalca

Lag. Cuchilla

Chopiraju

Vallunaraju

Ranrapalca

Huapi

Tulpacocha

Cayesh

Q. Llaca

Q. Cojup

Q. Cayesh

Maparaju

Churup

Quimarumi

Lag. Churup

Q. Quilcayhuanca

San Juan

Pitec

Q. Shallap

N

9°30'N

Lag. Rajucolta

Huantsan

To Huaraz

Rurec

To Huaraz

Q. Rajucolta

Cashan

E

Verdecocha

Rurec Sur

Chinchey & Huantsan

W

Uruashraju

Shacsha

Pumahuacanca

0   2   4   6km

Q. Cashan

To Olleros

Q. Rurec

Palcaraju from the SW

Ranrapalca from the NE

summit

NE slopes

SE ridge

Nevado RANRAPALCA 6162m 4 days D

The normal route is on the NE slopes from the col with Ishinca (5350m). This col can be gained from either Q. Ishinca to the N or Q. Cojup to the S, both approaches take 2d. There are a large number of harder routes on this popular and accessible peak.

ACCESS See map opposite. To approach up Q. Ishinca follow the description under Ishinca to a high camp at Lag. Ishinca, 1½d. To approach via the Q. Cojup follow the directions given above for Palcaraju but just before you get to Palcacocha climb up the grassy NW slopes to reach a large meadow. Bear L and walk directly towards Ranrapalca to reach Lag. Perolcocha (4900m), 6-8 from the road.. Two smaller, higher lakes can also be used as camps. The Ranrapalca-Ishinca col lies a few hundred metres above Perolcocha up moraines and scree slopes.

CLIMB The NE slopes, D is the route most often climbed now and is probably the best descent. It climbs easy snow on the L of the NE ridge then through seracs (60°), over a bergschrund, then up a 55° wall (ice, mixed or poor grade IV rock) to reach the summit plateau, 8h. The summit lies at the SE side of this plateau.

OTHER ROUTES The SE ridge, TD/ED starting just S of Perolcocha has been climbed on 65-70° snow and ice mostly on the LHS but turning many obstacles on the RHS, 2d. The beautiful **SW ridge**, seen clearly from Huaraz has also been climbed from Q. Llaca. Gain this ridge at c.5350m by the SW face and avoid difficulties higher up by climbing a rib on the SE face, 2d.

OTHER PEAKS The twin summited **Vallunaraju 5686m, AD,** one of the most prominent mountains seen from Huaraz, makes a good acclimatisation ascent. Climb from the road end in Q. Llaca (4400m) in about 6-8h finishing on the N ridge. From the head of the valley climb L of the stream. A pitch of grade IV rock leads to glaciated slabs, then higher up follow an easy ramp up and R to reach the col in the N ridge. Between Vallunaraju and Ranrapalca is the steep sided **Ocshapalca 5881m**, a long ridge which has a number of hard gully lines on its S face.

BEST MAP As for Tocllaraju.

Climbing in the
Quebrada Llaca

Nevado PUCARANRA 6156m
5 days   AD/D

Pucaranra is a bulky mountain, prominent at the head of the Q. Cojup but probably best climbed by the SE ridge from Lag. Cuchilla above the Q. Quilcayhuanca. Puca means red, ranra means stony ground.

ACCESS See map on page 98. Follow the access for Chinchey detailed below up the Q. Quilcayhuanca to beneath Tullpacocha. Then climb the zig-zags on the LHS of the stream descending from Lag. Cuchilla to reach pleasant campsites in meadows by the lake (4600m), 6-8h from Pitec.

CLIMB SE ridge AD/D. Climb moraine on the RHS of Lag. Cuchilla and turn a small crag on the R to reach the very broken glacier. Follow ramps L through seracs to gain a flatter area immediately below a shallow col in the SE ridge (c.5700m - camps possible). Climb the ridge above passing a couple of easy rock bands, 10h from Lag. Cuchilla.

OTHER ROUTES The SE face, AD/D has been climbed from a high camp just below the Pucaranra - Chinchey col (see Chinchey). Before reaching the col climb 50-55° slopes to the S of the E ridge avoiding mixed ground at the top. The **NW ridge, TD** has been climbed from Palcacocha at the head of the Cojup valley.

BEST MAP As for Tocllaraju.

Pucaranra from the W

NW ridge

Tullparaju

Chinchey

Nevado CHINCHEY 6222m
5 days   AD

The highest peak of the extensive Chinchey massif, but not as high as the 6309m often reported. The most common route is the W ridge, most easily reached from Q. Quilcayhuanca to the S. Chinchey means puma.

ACCESS From Huaraz via the village of Pitec (3800m), where donkeys can be hired for the walk up the Q. Quilcayhuanca. Camps can be made at the junction of Q. Cayesh (4050m), 9km, 3h. Continue up the LH valley to Tullpacocha then climb up the moraine on the LHS of the lagoon and grass slopes to reach rock slabs and the glacier above the lagoon. Climb the gully on the LHS of the glacier until forced onto the glacier itself and continue towards the Pucaranra-Chinchey col, camp at about 5100m, 6-7h. from Q. Quilcayhuanca.

The W ridge route can also be gained from Lag. Pucaranracocha at the head of the Q. Honda to the N - see under Palcaraju for access.

CLIMB W ridge, D. From the camp at 5100m climb the headwall on the LHS to reach the col, 5500m.. Climb the crevassed 30° slopes on or just S of the ridge to reach the short 55° summit pyramid, 6-8h.

OTHER ROUTES The **N ridge** has also been climbed direct from Pucaranracocha.

OTHER PEAKS For the keen, the incredible needle of **Cayesh 5721m, TD/ED** lies 7km S of Chinchey. It has been climbed by at least 5 very hard routes on the W face.

BEST MAP As for Tocllaraju.

Nevado HUAPI 5415m

3 days   F/PD

Huapi is an easy peak lying close to Huaraz which makes a good acclimatisation ascent. Great views of the Chinchey group from the summit. The peak is also known as Jatunmontepuncu, the great doorway mountain.

ACCESS See map on page 98. Approach via the Q. Cojup. Walk in along the relatively flat quebrada (as for Palcaraju) until directly below the peak, 4-5h.

CLIMB Steeply up grass and then scree to gain the glaciated SW ridge. Follow this to summit, crossing a few crevasses.

OTHER ROUTES Can also be climbed from the Q. Quilcayhuanca at about the same grade

BEST MAP As for Tocllaraju.

Huapi SW slopes

Nevado SAN JUAN 5843m

4 days   D

Nevado MAPARAJU 5326m

3 days   F/PD

These two popular peaks lie at the head of Q. Cayesh. Maparaju in particular has become popular in recent years due to its suitability as an acclimatisation peak. Both peaks are unnamed on the PIGM map.

ACCESS See map on page 98. Walk in up the Q. Quilcayhuanca, as for Chinchey, then up the Q. Cayesh (Callash). Camps can be made in meadows at several places in this valley (4200-4400m), 4-5h.

SAN JUAN CLIMB From the lower part of Q Cayesh climb the centre of the steep valley with two streams in it that leads to the 5200m col in the W ridge. This valley is a mixture of pastures, rock outcrops and finally moraine. The 5200m col can also be reached from Q. Shallap to the S. From the col climb by the S side of the W ridge on 50-60° snow slopes, going round a prominent rock foresummit and finishing up the S slopes.

MAPARAJU CLIMB From the head of the Q. Cayesh a path climbs the grassy S slopes to the Abra Villon (5000m). There are traces of an old donkey path, and a tricky rock step at 4500m. Cross onto the glacier just before the pass, cross the almost level glacier to the E and then a short steep slope to a basin. Cross this to the glacier below the summit then climb straight to the summit, 4h.

OTHER PEAKS The small peak W of the 5200m col in San Juan's W ridge is **Quimarumi 5459m, PD.** It is an enjoyable ascent from the col. **Chopiraju Oeste 5475m, F/PD** (on PIGM as Andavite) can be climbed easily by the S slopes from the Q. Cayesh

BEST MAP As for Palcaraju.

Maparaju from the W

Cashan Este, SW ridge

Nevado CASHAN Este 5716m   5 days   AD

One of the easier peaks in the Huantsán group. Cashan means spiny.

ACCESS See map on page 98. From Huaraz to the village of Macashca (PT) then up the N side of the long Q. Rajucolta (Q. Pariac on PIGM maps) to Lag. Rajucolta (4300m) (Lag. Tambillo on PIGM map), 2d. The quebrada can also be entered by crossing the broad col (4250m) SE of Pitec, without losing too much height.

CLIMB From the huts below Lag. Rajucolta follow the path S up the steep Q. Pumahuanca. Turn R and follow cairns over moraines then slabs to the glacier. Climb this and then the R sloping ramp to reach the E ridge. Follow this on snow to the summit, 1d.

OTHER CLIMBS Cashan can also be climbed at about the same grade from the Quebrada Rurec by the SW ridge. Access as for Uruashraju below, then climb steep hillside and moraines to camp on the ridge at about 5200m near the glacier edge.

BEST MAP As for Huantsán.

Nevado HUANTSÁN 6369m   8 days   TD

The highest peak of the southern Cord. Blanca and after Chacraraju probably the hardest big peak in the whole range. Very rarely climbed. Marked as 6395m on the DAV map.

ACCESS See map on page 98. As for Cashan to the Lag. Rajucolta. From here climb the small valley SE of the lake to a meadow then climb out the L flank of this valley and pass a small rock cliff and some ruins. Enter a small bowl and leave this by the L, following a stream which leads up to a base camp at Lag. Ahuac (4780m).

Huantsan from the W

CLIMB The easiest route to the summit traverses over **Huantsán Norte 6113m**. From Lag. Ahuac gain the W glacier and cross this under the W face of Huantsán heading towards Huantsán Norte. Climb the snow slopes on the RHS of the SW ridge of Huantsán Norte to gain this summit, then descend to the col with Huantsan (camp possible - 5950m). From here the main peak of Huantsán can be reached by the difficult NNW ridge, keeping mostly to the steep snow on the E side to avoid towers. 2d. from Lag. Ahuac, with camps or bivouacs. Huantsan Norte can also be reached from the Q. Shallap by the crevassed NW glacier and NW ridge.

BEST MAP AV sheet 0/3b 'Cordillera Blanca Süd' 1:100,000 or PIGM sheet 20-i 'Recuay' 1:100,000.

Nevado URUASHRAJU 5722m   5 days   AD/D
Nevado RUREC SUR 5380m   3 days   F

These peaks lie at the head of the exceptionally beautiful Quebrada Rurec. Uruashraju is an interesting snow peak with good views of Huantsán. The three Rurec Sur peaks make easy but scenic acclimatisation ascents.

ACCESS See map on page 98. From Huaraz via the village of Olleros (3500m) (PT). From Olleros follow the road E to a river fork then climb up L and continue through Canray Grande and along a broad ridge to enter the Q. Rurec, 2h. Walk up this beautiful quebrada on a good path on the LHS of the valley to campsites at the stream junction below Lag. Verdecocha (Tararhua), 4h.

RUREC SUR CLIMB Walk up the LHS of Verdecocha then over moraine and up a ramp sloping back R to the glacier. Easily up the glacier to any of the three summits, the central is highest, 4-5h.

URUASHRAJU CLIMB As for Rurec Sur to the glacier. Then traverse S and cross over the ridge coming down NW from the small Uruashraju N peak (5464m), some scrambling, grade I/II, to reach the glacier basin under the NW slopes of Uruashraju. Camp possible. From here climb the steep NW slopes and W ridge, avoiding numerous seracs, 2d from Verdecocha.

Uruashraju

5464m

Rurec Sur

Uruashraju and Rurec Sur
from the W

OTHER ROUTES URUASHRAJU Uruashraju can also be climbed from the Q. Pumahuacanca to
the S. Follow the Olleros to Chavin trail but cross the river by a bridge in a gorge before Qollotococha.
Then follow a path up into the Q. Pumahuacanca to the glacier edge SW of the summit, 7h. Climb the
S ridge, AD/D. Cross the glacier to the col (5250m) below the narrow S ridge, and follow this up to
the summit (45-65°), 4-6h. The **W ridge AD/D** can also be climbed from Q. Pumahuacanca, joining
the S ridge just below summit.
OTHER PEAKS Near the entrance to the Q. Rurec **Shacsha 5703m, D** has been climbed by the W
flank of the S ridge and the mixed NE ridge, gained from the Q. Rurec.
BEST MAP As for Huantsán.

New routing in
the Quebrada Rurec

Nevado YANAMAREY Norte 5237m   2 days   PD
Nevado YANAMAREY Sur 5197m   2 days   F

The N and S peaks of Yanamarey are easy peaks that make good acclimatisation ascents. They can both be climbed from the Q. Yanamarey and the S peak can in fact be climbed in one day from near the Punta Cahuish tunnel on the Chavin road. The name means black pestle.

ACCESS For the Q. Yanamarey drive from Huaraz via Catac to the large, beautiful lake of Querococha (3980m) (PT). Follow a path along the SE shore and up the valley to the obvious fork. The R fork leads up to good camps by lagoons (4600m) under Yanamarey Sur, the L to the S side of Yanamarey Norte. To climb both peaks a camp near the fork in the Q. Yanamarey at 4400m would make sense, 2-3h to the fork from Querococha.

YANAMAREY NORTE CLIMB Yanamarey Norte can be climbed easily by the rocky S side, II, 5-6h from the fork

YANAMAREY SUR CLIMB From the last lagoon in the valley W of the summit climb moraines to a L sloping rock ramp then back R over slabs to gain the glacier. Go up this moving R to join the S ridge and climb this to the summit, 5-6h from fork. The S ridge can also be joined from the Punta Cahuish tunnel.

OTHER ROUTES Yanamarey Norte can also be climbed from the Q. Araranca by the N slopes and the N ridge, 3d.

BEST MAP As for Huantsán.

Yanamarey Sur from the SW

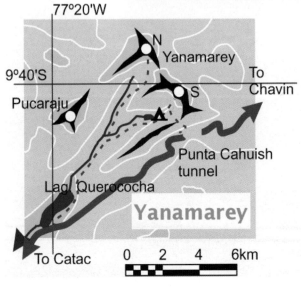

Mururaju from the S

Nevado MURURAJU (Pongos Sur) 5688m   3 days   AD/D

Mururaju is also known as Pongos Sur.

ACCESS See map on page 108. From Huaraz to Catac (PT) then walk via the Q. Queshque and Lag. Jarpococha (4250m) to the Lag. Pamparaju, 4650m, about 6-7h.

CLIMB From the Lag. Pamparaju climb rock slabs to the W glacier then up this to reach the narrowing W ridge. Climb this narrow ridge to the summit.

OTHER PEAKS Pongos Norte, 5630m, can be climbed from Catac via the Q. Cotush and the Q. Pamparaju (not to be confused with the lagoon of the same name mentioned above), then via the N glacier, grade n/k but about AD.

BEST MAP As for Huantsán.

Nevado RARIA Norte 5576m   3 days   PD
Nevado RARIA Sur 5504m   3 days   PD/AD

The two main peaks of the Raria massif, Raria Norte and Raria Sur can be combined from a camp in the Q. Huaillacu. This is a good area for a preliminary acclimatisation trip.

ACCESS From Huaraz drive via Pachacoto and up the Rio Pumapampa towards Pastoruri (plenty tourist buses go this way). Get out 4km before Pastoruri almost opposite the track up to the Mina San Anton and go down to the river (back-track slightly). Cross the river and walk NE up the Q. Huaillacu then over moraines to a camp by the beautiful Lag. Verdecocha (4650m) at the foot of the Raria peaks, 3h.

Raria Sur

To Raria Norte

behind

route behind pinnacle

Raria Sur from Verdecocha

RARIA NORTE From Verdecocha ascend the broad and easy SE glacier of the massif to the col between the peaks (5200m). Descend R to the base of the S slopes and climb these on snow and ice, 5-6h. The peak can also be climbed from the Q. Raria to the N. A good ski-mountainering ascent.
RARIA SUR Can be climbed from the 5200m col by the rocky N ridge, about PD or AD.
BEST MAP As for Huantsán.

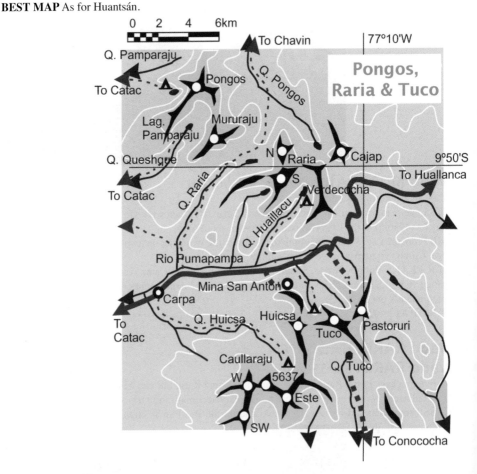

Pongos, Raria & Tuco

Nevado **HUICSA** 5476m	2 days	F
Nevado **TUCO** 5463m	2 days	PD
Nevado **PASTORURI** 5240m	1 day	F

These three peaks are enjoyable and easy climbs in a quiet part of the Cordillera Blanca, with easy access. Huicsa is called Challhua on the PIGM map. Tuco is Quechua for owl. It is called Huanaco Punta on the PIGM map. Pastoruri is a flattish glacier overrun with tourists, but does have nice views of the Huayhuash peaks to the S. These valleys are a good place to see condors.
ACCESS From Huaraz via Pachacoto and up the Rio Pumapampa road towards Pastoruri. In summer many tour buses go this way and it should be possible to arrange a lift on one of these buses. For Huicsa and Tuco leave the road about 2km before the Pastoruri turn off and walk up the valley (confusingly called Q. Pastoruri on the PIGM map) towards the N slopes of Tuco. Camps can be made where the

valley splits (4650m) or higher by a small lake (4850m) between Tuco and Huicsa.

HUICSA CLIMB The NE ridge can be climbed without axe or crampons. Climb up from the lake at 4850m to the col at 5050m then follow the NE ridge on loose rock.

TUCO CLIMB From the lake (4850m) climb easily up the NW glacier, using a hidden snow ramp to gain the N ridge. Finish up the N ridge, sometimes with a steep section (60°), only 4-5h in total from the road if acclimatised. The peak can also be climbed by the NE slopes at the same grade.

Tuco from the NW

hidden ramp

PASTORURI CLIMB Most of the tourists don't go far from the road and once you get away from them Pastoruri is a nice ridge with good views of the Cordillera Huayhuash. The highest point is right at the S end of the ridge. Pastoruri is a great place for some acclimatisation or to practice glacier techniques. Or even to ski!

BEST MAP As for Huantsán.

Este

Central

Caulliraju Este and Central from the NE

CAULLARAJU Este 5682m   3 days   PD
CAULLARAJU Central 5637m   3 days   F

The final group at the S end of the Cord. Blanca has some enjoyable and easy lower peaks. The Caulliraju massif is quite complex, with three main summit areas, the Este, Central and Oeste peaks. Each of these has in turn several sub-summits. The highest peak is the Este peak, lying S of the head of the Q. Huicsa.

ACCESS From Huaraz via Pachacoto and up the Rio Pumapampa road towards Pastoruri (PT). Leave the road at Lag. Patococha just before the Carpa checkpoint and approach up the Q. Huicsa valley, 1d.

ESTE CLIMB Climb either the NE face on snow or the NE ridge on rock.

CENTRAL CLIMB The second highest peak in the group, Caulliraju Central is a very easy ascent by the NW glacier and a reasonable ski descent.

OTHER PEAKS The Oeste peak, easily seen from the main road when approaching Huaraz, has two summits of almost identical height. Both are steeper and more difficult climbs, probably in the AD/D range.

BEST MAP As for Huantsán.

Caulliraju Central from the NW

To Huaraz | 77°W
Chiquian
Cord. Huayhuash
Cord. Raura
HUANUCO

Central Peru

To Trujillo
Cajatambo
Oyon
Huagaruncho
Huachon
CERRO DE PASCO

Lago Junin

Huacho
Canta
Cord. La Viuda
Santa Ana
LA OROYA
Morococha
Jallacate
HUANCAYO

Matucana
Tunshu
Chosica
Ticlla
Miraflores
12°S
LIMA
Llongote
Yauyos

PACIFIC
OCEAN

0   25   50   75km

Cañete
To Nazca, Arequipa

CHIQUIAN Access town for the Cordillera Huayhuash 3400m

The small town of Chiquian has become famous as the entry point to the spectacular Cordillera Huayhuash although the roadhead has now moved on to the village of Llamac at 3300m. This saves a long and hard days walk in both directions. The world famous Huayhuash trek now starts and finishes in Llamac, taking in a complete circuit of the mountains in about eight days. There are a number of good easy peaks that can be done on the way around this circuit, including Jurau, Leon and Suerococha.

To reach Chiquian turn off the main Lima to Huaraz road at Conococha. About 7h travel from Lima to Chiquian. There are direct buses from Lima but it may be easier to go via Huaraz. There are several buses a day from Huaraz to Chiquian, about 3h. There are regular minibus services connecting Chiquian to Llamac in about 1½h.

Facilities in Chiquian are a bit limited, but there are simple shops, hotels and restaurants. In Llamac there is very little other than basic shops, but it is easy to arrange pack animals here for base camp approaches because of the popularity of the circuit trek.

FOOD Several small grocery stores round the centre of Chiquian, but there is a much better choice in Huaraz (or even Lima).

FUEL If you need bencina blanca or camping gas it would be better to buy it in Huaraz or Lima. You can buy petrol and kerosene from shops in town.

The west face of Yerupaja from just below high camp

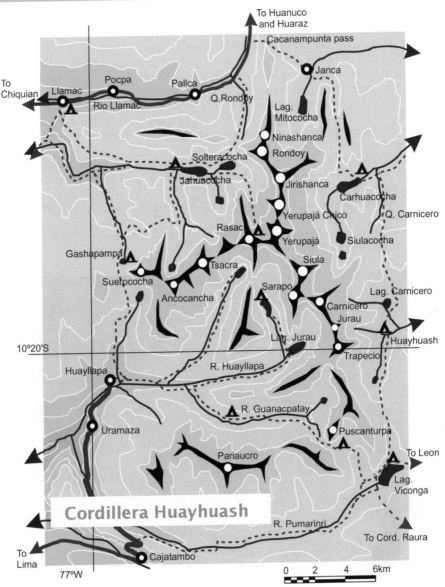

To Huanuco
and Huaraz
Cacanampunta pass
Janca
To
Chiquian Llamac Pocpa Pallca
Rio Llamac Q.Rondoy
Lag.
Mitococha
Ninashanca
Solteracocha Rondoy
Jahuacocha Jirishanca
Carhuacocha
Q. Carnicero
Yerupajá Chico
Rasac Siulacocha
Yerupajá
Gashapampa Siula
Tsacra
Suerocha Sarapo Lag. Carnicero
Ancocancha Carnicero
Jurau
Lag. Jurau Huayhuash
Trapecio
10°20'S
Huayllapa
R. Huayllapa
Uramaza
R. Guanacpatay
Pariaucro Puscanturpa
To Leon
Cordillera Huayhuash Lag.
Viconga
R. Pumarinri To Cord. Raura
To
Lima Cajatambo
77°W 0   2   4   6km

JIRISHANCA 6094m   7 days   TD/ED

At the N end of the range, Jirishanca is one of the most dramatic and difficult peaks in the Cord.
Huayhuash and one of the hardest 6000m peaks in the Andes. The name means 'peak of the humming
bird'.

ACCESS As for Yerupajá from Llamac to Solteracocha and onto the glacier. Once on the Yerupajá
glacier traverse L at c.5200m over chaotic glacier terrain to a corridor between the W face of Yerupajá
Chico and a minor peak (5545m), known as the Ghost Col. Descend to the base of the SW face of
Jirishanca and camp (5100m), 3d from Llamac. This access to the W face is becoming increasingly
difficult, but there is no obvious alternative

CLIMB The most straightforward route is the **SW face**. Start R of the central rocky face. Climb mixed or icy slopes to pass some seracs (65°). Continue up climbing around a second serac zone to the R and climb flutings towards the W ridge. On the ridge climb loose mixed ground to reach the summit crest and follow this S to the summit.

OTHER ROUTES The Cassin route gains the **W ridge** much lower on the mountain by mixed ground (70°, IV+). There are now a number of difficult (ED2-3) modern lines on the dramatic E face and NE ridge, reached from Carhuacocha (see the British magazine, High #April 2004).

OTHER PEAKS To the N lies **Rondoy 5870m, ED+** a very serious and difficult ascent by the **W face** to the col between the N and S summits. Further N is the more practicable **Ninashanca 5607m, D** which can be climbed from Lag. Mitucocha by the NE ridge, gained by a 45° snow couloir then a short rock pitch (III) followed by the corniced ridge.

BEST MAP As for Yerupajá.

Jirishanca SW face

Nevado YERUPAJÁ 6617m 7 days ED/ED+

Yerupajá, the highest peak in the Huayhuash is a spectacular wedge of snow and ice. It is the third highest peak in Peru after the two Huascarán summits, but is considerably more difficult and much more dangerous. There may have been only one or two ascents to the summit (with a safe descent) since the 1980's. The normal route was by the SW ridge, gained from the W but this has become problematic in recent years and the safest line is probably now on or near the NW ridge.

ACCESS From Llamac head SE over the high pass known as Pampa Llamac (4300m) to reach the Rio Achin valley coming down from Lag. Jahuacocha. The lake makes a good low base camp (4100m), 5-6h. From Jahuacocha go along the S side then up the moraine valley S of Solteracocha to the top. Traverse the seriously steep grassy slope on a good path then climb the small but steep moraine crest above followed by rock slabs to reach the moraine camp by a small stream, 4800m, 4h. Continue on moraines R of the glacier (rockfall hazard) until at about 5200m it is possible to get onto the glacier. Cross the flat glacier to a high camp at c.5300m between Yerupajá and Rasac, 3h from moraine camp.

CLIMB The normal route was by the **SW ridge**, the route of the first ascent. Climb the snow slope (55°) to the L of the S summit, now with a very difficult and dangerous section through the lower serac zone. A steeper gully (60°) to the L of the rocky pinnacle leads to the summit ridge which can be difficult if heavily corniced.

OTHER ROUTES The **NW ridge** currently appears to offer the fastest and safest way to the top and is probably the only route to have been climbed successfully to the summit since the 1980's. Most climbers have taken a line a little out onto the W face, but staying quite near this ridge. The **W face direct** is probably unjustifiably dangerous now. The **NE face** can be climbed with difficulty (65°/III) from Lag. Carhuacocha.

BEST MAP The best map is the 1:50,000 map of the range by the Alpine Mapping Guild, Boston, USA. Also reasonable are AV sheet 0/3c 'Cordillera Huayhuash' 1:100,000 or PIGM sheet 21-j 'Yanahuanca' 1:100,000.

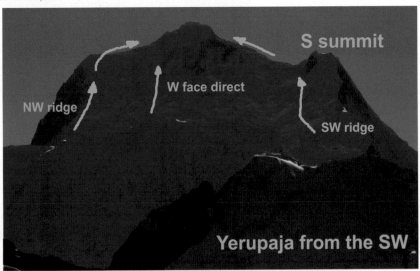

Yerupaja from the SW

Yerupaja from the moraine camp

Nevado RASAC 6017m   6 days   D

The easiest of the 6000m peaks in the Huayhuash, but by no means straightforward and like all Huayhuash peaks Rasac is getting harder every year. There may have been as few as 2 or 3 ascents in the last decade. Rasac lies just to the W of Yerupajá. The name Rasac is derived from the Quechua for toad.

ACCESS As for Yerupajá from Llamac to the camp in the glacier basin at c.5300m, 3d.

CLIMB By the **SE ridge**, several different lines are possible on this long and complicated route. The rock is reported to be dangerously loose, grade III-IV rock and some snow or ice to 50-60°, 10-12h.

BEST MAP As for Yerupajá.

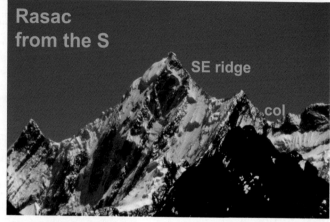

Rasac from the S

SE ridge

col

Nevado SUEROCOCHA c.5400m   4 days   PD

Perhaps the easiest snow peak in the Cordillera Huayhuash, Suerococha is a good viewpoint and is often climbed as part of the Huayhuash circuit. Also commonly known as Diablo Mudo,

ACCESS See map on page 112. This is just the first (or last) day of the standard Huayhuash circuit. From Llamac head SE over the high pass known as Pampa Llamac (4300m) to reach the Rio Achin valley coming down from Yerupaja. Continue up the Rio Ocshapata and up towards the Punta Tapush to a camp at a locality known as Gashapampa under the NW side of the peak (4600m), 1-1½d.

CLIMB From the camp go up the valley to about 4800m then climb up the orange coloured moraine on the LHS of the valley. Cross loose boulder slopes to reach the NW ridge and follow this passing the first smooth orange/brown rock wall by an easy scree gully on the L and the next rock buttress by ledges on the L. Once on the glacier follow the N ridge over an easy pinnacle (grade II) to the summit, 4-5h.

OTHER PEAKS The next peak to the E, **Ancocancha 5450m**, looks like an easy ascent from Q. Huacrish to the N. Climb by the smooth glacier on the W slopes, PD/AD

BEST MAP As for Yerupajá.

N ridge

summit

W couloir

Suerococha from the NW

Nevado SIULA GRANDE 6344m   7 days   D/TD

A mountain which has become famous because of Joe Simpson's exploits in a crevasse after falling during a descent of the normal route after completing the first ascent of the W face in 1985. These exploits are described and portrayed in the book and film "Touching the Void". The easiest route on this very difficult peak is the N ridge from the Lag. Carhuacocha.

ACCESS See the map on page 112. From the new roadhead above Llamac at Cuartelhuain (4200m) cross over the Cacanampunta pass (4700m). Walk on good paths SE to Janca, then S over the Punta Carhuac (4650m) to reach a base camp at Lag. Carhuacocha (4150m), 6-8h.

CLIMB From Carhuacocha walk up the valley to the W to reach the small lagoon under the W face of Yerupajá Chico (4400m). Climb S from here to gain the flatter upper section of the Yerupajá East glacier and go up this to the Yerupajá-Siula col (5730m), camps possible. Cross the bergschrund above and climb towards the N ridge, keeping L at first. Then climb a rock or mixed pitch (III) and continue along the narrowing crest to the summit. 3-4d from Carhuacocha.

OTHER ROUTES There are some very difficult lines on the W face.

OTHER PEAKS From the Lag. Carhuacocha base **Sarapo 6127m,TD** can be climbed in 3-4 days by the E face. Climb S past Siulacocha and Quesillacocha to gain the badly crevassed Sarapo glacier. Climb this by the S side to reach a snow plateau (5500m) beneath the E face of Sarapo. From here climb steeply to the summit on rock, ice and mixed ground, finishing by a couloir (60-65°) between seracs.

BEST MAP As for Yerupajá.

Siula from the NE

Jurau from the E

JURAU Sur (Quesillo) c.5600m   5 days   AD
JURAU Norte (Huaraca) 5537m   5 days   PD/AD

One of the easier peaks in the Huayhuash, the higher S peak, c.5600m, is also known as Quesillo.

ACCESS As for Siula to Carhuacocha then continue S for 5h. over the Punta Carnicero pass to Laguna Carnicero 4450m.

CLIMB From Laguna Carnicero go up to the NE glacier coming down between the peaks and climb this to the col. From here the N peak can be climbed by the steep S ridge on snow. The S peak has a short mixed section then a narrow corniced ridge to the summit.

OTHER PEAKS The very impressive **Trapecio 5644m,** has a number of hard lines on its dramatic SE face, but is an easier ascent by the NE face from the col with Quesillo. Grade about AD/D.

BEST MAP As for Yerupajá.

Puscanturpa Sur
from the S

S face

PUSCANTURPA Sur 5550m   5 days   PD/AD

One of the easier peaks in the Huayhuash, sometimes also known as Cuyoc or Puyoc. The peak lies immediately N of the Punta Cuyoc pass half way round the famous Huayhuash circuit trek and can be climbed from near the pass in a day. The length of time needed to complete the climb from the N and Llamac would be 7-8 days - the time of 5 days is for the shortest approach via Cajatambo or Huayllapa to the W.

ACCESS Quickest access is via the village of Cajatambo (3380m)(PT) lying SW of the Huayhuash. From here cross the steep pass to the N (4190m) on a new vehicle track to reach the Rio Pumarinri. Walk up the valley E and then NE to below the dam on Lag. Viconga on the Huayhuash circuit. From here continue up the trail on the LHS of the valley to the small lagoon (4850m) below the S slopes of the peak, 2d. From Llamac follow the circuit trek counter-clockwise S to Huayllapa then E up the Q. Guanacpatay to the Punta Cuyoc, 2-3d.

CLIMB From the small lagoon (4850m) which lies below the S slopes traverse R to the poorly defined SE rib on the R of the S face. Climb directly up snow or scree slopes towards the summit, passing or turning several rock bands to reach a shoulder. From here traverse L on the glacier until it is possible to climb to the summit L of the seracs.

OTHER PEAKS The slightly higher **Puscanturpa Norte 5652m** can be climbed with greater difficulty by the rocky SW ridge, gained from the W side of Punta Cuyoc (grade VI - good rock). There are now a large number of hard rock routes on this impressive face. **Puscanturpa Central 5442m** is a relatively easy ascent by the NE glacier from the Portachuelo de Huayhuash.

BEST MAP As for Yerupajá.

LEON HUACCANAN 5421m   5 days   F

An easy snow peak lying SE of the main Huayhuash range and (strictly speaking) part of the Cord. Raura, Leon makes an interesting and easy ascent from Lag. Viconga. It is marked as Kuajadajanka on the Alpine Mapping Guild map and is also known by locals as Leon Dormido.

ACCESS See the map on page 112, although the peak itself appears on the map opposite. Follow the access detailed for Puscanturpa above from Cajatambo to Lag. Viconga then go around the lake to a scenic camp in a meadow above the extreme N point of the lake, (4500m) 2d.

CLIMB From the camp at the N end of Viconga climb 50m to a shoulder then traverse on a path past a coal mine. Descend to a small boggy valley then climb up and R out the other side, over rock slabs to reach the Lagunas Aguascochas, 4700m. Walk past the lagunas to a moraine S of the most southerly lagoon and follow this to the foot of Leon, 2h. Follow cairns up and L over easy scrambling on rock ledges with a short detour R to pass a steeper buttress, to reach the glacier at 5000m, just L of the highest rocks.

Climb the glacier easily to the summit via the N slopes, 5-6h in total.

OTHER PEAKS To the S, **Quesillojanca 5348m, F** is another enjoyable ascent by the NW slopes from the same base camp, 7-8h.

BEST MAP As for Yerupajá.

Leon from the NW

Cerro SANTA ROSA 5706m   4 days   AD/D
Cerro YARUPAC 5685m   4 days   D/TD
Cerro CULE 5580m   4 days   PD/AD

These are the three highest peaks of the Cord. Raura which lies SE of the Cord. Huayhuash.

ACCESS Access in general is easiest from the village of Oyon (3630m) (PT) to the S of the range. Shops and lodging. Buses from Lima via Huacho. From Oyon follow the valley N to Pucallpa. For Santa Rosa go NE from here to the Mina Raura on a high plateau in the centre of the range at 4800m - about 20km. It may be possible to drive this section. For Yarupac go NW from Pucallpa past Lag. Surasaca to a base camp W of the peak (4400m). A road (condition n/k) now goes from Oyon to here and on to near Lag. Viconga in the Cord. Huayhuash.

All the peaks in the Cord. Raura could also be reached from Cajatambo to the W via Lag. Viconga (see under Leon above for details) and this may be the quickest access for Cule and even Yarupac.

SANTA ROSA CLIMB The normal route is by the glaciated N face from the Mina Raura road.

YARUPAC CLIMB Climb by the W ridge, no details but looks quite difficult and dangerous.

CULE CLIMB Also known as Kuli or Rumiwain, has been climbed by its attractive looking NW ridge. Grade n/k but not too difficult, probably PD/AD

OTHER PEAKS Near the Mina Raura is **Flor de Luto, 5529m** climbed by various routes on S side. **Condorsenja 5379m,** has been climbed easily from the N and NE.

BEST MAP PIGM sheet 21-j 'Yanahuanca' 1:100,000. Sheet 22-j 'Oyon' useful for access.

Cule

Yarupac Norte

Santa Rosa

Yarupac

Cord. Raura from the W

Climbing in the
Cordillera Raura

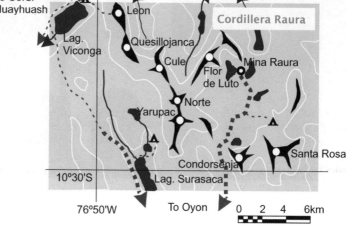

To Cord.
Huayhuash

Leon

Cordillera Raura

Lag.
Viconga

Quesillojanca

Cule

Mina Raura

Flor
de Luto

Yarupac

Norte

Santa Rosa

Condorsenja

Lag. Surasaca

10°30'S

76°50'W

To Oyon

0 2 4 6km

LIMA The capital of Peru, a sprawling coastal city   150m

Most people hate the dirty, smoggy sprawl of Lima, Peru's capital city. It does grow on you a little after a few days, but it is never a pleasant place. The city must have the world's most bizarre climate; Lima is drier than most of Arabia and is a tropical city at sea level but during the main climbing season, it's plagued by five months of dreadful cold mist with occasional outbreaks of thin drizzle.

Most climbers and tourists stay in the more affluent and modern area of Miraflores, although the old town around the Plaza de Armas is well worth visiting to see some beautiful colonial architecture.

SIGHTS There are some museums and archaeological sites worth seeing in and around the city. Particularly recommended are the Gold Museum and the ruins of Pachacamac to the S of the city. Miraflores has some good beaches in the Lima summer (November - March).

FOOD There are a number of big supermarkets in the affluent central area of Miraflores with a good choice of dried foods etc. (a much better choice than in provincial cities like Huaraz and Cuzco). One of the best is Wong at Benavides corner with Panama. There are other branches around town. In the old part of town there is a huge supermarket at the corner of Venezuela and Ugarte, in the area of Breña.

MOUNTAIN INFO The South American Explorers Club, located in Miraflores at Piura 135, is a reasonable source of information on mountaineering and a very good source for travel info in general and for up to date information on trouble spots. It is also a good place to contact other climbers in Lima if you're looking for a partner. Also worth trying are the Peruvian guides (AGMP) offices at Paz Soldan 225, San Isidro.

MOUNTAIN EQUIPMENT There is a fairly good shop 'Alpamayo' in the shopping mall at Larco #345, unit 27 on the central park in Miraflores, and another called "Tatoo" in the Larcomar shopping centre where Larco meets the Pacific Ocean. Both have a good range of camping equipment and some basic climbing equipment, e.g. karabiners, ice-axes.

Plaza de Armas, Lima

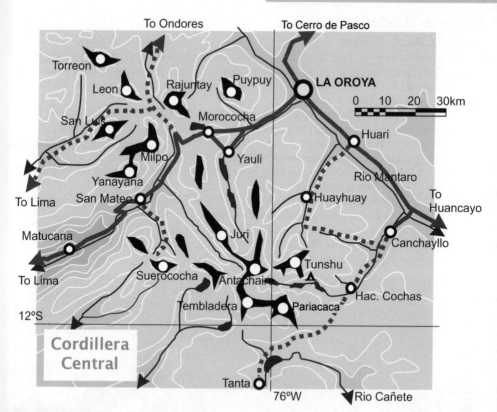

Nevado RAJUNTAY 5477m   2 days   N/K

Also commonly spelt Raujunte, this is the highest point of the Cordillera La Viuda which lies inland
from Lima and N of the main road and rail link to Huancayo. The mountains of the Cordillera la Viuda
rise from a high rolling plateau (4400-4800m) scattered with many small lakes. These peaks can be
reached easily in a day from Lima, though for acclimatisation it may be better to stay in the large town
of La Oroya (c. 3400m) for a couple of days. There are 4x4 tracks into most of the main valleys leading
to small mines.

ACCESS For Rajuntay approach up the Q. Chinchan, leaving the main Lima road at the large hairpin
bend 3km beyond Casapalca (about 10km before Morococha). From here a track heads NW to good
camping (4700m) beneath the S slopes of the peak.

CLIMB By W ridge. No details but easy, 1d.

OTHER PEAKS There are many other peaks just over the 5000m mark all with easy access. For many
of the northern peaks in the range such as **Torreon 5362m** access is probably easier from Ondores in
the Mantaro valley to the NE.

BEST MAP PIGM sheet 24-k 'Matucana' 1:100,000.

Nevado TUNSHU 5730m   4 days   AD
PARIACACA 5760m   4 days   PD

Pariacaca is also known as Azulcocha. These are the two highest peaks in the northern massif of the range which is generally known as the Cordillera Central. This lies S of the main Lima - Huancayo road and rail link. Being close to Lima the area has been opened up to mining and access is relatively easy along the many tracks.

ACCESS From Pachacayo in the Mantaro valley to the Hac. Cochas (PT) then walk or drive W for about 15km to base camps near Lag. Carhuacocha (4420m) about half way between the peaks. Access is also possible from Huari in the Mantaro valley by track to the village of Huayhuay then walk about 20km S-SW to reach the same area. It is possible to drive many of the old mining roads in this area.

TUNSHU CLIMB The NE ridge, from a camp by Lag. Tunshu. The ridge was first climbed in 1958 and consists of mixed rock and snow/ice.

PARIACACA CLIMB This is the peak which lies 5km SW of Tullocotococha and is unnamed on the IGM map. The previous edition of this guidebook called it Azulcocha. From Carhuacocha go around the W side of Tullocotococha to a high camp beneath the peak at about 4700m, 3-4h. From here climb over moraines to reach the glacier edge at 5300m, then use a snow ramp hidden on the left to gain the steep upper snow slopes. Climb these, 40°-50° to the summit,

Tunshu from the SE

Antachaire from the S

Tembladera from the E

OTHER PEAKS The peak to the W of Pariacaca, **Tembladera 5658m,** also known as Colquepucro, can be climbed easily by the S glacier F/PD. **Antachaire 5705m**, is also a relatively easy ascent from the S.

PARIACACA KEY WAYPOINTS Carhuacocha camp 11°56'43" 75°57'16" Tullucotococha camp 11°58'26" 75°58'27" Glacier edge 11°58'54" 75°59'22" Summit 11°59'20" 75°59'43"

BEST MAP Both peaks lie on PIGM sheet 24-1 'La Oroya' but sheets 24-k, 25-k and 25-l, will also be useful for access. All at 1:100,000.

Pariacaca peaks from the NE

Norte

Sur

Nevado TICLLA 5897m   4 days   PD/AD
Nevado LLONGOTE 5781m   4 days   N/K

These are the two highest peaks in the southern massif of the range which is generally known as the Cordillera Central. Ticlla is occasioanlly also known as Cotoni. These peaks get generally better weather than the Cordillera Blanca.

ACCESS There are two main possibilities, approaching from either the inland city of Huancayo or the coast at Cañete. From Cañete travel via Yauyos to the village of Miraflores (3650m) (no regular PT and only a few small shops). From Huancayo travel via Angasmayo and San Jose de Quero to reach Miraflores, there is reported to be a bus on Sundays only. From Miraflores a good pack animal trail in the Q. Tomapampa valley leads W and over a 4750m high pass to Lag. Huasacocha (4250m) under the S slopes of Ticlla, 5h.

TICLLA CLIMB A glacier ascent by the SW face and W ridge gained from Huascacocha to the S possibly with a higher camp at 4800m below the glacier edge, 3-4h. Climb onto the glacier and then head for the col at 5300m on the W ridge. Climb the glaciated W ridge getting steadily steeper reaching as much as 50°-60° beneath the summit.

OTHER ROUTES The dramatic 300m high **SE face** can also be climbed at about AD/D (50-60° snow and ice) from a camp in the upper Q. Cutunia.

LLONGOTE CLIMB S of Ticlla is the steep rock spine of Llongote which has only rarely been climbed. The best route appears to be the E ridge reached from the S at Lag. Llongote above Yauyos. Details n/k but believed to be mixed rock and snow about alpine D.

OTHER PEAKS There are a number of lower and relatively easy peaks in the area. **Uman Norte 5431m,** is fairly easy by the S ridge gained from the W. **Padrecaca 5362m, F** on the rocky E slopes/ridge, or by the **W ridge, AD**. Further E, **Ancovilca 5467m**, can be climbed by the attractive S ridge, on snow, possibly about AD.

If arriving in Miraflores from Huancayo have a look at the 300-500m overhanging limestone walls in the canyon between Tomas and Alis. There is now some rock climbing recorded here.

TICLLA KEY WAYPOINTS Pass on approach 12°17'48" 75°56'44" Laguna Huascacocha camp 12°17'40" 75°57'46" High camp 12°16'31" 75°58'36" 5300m col 12°15'30" 75°58'20"

BEST MAP PIGM sheet 25-l 'Yauyos' at 1:100,000.

Ticlla from the SW

SE face

W ridge

HUANCAYO A large inland city   3200m

Huancayo is a big inland city in the fertile Mantaro valley. It makes a good base for climbs in the Cordillera Huaytapallana and can also be used to access the other central Cordilleras. A scenic 8h. bus journey from Lima via La Oroya and over the Ticlio pass.

FOOD There is a supermarket at the junction of Giraldez and Real.

FUEL Bencina blanca and kerosene from ferreterias at the S end of Calle Real. Camping gas has not been seen.

MOUNTAIN TRANSPORT AND INFO Huancayo is so far off the tourist trail that it is hard to find much, but Lucho Hurtado at La Cabaña, Giraldez 652 knows a bit about the Cordilleras Central and Huaytapallana and can help with logistics.

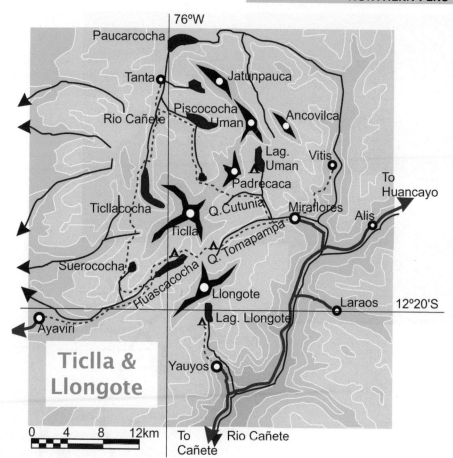

Ticlla & Llongote

0   4   8   12km

Cerro JALLACATE 5557m — 3 days — N/K
Cerro JALLACATE SUR c.5520m — 3 days — AD

Jallacate is the highest peak in the Cordillera Huaytapallana lying only 30km NE of the large inland city of Huancayo. The range are considerably wetter than the other Central Cordilleras and often cloud over in the afternoons.

ACCESS From Hauancayo via Hac. Acopalca to the pass at the head of the Q. Ronda (4600m). From here walk NW around a ridge to reach a camp at Lag. Lasuntay (4650m - Lazo Huntay on PIGM map). For Jallacate Sur head in a northeasterly direction over a col behind a small peak to reach campsites in the valley above the Laguna Cocha Grande.

JALLACATE CLIMB No details but reported to be fairly easy. Presumably a combination of the S slopes and SW ridge. The peak is quite heavily glaciated for its size.

JALLACATE SUR CLIMB From the camp in the valley above Cocha Grande cross steep moraines on the LHS of the glacier, before crossing onto the glacier at about 5000m. Climb the glaciated SW ridge, generally easy but with short sections to 60° or more to the summit.

KEY WAYPOINTS Camp at Cocha Grande 11°56'07" 75°02'35" Onto glacier 11°55'41" 75°02'55" Final steep section 11°55'11" 75°02'52"

BEST MAP PIGM sheet 24-m 'Jauja' at 1:100,000.

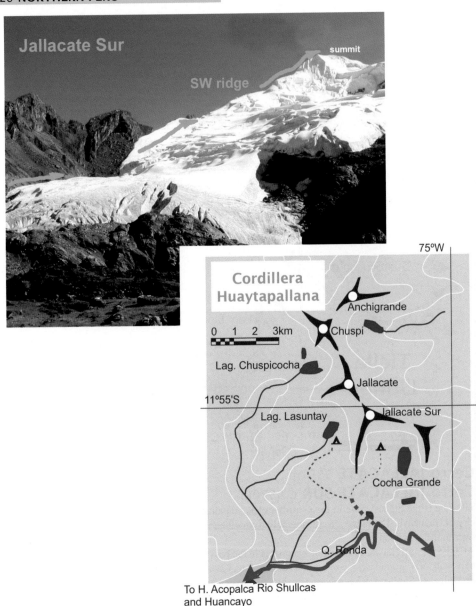

Jallacate Sur

SW ridge

summit

Cordillera Huaytapallana

75°W

Anchigrande

Chuspi

0 1 2 3km

Lag. Chuspicocha

Jallacate

11°55'S

Lag. Lasuntay

Jallacate Sur

Cocha Grande

Q. Ronda

To H. Acopalca Rio Shullcas
and Huancayo

HUAGARUNCHO 5723m

5-7 days   N/K

A difficult and isolated peak lying NE of Cerro de Pasco.

ACCESS From the large town of Cerro de Pasco via Huachon (PT). Then walk for 2-3 days to reach the N side of the peak.

CLIMB The first ascent and the easiest line is by the W ridge, gained from the N. It is difficult, with poor snow and ice, big seracs and bad cornices.

BEST MAP PIGM sheet 22l 'Ulcumayo' at 1:100,000.

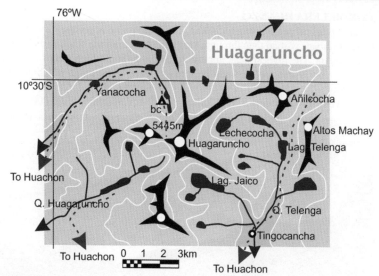

OTHER RANGES

South of the Cordillera Central are a number of lower isolated ranges, described briefly below. All these ranges are remote and very rarely visited by mountaineers, although Neate's bibliography does record ascents of many of the principal peaks.

CORDILLERA DE CHONTA

A compact range S of Huancavelica and best accessed from that city. The highest points are the northern outlier **Tanranu 5431m,** and in the main group **Turuyoc 5396m, Huamanrazo 5304m** and **Palomo 5308m**. Access from Huancavelica to the mining settlement of Santa Ines near Orcococha. The highest peaks have some small glaciers.

BEST MAPS PIGM sheets 27m and 27n at 1;100,000

Cuscuchille, Cordillera Huanzo

CORDILLERA HUANZO

A small range of peaks rising to 5400m. The Huanzo are accessible from the north via Puquio on the Nasca to Abancay road then through Antabamba, or from the south and Chivay via Caylloma and the Mina Arcata. The highest peak appears to be the 5450m+ high peak of **Toro Rumi**. The Cordillera Huanzo name is also applied to the eastern extension of the range which lies N of Coropuna and rises to 5510m.

BEST MAP PIGM sheets 30-q "Chulca" and 30-r "Cayarani", 1:100,000

Toro Rumi, Cordillera Huanzo

Sara Sara from the N

No. SARA SARA

Inca offerings and the remains of a girl child were found on the summit of this peak by Johan Rheinhard in the early 1990's and well documented in a film of the excavations. **Sara Sara 5505m, F** is a volcanic peak that should perhaps be counted as the most northerly summit of the Cordillera Occidental. Access from Chala on the coast road by a poor road to Laguna Parinacochas which lies W of the mountain. Easy ascents are by the N or NW slopes.

BEST MAP PIGM sheet 31p, 1:100,000

SOUTHERN PERU

INTRODUCTION

Some of the wildest and least explored ranges in the Andes lie in southern Peru, in the area around and south of Cuzco. Numerous compact ranges are found on the eastern edge of the Altiplano, where the high plateau meets the Amazon basin.

The peaks are all heavily glaciated and very Alpine, with some ranges rivalling the Cordillera Blanca and Huayhuash for spectacular peaks. There aren't many technically easy peaks in this part of Peru and there aren't many accessible peaks either. As a consequence it is a very quiet area and you will probably be the only team on your mountain even on the busiest peaks like Ausangate and Salcantay.

This chapter deals with the three main ranges around Cuzco; the Cordilleras Urubamba, Vilcabamba and Vilcanota. It also includes the peaks in the Peruvian Cordillera Apolobamba (on or near the Bolivian border) which are easiest to access from Peru via the city of Juliaca. The high volcanic peaks in southern Peru around Arequipa are described in the Cordillera Occidental chapter, from page 179.

Southern Peru is the best part of South America to visit if you want to see the real South America, with colourful highland Indians, Inca ruins, llamas and condors. The fantastic stone work of the many Inca ruins in and around Cuzco, including Machu Picchu, should not be missed.

GETTING THERE

The only easy way to get to the area is by flying to Cuzco via Lima, the Peruvian capital. See the Northern Peru chapter for details of flights to Lima. There are several flights daily from Lima to Cuzco with the domestic Peruvian airlines such as LAN and Avianca. The bus journey from Lima to Cuzco is a very long 33 hours, passing through areas that can be dangerous because of armed robbery etc. It is not recommended.

For the ranges further south, the Apolobamba and Carabaya, a flight from Lima to Juliaca is recommended.

SEASON AND WEATHER CONDITIONS

The climbing season in this part of Peru is the May to August dry season. The weather is a little less reliable than in Bolivia to the S and seems to be best early in the season (May and June). The ranges are near to the Amazon and have relatively wet climates with frequent afternoon storms and fresh snowfalls common even in the dry season. You can expect about 2-3 bad days per week. Temperatures are very cold with freezing levels about 3500m at night in the dry season. Within the area there is very wide variation, with the Apolobamba enjoying the most stable weather, followed by the Vilcanota. The Urubamba and Vilcabamba have the least stable weather.

CLIMBING CONDITIONS

Deep new snow is common even in season and because the mountains are rarely climbed this can lead to problems making a trail. Snow lines are at about 5000m. The western and southern slopes have noticeably more snow and ice, the eastern and northern slopes generally more rock. Where there is ice it is generally very good.

The naming of peaks in the area is very confused, particularly in the Cordillera Vilcanota where even the main 6000m peaks seem to be known by several different (but unfortunately similar) sets of names. The names used in this chapter for the Cord. Vilcanota are those widely used in mountaineering literature (e.g. Neate) but do not always correspond to local or PIGM usage.

CUZCO The ancient Inca capital, now a regional centre 3500m

Cuzco (or Qosqo) was the ancient capital of the Inca Empire and in and around the city are many traces of the fabulous architecture they left behind. No-one should come to this part of South America without spending some of their time exploring this fascinating archaeology. The city of Cuzco sits in a high basin at 3500m on a plateau between the rivers Urubamba and Apurimac. For mountaineers the city makes an ideal base for acclimatisation with the opportunity to see some of South America's most spectacular tourist sites while getting used to the altitude.

SIGHTS There are so many ruins around Cuzco that no guide could list all those worth seeing but Sacsayhuaman, an incredible toothed fortress which sits on the hillside immediately N of Cuzco is probably the most spectacular. There are also good views of Ausangate from here.

MACHU PICCHU Set on a spectacular neck of rock almost 1000m above the deep gorge of the Urubamba river, Machu Picchu is a sight that should not be missed. Manic mountaineers can console themselves for a 'wasted' day by ascending the steep peak which forms the classic backdrop to Machu Picchu, **Huayna Picchu, 2660m.** This ascent needs to be booked in advance online. There is a path to the top, but several steep staircases almost merit a UIAA rock grade. The path round the LHS of the peak to the Temple of the Moon is even more spectacular.

The 3 day Inca Trail to Machu Picchu starting at the rail halt known as km88 is worth doing, but it is now very busy and the permits are expensive. However it provides a great way of acclimatising, with passes up to 4200m and superb views of Salcantay and the Pumasillo group. The ruins which are seen along the way are increasingly spectacular as you walk towards Machu Picchu.

FOOD There are several big grocers shops near the centre of Cuzco. Try the one on the N side of Plateros.

FUEL White gas (bencina blanca) can usually be bought from hardware shops (ferreterias) in the market area out towards the station. Camping gas from many shops around the Plaza that also sell and rent camping equipment.

MOUNTAIN TRANSPORT AND INFO There are numerous agencies in and around the Plaza de Armas who can arrange mountain transport, donkeys and or porters. Most are set up for trekkers, and particularly for those doing the Inca Trail, but some may be able to help with arranging mules for the Vilcanota and more remote parts of the Urubamba and Vilcabamba.

MOUNTAIN EQUIPMENT There are many agencies around town renting and selling camping equipment. Climbing gear is harder to find.

Plaza de Armas, Cuzco

PUMASILLO 5991m
12 days   N/K

LASUNAYOC 5936m
10 days   AD/D

Pumasillo is the highest point of an extensive group of difficult peaks near the W end of the remote Cordillera Vilcabamba. The name means the Puma's Claw.

ACCESS From Cuzco by rail to Santa Teresa, then by mule via the Yanama pass (4770m) to the village of Yanama (3510m), S of the peak. From Yanama continue via Paccha (3900m) to reach a base camp under W ridge. About 4d.

PUMASILLO CLIMB The line of first ascent was the W ridge. Avoid the prominent rock buttress low down by climbing around the N side of it on the W glacier. Move back R to the W ridge. Climb over flutings and an ice bulge then follow the ridge to the summit ice formations. Grade n/k but very difficult, 2-3d.

LASUNAYOC CLIMB From the E side of the Yanama pass climb the valley N to the Lasunayoc col (5300m - E of the peak). Cross the col and climb the E slopes and ridge with some steep ice and seracs high up.

OTHER PEAKS Between Pumasillo and Lasunayoc is the difficult ice peak **Sacsarayoc 5918m** climbed by the E ridge. This ridge is gained by a long traverse from the Lasunayoc col across the N and E slopes of Lasunayoc.

BEST MAP PIGM sheet 2344 'Machupicchu' 1:100,000.

summit

W ridge

Pumasillo from the S

Lasunayoc from the S

E slopes

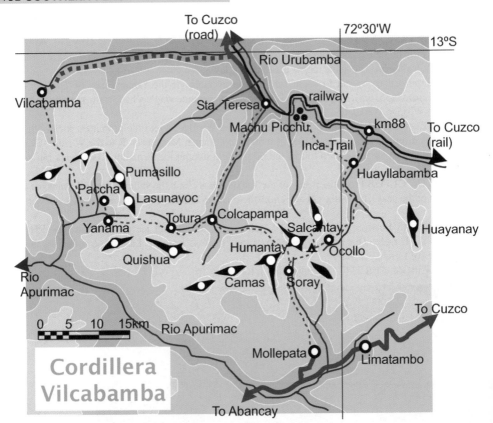

To Cuzco (road)

72°30'W

13°S

Rio Urubamba

railway

Vilcabamba

Sta. Teresa

Machu Picchu

km88

To Cuzco (rail)

Inca-Trail

Pumasillo

Huayllabamba

Paccha

Lasunayoc

Totura   Colcapampa

Yanama

Salcantay

Huayanay

Quishua

Humantay

Ocollo

Camas   Soray

Rio Apurimac

0   5   10   15km

Rio Apurimac

To Cuzco

Mollepata

Limatambo

Cordillera Vilcabamba

To Abancay

SALCANTAY 6271m — 8 days — AD
HUMANTAY 5917m — 7 days — AD/D

The massive Salcantay is the highest peak in the Cord. Vilcabamba. It has an impressive S face as does the neighbouring peak of Humantay.

ACCESS From Cuzco by bus, truck or jeep to Mollepata (2800m), then by mule to Soray (3850m), then E over the pass of Incachillasca to a small settlement. About 3d. This settlement can also be reached from km88 on the Machu Picchu railway by walking up the valley to the S through Huayllabamba, 2d., but this may require an expensive Inca Trail permit. From the settlement a further day will be needed up the pass to the N to reach a base camp in a pleasant meadow under the NE ridge.

SALCANTAY CLIMB The normal route is the NE ridge from a camp below the col at c.4500m. Gain the ridge by a rising traverse of the glacier to a snow saddle or, more easily, by a rocky crest leading to the same saddle. Bivouac possible on last rocks at c.5500m. The snow/ice ridge above is followed over several short steep sections to the summit.

HUMANTAY CLIMB The easiest ascent is from the NE, either up a shattered rock buttress or winding up the high E facing glacier to gain the summit ridge.

BEST MAP PIGM sheet 2344 'Machupicchu' 1:100,000.

NE ridge

Salcantay from the S

NE ridge

camp

Salcantay from the E

Nevado VERONICA 5682m   3 days   AD/D
Nevado SAHUASIRAY 5818m   5 days   N/K

These two peaks are the highest in the Urubamba range which lies N of the river of the same name. The peaks are relatively easy to get to from Cuzco and certainly more accessible than many others in SE Peru but have been strangely neglected by climbers. The range consists of several isolated massifs known as 'nudos'.

Veronica is a beautiful snow pyramid clearly seen from the upper Urubamba valley. It is also known as Huacay Huilcay, Waqaywillka or Padre Eterno.

ACCESS For Veronica travel from Cuzco via Ollantaytambo then up to the Abra Malaga pass (PT) on the road which leads to Santa Teresa and Quillabamba.

VERONICA CLIMB The normal route is by the NE ridge from Abra Malaga (4350m) and has got steeper and more complex in recent years. Grade n/k but about AD/D.

SAHUASIRAY CLIMB Sahuasiray is a steep peak sometimes mistakenly called Chainapuerto. This is the name given more specifically to a summit lying N of the main peak. The first ascent was by the E ridge gained from the S. Grade n/k but reported to be difficult.

OTHER PEAKS The peak E of Veronica is **Helancoma 5367m,** climbed on the SE side from

Ollantaytambo. The peak W
of Sahuasiray is **No. Chicon
(Media   Luna)   5530m,**
climbed from the village of
Urubamba to the SW.
BEST MAP PIGM sheet 27-r
'Urubamba' 1:100,000.

Veronica from the NE

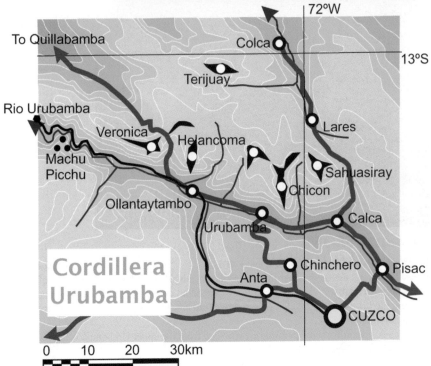

TINQUI The access town for the Cordillera Vilcanota   3800m
The town of Tinqui is the easiest place to start for almost all of the Cordillera Vilcanota peaks. It is
a 4h. drive from Cuzco via Urcos and there is regular public transport. There are basic shops and
accommodation and a cafe that serves great chips. Mules and arrieros can be rented from Cayetano
Crispin at the Hostal Ausangate. A small fee, per person, is payable for entry to the Cord. Vilcanota at
a wee booth on the outskirts of town.

TACUSIRI 5350m+

5 days   PD

Tacusiri is the most westerly main peak in the extensive Cordillera Vilcanota. The peak is marked on the PIGM map as Tacusiri but seems to be known as Sorimani in some sources. The ascent is an easy scramble from Pucacocha with fine views of the huge icefalls on the S and W sides of Ausangate.

ACCESS From Tinqui via Upis to Pucacocha (4600m). Beautiful campsite, 2d.

CLIMB From Pucacocha climb onto the low ridge lying due S and scramble to the summit over rock and scree on the S side of E ridge, 5-6h., PD.

OTHER PEAKS AND ROUTES Both Tacusiri and **Sorimani 5350m+** (to the N) can also be climbed from Pucacocha by the glacier col between them. The superb rock needle E of Sorimani has also been climbed at about grade VI/VII.

KEY WAYPOINTS See Ausangate below.

BEST MAP As for Ausangate.

AUSANGATE 6372m

8 days   AD

The highest peak in SE Peru and also the highest peak of the extensive and rugged Cordillera Vilcanota. Ausangate is a great wedge shaped mountain with a dramatic N face and a gentler but heavily glaciated slope to the S.

ACCESS From the village of Tinqui (3800m) (PT) around either the W (via Upis, Pucacocha, Ausangatecocha and a 5100m pass) or the E side (via Pacchanta, Pachaspata and Jampa) of Ausangate to reach a base camp (4800m) in the unnamed valley on the S side of the mountain above Pinaya. Either way 3d. There is a refugio here now, reported to be expensive and poor value.

CLIMB The normal route is on the E flank of the mountain. From base camp go up the narrow block filled valley on LHS of the Ausangate-Mariposa glacier. Climb scree slopes and pass the cliff above by a series of ledges on the R at about 5000m (difficult to find but marked) to gain easier ground and moraines. Go through the rock band at the top of the moraines in a series of easy zigzags to reach a high camp (5450m), 5h. From the camp climb the LHS of the E glacier, avoiding the icefall to reach a large glacier platform under the headwall. Climb the headwall on steep snow (more often mixed

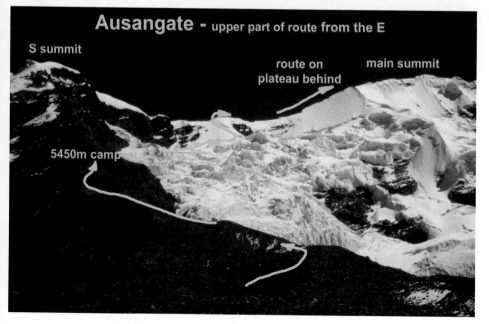

Ausangate - upper part of route from the E
S summit
route on plateau behind
main summit
5450m camp

ground in recent years) to reach the summit plateau at 6000m then over easier ground to the final steep summit pyramid. A higher camp on the plateau edge may be needed, especially if there is deep snow on the plateau.

KEY WAYPOINTS Tinqui 13°40'01" 71°19'21" Upis camp 13°45'07" 71°16'26" Pucacocha camp 13°48'57" 71°16'03" Ausangatecocha 13°49'32" 71°14'20" 5100m Pass 13°49'00" 71°13'22" Ausangate BC 13°49'00" 71°12'13" Ausangate high camp 13°47'50" 71°13'00" Summit 13°47'27" 71°13'57" See Campa below for the approach to Ausanagate base camp by the Campa pass.

BEST MAP PIGM sheet 28-t 'Ocongate', 1:100,000

Ausangate Headwall

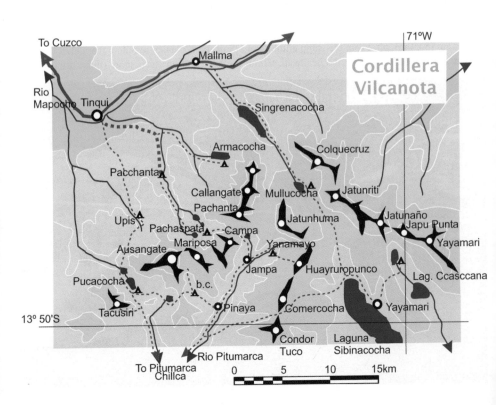

Nevado MARIPOSA 5808m   7 days   D/TD

This peak, one of the most dramatic in the Vilcanota, can be climbed from a base camp at Pachaspata. Mariposa is a challenging peak, a narrow ridge mostly rock on the NE side, beautiful steep snow and ice on the SW side. The name is Spanish for butterfly. On the PIGM maps Mariposa is known as Santa Catalina.

ACCESS From Tinqui via Pacchanta to a camp by one of the many lagoons in the Pachaspata area N of Mariposa (4800m), 1½d.

MARIPOSA CLIMB By the long SE ridge from Mariposa Sur (see below) or the col just north of it. No details of the exact difficulties, but the climb is easy to the foresummit (5650m) then is a narrow crest of either rock or snow.

OTHER PEAKS The small peak at the S end of the ridge, **Mariposa Sur 5460m, F/PD** can be climbed easily from either Pachaspata by the N glacier and E ridge or from Ausangate base camp by Lag. Cochajasa and the SW slopes. There are large crevasses either way but otherwise easy terrain.

BEST MAP As for Ausangate.

Nevado HUAYRURO PUNCO 5550m   5 days   F
Nevado CAMPA 5500m   5 days   F

These two peaks are two of the easiest ascents in the Vilcanota and both give good views. Campa is climbed from the pass to the E known as the Campa pass. Huayruro Punco is climbed from the valley N of the peak. Both are good acclimatisation ascents. On the PIGM map Campa is marked as Maria Huamantilla.

ACCESS For Campa go from Tinqui (PT) via Pacchanta to a camp by one of the many lagoons in the Pachaspata area N of Mariposa (4800m), 1½d. For Huayruro Punco carry on over the Campa pass (5100m) and then cut across the low ridge from Ticllacocha to reach a camp by the houses at Yanamayo, also known as Asiro, 2½d.

CAMPA CLIMB From Pachaspata follow the well worn trail up towards the Campa pass (5100m). Turn R before the pass and climb over loose boulders to reach the NE glacier. Climb this and the easy N slopes to the summit, 5h.

HUAYRURO PUNCO CLIMB The peak can be climbed quite easily from Yanamayo by either the N or NE ridge via the Pampa Puca Puca. Both ridges have snow as well as some scree and rock, but it is not necessary to cross the glaciers, 5h.

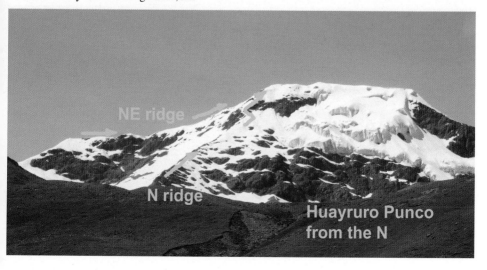

Huayruro Punco from the N

OTHER PEAKS Campa II can be climbed from Pachaspata by the N side. Difficulty n/k.

CAMPA KEY WAYPOINTS Pacchanta 13°43'12" 71°14'36" Pachaspata camp 13°46'07" 71°10'55" Campa ascent start 13°45'59" 71°10'58" Campa pass 13°46'05" 71°10'36"

H.P. KEY WAYPOINTS Asiro camp 13°46'38" 71°08'24" Pampa Puca Puca 13°47'02" 71°07'38" NE-ridge start 13°47'04" 71°07'10" H.P. summit 13°47'28" 71°06'57" Pinaya 13°49'32" 71°11'31"

BEST MAP As for Ausangate.

Campa from the NW

CALLANGATE 6110m

6 days   N/K

There are five main summits in the Callangate chain. The highest peak is marked as Collpa Ananta on the PIGM maps, but is often known as Callangate V. To add to the confusion it is also known as Chimboya in many sources!

ACCESS See the map on page 136. From Tinqui to Lag. Armacocha at 4550m. 1d.

CLIMB The first ascent in 1966 was by the W ridge from Armacocha. Grade n/k but will not be easy.

OTHER PEAKS At the S end of the chain and overlooking the Campa pass the steep needle of **Pachanta 5727m**, can be climbed from Ticllacocha via the col to the N linking it with Ccapana. **Ccapana 5725m,** can also be climbed without great difficulty from Ticllacocha via the NE glacier with a short ice-wall to finish. Both ascents 1d. The peak at the N end of the range, **Callangate I, 6000m**, was first climbed from the S in 1957, mixed snow and rock, not easy.

BEST MAP As for Ausangate.

Collpa Ananta

Callangate I

Callangate peaks from the NW

Callangate peaks from the S

JATUNHUMA 6093m
7 days   AD/D

Also known as Pico Tres on the PIGM map.

ACCESS See the map on page 136. From Tinqui via Pacchanta and Pachaspata to Lag. Ticllacocha at 4800m, 2d.

CLIMB From Ticllacocha go over the wide glacier plateau on the W side of Jatunhuma to a high camp at c.5300m. Then climb by the NW buttress, the line of the first ascent in 1957. Steep snow and ice and there may be problems getting through seracs about 150m below the summit, 2-3d. from Ticllacocha. Grade n/k but about AD/D.

OTHER PEAKS The subsidiary peaks to the SE, Jatunhuma II and III are relatively easy ascents from the glacier plateau on their NE flanks, which is reached from Ticllacocha by going around the S side of the peaks.

BEST MAP As for Ausangate.

Jatunhuma from the W

NW buttress

Vicuña, Cordillera Vilcanota

JATUNRITI 6106m 5 days AD

This is the peak lying about 6km ENE of Jatunhuma sometimes also known as Nañaloma or Yanaloma, but marked on the PIGM map as Chumpe. The name Jatunriti means big snow peak.

ACCESS See the map on page 136. From Mallma on the road about 20km E of Tinqui walk past the beautiful Singrenacocha then up to a base camp above Lag. Mullucocha (4600m) in the broad valley NW of the peak, 1d. This is as far as pack animals can go.

CLIMB The normal route is by the NW glacier and ridge. From Lag. Mullucocha follow a cairned path up the RHS of the moraines towards Lag. Huarurumicocha (4970m). From here climb moraines on the RHS (S) of the big glacier E of the lake to reach a camp at about 5400m, 1d. In some years the glacier may be easier to walk up than the moraines. Above the camp join the glacier and find a way through the difficult crevasse field (usually best in the centre) Move L to an easy angled snowfield that leads towards the col above, but just before the col move R to gain the NW ridge by a steep snowfield. Follow the NW ridge to the summit with a couple of steep ice pitches.

OTHER ROUTES Jatunriti can also be climbed from the S at about the same grade.

OTHER PEAKS A subsidiary peak called **Colquecruz 6102m** (known as Alcamarinayoc on the PIGM map) lies to the NW. The first ascent was by the NW slopes from a base camp at 4800m. Grade likely to be about D or TD.

BEST MAP As for Ausangate.

Jatunriti from the S

YAYAMARI 6049m 10 days AD

This is the remote peak lying about 12km SE of Jatunriti and marked on the PIGM map as No. Montura. There are only a few recorded ascents of this very remote peak. The name Yayamari means 'father of the little lakes'.

ACCESS See the map on page 136. Access is long and difficult but best as for Ausangate to the village of Chillca then through the pass immediately S of Comercocha, known as Condor Pasa, to the settlement of Yayamari at the N end of the huge Lag. Sibinacocha. Then go E towards the W slopes of the peak and a base camp at the beautiful Lag. Sorañaña, 5000m, 4-5d from Tinqui. Locals here may want payment in return for camping. The much shorter route from the town of Mallma to the N via Singrenacocha crosses high glaciers and is not suitable for pack animals.

CLIMB The first ascent was from the S and the second (in 1983!) was from the NW. The peak has big and complicated glaciers but appears to be easier angled than most Vilcanota peaks. The S ridge route appears to be safer, climbing a steep snow ridge to the S summit (5800m) then following the ridge N to the main summit. The NW face route is probably easier but is threatened by some big seracs.

OTHER PEAKS This area of the Vilcanota has a number of interesting peaks which can all be climbed from the same base camp as Yayamari. **Jatunñaño Punta 5812m, PD** can be climbed by going round the S side of Lag. Sorañaña then climbing either the broad glaciated S ridge or by following the long SE ridge over several subsidiary summits. **Japu Punta 5852m, AD/D** a northern summit of Yayamari can be climbed from the col to the W. There are some complex crevasses and a steep finish of 80m on 60° snow.

BEST MAP PIGM sheet 28-u, 'Corani' 1:100,000, and sheet 28-t 'Ocongate' useful for access.

Yayamari from the W

S ridge

NW face

Jatunñaño Punta from the S

ALCCACHAYA 5780m   8 days   F
SAN BRAULIO 5675m   8 days   F

These two very remote peaks lie in the heart of the southern Vilcanota near the Chimboya pass. Alccachaya is also known as "Intermedio".

ACCESS Access is long and difficult although a new road to a mine at the Chimboya pass may make things easier. Alccachaya can be accessed from the village of Tinqui to the north and through the Vilcanota mountains but this is an extremely long but scenic 6 day trek. Shorter access from the remote village of Corani (reached from Juliaca via Azangaro and Macusani) by the valley of the Rio Chimboya around the N side of the Ritipampa ice-cap and over the 5100m Chimboya pass, then N up the Q Mates to a camp at 4900m, 3d.

ALCCACHAYA CLIMB The easiest route is by the NE glacier, a very decayed glacier now. 5-6h. from the Q. Mates camp.

Alccachaya from the W

S ridge

On the S ridge of Alccachaya

OTHER ROUTES The S ridge is an excellent route. From the Rio Mates camp climb onto the ridge at its southern end by several routes, on scree or rock. Then follow this S ridge over a level rocky section to the final steep 50-60° snow slopes to the summit.

SAN BRAULIO CLIMB San Braulio can be climbed from the Q. Mates camp by either the W or S glaciers, 5h.

OTHER PEAKS The remote and impressive peak of **Auzangate 5714m**, details not known, but probably easier reached via Tinqui and the town of Marcapata to the north

BEST MAP PIGM sheet 28-u, 'Corani' 1:100,000. Sheet 28-t 'Ocongate' will be useful for the northern access.

Auzangate from the S

RITIPAMPA de QUELLCAYA 5680m   8 days   F

Highly unusual in the Peruvian Andes, the Ritipampa is an almost flat glacier plateau 5400 to 5700m high, about 15km long by 5km wide, rising 400m above the surrounding terrain and generally with quite steep sides. The highest point, known as Coyllor Puñuna, is towards the centre-east of the plateau.

ACCESS Long and difficult. It is probably best via the town of Sicuani and then the small villages of Santa Barbara and Antonio Palma to the NE. It is also possible to approach through the Cordillera Vilcanota, passing Laguna Sibinacocha, 4-5d.

CLIMB Easiest by routes on the N and W sides from the Rio Phinaya valley.

BEST MAP PIGM sheet 28-u, 'Corani' 1:100,000

Ausangate   Ritipampa de Quellcaya   Yayamari

YANA CUCHILLA 5472m
CUNURANA 5420m

2 days   N/K
2 days   N/K

These are the two most accessible peaks of the Cordillera La Raya, lying just 10km E of the main Cuzco-Juliaca road and rail links. The Cordillera La Raya are due south of the main Vilcanota range. Access to these peaks and others in the SW part of range is relatively easy due to the proximity of the Cuzco-Juliaca railway which runs SW of the range.

ACCESS From Cuzco via Sicuani or Juliaca via Ayaviri by the railway (or parallel road) to the Abra La Raya pass at 4300m. The pass lies just NW of the village of Santa Rosa.

YANA CUCHILLA CLIMB Climb from just over the N side of the Abra La Raya by the rocky N ridge, 5-6h.

CUNURANA CLIMB From the village of Santa Rosa directly by fairly easy snow and ice on S face, 5-6h.

BEST MAPS PIGM sheets 29-t 'Sicuani', 29-u, 'Nuñoa' and 30-u 'Ayaviri' all at 1:100,000

Yana Cuchilla
from the S

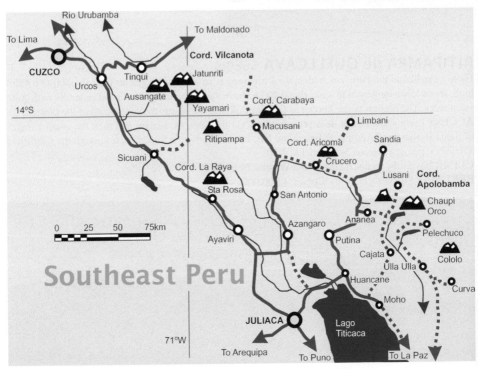

Southeast Peru

Cunurana

Cuddling an Alpaca,
Cordillera Carabaya

Allincapac from the S

Nevado ALLINCAPAC 5805m   4 days   D/TD
CHICHICAPAC 5614m   3 days   PD

These are the two highest peaks of the Cordillera Carabaya, the name generally given to the steep and compact massif E of the remote town of Macusani. Allincapac is also known as Schio. Allincapac is now a difficult and dangerous ascent because the summit plateau is isolated by seracs on all sides. There is some good mountain rock climbing potential in this range and generally good mountaineering on all the lower peaks.

ACCESS Easiest access is from the city of Juliaca via Azangaro to the town of Macusani. From the road 5km N of Macusani follow the valley NW on a dirt road for about 10km, and then on a path to a base camp near Lag. Chambiné (4600m), 3-4h. For the E glacier of Chichicapac access is better by Lag. Chungara to the NE of Macusani. Take the Ayapata road to Lag. Chungara, then walk in along the W shore to scenic base camps, 2h.

CHICHICAPAC CLIMB The easiest route on Chichicapac is now the E glacier. From a base camp at 4700m in the valley NW of Lag. Chungara go up the valley to the N that leads past a small lagoon to the E glacier. Climb this easily to join the NE ridge and follow this to the summit, 5-6h.

OTHER CLIMBS Both peaks were first climbed from near Lag. Chambiné in 2-3d., Chichicapac by the W ridge, grade about AD, Allincapac by the difficult E face. The final section of Allincapac through the serac ring will be easiest and safest from the N, grade at least D.

OTHER MOUNTAINS The mountains at the S end of the range are generally easily accessible and easy to climb. One of the highest peaks is the remote **Balansani 5354m, F.** Further S the peak of **Queroni 5259m**, is only 15km E of Macusani and can be climbed directly by the S or SE slopes.

One of the most accessible peaks, **Quenamari 5294m, F** is 20 km SE of Macusani and is an easy climb from the mines on the N and NE slopes.

BEST MAP PIGM sheet 28-v 'Ayapata' for the northern peaks and 29-v 'Macusani' for the southern ones, both at 1:100,000.

NE ridge

Chichicapac from the SE

Climbing the E glacier on Chichicapac

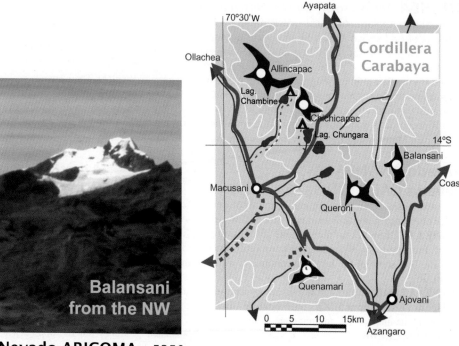

Balansani from the NW

Nevado ARICOMA c.5350m   5 days   N/K

This is the highest peak in the Nudo Aricoma, the small range lying between the Cordillera Carabaya and the Cord. Apolobamba. The peaks are about 60-80km E of Macusani in a very remote part of Peru. The peaks are all on the N side of the Rio Carabaya, also known as the Rio Crucero.

ACCESS Access is best from Juliaca via the town of Ananea which lies about 40km SE of the peaks. It is also possible to reach the range via Azangaro and Crucero to the W.

CLIMB Nevado Aricoma rises above the NE end of Lag. Aricoma. It is best climbed from a pass to the N on the Ananea to Limbani road. Grade n/k but not too difficult.

BEST MAPS PIGM sheet 29-x 'Limbani' at 1:100,000.

Nudo Aricoma from the SE

ANANEA Access town for the Peruvian Apolobamba 4700m

The Cordillera Apolobamba straddle the Peru-Bolivia border and lie to the NE of Lake Titicaca, about 250km N of La Paz and 300km SE of Cuzco. Described here are the northern peaks best accessed from Juliaca in Peru; see the Bolivia chapter for the southern peaks (pages 153-157) and a map on page 154.

Ananea is a desolate mining village at a height of over 4700m. It gets cold at night. There are reasonable shops, a few simple hostels and you can usually arrange transport to the mountains. Bus transport from the nearest city (and airport) at Juliaca is relatively frequent due to the nearby large mining settlement at La Rinconcada. A good place to stay is the hostal next to the church near the top of the town. The owner, Juan Monrroy can also help arrange local transport.

Nevado ANANEA 5853m   4 days   PD
Nevado CALLIJON 5829m   5 days   PD

These two peaks at the northern end of the Apolobamba lie wholly within Peru near the Peruvian village of Ananea. Callijon is marked on the PIGM map as 'Ananea Grande'.

ANANEA ACCESS See the map on page 154. Easiest from Juliaca to the village of Ananea (described above). From here you'll need to hire transport to reach the Laguna Pararani, S of the peak. Walk in along the NW shore of the lake and continue to a base camp by the scenic Laguna Callumachaya, 4700m, 2h.

ANANEA CLIMB Ananea can be climbed by a prominent and long rising ramp on the N side of the SE ridge to a high camp at 5100m, 3h. From here climb onto the SE ridge and follow this to the summit plateau and the final steeper summit cone, 5-6h.

CALLIJON CLIMB The easiest ascent is by the long glaciated N slopes but the approach to these is quite long and complicated. From Ananea village drive to the Paso Iscaycruz then descend slightly towards Lusani. Climb up and over a 4800m pass to the W to reach a camp in the upper Rio Choquechambi at about 4600m. From here to the summit in one long day. This camp could also be reached from Lag. Callumachaya by climbing up and over the glaciated col east of Callijon, but this approach involves some short sections of ice and rock climbing (about AD). The E face can be climbed at about the same grade.

OTHER PEAKS The most northerly peak in the Apolobamba, **Ñocaria, 5412m, F** can be climbed easily by the S slopes in one day from the village of Ananea. The peak of **Lunar (Ananea Oeste) PD** is an easy but interesting ascent from the 'wild west' mining settlement of Lunar directly up to the glacier tongue then along the W ridge.

BEST MAP PIGM sheet 30-y 'La Rinconada' 1:100,000.

Callijon from the SE   N slopes

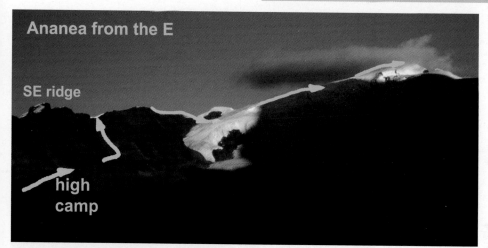

Ananea from the E

SE ridge

high camp

Nevado PALOMANI GRANDE 5768m   5 days   PD
Nevado PALOMANI TRANCA c.5600m   5 days   AD/D

The pyramidal peak of Palomani Grande sits isolated on the W edge of the Apolobamba on the Peru-Bolivia border. It can be climbed from either Peru or Bolivia. Palomani Tranca is a complicated summit a few km S of Grande, with a central peak, a highest east peak, a south peak and a minor west peak.

PERUVIAN ACCESS See the map on page 154 for access details. From Juliaca in Peru via Ananea and Trapiche to small settlements on the N shore of Lag Suches. From here walk along the shore for 3-4h to reach a camp at 4800m in the Quebrada Palomani, W of the peak.

BOLIVIAN ACCESS Easiest from La Paz to the village of Suches on the S shore of Lag. Suches and then further E along a 4x4 track. A good base camp is the large Lag. Chucuyo (4850m), E of the peak. Access is also possible from the Paso Pelechuco road in Bolivia by climbing over a low hill to the N

PERUVIAN CLIMB From the Peruvian side the easiest route is the long N ridge, PD, 5-6h. This is gained easily from the N end of the Quebrada Palomani. over the minor summit of **Palomani Cunca, 5600m**. From Q. Palomani the S face can be climbed by a number of lines all at about AD. Climbing the W glacier to reach the basin beneath the S face is easier and less exposed to serac danger than it appears.

BOLIVIAN CLIMB From Bolivia Palomani can be climbed by either the N or E ridges (both at PD/AD) from Lag. Chucuyo on rock and snow, 4-5h.

PALOMANI TRANCA CLIMB
The highest eastern peak has been climbed by the difficult and rocky N ridge from the basin under Palomani Grande. The central peak is an AD snow climb from the Quebrada Palomani. It would be possible to traverse to the highest peak from here at about AD/D.

BEST MAP As for Chaupi Orco, page 154.

Villagers, Cordillera Apolobamba

Palomani from the S

S rib

SW rib

N ridge

E ridge

On the summit of Palomani
after the first ascent of the S rib

BOLIVIA

INTRODUCTION
With very stable weather, accessible peaks, excellent climbing conditions and an interesting culture Bolivia makes a fine destination for a mountaineering expedition. Included in this chapter are almost all peaks in Bolivia, described as usual from N to S, starting with the Cordillera Apolobamba (but excluding a few peaks shared with Peru), followed by the Cordilleras Real, Quimsa Cruz and Lipez (see map on page 189). The volcanic peaks on or near the Chilean border (including Sajama the highest peak in Bolivia) are included in the Cordillera Occidental and are described in the next chapter. By far the most popular range in Bolivia is the Cordillera Real, particularly the southern half and the peaks of Illimani, Huayna Potosi and Condoriri. This popularity is largely due to easy access but the range is also a very attractive one with several dramatic 6000m peaks which have relatively easy ascents by their normal routes. Also relatively busy are the northern Cordillera Real around Sorata. Other areas of the Cordillera Real are generally very quiet due to more difficult access. For the same reason the Cordillera Lipez, Cordillera Apolobamba and the Cordillera Quimsa Cruz are all quiet.

GETTING THERE
At the moment there are no direct flights to the Bolivian capital La Paz from anywhere in Europe although Lufthansa, Air France and KLM will get you there with a change of plane at Lima in Peru. Other options from Europe are with American Airlines via Miami, or with Avianca via Bogota in Colombia. From the USA there are daily flights from Miami with American and the Bolivian airline Boliviana.

SEASON AND WEATHER CONDITIONS
Climbing in all areas is best from May to August. This is winter so temperatures are very low, but it is the dry season and rain and clouds are at a minimum. Bolivia has the most stable weather of any destination in the Andes at this time of year with often only 3 or 4 bad days in a month. Climbing is still reasonable in September and October, with noticeably warmer temperatures and afternoon cloud. Most snowfall is in the summer months of December to March. The Cordillera Lipez are dry enough for climbing to be possible all year round.

CLIMBING CONDITIONS
Most of the peaks in the Cordilleras Real, Apolobamba and Quimsa Cruz are alpine in nature and ascents are normally largely on glaciers, although both the Quimsa Cruz and Apolobamba have quite a lot of exposed rock. In dry years the mountains can become very icy due to low winter temperatures and may be considerably harder. Snow and ice are very stable in the Cordillera Real due to the low night temperatures and avalanches are almost never seen in season. The Apolobamba have a slightly wetter climate and fresh snow is more likely to be encountered as well as more frequent problems with afternoon cloud and mist.

OTHER GUIDEBOOKS
Bolivia - A Climbing Guide, Brain, 1999. Good detail on the main areas around Condoriri, Illimani and Illampu, but a bit restricted on other areas. It doesn't always describe the easiest route on a peak. Southern Cordillera Real, Pecher and Schmiemann, 1977, out of print and out of date, hard to find. Every couple of years local author Alain Mesili brings out a new climbing guidebook to the Bolivia Andes, seemingly with a different title every time. Worth looking for the latest edition in La Paz.

LA PAZ The capital city of Bolivia and a good base   3700m

Most visiting mountaineers arrive in La Paz. It makes an excellent base, particularly for the southern Cordillera Real. At an altitude of 3700m it is a very good height for acclimatisation although some people are ill for several days on arrival. It has an international airport, all the facilities of a capital city, cheap hotels, good restaurants. Roadheads for most peaks in the Cordillera Real can be reached in a few hours, sometimes on public transport.

SIGHTS Tourist trips to the pre-Inca ruins at Tiahuanaco, the islands of the legendary Lake Titicaca and Chacaltaya mountain (5395m) can all be recommended while acclimatising. In town the traditional market area uphill from Calle Sagarnaga is well worth a look.

FOOD There are good outdoor markets in the budget hotel area around Sagarnaga and Santa Cruz. For supermarkets go to the affluent suburbs a long way downhill in the area around Avenida Arce. There are several branches of "Hipermaxi" in this area and Supermercado Ketal on the corner of Arce and Pinilla can also be recommended.

FUEL Bencina blanca can be bought in the ferreterias near the foot of Calle Santa Cruz and in some of the trekking agencies on Sagarnaga and Illampu. Camping Gas from the climbing shops mentioned below.

MOUNTAIN TRANSPORT AND INFO Try the Club Andino Boliviano, Calle Mexico 1638. There are many companies on Sagarnaga offering guided climbs and transport, Bolivian Journeys and Andean Summits can be recommended, also several agencies in the 'Galeria Doryan' at Sagarnaga 189.

CLIMBING EQUIPMENT There are several shops selling camping, trekking and climbing equipment on Calle Illampu, mainly between Santa Cruz and Sagarnaga. Several of the agencies in the shopping centre at Sagarnaga 189 also have rented and second hand gear.

Illimani from La Paz

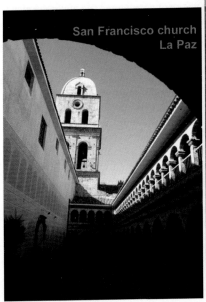

San Francisco church
La Paz

PELECHUCO Access town for the Bolivian Apolobamba 3600m

The Cordillera Apolobamba straddle the Peru-Bolivia border and lie to the NE of Lake Titicaca, about 250km N of La Paz and 300km SE of Cuzco. Described here are the southern peaks best accessed from Bolivia; see the preceding Southern Peru chapter for the northern peaks of Ananea, Callijon and Palomani which are easiest to reach from Juliaca in Peru. The Apolobamba are prone to slightly poorer weather than the Cord. Real.

The friendly wee town of Pelechuco is the best base for organising an expedition into the northern or central Bolivian Apolobamba but a few of the most southerly peaks are better accessed from Curva. Pelechuco has only very basic shops and facilities and an infrequent bus service along a very rough road from La Paz (up to 24h.). You can hire mules and get some information at the Hotel Llataymanta. The town is shrouded in mist almost every afternoon.

There is a popular 3 day trek from Pelechuco to Curva via Hilo Hilo and this is one way of reaching some of the more remote peaks in the Southern Apolobamba.

CHAUPI ORCO 6044m 7 days PD

Chaupi Orco lies in the N of the Cordillera Apolobamba on the Peruvian-Bolivian border and is the highest point in the range. The area S from Chaupi Orco to the peaks of Soral, Ascarani and Katantica is a large ice plateau. The peak is named Viscachani on both the PIGM and BIGM maps. Chaupi Orco means 'central mountain'. Neither the Peruvian nor the Bolivian map gives a spot height but there is a 6000m contour on the Peruvian map and SRTM data confirms that it is over 6000m.

ACCESS Access to Chaupi Orco is difficult but easiest via the small town of Pelechuco (3600m)(PT). From Pelechuco it is a 2d. walk to El Rincon (4300m) in the valley E of the peak, via Nacara, Paso Sanchez and Lago Soral (Celeste on BIGM) and crossing three passes of up to 4800m E of the peak Soral. It is also difficult but possible to reach the Peruvian side of the peak from the city of Juliaca. Approach via the very remote village of Ananea (only basic services).

CLIMB From El Rincon follow moraines and rubble on the LHS of the valley to the NW to establish a high camp by a small lake at the edge of the glacier (c.5100m). From here go due W to reach a broad col (5500m) at the foot of the SE ridge. Follow the SE ridge for 2km to the summit passing or turning several minor difficulties.

OTHER ROUTES The E or **NE ridge** can also be climbed from El Rincon at about AD (see Brains

guide). Ascents have also been made from the W but no details are known of the exact route or the difficulty.

OTHER PEAKS Brief details of some other ascents in the area follow. **Chaupi Orco Norte 6000m, PD** (probably less than 6000m) has been climbed from El Rincon by the SE face. **Soral Este 5471m** can be climbed from a camp in the unnamed valley to the N by the N ridge. To the SW of Chaupi Orco, **Salluyo c.5650m** has been climbed from Peru by the W slopes.

BEST MAP BIGM sheet 3041 'Pelechuco' 1:100,000 or PIGM sheet 30-y 'La Rinconada' 1:100,000 available in Lima.

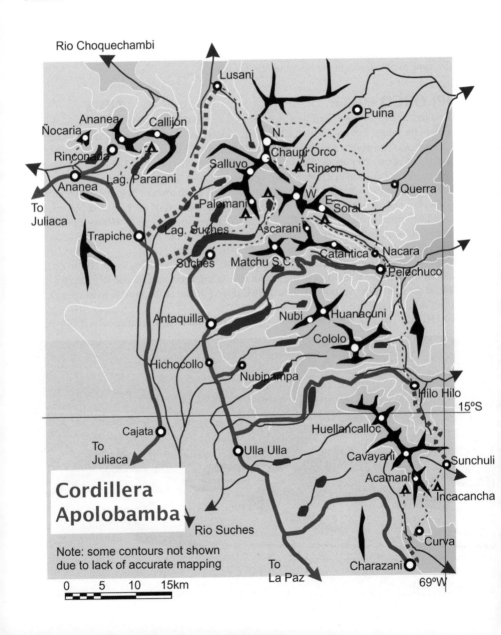

SORAL OESTE 5641m
5 days   F/PD

ASCARANI 5580m
5 days   PD

These two peaks can be climbed in one day each from a high camp at the glacier col (Col Ingles) at the head of the Nacara valley. There are several other excellent small peaks in the area. When first climbed Ascarani was described as a beautiful snow pyramid, but these days most of the snow has melted away leaving steep rock.

ACCESS From Pelechuco (3600m)(PT) it is a long days walk to a camp at the head of the Nacara (Macara) valley at 4600m, 7h. Then a further 4-5h. to walk up moraines on the LHS of the valley on faint paths to reach the glacier col (Col Ingles) N of Ascarani. Several camps are possible at 5250m.

SORAL OESTE CLIMB Easiest from El Rincon to the N (see Chaupi Orco) at about F/PD. Soral Oeste can also be climbed by the S ridge, a beautiful snow crest, from a camp in the Col Ingles. Cross the glacier and gain the ridge from the RHS. Climb the steepening ridge to the summit, 4h, PD/AD.

ASCARANI CLIMB From the camp in the col climb by the NW ridge. It is best to stick fairly close to the edge of the glacier or even stay on the rock. There are several short easy rock steps before a final 30m pitch of 45° ice just below the summit, 3h.

OTHER PEAKS The peak at the W end of the Soral Oeste chain, **Montserrat 5655m, F** can be climbed by the S slopes finishing with a scramble along a rocky ridge. The peaks S of Ascarani **Matchu Suchi Cuchi c.5660m, F** and **Catantica c.5650m, F** can be climbed in one long day from the col

camp or more easily from a glacier camp S of Ascarani. They have no technical difficulties but hard route finding to cross the glacier. Both have more interesting routes on their steep S faces above the Paso Pelechuco.

BEST MAP BIGM sheet 3041 'Pelechuco' 1:100,000.

Ascarani from the N

Soral Oeste from the S

COLOLO 5915m   5 days   D

The steep triangular peak of Cololo is the highest peak in the southern Cordillera Apolobamba and one of the most beautiful. It is marked on the BIGM map as Khala Phusa.

ACCESS There are occasional trucks or buses going from La Paz via Ulla Ulla (4300m) to Pelechuco which can be used for access to this part of the range. To get to a base camp for Cololo turn E off the road about 15km N of Ulla Ulla to reach the village of Nubipampa. Mules can be hired here for the 7km walk along the shore of Lago Nubi and then 2km further up the valley to a camp between two large lakes (4720m).

CLIMB Climb by the glacier which lies N of the W ridge, (probably with a high camp) then use a hidden rock ramp to reach the W ridge. There are ice steps up to 60° on the spectacularly exposed ridge.

OTHER ROUTES Ascents have also been made by the very loose rock of the **N ridge D**, gained from either the E or the W.

OTHER PEAKS To the N, **Nubi 5710m**, can be climbed from the same base area. The difficult. **Huanacuni 5798m** can be climbed from Agua Blanca above Pelechuco by the E slopes and corniced S ridge.

BEST MAP BIGM sheet 3041 'Pelechuco' 1:100,000.

Cololo and Huanacuni from the N

HUELLANCALLOC 5825m   5 days   F/PD

Huellancalloc is unnamed on the BIGM Pelechuco sheet but lies 9km SSW of Hilo Hilo. It is a big, easy angled peak that would probably make a good ski ascent.

ACCESS Drive from La Paz via Ulla Ulla to the village of Hilo Hilo (3800m - a.k.a Illo Illo).

CLIMB From Hilo Hilo walk up the valley to the SW to a high camp at c.4800m just where the valley turns to the S and the N slopes of Huellancalloc become visible, 1d. Climb from here by the easy N slopes, grade about F/PD.

BEST MAP BIGM sheet 3041 'Pelechuco' 1:100,000

ACAMANI 5400m+   5 days   PD/AD
CAVAYANI 5484m   6 days   F/PD

At the extreme southern end of the Apolobamba are the peaks of Acamani (often spelt Akamani) and Cavayani. Cavayani is also known as Isquillani. Acamani is a sacred peak of the Kallahuaya medicine men.

ACAMANI ACCESS From La Paz get to the town of Charazani (daily PT, shops and hostals) and then on to the village of Curva. Curva is the start of a popular trek to Pelechuco so donkeys are easy to find. From Curva follow the track N out of the village towards Canisaya but 2km before this village drop down into the main valley and go up the LH of two streams on the opposite side (Rio Acama). Continue past a small hidden lagoon at 3900m and then more steeply up to a high camp at 4700m on the moraines above the Lag Glaciar (Canchani on BIGM map), 8h.

ACAMANI CLIMB From the camp climb the RHS of the glacier but move gradually L to reach the col between Acamani and the N summit (5189m). From here climb the NW ridge of Acamani on snow to 50° and with one short rock step (I or II), 4h.

CAVAYANI CLIMB As above but take the RH of the two streams over a pass and continue along the trek towards Hilo Hilo over a second pass to reach the large valley beneath the Sunchuli pass. (This point can also be reached by road from the N over the Paso Sunchuli) From a camp in this valley climb the E glacier. Go R at the top of the glacier and climb a 150m snow ramp to reach the snowy NE ridge of Cavayani, then easily to the summit.

OTHER PEAKS To the NE of Cavayani is the pyramid of **Cuchillo, c.5400m, PD** which can be climbed easily by the NE ridge from the road at Paso Sunchuli.

BEST MAP BIGM sheet 5748-I 'Khata' 1:50,000.

Acamani from the SW   from Lag. Canchani

Cuchillo from the SE

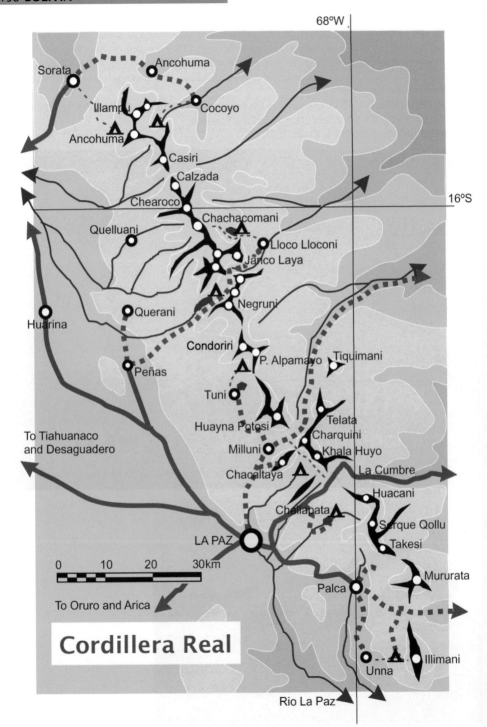

68°W

Sorata

Ancohuma

Illampu

Cocoyo

Ancohuma

Casiri

Calzada

Chearoco

16°S

Chachacomani

Quelluani

Lloco Lloconi

Janco Laya

Negruni

Huarina

Querani

Condoriri

Peñas

Tiquimani

P. Alpamayo

Tuni

Telata

Huayna Potosi

Charquini

To Tiahuanaco
and Desaguadero

Milluni

Khala Huyo

Chacaltaya

La Cumbre

Huacani

Challapata

LA PAZ

Serque Qollu

0   10   20   30km

Takesi

Mururata

To Oruro and Arica

Palca

Cordillera Real

Unna

Illimani

Rio La Paz

SORATA Base town for the northern Cordillera Real 2700m

Sorata is an idyllic little tourist town which makes a great base for trekking or climbing in the northern Cordillera Real. There is regular public transport from La Paz (about 5h.), plenty of hotels and good shops including a well stocked delicatessen. Pack animals are easily obtained from the arrieros association beside the Residencial Sorata. Many climbers stay in the Res. Sorata and it is usually a good source of information on current climbing conditions.

Nevado ILLAMPU 6368m   5 days   AD/D
Pico SCHULZE 5943m   5 days   PD/AD

Illampu is the most difficult of the high peaks in Bolivia. It is part of the Sorata massif at the extreme northern end of the Cordillera Real. Illampu was first climbed in 1928. Pico Schulze is a western outlier of Illampu which gives a fine climb.

ACCESS From Sorata (2700m)(PT) take hired transport to the village of Ancohuma (also known as Ancoma) where mules can be hired. Follow the valley S and SW to a camp at the tongue of the N glacier coming down between Schulze and Illampu (4700m). This point can also be reached more directly (and more strenuously) from Sorata via the Huilacota pass with pack animals. Continue up the RHS of the N glacier, including several steep sections, to a high camp in the upper basin under P. Schulze at 5600m, 2d.

ILLAMPU CLIMB The normal route is by the **W ridge, AD**. There is a steep 300m headwall of 45/55° snow and ice to gain the ridge from the upper basin of the N glacier. The ridge is then followed to the summit, mostly 30° but with a steeper section of 60° just before the summit.

OTHER ROUTES ON ILLAMPU Many harder routes have been climbed including the **E face direct, D** 50/60° and the **NE face and ridge, D**. For access to this area see Ancohuma E face routes.

PICO SCHULZE CLIMB The easiest route on this peak is by the SE ridge gained at point 5765m from the Illampu high camp to the N. There are also some obvious harder routes on the E face.

BEST MAP AV # 0/8, Cordillera Real - Nord, 1:50,000 or BIGM sheet 5846-I 'Sorata' 1:50,000

Illampu from the S

W ridge

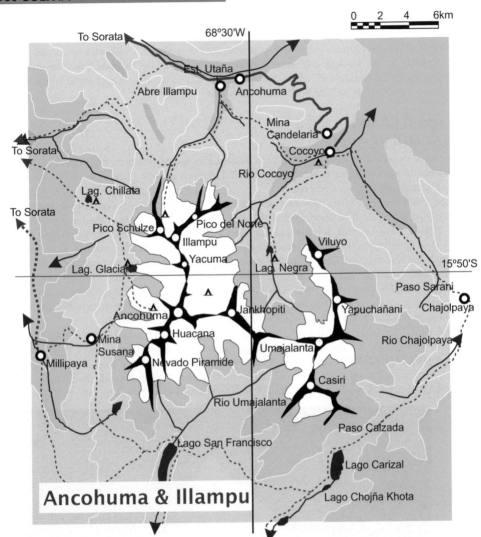

Ancohuma & Illampu

ANCOHUMA 6427 m   6 days   PD/AD

Ancohuma is the highest point of the Sorata massif. Its height has been disputed but reports in the 1970's that it was 7014m high were greatly exaggerated. The alternative spelling of Jankhouma, and several other variations, are often used. The most common ascent route is now directly from Sorata by the W side, finishing on the SW ridge (PD+) though routes from the E side used to be more common and are still described below.

ACCESS The normal approach from the W follows the popular 2 day walk from Sorata to Lag. Glaciar. This follows tracks SE from Sorata (local guide recommended) to cross the valley and work up through fields and pasture to a camp at Lag. Chillata, 6h. There are poor Inca ruins above. This is as far as mules can go. The second day crosses a col on Cerro Titisani before rising up to the impressive base camp at Lag Glaciar 5038m, 5h.

CLIMB The **SW ridge, PD+** is described here. From Lag Glaciar go up a 300m boulder slope S of the camp to reach the glacier. Stay on rocks on the RHS of the glacier until forced onto the ice at 5500m. Regain the moraine on the R of the glacier higher up to a camp on snow at 5700m, 5-7h. Various campsites are possible lower and higher. From here go up the slope behind the camp to the wide plateau below the SW ridge. Head straight for the summit initially and gain the W face. Move up L then R to gain the SW ridge by 1 or 2 steep pitches (45-50°). Follow the SW ridge to the top, 6h. The **NW ridge, AD** can also be climbed from the same high camp.

OTHER ROUTES The NW ridge gained (unusually) from the **E side** of the peak used to be the most common route to the summit. The SW ridge was also climbed from the E side and the valley has many other attractive ascents, two of which are described below. For all these routes travel from Sorata to the road end at Cocoyo (3500m), where llamas can be hired. From Cocoyo follow a good path high above the S slopes of the valley to a base camp by Lag Negra (4650m)(marked as Chamach Kota on the AV map) in the high basin E of the peak, 7h. From Lag. Negra go up the valley to the SW of Leche Cota to gain the glacier plateau N of Jankhopiti, various high camps are possible. The **NW ridge** is gained from the glacier plateau by a broad snow ramp leading onto the NE ridge. Then make a rising traverse across the N flank to the NW ridge. The NW ridge route is mostly snow with some III-IV rock. The exposed **SW ridge, PD** is also gained from the glacier by a steep pitch or two of ice (another high camp may be necessary).

The SW ridge can also be reached from Lag. San Francisco to the S. This is quicker but with more objective danger.
OTHER PEAKS Try **Jancopiti 5875m, PD** climbed by the N ridge.
SUMMIT WAYPOINT 15°51'12" 68°32'27"
BEST MAP AV # 0/8, Cordillera Real - Nord, 1:50,000 or BIGM sheet 5846-II 'Warizata' 1:50,000

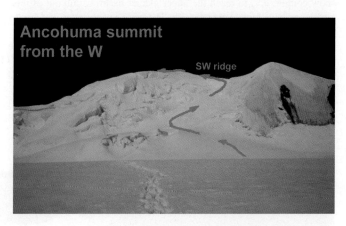

Ancohuma summit from the W

SW ridge

UMALAJANTA 5723m
VILUYO 5540m

5 days   F
5 days   PD

These two peaks lie E of Ancohuma and can be climbed from a base camp by Laguna Negra in the valley S of Cocoyo.

ACCESS From Sorata via Cocoyo to Laguna Negra (4650m)(marked as Chamach Kota on the AV map) as described for routes on the E side of Ancohuma above, 2d.

UMALAJANTA CLIMB By the NW slopes. From Lag Negra walk up the main valley to a high camp by lagoons at 5000-5100m, 4-6h. From this camp go up scree slopes to the NW glacier aiming W of the obvious triangular rock face. Continue up the glacier to the col E of spot height 5578m, then walk E to the summit, 4h.

VILUYO CLIMB By the NW glacier. Climb up the slope S from Lag Negra and cross scree L to gain a moraine ridge. Follow this till it meets a rock ridge on the LHS of the glacier. Follow the RHS of the ridge along the edge of the glacier until forced onto the glacier. Climb this easily to finish on the summit rock, 5h.

OTHER PEAKS Try **Yapuchañani 5526m, PD** climbed by the NW slopes.
BEST MAP As for Ancohuma.

Nevado CHEAROCO 6104m   6 days   AD/D
Nevado CHACHACOMANI 6074m   4 days   AD

Both of these peaks are rarely climbed due to the difficult access and lack of information. Due to problems with locals in the valleys to the W it is safest to reach these peaks by the more complicated access from the new road through the Khara Kota (Caracota) valley which passes SE of them.

ACCESS From La Paz via Peñas and the Khara Kota valley, then on the new road past the peak Janco Laya to reach the settlement of Lloco Lloconi also known as Janco Lacaya. From here walk over a pass to the NW, drop a few hundred metres then traverse left to reach a base camp at Lechecota, 4500m, for Chachacomani (3h.). For Chearoco continue on for another day via Palca to the upper Chiquini valley, or climb the valley and cross the glaciated col on the E side of Chachacomani (as for approach to Chachacomani high camp) If you want to risk the troublesome locals the peaks can be climbed from the W by the Quelluani (Kelluani) river to a base camp at 5000m.

CHACHACOMANI CLIMB The normal route is now from above Lechecota by the **E slopes, AD**. From Lechecota climb 250m boulder slopes to the NW to reach a hanging valley full of very difficult glacier rubble and a poor high camp at about 5000-5200m. From here climb a moraine then a wide snow couloir, 45°, to reach the upper glacier basin. Climb out of this by the 100m 45-50° headwall, which can have high avalanche risk. There are easier routes on Chachacomani by the W side from the Quelluani valley, although this way has access problems.

CHEAROCO CLIMB The most straightforward route is the **SE ridge** from the Chiquini valley. This is a fairly steep and winding glacier climb at about AD. The **E face D/TD** gives a harder climb, 55°.

OTHER PEAKS To the N, **Calzada, 5650m PD/AD,** can be climbed by the W slopes from a camp at the head of the Calzada valley.

BEST MAP BIGM sheet 5946-III which covers the peaks is not currently available, though it definitely does exist! Best available map is the Cordillera Real map by Liam O'Brien, 1:135,000.

Chearoco from the E

SE ridge

Chachacomani from the E

to upper basin

Chachacomani from the S

normal route

direct

upper basin

JANCO LAYA 5545m   2 days   F
JALLAWAYA 5670m   3 days   PD

These peaks make excellent objectives for a short expedition or for acclimatisation ascents. Jallaway is also known as Jacha Pata.

ACCESS From La Paz via Peñas to the Khara Kota (Caracota) valley. Cross the pass (4980m) at the head of the Caracota valley by the 4x4 track and continue down to a pleasant camp (4600m) at the foot of the SE ridge of Janco Laya. For Jallaway continue following the access described above for Chachacomani to the beautiful (aren't they all?) Lechecota at 4500m.

JANCO LAYA CLIMB The normal route is on the SE ridge, over scree then glacier.

JALLAWAYA CLIMB From the SW corner of Lechecota follow the stream up and SE to gain the hidden valley of the Rio Huarca Jahuira. At the second meadow turn R and climb steeply to a lagoon at 5000m. From here go on to the tongue of the RH glacier then cross to the LH glacier by easy rock slabs (grade II-III). Continue over glacier col to the upper basin and the summit.

OTHER PEAKS To the north of Lechecota are several other good peaks. Amongst the easiest is the central peak of the **Tres Marias c.5400m, AD** climbed by the central glacier from the valley NW of Lechecota. A short and easy climb of PD to the SE summit or continue on northwards to the main summit at about AD/D

BEST MAP BIGM sheet 5945-IV, 1:50,000

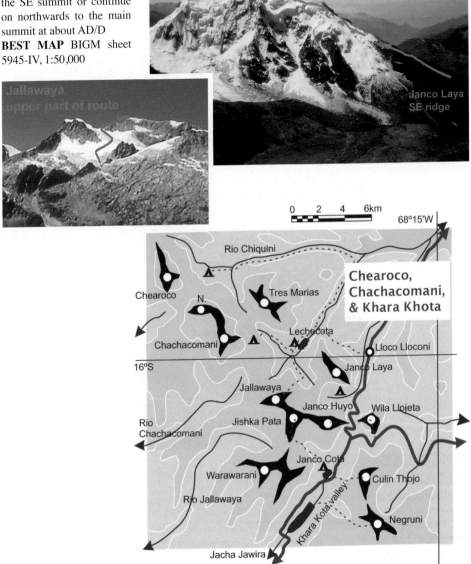

Jallawaya
upper part of route

Janco Laya
SE ridge

0 2 4 6km

68°15'W

Rio Chiquini

Chearoco, Chachacomani, & Khara Khota

Chearoco

N.

Tres Marias

Chachacomani

Lechecota

Lloco Lloconi

16°S

Janco Laya

Jallawaya

Janco Huyo

Wila Llojeta

Jishka Pata

Rio Chachacomani

Janco Cota

Warawarani

Culin Thojo

Rio Jallawaya

Khara Kota valley

Negruni

Jacha Jawira

To Peñas and La Paz

JANCO HUYO 5512m	1 day	F
JISHKA PATA 5508m	1 day	F
NEGRUNI 5468m	1 day	F
CULIN THOJO 5368m	1 day	F
WILA LLOJETA 5244m	1 day	F

These five peaks around the beautiful Khara Khota valley make excellent objectives for a short expedition or for acclimatisation ascents and can be climbed from just one campsite, or combined with ascents of Janco Laya. Many of the peaks can be traversed to give great days out, and all are good for ski ascents and descents early in the season.

ACCESS From La Paz drive via Peñas to the head of the Khara Khota valley, where a base camp can be set up at 4700m by the beautiful Lag. Janco Cota. A 4x4 will be needed for this rough road.

JANCO HUYO CLIMB From Lag. Janco Cota follow the main valley to the pass SE of Janco Huyo at 4950m. From the pass climb easily through rock outcrops and a narrow rocky ridge to reach the glacier (5200m) then follow the broad glaciated SE ridge to the summit, 4-5h.

Janco Huyo from the SE

SE ridge

Janco Laya

summit lies behind

Jishka Pata from the SE

JISHKA PATA CLIMB From the N end of Lag. Janco Cota climb into the hanging valley to the NW and get onto the glacier at 4950m, Follow this easily up to a col at 5300m, then over a couple of small bumps to the main summit of Jishka Pata. A great ski peak with stunning scenery.

NEGRUNI CLIMB Also spelt Nigruni. Either directly from Janco Cota by the chopped up NW glacier or from 2km further S in the Khara Khota valley by the steep SW glacier, 5-6h.

CULIN THOJO CLIMB From Janco Cota directly by the W slopes and a tiny remnant glacier, 3-4h. On skis a better ascent is to go up the valley just S of the peak passing the Mina Natividad at 5000m, then onto the easy angled S and SE glacier.

WILA LLOJETA CLIMB At the head of the valley the road forks at about 4900m. Climb either fork of the road to either the S or W col and then easily to the summit, 3-4h. A great wee ski peak.

BEST MAP BIGM sheet 5945-IV, 1:50,000

Negruni from the W

Wila Llojeta from the W

S ridge

W ridge

Campsite in the Khara Khota valley

Skiing on Janco Huyo

Cerro CONDORIRI 5648m   3 days   AD/D
PEQUEÑO ALPAMAYO 5410m   3 days   PD

Condoriri is one of the most beautiful peaks in Bolivia, if not in the entire Andes. The highest central peak is known as the Cabeza del Condor (head of the condor) and on either side are the Ala Izquierda and Ala Derecha (the condors left and right wings). Condoriri is climbed by a sensational route, is fairly easy to reach and is justifiably popular. The nearby peak of Pequeño Alpamayo, a beautiful snow pyramid is also frequently climbed. There are many other good mountaineering routes accessible from the same base camp.

ACCESS From La Paz via Estancia Tuni (4400m) where animals can be hired. Getting here is difficult without a private hire vehicle. From Tuni go around the S end of the large Lag. Tuni, then turn N and follow the valley to Lag. Chiar Cota (4700m), 2h. The organised base camp here now has toilets and a tap and there is also an obligatory guardians fee. It can be busy.

CONDORIRI CLIMB The normal route is the **SW ridge, AD/D** from Lag. Chiar Cota. Follow a path N to a hidden wide scree couloir through the rock band. Alternatively climb a snow gully on the extreme L of this rock band. Follow either of these up L to reach the Condoriri glacier (SW of summit). Climb this glacier towards the summit pyramid. Climb up to the SW ridge by a 40/50° snow gully through a rock band to reach a prominent notch. Then follow the exposed ridge on loose rock or ice to the summit, 6-8h. This climb is becoming more dangerous due to the lack of snow in recent years exposing much loose rock.

OTHER ROUTES ON CONDORIRI The **SE face D/TD** of Cabeza del Condor can be climbed direct, 55° snow, sometimes with rock bands of grade V.

PEQUEÑO ALPAMAYO The beautiful snow pyramid of Pequeño Alpamayo, also called Alpamayo Chico lies E of Condoriri and can be climbed from the same base camp. From Lag. Chiar Cota follow the path NE up past Lag Quellual Cota and up a moraine on the RHS of the main glacier. Above the crevasses drop down to the glacier and go up and L to reach the col between Huallomen (Wyoming) and Tarija. Continue up snow to reach the rocky top of Tarija. Scramble down and pass a pinnacle on the R to gain the SW snow ridge of Pequeño Alpamayo, 5-6h.

OTHER PEAKS The subsidiary peak to the W of Cabeza del Condor, known as the **Ala Izquierda 5540m** has been climbed on steep snow by the **SE face D**, 50/55° and by the **E ridge AD**. The four obvious gullies on the SE face of **Ala Derecha 5330m** have all been climbed at D or TD. Brains guidebook has more detailed descriptions of technical routes in this area.

Easier peaks include **Jahuaca (Ilusion) 5350m PD** which can be climbed by the W slopes from the moraine above Lag. Quellual Cota. To the SE of the base camp the summit of **Jallayco (Mirador) 5224m** offers good views of the Condoriri group.

BEST MAP BIGM 1:50,000, sheets 5945-II 'Milluni' and 5945-III 'Peñas'.

Pequeño Alpamayo from the SW

Condoriri from the S

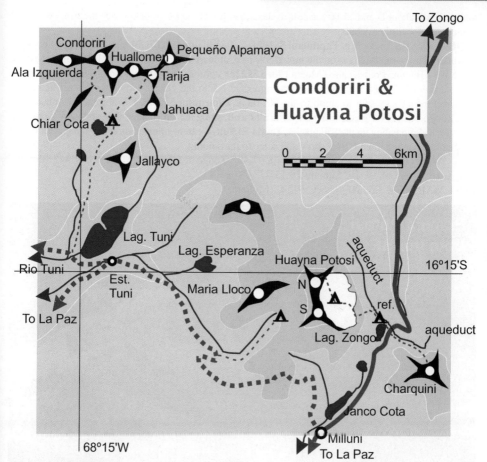

Condoriri &
Huayna Potosi

Cerro HUAYNA POTOSI 6088m 3 days PD

A fine triangular peak which dominates the view as you come in to land at La Paz airport. There are two summits, the N is slightly higher, the S a slightly more difficult climb. Reputedly the easiest 6000m peak in the Cordillera Real but in some years Illimani may be easier. The impressive and accessible W face has a large number of long and difficult routes. Also known as Cacca Aca.

ACCESS Hire private transport all the way to Zongo Pass (no PT). There is a refugio a little above and W of Lag. Zongo here, all facilities but not much space. Porters can usually be hired here.

CLIMB From Lag. Zongo, cross the dam and follow an aqueduct to a small stream. Ascend this through moraines, then go L to a prominent moraine rib. Trend L up broken rock behind to gain the glacier at 5200m (small hut at 5150m, and camp possible). Cross the glacier in a wide RH arc to the snow ridge on the R coming down from the S summit. Underneath this ridge is Camp Argentino at c.5500m (5h. from dam). Higher camps are also possible. Take care at this camp as there are a number of dangerous crevasses in the area. From the camp climb up the steep slope above to a short but exposed section on the ridge coming down from the S summit. Then traverse R across easier snow slopes to reach the NNW ridge. Follow this ridge back to the summit, very exposed but easy, 5-6h. from camp.

OTHER ROUTES The **S peak** is harder, about AD/D and can also be climbed from Camp Argentino by the SE face or the SW ridge. There are also many routes on the imposing 1000m W face of the mountain, all about D and 55-60°, access as described for Maria Lloco below. See the Brain or Mesili guidebooks for further details.

OTHER PEAKS To the N is **Tiquimani 5519m**, (called Illampu on BIGM maps). This is a very hard mountain. The normal route is on the mixed SW face, at least TD, 60/65° and V/VI. To climb the peak to the W of Huayna Potosi, called **Maria Lloco 5522m**, approach via Milluni along a track to the ridge above and S of Carmen Pampa. Follow the aqueduct NE to the glacier. Go up the glacier and curve round behind a rocky spur to climb by the NE ridge. **Charquini 5392m, F** is normally climbed from Lag. Zongo by the NW glacier after a pleasant walk along the aqueduct. Other routes look possible from the Kaluyo valley up the SW glacier. **Telata 5336m, F** can be climbed direct by the glacier on the SW flank to a notch, then L over snow and scree to the summit.

KEY WAYPOINTS Parking 16°17'14" 68°07'49" Zongo refugio 16°16'54" 68°07'44" Moraine refugio 16°16'32" 68°08'16" Summit 16°15'47" 68°09'14"

BEST MAP BIGM 1:50,000, sheet 5945-II 'Milluni'.

Huayna Potosi from the SE

S summit — SE face — N summit — SW ridge — N ridge — camp

CHACALTAYA 5395m — 1 day — F
KHALA HUYO 5324m — 2 days — PD

These two lower peaks make ideal acclimatisation ascents. Many companies offer day tours to Chacaltaya from La Paz, driving up to 5180m where there is hut and used to be a ski-tow. The mountain also makes a fine easy day walk from the Kaluyo valley at the far side. The peaks can be climbed as a combination from a high camp here. Khala Huyo is also spelt Kaluyo and is sometimes known as Wila Mankilisani or Huila Manquilisani!

ACCESS To get to the Kaluyo valley from La Paz take a bus or a taxi up the tar road to La Cumbre pass (4800m)(PT) 1h. Walk W over a low pass and descend into the Kaluyo valley. Good camping at lagoons, 2h.

KHALA HUYO CLIMB Climb the LHS of the rectangular SW glacier (30-40°) then an easy 10m gully in the top LH corner of the glacier to reach the ridge. Climb the shattered rock ridge (II) turning the first pinnacle on the RHS. Easier climbing leads to the summit, 4h.

CHACALTAYA CLIMB Take a day tour from La Paz to the Club Andino lodge at 5180m and then stroll very easily to the summit, ½h., if acclimatised. The peak can also be climbed from a Kaluyo valley camp in about 4-6h. Normally no snow on either route. The ridge to the N of the peak makes a fine walking traverse.
BEST MAP BIGM 1:50,000 sheet 5945-II for Khala Huyo, sheet 5944-I for Chacaltaya.

Khala Huyo from the SW

route goes behind

The old ski station at Chacaltaya above La Paz

SERQUE QOLLU 5546m   2 days   N/K

Also spelt Serkhe Kkollu or Sirki Qullu.

ACCESS About 15km out of La Paz on the way to La Cumbre is Lag. Incachaca. Take the track from here over the ridge to the E and a second larger lake, Lag. Challapata (4200m).

CLIMB Follow the valley up and E from Challapata to Lag. Serque Cota (4800m), ½d. Climb from here, 1d., grade and exact route n/k.

OTHER PEAKS Further N is **Huacani 5321m**. From the camp at Lag. Serque Cota (4800m) climb the main peak which lies to the N, 1d. Some snow, difficulty n/k. Further S is **Jati Qollu 5421m, PD/AD** also spelled Hati Kollu, which can be climbed in 2d. by the SE ridge from above the village of Palcoma with a high camp at Lag. Jacha Khasiri.

BEST MAP BIGM 1:50,000, sheet 6044-IV 'Chojlla'.

Jati Qollu

Serque Qollu
from the SE

MURURATA 5869m   3 days   F

In legend the god Thunupa was angered by the arrogant Mururata. He knocked off the head of Mururata with his catapult and it became Volcan Sajama. Mururata was left headless and the flat topped summit is prominent from La Paz to this day! Mururata is one of the easiest and most scenic of the big peaks in the Cordillera Real.

ACCESS From La Paz via Ventilla to Estancia Choquecota (3900m)(PT) From Choquecota with 4x4 it is possible to to drive up the main valley on a track (which goes to the San Francisco mine) for about 3km then take the valley to the E, marked as Takesi Uma, for about another 3km to several possible base camps at 4300m-4400m.

CLIMB From the base camp climb steeply S into the hanging valley below Mururatas W glacier and good high camps just before the glacier (4900m), 2-3h. It is necessary to climb the slopes about 1km to the W of the stream coming from the glacier because it flows through a gorge. From the high camp climb onto the glacier and follow it easily to a col at 5500m with Co. Arcata. Then continue across the wide summit plateau to the top, normally very few crevasses. The glacier can be arduous in deep snow but for the same reason Mururata makes a good ski-mountaineering ascent. 6-8h. from camp.

OTHER PEAKS Co. Arcata 5658m, F, also spelt Arkhata, can be climbed from the same high camp, even in the same day by a fit group. Either by way of the W glacier and col as above, or by the ridge known as 'Cumbres del Mururata' to the S of the glacier.

KEY WAYPOINTS Base camp 16°30'10" 67°52'52" Entrance to hanging valley 16°30'42" 67°52'24" High camp 16°30'37" 67°51'43" Glacier snout 16°30'32" 67°51'09" Arcata col 16°30'41" 67°50'13" Summit 16°31'06" 67°48'52"

BEST MAP AV # 0/9, 1:50,000 or BIGM 1:50,000 sheet 6044-III

route lies behind
Arkhata summit

W glacier

Mururata from the W

Mururata ski ascent

Nevado ILLIMANI 6438m   4 days   PD/AD

The highest peak of the Cordillera Real and a mountain which dominates La Paz. Illimani is a fine long ridge running NW-SE, continuously over 6000m for 8km, with the highest point, known as Pico Sur, near the S end. Large glaciers descend its flanks to c.4800m. Illimani was first ascended by Conway in 1898. The first traverse over the full ridge was done in 1972.

ACCESS Normally from La Paz via Palca to Estancia Unna (No PT - 3600m). Pack animals can be hired here for the 4h. walk to the base camp (4450m) at Puente Roto. Puente Roto can also be reached from the N by an old 4x4 mine road (blocked 8km to the N) and then almost level walking for 8km, or from Cohoni (3500m)(PT) to the S.

CLIMB From Puente Roto climb scree to pass a rock band (4800m) on the R. Go up to the col in the ridge to the S (4950m). Continue up the rock ridge above, which becomes steeper and more exposed (II) to reach the Nido de Condores camp (5450m), 4-6h. From Nido de Condores go up the small forepeak and follow the snow ridge to a level area and possible high camp (5800m) then up the shoulder above avoiding crevasses and ice walls. Usually fairly easy, but sometimes with one or two serious ice pitches. Move L before the top to gain the summit ridge N of the summit. Follow the fine summit ridge S, 5-7h from the Nido camp.

Illimani from the W

Nido camp

from Puente Roto

OTHER ROUTES Routes on the **N peak 6403m** include one directly below the summit on steep snow by the **SW face direct, D, 50-60°**. Gain the face by traversing L from the normal S peak route at the level area at 5800m. The N peak has also been climbed directly from Puente Roto by the prominent triangular snowfield to the N of the Nido **D**. Illimani has also been climbed by the long **N ridge D 40/50°** and several complete N-S traverses have been done.

OTHER PEAKS SW of the Puente Roto base camp **Sonaka 4615m F,** is a half day excursion with an excellent view of the normal route on Illimani.

KEY WAYPOINTS Puente Roto (general area) 16°38'54" 67°49'34" Col in ridge 16°39'26" 67°48'36" Nido de Condores camp 16°39'16" 67°48'06" Summit 16°38'00" 67°47'27"

BEST MAP AV # 0/9 1:50,000. Or BIGM 1:50,000 sheet 6044-III.

Illimani Norte from Nido camp

W ridge

summit

direct

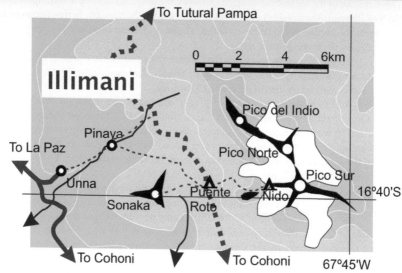

To Tutural Pampa

0   2   4   6km

Illimani

Pico del Indio

Pinaya

To La Paz

Pico Norte

Pico Sur

Unna

16°40'S

Sonaka

Puente Roto

Nido

To Cohoni

To Cohoni

67°45'W

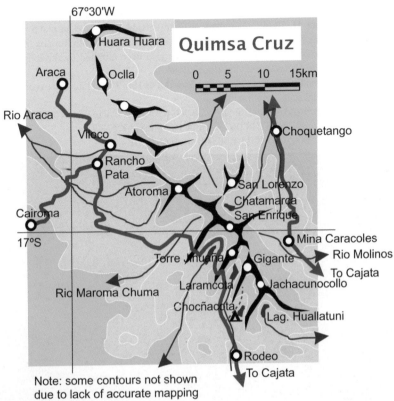

Note: some contours not shown
due to lack of accurate mapping

Cerro GIGANTE 5748m
JACHACUNOCOLLO 5721m

3 days   AD/D
3 days   F

These are two of the highest peaks in the Quimsa Cruz range, an isolated and compact group which lie to the S of Illimani. The heights here are taken from the BIGM map, but in many sources Jachacunocollo is given as the highest in the range at 5800m. The peak of Torre Jihuaña is also very high and is another contender for the highest in the range.

There is generally less snow and ice in the Quimsa Cruz than in the Cordillera Real but all the highest summits are glaciated. Glaciers are retreating rapidly. Jachacunocollo is also known locally as Tres Marias and is marked on the BIGM map as Don Luis.

ACCESS Access to the range is not very easy without private transport. From La Paz to Panduro on the Oruro road then to the village of Cajata (4400m) (PT). From here access to the mountains in general can be made up mine roads, either walking, driving or hitching on mine lorries. For Gigante and Jachacunocollo follow a good track past Rodeo which leads to a mine at Chocñacota on the W slope of the mountains. From Chocñacota a short 2h. walk leads to Lag. Congelada (4880m) which makes an excellent base camp.

GIGANTE CLIMB Gigante has become more difficult as the glaciers have retreated. The easiest route is probably still the S ridge. From Lag. Congelada climb through steep scree and rock bands to the W to reach the glacier edge at 5200m (high camp possible). Cross the glacier basin easily and gain the S ridge of Gigante by a steep mixed slope, 6-8h. The W/NW ridge has also been climbed and there is also a reasonable route by the short steep NE ridge from a glacier saddle (grades n/k but probably about AD/D).

JACHACUNOCOLLO CLIMB From Lag. Congelada gain the glacier basin as described for Gigante then climb the **N ridge** of Jachacunocollo on loose grade I rock, 6h. The mountain can also be climbed by the pleasant snow crest of the **W ridge PD**, gained from a glacier shelf NE of Lag. Congelada.

Jachacunocollo
from the SW

OTHER PEAKS The other main summits in this area of the Quimsa Cruz are generally easiest to access and climb from the W. **Santa Rosa 5550m, F** can be climbed by the rocky E ridge from above Lag. Congelada in 4h. **Torre Jihuaña 5700m+** is a very steep and loose rock tower that may be the highest peak in the range. It is best approached from the Lag. Laramcota. **San Enrique 5600m,** can be climbed by the S face on straightforward 40-50° snow. **San Lorenzo 5508m** can be climbed from Lag. Chatamarca above the Mina Caracoles. **Atoroma 5580m, AD** unnamed on the BIGM map, has been climbed by a snow ridge from the SW.

E of the Mina Caracoles road is another massif whose highest point is **San Roque 5520m.**

There are many interesting lower peaks in the northern Quimsa Cruz around Araca, with some of the best quality rock climbing in the Bolivian Andes. A detailed German guide is available in a few places in La Paz.

BEST MAP BIGM sheet 6143-III 'Mina Caracoles' for Gigante, Atoroma and Jachacunocollo. Sheets 6142-IV and 6142-I both at 1:50,000 cover the outlying peaks of the Cordillera Quimsa Cruz.

High on Jachacunocollo, Quimsa Cruz

Cerro UTURUNCO 6008m   3 days   F
Cerro NUEVO MUNDO 5929m   3 days   F

Uturunco, an active volcano, is one of the most isolated yet easiest 6000m peaks in South America. Nuevo Mundo is the second highest summit in the remote Cordillera Lipez in SW Bolivia. Uturunco means jaguar.

ACCESS See page 189 for a general location map. Access for Uturunco from Uyuni via Mallqu to Quetena Chico which lies NW of the mountain. For Nuevo Mundo drive via San Pablo de Lipez to San Antonio de Lipez. A private 4x4 vehicle will be essential to reach these peaks.

UTURUNCO CLIMB From Quetena Chico a usable vehicle track runs to about 5800m on the N flank of the mountain (mine workings). From here stroll easily up scree in 2h to the summit.

OTHER PEAKS Nuevo Mundo, is an easy ascent with little or no snow. There are many other easy but remote peaks in this area, many surely still waiting first ascents.

BEST MAP BIGM sheets SF-19-8 and SF-19-12, both 1:250,000.

Uturunco from the SW

CORDILLERA OCCIDENTAL

INTRODUCTION

The Cordillera Occidental is the name given to the chain of volcanic mountains which stretches from near Arequipa in southern Peru, down along the Chile-Bolivia border to the northern edge of the Puna de Atacama where Bolivia, Chile and Argentina meet. The mountains are almost all easy ascents although a few, such as Solimana and the highest peak Sajama, are more eroded and slightly steeper. The mountains rise in isolation from a generally high plateau (the Altiplano) at about 4200-4400m giving splendid views from the summits. There are active volcanoes throughout the length of the range. Water is often scarce.

The scenery in the area is superb with an enduring sense of remoteness and desolation. The air is beautifully sharp. Small villages lie scattered over the vast Altiplano, dwarfed by the volcanic peaks and battered by dust storms. In the wetter areas there are large flat swamps known as 'bofedales' where llamas and alpacas graze in their hundreds. Wildlife is easily seen and much more numerous than in the classic climbing destinations such as Cordillera Blanca and Cordillera Real. Vizcachas, rheas, flamingos, condors, humming birds and vicuñas are all commonly seen.

GETTING THERE

For the Peruvian Occidental the best base is Arequipa with daily flights from Lima on the domestic Peruvian airlines e.g. LAN, Peruvian and Avianca. See the Northern Peru chapter for details of flights from Europe and the USA to Lima.

For the northern Chilean and Bolivian Occidental either fly via Santiago to Arica or fly to La Paz and approach overland from Bolivia (see Bolivia chapter). There is not much to choose between these two options in terms of convenience, but the approach via La Paz definitely has the advantage as far as acclimatisation is concerned.

For the southern Chilean Occidental the best approach is to fly to Calama via Santiago. See the High Andes chapter for details of international flights to Santiago.

SEASON AND WEATHER CONDITIONS

Ascents can be made of all the peaks in the Cordillera Occidental at any time of year. The area has a very dry climate and although it experiences the same summer wet season as the rest of Peru and Bolivia (December-April) mountain conditions are not too badly affected. Recent storms with snowfall may in fact reduce water problems in some areas due to a lower snow line. Temperatures are noticeably colder in the mid-winter months of June-August, but climbing is still possible. On balance, probably September and October are the best months to climb here.

CLIMBING CONDITIONS

This is a very dry area, particularly in the south around Calama. Water is hard to obtain on many peaks until the snow line is reached. Only the highest peaks, over 6000m, have permanent snowfields or glaciers. Navigation on some of the almost flat summits could be a problem in cloud.

Snow conditions are generally very stable although hard windslab can be found high on some of the peaks. Due to the very dry climate the snow does not normally turn soft later in the day. Approaches over ash and scree can be arduous and these mountains suffer more than any others in the Andes from bad penitentes. These can be as high as 5m on some peaks and make travel 'against the grain' almost impossible.

OTHER GUIDEBOOKS
'En las Cumbres de Arequipa', 1999, by Pablo Masias Nunez del Prado. Yossi Brain's Bolivia climbing guide covers a few of the peaks in Bolivia.

AREQUIPA The main city of SW Peru
2325m

Arequipa is a pleasant and relatively prosperous city in southern Peru. It sits in an oasis at 2325m at the foot of the volcano El Misti. There is a particularly beautiful Plaza de Armas, with Volcan Misti forming a stunning backdrop.

SIGHTS The nearby Colca canyon is worth a visit. There are many organised tours to this vast canyon which is supposedly the deepest canyon in the world. It is one of the best places in the Andes to see condors. The town of Chivay at 3600m would be a good acclimatisation base.

FOOD There is a good supermarket on the SW corner of the Plaza de Armas.

FUEL Camping gas and bencina blanca can be bought from one of several outdoor shops on Jerusalen, near the corner with Ugarte. There are many petrol stations around the central area.

MOUNTAIN INFORMATION A good source is Carlos Zarate who can be contacted online or through his office at Santa Catalina #204, near the Plaza de Armas. Also try the Casa de Guias of the AGMP at Desguadero 126, San Lazaro.

MOUNTAIN TRANSPORT Try the tour agencies towards the N end of Jerusalen or Carlos Zarate.

CLIMBING EQUIPMENT
There is no known source for climbing equipment in the city, although the shops on Jerusalen sell some basic camping and trekking equipment.

Volcan Misti from the Plaza de Armas, Arequipa

Nevado SOLIMANA 6093m

3 days　　　PD

A steep and eroded volcanic massif with an impressive S face overlooking the 3000m deep Chichas canyon. There are four main peaks on a ridge running for 1km in an arc around the top of the canyon. The highest point is the central of three summits near the NE corner of this arc.

ACCESS From Arequipa as for Coropuna but continue towards the village of Cotahuasi for 30km until the next pass at Visca Grande (4650m)(PT). From here walk W, then SW to reach huts at Sora on the N slope of the mountain.

CLIMB Up the N or NW side, including a glacier from 5300m, steep snow and ice and some loose rock, grade n/k but probably about PD.

OTHER PEAKS The S peak, known as **Senta 5898m,** can also be climbed from the E, best to leave the road a little further S at the Quebrada Angostura.

BEST MAP PIGM Sheet 31-q 'Cotahuasi', 1:100,000.

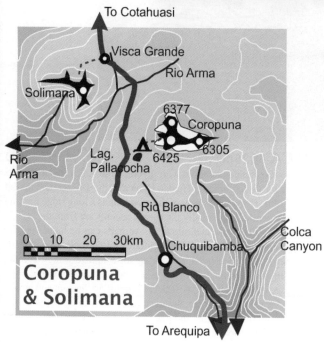

Coropuna & Solimana

Nevado COROPUNA 6425m · 3 days · F

A complex volcanic mountain with an 8km long plateau over 6000m in height. The peak on the SW corner of the plateau, known as Bingham, appears to be the highest but this may vary with snow build up. The name means 'shrine on the plateau'. Remains of clothing from Inca ascents have been found as high as 6000m.

ACCESS Easiest from Arequipa in southern Peru via the small town of Chuquibamba (3000m - last food and fuel) then along the Cotahuasi road (PT) to Lag. Pallacocha (4750m). This lagoon can't be seen from road but is at the highest point of the road when the road is nearest to Coropuna. 8h drive from Arequipa.

CLIMB The highest point is just behind the RH of two domes seen from Pallacocha. The normal route on this peak is by the W rib. High camps can be made at 5600-5800m, 1d. Then follow the RH of two prominent rock ribs and the glacier slopes above (small crevasses only). Go over the foresummit and on to the highest point. Navigation would be very difficult in cloud. Coropuna can probably be climbed from several other directions just as easily.

OTHER PEAKS Other peaks of the Coropuna massif would make easy ascents and a ski traverse would be an interesting expedition, although bad penitente snow conditions might make it difficult.

KEY WAYPOINTS Laguna Pallacocha 15°34'39" 72°43'10" High camp 15°33'02" 72°41'03" Summit 15°32'46" 72°39'39"

BEST MAP PIGM sheet 32-q, 'Chuquibamba', 1:100,000

Nevado HUALCA HUALCA 6025m · 3 days · PD

Hualca Hualca is an extinct volcano and is a complex mountain with several large valley glaciers on its southern flanks. A ceremonial puma skin was found high on Hualca Hualca in the 1980's. The massif has at least seven major summits over 5800m. The general form of the mountain is a long ridge running E to W, with a spur heading SE from the E centre. Logistically the easiest ascents are from the N.

ACCESS From Arequipa via Chivay to the village of Pinchollo (PT). Animals can be hired here for the climb to the N side of the mountain. Follow a track which deteriorates into a footpath and leads to a small dam at 3900m. From here head over open hillsides making for a narrow valley coming down from the W end of the mountain, then follow this valley up to a small geyser at 4350m, 3-4h. Alternatively, about 2km beyond the village of Pinchollo a 4x4 track leads uphill to the dam and geyser but may be difficult to drive. From the geyser (or a bit earlier, the river gets harder to cross the higher you go) climb the hillside on the LHS (W side) of the river and get over an old moraine into a small hanging valley, un-named on the PIGM map, that leads up to the summit. High camp can be made at 4800-5000m in this valley, 3h. from geyser.

HUALCA HUALCA CLIMB There is much debate about which actual summit is highest; the author believes it is probably the central and snowiest summit. But others have reported the peak furthest E to be higher! Two routes are in common use. From the high camp climb the valley to reach the glacier/snowfield and head up and R to the central, and snowiest of the three summits. Or head from the camp more directly to gain the ridge near the col between the central and the E summit and follow this ridge to the top.

OTHER ROUTES Hualca Hualca can also be reached from the Sallalli area (see Ampato for access). Head N and then E to Pampa Tacujani, high camp, 5200m. The normal route is up the RHS of the E glacier then N to the ridge and back W to the summit - grade just F to the main summit but the final 20m rock pinnacle is more difficult.

KEY WAYPOINTS Dam 15°37'52" 71°51'09" Valley Entrance 15°39'01" 71°51'00" Geyser 15°40'31" 71°51'44" High camp 15°41'47" 71°51'05" Central Summit 15°43'13" 71°51'37" E summit 15°43'17" 71°51'25"

BEST MAP PIGM, sheet 32-s, 'Chivay', 1:100,000

Approach summit from W

camp

From Sallalli

Hualca Hualca from the NE

Hualca Hualca from the N

E summit   summit

Nevado AMPATO 6288m   3 days   PD
Nevado SABANCAYA 5976m   3 days   F

These two volcanoes in a remote setting lie only 100km from Arequipa. Sabancaya was erupting, throughout the 1990's, throwing off a plume of ash every 2h in 1994 and was still smoking in 2013. In 1995 the rapidly retreating glacier on Ampato revealed the corpse of a young girl killed by a sharp blow to the skull approximately 500 years ago.

ACCESS Easiest from Arequipa along the Chivay road (PT) and then turn W to get to the remote settlement of Sallalli - also known as Cajamarcana (4400m, water and good campsites). 4h drive. There are no facilities at Sallalli. With a 4x4 it is possible to drive to about 5100m up a track beginning 1km SW of an irrigation canal. From either camp walk up the unnamed valley which comes down from the col between Ampato and Sabancaya. A high camp can be established at about 5200m. Both peaks can also be approached from Cabanaconde (PT) in the Colca canyon past Lag. Mucurca in 2d.

AMPATO CLIMB Several possible routes on the N and E sides of the mountain. The glacier is now only above 6000m. This is in very poor state with many penitentes. The normal route was via the NE slopes, over the N summit, but this is hard work if the penitentes are bad. The E rib is also possible at the same grade.

SABANCAYA CLIMB Sabancaya can be climbed easily using the same approach and high camp as Ampato and then up the S slopes. Ash and some ice.

SUMMIT WAYPOINT Ampato summit 15°49'18" 71°52'45"
BEST MAP PIGM, sheet 32-s, 'Chivay', 1:100,000

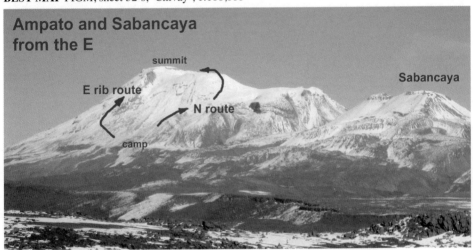

Ampato and Sabancaya from the E

Nevado MISMI 5598m   3 days   F
Nevado HUARANCANTE 5425m   1 day   F

These two smaller peaks lie N and S of the Colca canyon respectively. A small spring on the N side of Mismi is famous as the ultimate source of the Amazon river. Both can be climbed relatively easily from the town of Chivay and both make good acclimatisation ascents for bigger peaks. Chivay itself is a pleasant and friendly town with hotels, cafes and a good market.

MISMI ACCESS From Arequipa via Chivay to the village of Tuti (PT). Animals can be hired here for the 2d. walk to the N side of the mountain, via the abandoned village of Ñanallacta, by the Rio Mismi. A camp can be made at the Rio Mismi, then another beneath the N slopes of the peak at about 5150m. Alternatively a 4x4 track heads towards the mountain from about 4km N of Tuti, how near this track gets to the peak is n/k.

MISMI CLIMB The ascent is an easy walk up the N slopes to the highest point.

HUARANCANTE ACCESS & CLIMB Huarancante can be climbed easily in a day from Chivay if you are acclimatised. Take a taxi or early bus to the 4900m Patapampa pass. From the high point of the road here head E across open terrain to a radio mast. From the mast climb to the **Nevado Chucura 5284m**, foresummit. Then follow the ridge eastwards to finish up the SW ridge of Huarancante, 4h. from road. It's possible to descend from the summit directly back to Chivay via valleys and pastures.

KEY WAYPOINTS Abandoned village 15°31'25" 71°34'03" Rio Mismi camp 15°31'36" 71°37'11" High camp 15°30'05" 71°40'29" Mismi summit 15°31'11" 71°40'42" Patapampa 15°45'06" 71°34'59" Radio mast 15°44'33" 71°33'53" Nevado Chucura 15°44'34" 71°32'16" Huarancante summit 15°43'49" 71°31'31"

BEST MAP PIGM, sheet 32-s, 'Chivay', 1:100,000 for Huarancante, plus sheet 31-s "Cailloma" for Mismi.

summit

SW ridge

Huarancante from the W

Mismi from the S

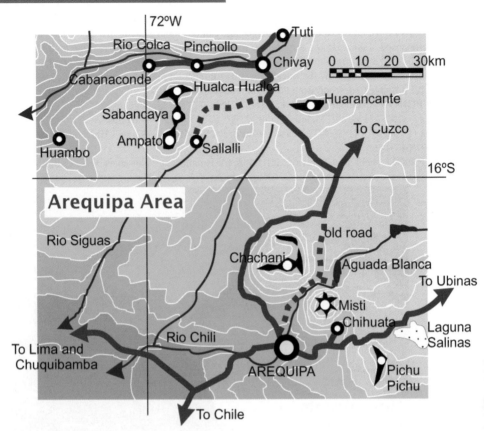

Nevado CHACHANI 6057m   1 day   F

A complex massif with many summits but very little snow. With good previous acclimatisation it can be climbed in a day from Arequipa, but most parties camp for a night or two. Like Misti this is a popular summit with backpackers! There are archaeological remains near the summit.

ACCESS From Arequipa follow the old road to Chivay to beyond the Aguada Blanca turn off. The road continues N along the E flank of Chachani to Cutipampa. At about km 48 turn off onto a 4x4 track that leads W and higher (up to 5000m), 3-4h drive from Arequipa. No public transport.

CLIMB From the end of the 4x4 road walk up a zigzag trail to the SW to reach a camp in walls at 5200m, 1h. From this camp follow a good trail S and up to a col at about 5550m. Drop slightly down the other side of the col and follow a trail which traverses W, then climbs back up to a 5602m col, then over a sandy foresummit, 5950m, to reach the main summit, 5-6h. from the camp. While there is no permanent snow on the route, there are often fresh snowfalls.

OTHER ROUTES Chachani can also be climbed from the western and southern sides.

SUMMIT WAYPOINT Chachani summit 16°11'39 71°31'54"

BEST MAP PIGM sheet 33-s, 'Arequipa'. 1:100,000, sheet 33-t for the approach

5950   main summit

Chachani
(from the NW)

Chachani from the E.

Volcan Misti from Chihuata

Volcan MISTI 5822m   2 days   F

This perfect volcanic cone sits right above Arequipa in southern Peru. It is climbed very often and is something of a tourist mountain, people reaching the summit even in trainers and sandals. There is no water on the mountain except at the Aguada Blanca reservoir. There is usually no snow either. The mountain is another peak that was climbed frequently by the Incas.

ACCESS Two approaches are commonly used. **1.** The best approach is a 3h drive from Arequipa to the Aguada Blanca reservoir which gives a height advantage. With permission it is possible to drive over the dam and up to about 4300m – you can obtain a permit from various trek agencies in Arequipa. **2.** The longer climb but easier access without a 4x4 is from the shanty town of Apurimac San Luis (PT) on the N side of Arequipa. The shanty town is not safe to walk through due to robberies, and this route may not be used much now.

CLIMB There are two normal routes. **1.** The easier and more pleasant climb is from the reservoir of Aguada Blanca (3700m) on the NE side. There is no water on this route. Head initially for the prominent NE rib. There are a few tent sites at 4600m here, ½d. From these campsites follow the path which takes a rising traverse up the N slopes to the summit, 6-8h. There is bad scree in places. The high camp on this route can also be approached from the village of Chihuata (PT) to the S, 1d.

2. By the S side of the mountain, directly from Apurimac San Luis. Head for Tres Cruces (3000m) then up under pylons to Los Pastores at 3300m. From here follow the path up a rib past a possible camp at 4200m, no water, 1d. Then continue to the summit in one very long day, 8-10h.

SUMMIT WAYPOINT Misti summit 16°17'49" 71°24'40"

BEST MAP PIGM sheet 33-t, 'Characato', 1:100,000

Nevado PICHU PICHU 5655m   2 days   F
Volcan UBINAS 5672m   2 days   F

Pichu Pichu is a long ridge which dominates Arequipa's eastern skyline. The remains of a young woman, an Inca sacrifice victim, were found with various wooden and copper items on the summit ridge. The highest peak is the centrally located Co. Crespon Grande. Ubinas is an active volcano with a huge crater located a little further from Arequipa.

PICHU PICHU ACCESS AND CLIMB From Arequipa to Lag. Salinas to the N of the summit. Walk S then climb the E slopes of the mountain, no permanent snow and very easy.

UBINAS ACCESS AND CLIMB From Arequipa to Lag. Piscococha W of the summit. Head for an obvious valley just L of summit to camp, no water, 2h. From here climb straight to the crater then round to the summit, 4h. Other routes are also possible.

BEST   MAP
PIGM sheet 33-T,
'Characato',
1:100,000

Ubinas from the SW   summit

N slopes

E slopes

Pichu Pichu from the NE

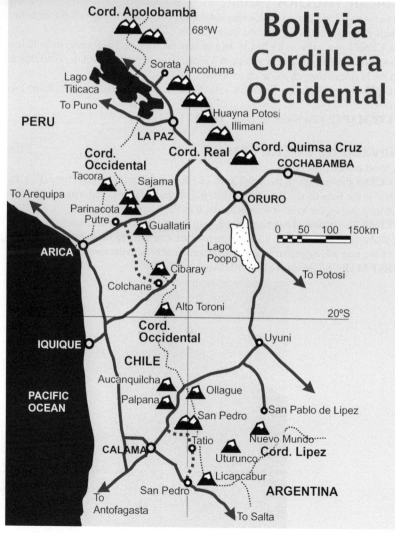

ARICA A Pacific port in northern Chile — Sea Level!

Arica is the only big city in this northern part of Chile but being at sea level it makes a poor base for mountaineers. However it is the most convenient city to fly to and makes a good starting point. Wherever you are climbing the beautiful Volcan Parinacota is well worth a visit for the quality of scenery and the rare wildlife (vicuña, rhea and flamingo) which can be seen nearby. There are daily flights from Santiago and La Paz to Arica and many buses every day from Santiago (a comfortable but long 28h. journey) and a few buses per week from La Paz, 10h.

FOOD There are several large supermarkets in the centre of town.

FUEL No knowledge of camping gas or bencina blanca being available.

MOUNTAIN TRANSPORT For private transport to Putre, Parinacota etc., try one of the tour operators or hire a 4x4.

Volcan TACORA 5980m — 3 days — N/K

A famous volcano just on the Chilean side of the Peru-Chile border, visible from the city of Tacna in southern Peru but best approached from Arica in Chile.

ACCESS From Arica or La Paz by 4x4 or take the train (2-3 per week) to Villa Industrial (4100m), about 40km before the border village of Visviri. From here roads (20km - condition n/k) lead to mines on the N side of the volcano at up to 5000m.

CLIMB By the N slopes. Grade not known but likely to be a very easy volcano ascent with little or no snow.

BEST MAP ChIGM Sheet SE 19-6, 'Visviri', 1:250,000

Nevado de PUTRE 5840m — 2 days — F

A small eroded peak NE of Putre.

ACCESS From Arica to the small town of Putre at 3500m by a good road (PT). Putre is a pleasant town at the base of the mountain which has shops, cafes etc. and makes a good intermediate base before going higher to do 6000m peaks such as Parinacota and Guallatiri.

CLIMB The mountain can be climbed from several directions including directly up from Putre, but is probably easiest from the Lauca National Park entrance station at Las Cuevas (4500m). From here gain the long NE ridge and follow this on scree and rock to the summit.

BEST MAP ChIGM sheet SE 19-10, 'Arica', 1:250,000

Nevado de Putre

Volcan PARINACOTA 6342m
2 days   F

Volcan POMERAPE 6282m
2 days   PD

These two peaks on the Chile-Bolivia border are known collectively as the Payachatas (the twins). Seen from the Chilean side under snow, Parinacota is one of the most beautiful volcanic cones and has a deep crater. The last eruption of Parinacota was about 2000 years ago, and lava flows, cinder cones etc., can be seen on the volcanos southern flanks. Parinacota is Aymara for 'lake of the flamingos'. Pomerape, or Pomarata, means 'peak of the puma'.

CHILEAN ACCESS Some climbers have been asked to produce the Difrol border permit when climbing here. See under Ojos del Salado, page 226 for more details of how to obtain this permit online at www.difrol.cl .

From Arica in Chile on an asphalt road via Putre (3500m) to get to Parinacota village (4500m) (PT). There is a mountain refuge at Parinacota with limited facilities and a small shop and cafe nearby at Chucullo. From the NW corner of Lago Chungara a 4x4 track gives access for about 5km towards the volcano. From the end of this track walk over pumice and lava to camps at 5200m or so on the S or SW side of Parinacota. With a 4x4 access may be better via Caquena (especially if you want to climb both peaks), from where you can drive to about 4900m at a place called Rinconada, directly below the 5350m col which separates the peaks. Water is only available from snow, which is often as high as 5500m.

BOLIVIAN ACCESS The peaks can also be approached from the E via the village of Sajama in Bolivia. With a 4x4 it is possible to drive to about 4900m below the 5350m col or pack animals can be hired in the village for the walk, 1d walk to this spot. The usual camp on the E side of the peaks is just a little higher at 5150m.

PARINACOTA CLIMB This perfect volcanic cone can be climbed easily from any direction. Snowfields on the S and W (Chilean) sides are more aesthetic and often easier than the bare scree slopes on the N and E sides The most frequently climbed lines are on or near the S rib from Chungara, up the NW face from Rinconada or up the N rib above the 5350m col. The highest point is on the NW side of the crater rim.

Parinacota is a great ski mountain if there is good snow; the best route for skiing is near the S rib.

POMERAPE CLIMB Pomerape can be climbed from several directions. From the Chilean side the normal route is by the **SW flank PD**, glaciated, and possibly icy. From the Bolivian side the easiest route is the **E ridge, F**. Pass the rock band at 5800m on the extreme L. Easy snow slopes with a few crevasses then lead to the summit. The **S ridge PD** is mixed snow and rock (III) - climb from the camp just below the 5350m col.

OTHER PEAKS Try **Condoriri 5762m, F** to the N, mostly scree but with some snow on the summit. Most other lower peaks have no snow and little interest.

PARINACOTA S RIB WAYPOINTS End of track near Chungara 18°12'12" 69°11'18" Lava tongue 18°12'10" 69°09'47" Camp at 5200m below S rib 18°11'14" 69°08'47" S rib (5700m) 18°10'35" 69°08'19" Parinacota NW summit 18°09'38" 69°08'33"

BOLIVIA HIGH CAMP Bolivia (5150m) camp 18°09'07" 69°07'23"

BEST MAP BIGM sheet 5739-I, 1:50,000 or ChIGM sheet SE 19-10, 'Arica', 1:250,000

Parinacota from the SW

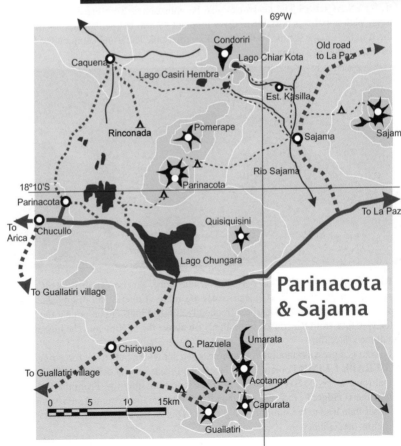

Parinacota & Sajama

Nevado SAJAMA 6550m
3 days   PD

Sajama is Bolivia's highest mountain, being about 100m higher than any peak in the Cordillera Real. It is also the highest peak in the Cordillera Occidental. Sajama is an eroded volcano with some big and unstable cliffs. It is a slightly harder ascent than any of the other major peaks in the Cordillera Occidental, particularly in icy years, and also suffers from huge penitentes. The village of Sajama at its base is a friendly little place with very basic shops and lodging available. Mules and porters can be hired here.

ACCESS Access is easiest from La Paz but is also possible from Arica in Chile. Get to the village of Sajama (4250m)(PT). The La Paz-Arica road, with frequent buses, passes about 15km S of the village. Mules can be hired in the village to reach the normal base camp (4800m) by the Rio Aychuta (there is now a toilet and a water spring here), 4h. In the wet season (November-March) it is reported to be difficult to find someone willing to go. Red barked queñoa trees near this base camp are said to be the highest trees in the world, but they look pretty small compared to California's giant Sequoias!

CLIMB Several routes are possible on the S, W and N sides of mountain. The normal route is by the NW ridge though in some years the SW ridge may be easier. The **NW ridge** can be reached from the normal base camp at Aychuta. Climb up scree slopes on the N side of the valley and cross scree fields past a potential camp (4900m) to join the NW ridge. Go up the ridge and climb a wide gully between old lava flows to a high camp (5650m) behind a pinnacle, 5h from Aychuta. From the camp carry on up the ridge on scree or snow, including one steeper section with poor rock, then finish on the glacier with many false summits, 7h.

OTHER ROUTES The mountain is also frequently climbed by the slightly harder **SW ridge** for which a base on the SW side of mountain will be better than Aychuta. From Aychuta a route on the curving **W glacier,** to join the SW ridge at c.6000m is also possible, this is probably the easiest line on the mountain though there is steep scree and some rockfall danger. On this route a high camp at c.5800m is possible above the bend in the glacier.

KEY WAYPOINTS Base camp 18°06'41" 68°55'01" High camp 18°06'02" 68°53'41" Sajama summit 18°06'30" 68°52'57"

BEST MAP BIGM, sheet 5839-IV, 1:50,000

Sajama from the W

SW ridge

NW ridge

W face

Volcan GUALLATIRI 6063m   2 days   F
Volcan ACOTANGO 6052m   2 days   F
Cerro CAPURATA 5996m   2 days   F

These three volcanoes lie on or near the Chile-Bolivia border and are known as the Quimsachatas. Guallatiri is very active and erupted in 1960. It is a contender for the world's highest active volcano as it appears to be the highest volcano which has actually been seen to erupt lava. Guallata is Aymará for goose. All three peaks are easy volcanoes with small permanent snowfields, which can be climbed from most directions.

ACCESS See map on page 192. There are several possibilities, but access is easiest from the Chilean side. The mountains can be approached direct from the Arica-La Paz road (PT) at Lago Chungará about 15km to the N on the Chilean side of the border. The shortest approach is from a place called Chiriguayo on the Chungara-Guallatiri village road where an old mining track (4x4) reaches 5100m on the N side of Guallatiri, with a branch road reaching 5000m in the Q. Plazuela at the foot of Acotango and Capurata. Acotango can also be reached from the Bolivian side by an old mine road that provides 4x4 access to 5000m or so. There is no water at campsites on either side.

GUALLATIRI CLIMB Guallatiri is best done from the top of the mining track at about 5100m, by either the NE or NW ridges. There is a small uncrevassed glacier on top of Guallatiri, 5-6h.

ACOTANGO CLIMB From the mining track at 5100m in the Q. Plazuela climb by the NW rib and summit snowfields. From the Bolivian side at 5000m climb the N ridge by the E side, sandy paths the whole way. There is a big glacier on the S side of Acotango.

CAPURATA CLIMB From Q. Plazuela climb the N ridge over several small pinnacles, starting at the Acotango-Capurata col. Some climbers have found this summit to be over 6000m on GPS readings.

OTHER PEAKS The next major summits south are four or five eroded volcanoes surrounding the Salar de Surire. These are not very inspiring mountains but the Salar is a beautiful place with a hot spring, fresh drinkable water and flamingos.

GUALLATIRI KEY WAYPOINTS Guallatiri parking 18°24'17" 69°06'00" Start of NE rib 18°24'27" 69°05'25" Snowline 18°24'53" 69°05'27" Summit 18°25'21" 69°05'29"

ACOTANGO & CAPURATA KEY WAYPOINTS Acotango & Capurata parking 18°23'37" 69°05'03" Acotango, top of track 18°20'00" 69°05'57" Acotango summit 18°19'04" 69°02'32" Acotango-Capurata col 18°24'10" 69°03'32" Capurata N pinnacle 18°24'28" 69°02'51" Capurata summit 18°24'53" 69°02'43"

BEST MAP ChIGM sheet A-017 'Volcan Guallatiri', 1:50,000

The Quimsachata volcanoes from the N

Acotango   Capurata   Guallatiri

NW rib   N ridge   NE route   NW route

Volcan ISLUGA 5501m
Cerro CIBARAY 5869m

2 days   F
2 days   N/K

Between the giant volcanoes around the Lauca National Park and the big peaks by Calama there are many lower peaks. Two of the more prominent and more easily accessible are the active volcano Isluga (last eruption 1960) and Cibaray, on either side of the Chile-Bolivia border near the village of Colchane (3600m). Cibaray, which is also known as Carabaya, has a 10km long summit ridge, with the highest point at the W end.

ACCESS There are buses from Iquique to Oruro passing through Colchane (small shops and cafes) several times per week. For Isluga head to the village of Enquelga (hot springs) on the S flank of the volcano.

CLIMBS Isluga is best climbed from the S. Cibaray can be climbed directly from Colchane, but it is probably better to cross the border officially and climb from Pisiga in Bolivia. Both ascents will be easy, normally with no snow.

BEST MAP ChIGM sheet SF-19-15, 'Pisiga Chile', 1:250,000.

Isluga church and Volcan Isluga

ALTO TORONI 5995m

2 days   F

This remote peak on the Chilean-Bolivian border is also known as Co. Sillajgual. It is the highest summit for several hundred kilometres between the group around Parinacota and the high peaks around Ollagüe. The author made an ascent in 2013 and "discovered" a large Inca ceremonial platform on the summit that had never been previously reported (see photo on page 333). The ChIGM height of 5982m probably refers to the bottom of the crater. GPS and digital elevation data indicate a height of 5995-6000m.

ACCESS From Pica via the Salar de Huasco to the small village of Lirima which has a very basic shop. Then continue by minor roads to the tiny settlement of Chaviri at 4300m, S of the peak. From Chaviri follow the wide quebrada NW for several kilometres, then head steeply up the RHS of the main valley into a hanging valley SW of the peak where a high camp can be made at 4800m.

CLIMB From the high camp climb up and L to reach a 4950m col at the start of the long SW ridge.

Follow this ridge easily to snow slopes below the lower western summit. Climb these and cross the shallow crater to reach the higher eastern summit with a large Inca platform on site.

It would also be easy to climb Alto Toroni by the SSW ridge, although it might be harder to find a good high campsite.

KEY WAYPOINTS Chaviri 19°49'05" 68°43'42" High camp 19°46'41" 68°43'47" 4950m col 19°49'21" 68°43'51" Below W summit 19°45'31" 68°42'20" Summit 19°45'10" 68°41'48"

BEST MAP ChIGM sheet SF-19-15, 'Pisiga Chile', 1:250,000.

Alto Toroni from the S

SW ridge

SSW ridge

summit lies behind

to camp

CALAMA A Chilean mining town in the Atacama desert   2350m

Calama is a dirty and unexciting town in a small oasis in the middle of the driest part of the Atacama desert at an altitude of 2350m. Until 1991 when 1cm of snow fell it had never been known to rain or snow here. It can be a useful base for climbing peaks in the southern Chilean Occidental and northern Puna, although most tourist services have now moved to the much more pleasant village of San Pedro de Atacama.

There are daily flights from Santiago to Calama. There are also many buses daily from Santiago (24h.) and also northwards to Arica, etc.

FOOD There are two supermarkets on Vargas near the centre of the town and a large one in Mall Calama 1km N of the town centre on Balmaceda.

FUEL White gas and camping gas from the large "Sodimac" hardware store in the Mall Calama.

Cerro AUCANQUILCHA 6176m   2 days   F
Volcan OLLAGÜE 5868m   2 days   F

These two big volcanoes north of Calama both have old mine workings on them - those on Ollagüe at 5600m, those on Aucanquilcha are at almost 6000m. Vehicle tracks leading to these mines are now impassable higher up, but leave the peaks as very easy ascents which can even be done, or at least descended, on a mountain bike! See photo on page 202. There is no running water on the mountains but Aucanquilcha usually has a little snow near the summit.

ACCESS For both peaks get transport from Calama to the small village of Ollagüe (3700m)(PT) which has accommodation, basic shops and one cafe. No buses use this road but there is a once weekly train from Calama.

AUCANQUILCHA CLIMB Aucanquilcha can be climbed from the village of Ollagüe in 2 or 3 days by the old mine roads on the E and NE flanks. There is no water on the mountain. With 4x4 transport it is possible to drive to the base of the mountain at about 5100m although the road is now deteriorating. The ascent can then be done in one long day. The cableway station at the end of the road at 5250m makes a good camp. From here follow the zig-zagging road above to the upper cableway station at just under 5850m. Then walk L and upwards through the mine workings and climb the N slopes of the summit cone on scree and snow, 5-6h from the 5250m camp.

OLLAGÜE CLIMB Ollague can be climbed from the village in 2 days by the old mine road which reaches 5600m on the WNW side. There are craters near the summit with fumaroles. The summit is 200m higher and NE of the road end. With 4x4 transport the ascent could be done in one long day from the old mining settlement at c.4500m.

Volcan Ollagüe from the N

Aucanquilcha from the N

AUCANQUILCHA KEY WAYPOINTS Cableway camp at 5250m 21°12'01" 68°28'07" Top cableway station 21°12'53" 68°28'22" Summit 21°13'15" 68°28'06"

BEST MAPS ChIGM sheets 2100-6810 and 2115-6800, 1:50,000 or sheet SF-19-7, 'Ollagüe', 1:250,000

Cerro PALPANA 6035m

3 days   F

A big and easy volcano about half way between Aucanquilcha and San Pedro volcano, lying W of the beautiful Salar de Ascotan, on which there are many flamingos. Watch out for the minefield on the N approach.

ACCESS From Calama follow the road to Ollagüe as far as the Salar de Ascotan (3700m).

CLIMB Palpana can be climbed easily by either the S scree slopes or via the broad col which lies N of the mountain. A 4x4 can reach over 4000m on the S route, turn off the Ollagüe road onto a faint track very near km149. On either the N or S route a high camp will be needed, probably carrying water.

KEY WAYPOINTS km149 turn-off 21°31'41" 68°21'36"

BEST MAP ChIGM sheet SF-19-7, 'Ollagüe', 1:250,000 or 1:50,000 sheet (number n/k).

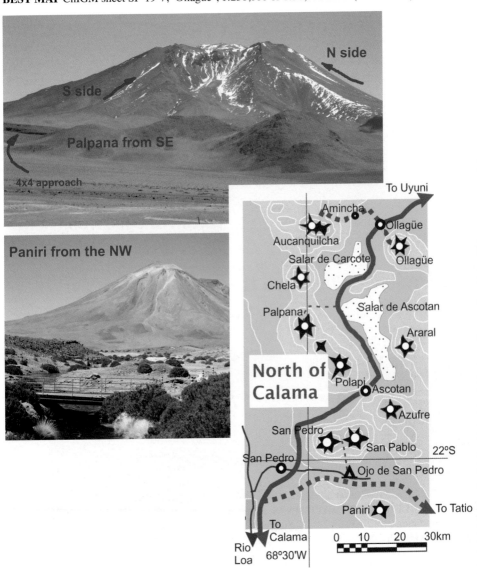

Palpana from SE

N side

S side

4x4 approach

Paniri from the NW

To Uyuni

Amincha

Aucanquilcha

Ollagüe

Ollagüe

Salar de Carcote

Chela

Palpana

Salar de Ascotan

Araral

North of Calama

Polapi

Ascotan

Azufre

San Pedro

San Pablo

22°S

San Pedro

Ojo de San Pedro

Paniri

To Tatio

To Calama

Rio Loa

68°30'W

0   10   20   30km

Volcan SAN PEDRO 6145m   3 days   F
Volcan SAN PABLO 6110m   3 days   F

A pair of very high volcanoes N of Calama and seen from the outskirts of the city. San Pedro is active with much new lava visible. Like many volcanoes in the Cordillera Occidental it last erupted in 1960. There is no water higher up on these mountains and often snow only very near the summits.

ACCESS From Calama there are several possibilities. The easiest is probably via Estacion San Pedro (PT) then the minor road for 20km E to the Ojo de San Pedro (3650m) on the S side of the mountains. There is running water here - a good base camp. A vehicle track leads up just W of the valley coming down from the col between the peaks to about 4200m. The volcanoes can also be approached from the N but there is no water on this route and less likely to be any snow.

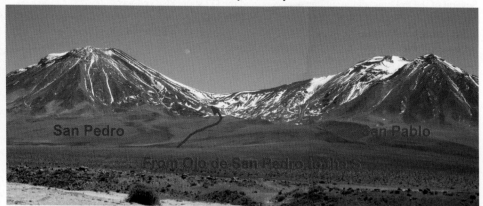

CLIMBS Both peaks can be easily climbed from the Ojo de San Pedro via the high col between them. There are good places for a higher camp just below this col at about 5100m, often with some old snow., about 5-6h. walk from Ojo de San Pedro. From this camp both peaks take about 5-6h. Or can be combined in a long 10-12h. day by the well acclimatised. Routes are straightforward, but a deviation to the R is needed high up on San Pablo to pass a rock band at 6000m.

OTHER PEAKS Immediately south of these two volcanoes are several high peaks including **Paniri 5946m, F** which can be climbed by the NW slopes from near the Ojo de San Pedro. There are extensive ruins on the summit.

KEY WAYPOINTS Ojo de San Pedro camp 21°58'37" 68°21'10"
High camp 21°53'22" 68°22'10"
Edge of Col 21°53'14" 68°22'20"
San Pedro summit 21°53'16" 68°23'29"
BEST MAP ChIGM 1:50,000, sheet(s) not known or sheet SF-19-7, 'Ollagüe', 1:250,000.

SAN PEDRO de ATACAMA A tourist town in the Atacama 2400m

San Pedro de Atacama is a pleasant tourist town near the Salar de Atacama. It is a useful base for climbing peaks in the southern Chilean Occidental and northern Puna de Atacama. There are frequent buses from Calama, including frequent direct transfers from the airport. There are regular tours from San Pedro to the geysers at Tatio (4400m), which are worth a visit.

ROCK CLIMBING There is some very good rock climbing at Socaire on wonderful pocketed volcanic rock. It can be found in a gorge just R of the road from Socaire up to the Paso Sico, 100km S of San Pedro.

FOOD There are several small supermarkets in town.

FUEL White gas and camping gas from the hardware store in the ferreteria in Poblacion Licancabur. Several of the trekking and mountain agencies, and the O2 shop, also sell gas.

MOUNTAIN TRANSPORT AND INFORMATION There are many agencies in town offering guided climbs and vehicle services. Azimut 360 and Turismo Vulcano are longer established and seem the most knowledgeable for climbing information.

Cerro SAIRECABUR 5971m — 2 days — F
Volcan LICANCABUR 5930m — 2 days — F
Cerro TOCO 5611m — 1 day — F

Sairecabur is an excellent viewpoint sometimes recorded as 6040m high, but digital mapping and handheld GPS data denote a height just under 6000m. Licancabur is a perfect isolated cone with archaeological remains on the summit and a crater lake which is usually frozen. The world's highest sub-aqua dive was done here in search of Inca treasure. Because of its proximity to the tourist town of San Pedro de Atacama it is climbed relatively often for an Atacama volcano. There is no drinking water on any of the peaks in this area and often no snow either. A map appears in the next chapter (Puna de Atacama) on page 205.

SAIRECABUR ACCESS From San Pedro follow the Tatio geysers road for approx. 40km, then turn R and drive up a track (4x4) to the Azufrera Saciel at 5400m on the N side of the mountain.

SAIRECABUR CLIMB From the car park at 5400m, walk through the col to the Bolivian side of the mountain, then climb a steep sandy slope to the S for 200m. Turn R and follow a blocky lava ridge to the summit. 4-5h. from the top of the 4x4 track.

LICANCABUR ACCESS From San Pedro de Atacama, take the new asphalt road to the Bolivian border at Hito Cajon. From here drive around the N side of Juriques (in Bolivia) and then along the S shore of the Laguna Verde. Then follow vehicle tracks up to a tongue of lava at 4500m.

LICANCABUR CLIMB From the tongue of lava a short walk up the RHS of the tongue gets you to a camp in Inca ruins at 4700m. From here climb steeply up to the summit trying to make use of the more stable lava ribs, 6-8h. Licancabur can also be climbed by the N ridge from the pass to the N, although the access up the track to this pass by vehicle directly from San Pedro (which is very short), is now unfortunately difficult 4x4 terrain and completely washed out at c.4000m.

TOCO ACCESS & CLIMB Toco was often climbed by the SW slopes but access through the new ALMA telescope complex may now be restricted. For this route leave the main Paso de Jama road at a sign 500m before the Bolivian frontier access, on a 4x4 track which leads to a telescope at 5150m. Follow the road past the telescope and up to 5280m, then the obvious path heading L up a valley to the summit, 3h.

It is also possible to climb Toco by the N slopes from the high point of the asphalted Paso de Jama road at about 4750m. Head for the col between a steep light coloured cone and a longer lump shaped hill (the summit), steep scree and perhaps a little snow at the top. Then follow the short ridge to the summit, 3-4h. from the road.

OTHER PEAKS Licancaburs neighbouring peak of **Juriques 5704m**, **F** is easiest to climb from the Hito Cajon frontier post to the SE (4500m) but could also be climbed from the Lag. Verde.

LICANCABUR KEY WAYPOINTS Camp at ruins 22°49'56" 67°51'23" Summit 22°49'59" 67°52'58"

SAIRECABUR KEY WAYPOINTS Car Park 22°42'39" 67°53'27" Top of sand 22°42'48" 67°53'07" 5850m 22°43'03" 67°53'14" Summit 22°43'08" 67°53'25"

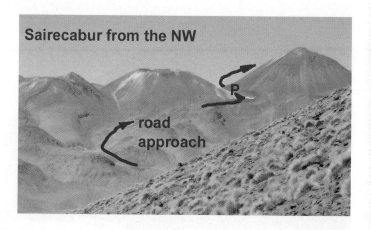

Sairecabur from the NW

road approach

Nearing the summit of Sairecabur

TOCO KEY WAYPOINTS Southern parking 22°57'29" 67°47'08" Top of road 22°57'21" 67°46'38"
Col 22°56'47" 67°46'35"   Summit 22°56'46" 67°46'31"
Northern parking 22°54'59" 67°45'36" Start of steep climb 22°56'27" 67°45'59" Then waypoints for
the col and summit as above.
BEST MAP ChIGM SF-19-11-12, 'Calama', 1:250,000 is adequate.

from
Lag. Verde

N ridge

Licancabur from the N

summit

Toco from the N

Mountain biking at 5500m
on Volcan Ollague

PUNA DE ATACAMA

INTRODUCTION

The bleak and inhospitable surroundings and constant desolate wind of the Puna de Atacama are not to everyone's taste, but the immense views and the wonderful clarity of the air leave a deep impression on most climbers who visit the area. Once very remote, the Puna has really opened up since the first edition of this book was published in 1996, and ascents of many of the peaks are now much more common.

The Puna de Atacama is a high plateau mostly over 4000m above sea level and over 300 kilometres wide. The Puna extends from southern Bolivia and northern Chile into NW Argentina. Rainfall is very low and there are many peaks over 6000m with little or no permanent snow on them. Peaks and access roads for the whole Puna are shown on the map on the next page.

The Puna has the greatest concentration of high peaks in the Andes, with over 30 principal 6000m summits and six of the ten highest Andean peaks. There are also undoubtedly many peaks of over 5000m awaiting first ascents. Over the last few decades there were various reports that the Puna peaks of Ojos del Salado and/or Pissis were higher than Aconcagua, with Ojos once being surveyed as high as 7104m. The latest satellite topography data clearly puts Aconcagua first, Ojos second and Pissis third.

Some of the highest summits were climbed at the time of the Inca empire, over 400 years ago. Remains and ruins (as well as treasure and sacrifice victims) have been found on numerous peaks and have given rise to the unusual sport or science of high altitude archaeology. To date the highest ruins which have been found are the two small huts just under the summit of Llullaillaco at over 6700m. These are also the highest ruins that have been excavated by archaeologists, who discovered a number of 'mummies'. See page 332 for more details.

The peaks are described in four areas. Firstly the peaks of the NW with access usually from San Pedro de Atacama in Chile. Secondly the peaks of the NE with easy access only from Salta in Argentina, thirdly the peaks of the SW around Ojos del Salado with access from Copiapó in Chile or Catamarca and Fiambalá in Argentina and finally the peaks of the SE around Pissis and Bonete with access easiest from Jagüe or Fiambalá in Argentina.

GETTING THERE

Many mountains can be approached from either Chile or Argentina. For Chilean approaches fly out to Santiago and then either fly or take the bus to one of the two main centres, Calama (described above in the Cordillera Occidental chapter, page 198) or Copiapó, described below on page 219. For the Argentine side of the mountains fly out to Buenos Aires then on to Salta for the Nevados de Cachi and Llullaillaco. To reach the Ojos del Salado and Pissis regions from Argentina fly from Buenos Aires to either Catamarca or La Rioja and then travel by bus to Tinogasta or Fiambalá. See the High Andes chapter for details of international flights to Santiago and Buenos Aires from Europe or North America.

SEASON AND WEATHER CONDITIONS

Because of the dry nature of the terrain climbs can be made at any time of year in most of the Puna. The spring months of September to December are reckoned to be best for the Salta ranges. There are lots of different opinions about when to climb in the area around Ojos del Salado and Pissis. The summer is probably least windy and warmest, particularly by February, but electrical storms and snowfall are more common. The spring months of November and December are drier but windier, but are probably the best on balance. The area is one of the windiest in the world (and the author is Scottish!!) so wind is likely to be the biggest weather problem encountered on all these peaks - expect at least 2-3 very windy days per week.

CLIMBING CONDITIONS

Almost without exception the peaks are of volcanic origin and are technically very easy ascents over scree and snow slopes. A notable exception is the rock tower of the Chilean summit of Ojos del Salado. Crampons will only occasionally be needed for the highest peaks. The problems of an ascent are usually confined to the extreme remoteness and lack of water and the constant cold and windy conditions. These hazards should not be underestimated.

Water (or snow) is generally more easy to obtain on the Argentine side of the range.

OTHER GUIDE BOOKS "+6500", in Spanish by Dario Bracali, Ediciones Vertical, covers the peaks over 6500m in good detail.

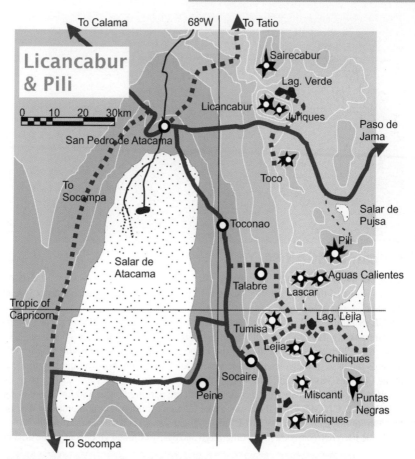

Cerro de PILI 6046m 　　　　　　　　2 days 　　　　F

The highest point on the vast plateau E of the Salar de Atacama, Pili is also known as Acaramachi. Pili is a fine conical volcano known to have had Inca ascents. The first ascensionists found Indian gold and silver statuettes, textiles, feathers and hair. There is a spectacular blood red crater lake in the deep crater.

ACCESS From San Pedro in Chile via the asphalt road towards the Paso de Jama as far as the Salar de Pujsa. The road passes 20km N of Pili so a 4x4 can be useful to approach down the W side of the Salar to a camp at 4500m beneath the prominent Co. Negro de Pujsa (normally water available). Otherwise this is a very long 4h walk from the road to camp.

CLIMB From the camp climb onto the ridge between Co. Negro and Pili, then onto the N shoulder of Pili. It is easiest to go up and over the top of this 5470m hill, then drop about 20m to the N col. Finally climb steeply up the loose scree of the summit cone, 6-8 hours.

OTHER PEAKS Just over the border in Argentina, NE of the Paso de Jama, is the very high volcano, **San Pedro 5860m, F.** This peak is easiest to access from Argentina, via Susques, El Toro and Ichaca, then climb by the N or NE side.

PILI KEY WAYPOINTS Camp 23°15'09" 67°36'28" North top 23°16'31" 67°37'12" North Col 23°16'57" 67°37'12" Summit 23°17'33" 67°37'03"

BEST MAP ChIGM sheet 2300-6700 'Toconao' 1:250,000.

Pili from the NE

5470m

Volcan LASCAR 5641m
1 day   F

Cerro MIÑIQUES 5890m
2 days   F

Lascar is one of the most active volcanoes in the Andes. Miñiques is an extinct volcano rising above the scenic Laguna Miñiques.

ACCESS From San Pedro drive S through Toconao, then towards Socaire. For Lascar turn off before Socaire passing Talabre to reach the Laguna Lejia (4400m). There are good campsites in a sheltered "lava bay" 20m above the S side of the lagoon. Then drive N along the W edge of the lake (4x4) towards the base of the volcano and a parking area at 4800m. For Miñiques continue through Socaire to the Lagunas Miscanti and Miñiques (4200m).

LASCAR CLIMB Easily up the S slopes from the parking area at 4800m. There is a good path, 4h.

MIÑIQUES CLIMB From the S end of the Laguna Miñiques climb S onto the W shoulder then up to the summit on steep scree, the last 100m or so are a steep and loose scramble, 8-10h.

OTHER PEAKS There are many other high and easily climbed volcanoes in the area including **Aguas**

Corona, Lascar and Aguas Calientes
from the Laguna Lejia

Calientes 5924m, Chilliques 5778m and **Tumisa 5658m**. The peak to the SW of Lascar, **Co. Corona 5301m**, is the highest mountain on the Tropic of Capricorn, the actual highest point on the tropic being on this peaks S ridge. It is an easy ascent from the 4x4 track to Lascar, 3-4h.

LASCAR KEY WAYPOINTS End of 4x4 track 23°23'23" 67°43'41" Crater Edge 23°22'00" 67°43'57" Summit 23°22'07" 67°44'14"

BEST MAP ChIGM sheet 2300-6700 'Toconao' 1:250,000.

Miñiques from the N

Volcan SOCOMPA 6051m   3 days   F
Cerro SALIN 6029m   5 days   F
Cerro PULAR 6233m   5 days   F
Cerro ARACAR 6095m   5 days   F

A group of high volcanoes lying S and E of the Salar de Atacama. All have produced evidence of Inca ascents. Salin and Socompa lie on the Chile - Argentina border. Pular, with an Inca altar on the summit, is entirely in Chile and Aracar lies inside Argentina. Access to Socompa is relatively easy, but the others are more difficult to reach. Pular is Atacameñan for 'eyebrow'.

ACCESS Very difficult without private transport. Trains no longer run on the railway to Estacion Socompa. The road to Estacion Socompa is OK for a high clearance two wheel drive, 1d. from Calama or Antofagasta. With a private 4x4 transport a roadhead for the other peaks could be reached in 2 days from Calama or Salta in Argentina.

SOCOMPA CLIMB Volcan Socompa is an easy ascent by the S slopes from the road at Estacion Socompa (3850m). The best route follows the frontier rib, it's long and steep and will take most mortals 2 days.

OTHER CLIMBS Pular and Salin are probably best climbed from near Estacion Socompa, approaching round the E side of Volcan Socompa (This may be possible with a 4x4 in good conditions). Aracar may be easier to reach from the railway to the S at Taca Taca. Ascents are all easy and all peaks have very little or no snow on them in a normal year.

BEST MAP ChIGM sheet 2400-6715 'Sierra Almeida' 1:250,000 covers all the peaks though Aracar is only partly shown. AIGM sheet 2569-II 'Socompa' covers the Argentine side of the border.

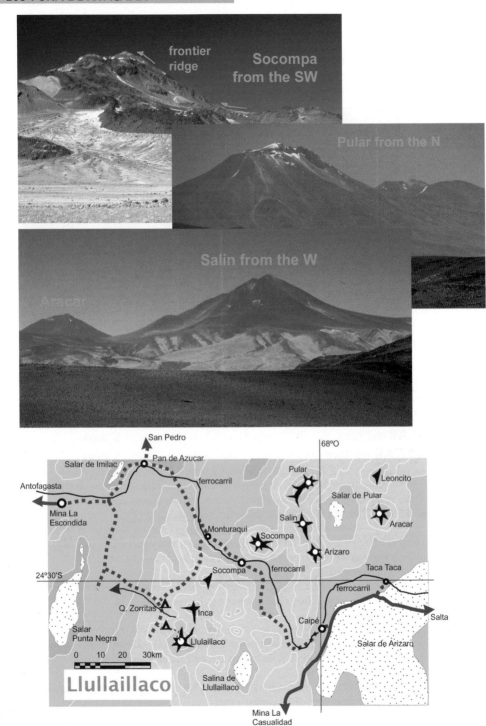

frontier ridge

Socompa from the SW

Pular from the N

Salin from the W

Aracar

San Pedro

Pan de Azucar

Salar de Imilac

ferrocarril

Pular

Leoncito

Antofagasta

Salar de Pular

Mina La Escondida

Salin

Aracar

Monturaqui

Socompa

68°O

24°30'S

Socompa

Arizaro

ferrocarril

Taca Taca

ferrocarril

Salta

Q. Zorritas

Inca

Caipé

Salar Punta Negra

Llulaillaco

0   10   20   30km

Salar de Arizaro

Llullaillaco

Salina de Llullaillaco

Mina La Casualidad

Volcan LLULLAILLACO 6739m

4 days   F

Volcan Llullaillaco is the mountain on which are found the highest archaeological ruins in the world. They lie just below the summit. The supposed first ascensionists in 1952 were reported to be very surprised to find ruined walls and houses on the summit area. The mountain was climbed at the time of the Inca empire for religious purposes, see page 332 in the appendix for further details. Llullaillaco, the 7th highest Andean peak, is also an active volcano with eruptions reported from the last century. The name means 'water of memory', a rather haunting name for such a remote desert peak.

CHILEAN ACCESS From Calama via San Pedro de Atacama. It is possible with a 4x4 to go all the way to Q. de Las Zorritas (4100m) NW of the mountain where there is a small hut and fresh water. To get to Zorritas is simplest via Estacion Monturaqui and then an old track that heads S. It is also possible to drive via Pan de Azucar and the N end of Salar Punta Negra, then look for the track heading E and up to Q. Zorritas. This area has many water pumps (no water) and dead end roads which make finding the right track difficult. From Zorritas head S on a track for ½h. then take a marked 4x4 track L towards the volcano and a vehicle base camp at 4600m.

ARGENTINE ACCESS From the La Casualidad mine in Argentina drive 10km towards Mina Julia, then keep on the W side of the Salina de Llullaillaco to a camp at about 4900m.

CHILEAN CLIMB By the N or NW sides several routes are possible. The small glacier (no crevasses) R of the obvious lava flow on the NW flank is probably the most interesting and frequently climbed line. Higher camps at c.5100m and on the glacier edge at 5900m are usually made. The summit climb is a long and hard day over lava boulders. Cross the glacier to a small col at 6250m, then climb onto a lava ridge from 6400m to 6500m and follow this to the summit plateau.

ARGENTINE CLIMB From the camp at 4900m go up to a high camp at 5900m just below the N saddle, then up to the summit.

OTHER PEAKS 15km to the N of Llullaillaco **Co. Inca 5540m, F** can also be climbed from Zorritas base camp.

LLULLAILLACO WAYPOINTS Q. Zorritas refugio 24°37'15" 68°35'17" Vehicle camp at 4600m 24°40'30" 68°34'54" Camp (5100m) 24°41'20" 68°33'43" Glacier edge camp 24°42'20" 68°32'47" Climb to lava ridge 24°43'00" 68°32'30" Ruins on summit plateau 24°43'07" 68°32'19"

BEST MAP ChIGM sheet 2430-6820 'Volcan Llullaillaco', 1:50,000. AIGM sheet 2569-II 'Socompa' covers the Argentine side of the border.

Llullaillaco from the W

SALTA The principal city of NW Argentina 1200m

Salta is a pleasant city in NW Argentina and a good base for trips into the northern Argentine Puna. There are several flights a day from Buenos Aires and many buses.

SIGHTS There are some nice colonial buildings around the centre of the city. Co. San Bernardo has good views of the city, with a cable car or trail to the summit. The Q. de Humahuaca lies beyond the smaller city of Jujuy, 80km N of Salta, and contains several important archaeological ruins from the time of the Incas, the best is probably the fort of Pucará.

FOOD There are several large supermarkets near the centre of town e.g. on Mitre near Plaza Guemes.

FUEL A few small shops in the central area sell camping gas. A source for bencina blanca is n/k.

MOUNTAIN EQUIPMENT For very basic camping supplies (including gas canisters) try the small shops at Zuviria 211 or Caseros 878.

Nevado de CHAÑI c.5930m 5 days F

Chañi lies about 100km N of Salta, near the small city of Jujuy. It is one of many peaks in NW Argentina that has Inca ruins on the summit. The altitude given here is from the SRTM data.

ACCESS From Salta travel via Jujuy to the settlement at Leon (1622m) (PT). From here walk up the valley to reach the E side of Chañi. 2-3d.

CLIMB By the E side. Easy, very little snow.

SUMMIT WAYPOINT 24°03'47" 65°44'45"

BEST MAP AIGM 1:250,000 sheet 2566-II 'Salta'.

S face of Chañi

Queva from the SE

Nevado QUEVA c.6140m   5 days   F

Also known as Quehuar, Pastos Grandes or Quironcollo. An Inca grave on the summit containing a mummy was dynamited by local treasure hunters.

ACCESS From Salta to San Antonio de los Cobres (3800m)(PT) where there is accommodation, shops and cafes. Then onwards towards the small village of Santa Rosa de los Pastos Grandes (3900m) for the southern route.

CLIMB From the village of Santa Rosa a track leads 7km towards the mountain ending at 4200m. Continue up the valley passing the stream source at 4850m, and then climb easily up the S slopes of the peak, 2-3d.

OTHER ROUTES It is also possible to climb Queva by the N and NE slopes, but there is normally no snow on this route and less water.

OTHER PEAKS Just NW of San Antonio is the prominent volcano **Tuzgle 5486m, F**. It can be climbed easily in about 4-5h. by an old mine road on the SW side. This road can be driven (4x4) to about 5000m. There is much interesting mine archaeology on the ascent.

Nearer Salta, **No. Acay 5770m, F** is sometimes quoted as being over 6000m. Climb the W slopes from the road at Abra del Acay (5000m), hard work over very rough ground. Or a longer but easier climb can be made from the road near Encrucijada (3500m) to the NE.

QUEVA WAYPOINTS Track ends 24°24'34" 66°40'22" Last water 24°20'51" 66°44'07" Summit 24°18'30" 66°43'57"

QUEVA BEST MAP AIGM 1:250,000 sheet 2566-I 'San Antonio de los Cobres

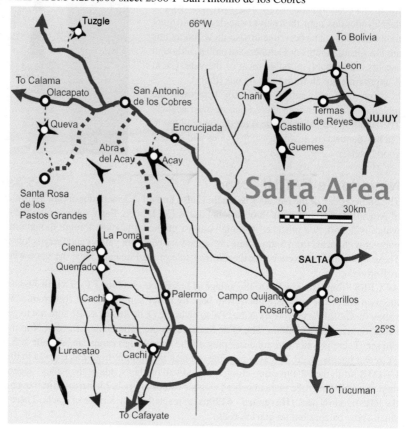

Cachi town

The S face of Nevado del Acay

CACHI A sleepy wee town   2700m

Cachi is a beautiful and sleepy wee town at the foot of the Nevados de Cachi, themselves a neglected and quiet mountain range. The best time to visit these mountains are the spring months of October-November, although ascents are probably possible most of the year. Cachi is approximately 5h from Salta by bus (daily).

It is possible to arrange mules for trips into the mountains here, although there is no agency as such. Try asking in the cafe near the river on the road out to Cachi Adentro. The town has shops, cafes and several good hotels.

Nevado de CACHI 6380m   5 days   F

The highest peak of the Nevados de Cachi is also known as Libertador or San Martin after the liberator of Argentina. Another name in occasional use is Co. Blanco. Early sources give the height as 6720m, which is definitely a mistake. Although almost unknown to most foreign mountaineers this range is popular with locals from Salta. There are some very beautiful valleys and there is lots of wildlife to see. These mountains are wetter than the Chilean side of the Puna and have the same wet and dry seasons as Bolivia.

ACCESS From Cachi by bus to the village of Las Pailas (3000m)(PT) or a little higher at 3200m where the road ends. The peak is hidden from here by lower summits in the foreground. Walk up the wide valley (beautiful cactus forest) to the NW to enter the Q. de los Arcas. Be sure not to go up the first deep valley on the right at 3400m. The Q de los Arcas is the valley that is furthest N in the mountains you can see. There is water and good camping all the way. A high camp can be made at 5250m a bit below a circular headwall, 2d. It is also possible to reach the summit from Las Cuevas to the south.

CLIMB From the 5250m camp climb the headwall on the N side of the valley - steep and a bit loose - then cross NW over the plateau behind (higher camps are possible here). Climb over or contour round the RHS of a low peak (**Hoygaard - 6120m**) to reach the long S ridge of Cachi. There are usually some small snow patches but no glacier, 6-8h.

Nevados de Cachi from the SE. No. Cachi lies behind. Antifeatro. Las Arcas. Q. de los Arcas

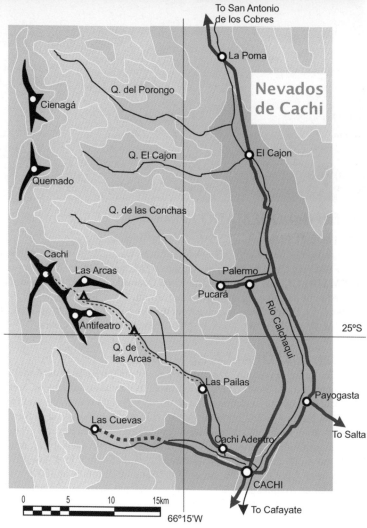

OTHER PEAKS From the high camp in the Q. de los Arcas a couple of other minor 6000m peaks can be tackled. The double summitted peak to the N is **Co. de los Arcas c.5950m, F.** It could easily be climbed from the plateau mentioned above by the SW side. The peak to the S is **Antifeatro c.6020m F** and could be climbed from the N after reaching the plateau.

KEY WAYPOINTS Road end 25°00'53" 66°15'01" Piedra Grande camp 24°59'00" 66°17'34" Pila de Piedra camp 24°57'35" 66°19'21" High camp 24°57'10" 66°20'47" Top of Headwall 24°57'14" 66°21'17" Hoygaard-Cachi col 24°56'36" 66°22'38" Summit 24°55'57" 66°23'26"

BEST MAP AIGM 1:250,000 sheet 2566-I 'San Antonio de los Cobres'. Sheet 2566-III 'Cachi' is useful for access.

Quemado from the SE · Cienaga

Morro del QUEMADO 6184m
5 days   F
Cerro CIÉNAGA 6050m
5 days   N/K

These two peaks lie to the N of Nevado de Cachi. Quemado is sometimes known as Palermo.

ACCESS From Cachi by bus to the village of El Cajon (2800m)(PT).

QUEMADO CLIMB From El Cajon climb Quemado by the Q. El Cajon. The Q. de los Conchas is reported to be passable but is very difficult terrain.

CIENAGA CLIMB Climb Cienaga from the village of El Cajon by the Q del Porongo.

BEST MAP AIGM 1:250,000 sheet 2566-I 'San Antonio de los Cobres'.

Volcan ANTOFALLA c.6440m
5 days   F

Antofalla, an active volcano, is one of the remotest 6000m peaks in the Andes, located about 80km NW of Antofagasta de la Sierra. There are extensive Inca ruins on the summit. Some sources quote a height of only 6100m but this is definitely false, the above height is from the satellite topography data.

ACCESS The best access is via the remote village of Antofagasta de la Sierra, which can be reached from San Antonio de los Cobres on the Salta-Calama road. You can also get to Antofagasta de la Sierra from the town of Belen to the S in Catamarca province (occasional PT). Antofagasta has some small hotels and shops and petrol. From Antofagasta de la Sierra a long 4x4 drive is needed to reach the settlement of Antofalla on the shores of the Salar de Antofalla at 3500m. With 4x4 it is possible to reach Salar de Archibarca (4080m - small refugio and water source) and indeed to continue to about 5000m on the N side of the peak. It is also possible to reach the Salar de Archibarca from the Mina La Casualidad 60km to the NW of the peak.

CLIMB Climb easily up the N slopes to a high camp at 5500m, 3-4h. From here climb scree and boulder slopes to the summit, which is visible from the camp, 5-6h.
BEST MAP AIGM 1:250,000 sheet 2569-IV 'Antofalla'.

Antofalla from the N

The summit shrine on Antofalla

Sierra LAGUNA BLANCA 6012m

3 days   F

Cerro GALAN 5912m

3 days   F

Laguna Blanca is sometimes quoted as high as 6195m, but the AIGM 1:100,000 map shows it as 6012m, broadly in agreement with the SRTM data. The height quoted here for Galan is also supported by the SRTM data.

Galan lies 60km E of Antofagasta de la Sierra. The summit lies at the centre of an enormous volcanic caldera over 40km across (and reputedly the world's largest). The peak known as Laguna Blanca lies about 50km SE. The peaks are shown on the map at the start of this chapter, page 204.

GALAN ACCESS As for Antofalla then by 4x4 from Antofagasta de la Sierra to the Lag. Diamante (4600m) which lies 15km SW of Galan.

GALAN CLIMB By the SW slopes from Lag. Diamante, easy. Also possible by the N slopes.

LAGUNA BLANCA ACCESS Laguna Blanca lies only 20km E of the road (PT) between Belen and Antofagasta de la Sierra. From about 9km S of El Peñon drive more or less due E to reach a dry base camp at the area known as Vega Agua Colorada, c.4500m.

LAGUNA BLANCA CLIMB From Vega Agua Colorada climb Laguna Blanca in 2-3 days with a high camp at about 5200m where the valley turns to the N.

OTHER ROUTES Laguna Blanca can also be easily climbed from the village of Laguna Blanca by the E slopes.

KEY WAYPOINTS Turn off S of El Penon 26°32'58" 67°14'39" Base of Laguna Blanca summit 26°32'20" 67°04'20" Laguna Blanca summit 26°32'02" 67°03'40"

BEST MAP AIGM 1:250,000 sheet 2566-III 'Cachi' covers Galan and 2766-I 'Santa Maria' covers Laguna Blanca. 1:100,000 sheet 2766-7 'El Peñon' shows Laguna Blanca in good detail.

Relaxing at the Laguna Verde

Laguna Blanca from the E

Cerro SIERRA NEVADA 6140m   4 days   F
Cerros COLORADOS 6080m   6 days   F
Cerro VALLECITOS 6120m   6 days   F

These three very remote peaks lie between 40 and 80km N of the Paso de San Francisco road. The names are all Spanish. Sierra Nevada means 'snowy mountains', Cerros Colorados means 'red hills' and Vallecitos just means 'little valleys'. Sierra Nevada is sometimes known by the name of its east summit, Cumbre del Laudo. The first ascent of the highest point appears to have been made only in 2000, and using the "description" provided in the 2nd edition (1999) of this guidebook! There are many minefields in this area so take care.

SIERRA NEVADA ACCESS Sierra Nevada lies on the border 25km E of the Rio Juncalito. There is a 4x4 track from the Chilean mining town of El Salvador to the thermals here and then on to the Lag. del Jilguero, which lie NW of the summit at 4200m.

SIERRA NEVADA CLIMB Ascend SE up the Q. El Arenal then over several minor ridges to a point just S of the summit, then directly up to the summit.

COLORADOS AND VALLECITOS ACCESS Drive (4x4) via Antofalla village down the W shore of the Salar de Antofalla to Vega de Oro Huasi. Then approx. 50km cross country to a camp at 5000m on the N slope of the mountains. The peaks can probably also be approached and climbed from the Rio Juncalito in Chile.

COLORADOS AND VALLECITOS CLIMBS From the 5000m camp Colorados can be climbed easily in 8-10h. Vallecitos is also an easy climb.

BEST MAP ChIGM sheet 2600-6730 'Laguna Verde' 1:250,000 or AIGM sheet 2769-II, 'Paso de San Francisco' 1:250,000

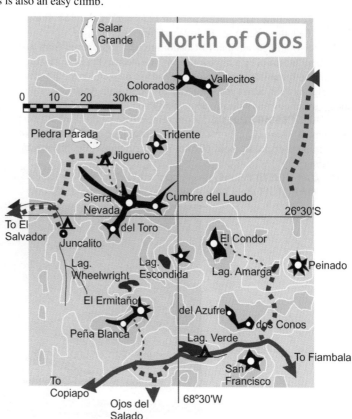

Colorados from the S   Vallecitos

Cerro el CONDOR 6414m
Cerro PEINADO c.5850m

5 days   F
4 days   F

The large wedge shaped peak of El Condor is also known as Volcan Sarmiento. Peinado is an impressively steep sided and dark black volcanic cone composed of fresh lava and ash. It will be hard work to climb. The highest point of El Condor is at the SE side of the crater. Recent SRTM data indicate both these peaks are higher than previously thought.

ACCESS Both Peinado and El Condor are best approached from just on the Argentine side of the Paso San Francisco, by a mining track which leads to the Lag. Amarga at 4000m. This section of road may not be reversible (steep and sandy) and so a much longer drive back W and then N of Peinado to Antofagasta de la Sierra may be required! From Lag. Amarga it is possible to drive W for about 1h. then S up an obvious valley to about 5000m on the N side of El Condor.

CONDOR CLIMB From the 5000m vehicle base camp climb R (west) over rough terrain and large boulders to a high camp at 5600m, 5-7h. From here climb the gully direct to the summit, very hard work through rocks at about 6000m. The S summit is the highest, but is not obvious to see while ascending.

PEINADO CLIMB Peinado is very hard work. Climb from a vehicle base camp at Lag. Amarga.

BEST MAP AIGM sheet 2769-II, 'Paso de San Francisco' 1:250,000

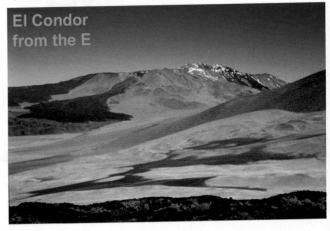

El Condor from the E

Peinado from the S

COPIAPÓ Main access city for the Chilean Puna   370m

Copiapo is a small city in a fruit growing region and the most important access for Ojos del Salado and the Chilean side of the Puna. There are flights daily from Santiago or buses day and night which take about 12h.

MOUNTAIN TRANSPORT AND INFO A 4x4 is necessary for approaching many of the peaks in the area. There is reported to be a list of 4x4 drivers kept at the tourist office. You can also hire a vehicle, with or without a driver, at several of the car hire agencies - Rodaggio are particularly good, although their vehicles are a bit old they have petrol 4x4's and will supply chains, sandboards etc.

MOUNTAIN EQUIPMENT Not known, although some basic camping equipment can be bought.

FOOD Near the centre there are supermarkets on Los Carrera one block W of the plaza. Also a large supermarket and hardware store 2km E of town centre on Av. Copyapu.

FUEL Camping gas from the large Sodimac hardware store across the river from the city centre.

Cerro COPIAPÓ 6052m   3 days   F
Cerro TRES QUEBRADAS 6239m   5 days   F

Co. Copiapó, an active volcano, is another of the high peaks in this area with "Inca"ruins near the summit. Ruins including terraces, retaining walls, fireplaces and altars have been discovered. Co. Tres Quebradas is also known as Co. de Los Patos. There is little snow on these peaks.

ACCESS For both peaks the best access is from the N (Chilean side). A road runs S from the main Copiapó-Paso San Francisco road. This leaves the main road at the E side of Salar de Maricunga and goes up the Q. Vega Redonda to the Mina Marte (c.4200m). The track continues to Lag. del Negro Francisco S of Co. Copiapó where there is now a refugio. The Argentine side of Tres Quebradas could also be approached from the Valle Ancho to the south (see Pissis).

COPIAPÓ CLIMB Copiapó is an easy ascent from the Mina Marte to the E.

TRES QUEBRADAS CLIMB The W summit is 5980m and lies on the Chilean border. The peak can be climbed from the Mina Marte (4x4 may get you closer) in several days over the easy W slopes.

BEST MAP ChIGM sheet SG-19-14 'Copiapó' 1:250,000 shows the summit of Co. Copiapó but not the approach. The western approaches to both peaks are shown on ChIGM sheet 2600-6815 'Copiapó' 1:500,000. For Tres Quebradas the 1:250,000 Argentine map AIGM sheet 2769 III y IV, 'Fiambala'.

Copiapo from the SE

Tres Quebradas
from the SE

Cerro el ERMITAÑO 6146m — 2 days — F
Cerros PEÑA BLANCA 6030m — 2 days — F

El Ermitaño and Peña Blanca are two neighbouring peaks in Chile to the N of the road to the San Francisco pass. They are sometimes climbed as acclimatisation peaks before an ascent of Ojos del Salado. Ermitaño means the hermit, Peña Blanca means the white stone or cliff.

ACCESS See map on page 225. As for the base area of Ojos del Salado to the ruined hosteria or the campsite by the Laguna Verde thermal spring.

CLIMB The peaks, which lie about 15km N of the road can be climbed easily by the S side in one long day (6-8 hours for Peña Blanca and 10-12 hours for Ermitaño). Leave the road at about km243 just above and W of the steep descent at Barrancas Blancas. It is also possible with a 4x4 to drive cross country to about 5000m on the SE side of Ermitaño, giving a shorter summit day of about 6-8 hours for this peak. There are normally only small and isolated snow patches on both peaks.

BEST MAP ChIGM sheet 2645-6830, 'Rio Peñas Blancas' 1:50,000

Peña Blanca
from the S

El Ermitaño

Nevado TRES CRUCES Sur 6748m   3 days   F
Nevado TRES CRUCES Central 6629m   3 days   F

The Tres Cruces massif is one of the highest in the Andes, with two major 6000m summits and a minor one. Tres Cruces Sur lies on the border with Argentina, but the rest of the massif is entirely in Chile. Tres Cruces has more snow and ice than other peaks in the area and there is a large glacier on the SE side of Tres Cruces Sur. Tres Cruces is Spanish for three crosses.

ACCESS See map on page 225. Much easier from the Chilean side. From Copiapó take the San Francisco pass road until just after it climbs out of the Rio Lamas valley, km211. Leave the road here and drive (4x4) up a sandy fan R of an old lava flow to a dry base camp at 4800m. Access to any of these peaks from Argentina involves a long and difficult 4x4 drive via the Lag. Verde, Lag Tres Quebradas and Rio Salado.

TRES CRUCES CLIMBS Establish a second camp at 5400m below the col between Tres Cruces Sur and Central. **Tres Cruces Norte 6030m, F** which is only a few metres short of having enough prominence to be a major 6000m summit, can be climbed from here by the easy S slopes in one day via the col at 5641m. For the two higher summits of Sur and Central a high camp beside the small lake at 5940m in the crater 1km W of the 6008m col is recommended (see photo page 343). From here climb Central by the S glacier or SW scree slopes, 4-5h. For Tres Cruces Sur climb towards the 6008m col but head S up a rib before reaching it. Then climb up snow fields to the shoulder at 6440m. Scramble up and through large and complex lava blocks to the summit, 5-6h.

OTHER PEAKS To the S of Tres Cruces Sur is **Puntiagudo 5980m, F** one of the highest peaks in the Andes to not quite make it to 6000m. It is another easy climb from the San Francisco road.

KEY WAYPOINTS Parking 27°05'22" 68°51'00" 5400m camp 27°05'00" 68°48'48" High camp 27°05'00" 68°47'40" Shoulder on Sur 27°05'41" 68°47'06" Summit of Sur 27°05'54" 68°46'42 Summit of Central 27°04'08" 68°47'05"

BEST MAP ChIGM sheet 2700-6845 'Macizo Tres Cruces' 1:50,000.

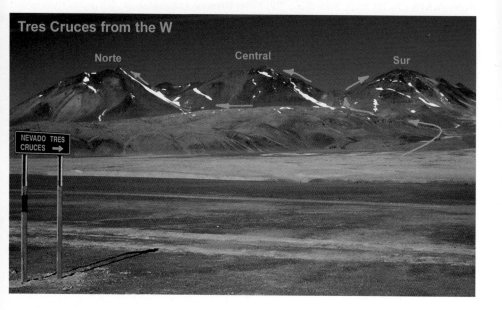

Tres Cruces from the W

Norte   Central   Sur

NEVADO TRES CRUCES →

Cerro SOLO 6205m

2 days   F

Solo is a sandy cone located between the Tres Cruces massif and Ojos del Salado.

ACCESS Much easier from the Chilean side. Approach using a 4x4 from km228 on the San Francisco pass road to the N side of the peak and a dry base camp.

CLIMB Solo is a very sandy climb - swim up the slopes from a camp to the N.

BEST MAP ChIGM sheet 2700-6830, 'Nevado Ojos del Salado', 1:50,000.

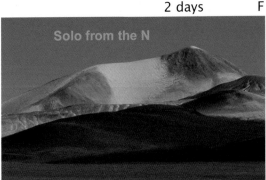

Solo from the N

Cerros BARRANCAS BLANCAS 6119m
1 day   F
Cerro VICUÑAS 6067m
1 day   F

These two peaks lie in Chile S of the road to the Paso San Francisco and are outlying peaks of the Ojos del Salado massif. Both are easy ascents, and are climbed relatively frequently as warm up peaks for Ojos del Salado. Vicuñas takes its name from the wild relative of the llama occasionally seen in the area, Barrancas Blancas means 'white canyons' and takes its name from the area of the same name by the main road to the north.

ACCESS See map on page 225. As for Ojos del Salado to the base area.

BARRANCAS BLANCAS CLIMB Barrancas Blancas is best climbed from the road at km241 by the prominent reddish colour central ridge on the N slopes, 8-10 hours. Pass the rock outcrop at 5900m on the L.

VICUÑAS CLIMB Vicuñas is best climbed by its E slopes from the 4x4 road to the lower refugio on Ojos. Leave the road at a height of about 4800m where it turns sharply E out of the quebrada. Climb directly up the E slopes, 6 h.

BEST MAPS ChIGM sheet 2645-6830, 'Rio Peñas Blancas' 1:50,000 shows Barrancas Blancas and ChIGM sheet 2700-6830, 'Nevado Ojos del Salado', 1:50,000 shows Vicuñas. ChIGM sheet 2600-6815 'Copiapó' 1:500,000 shows both peaks and access roads.

Barrancas Blancas from the N

Vicuñas from the hut on Ojos

E slopes

Nevado el MUERTO 6510m   3 days   F

Muerto is a high peak on the border NE of Ojos del Salado and best climbed from the Chilean side. El Muerto is Spanish for 'the dead one'. Satellite topography data indicates that this peak is definitely a wee bit over 6500m, the ChIGM height is just 6488m.

ACCESS As for Ojos del Salado.

CLIMB For El Muerto traverse E from the lower refugio on Ojos and set up a camp in the col (5500m) between Ojos and El Muerto. Climb easily over scree, sand and snow slopes to the summit.

OTHER PEAKS The peak to the E, lying between Muerto and El Fraile has become known as **El Muertito 5988m, F**. It has a height very close to 6000m and a prominence very close to 400m, so it may or may not be a major 6000m summit. It was first climbed in 2010, approaching from the main road to the N, and a deep crater lake was seen.

MUERTO SUMMIT WAYPOINT 27°03'27" 68°29'01"

BEST MAPS ChIGM sheet 2700-6815 'Cerro El Fraile' 1:50,000, with sheet 2700-6830, 'Nevado Ojos del Salado' useful for access from the Chilean side.

Muerto from the W

Cerro MEDUSA 6120m   5 days F
Volcan del VIENTO 6028m   6 days F

These two peaks lie S and E of Ojos del Salado and make good acclimatisation peaks for that mountain if approaching from the E (Argentine side). Medusa is however quickest to approach from Chile. Medusa was wrongly named Volcan del Viento in the first two editions of this guidebook. The real Volcan del Viento, 6028m, does not appear as a 6000m peak on any Argentine map.

ACCESS As for Ojos del Salado to either the Chilean or Argentine side.

MEDUSA CHILEAN CLIMB For Medusa traverse E between Ojos and Muerto to reach a high camp in a flat area at 5500m N of the peak. Climb to the summit easily from here.

ARGENTINE CLIMBS Both peaks can also be climbed in short days from camps between the two peaks near El Arenal in Argentina. About 4-5h each, with easy terrain on both.

OTHER PEAKS The subsidiary 6000m peak of **Medusa NE 6065m F,** can also be climbed from El Arenal in a long day by going around the E side of Medusa.

KEY WAYPOINTS Camp between peaks 27°09'38" 68°28'06" Medusa summit 27°07'38" 68°29'08" Volcan del Viento summit 27°11'27" 68°28'24"

BEST MAPS ChIGM sheet 2700-6815 'Cerro El Fraile' 1:50,000, with sheet 2700-6830, 'Nevado Ojos del Salado' useful for access from the Chilean side. Sheet 2769-IV y III 'Fiambala' 1:250,000 for the approach from Argentina.

Medusa from the S (after heavy snowfall)

Medusa NE

Armadillo, Puna de Atacama

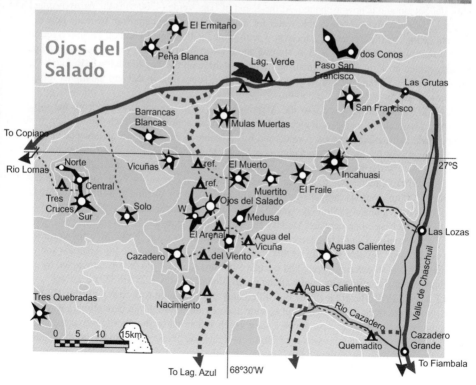

Ojos del Salado

El Ermitaño

Peña Blanca

Lag. Verde

dos Conos

Paso San Francisco

Las Grutas

San Francisco

Barrancas Blancas

Mulas Muertas

To Copiapo

Rio Lomas

Norte

Vicuñas

ref.

El Muerto

ref.

Incahuasi

27°S

Central

Muertito

El Fraile

Tres Cruces

Sur

Solo

W

Ojos del Salado

Medusa

El Arenal

Agua del Vicuña

Aguas Calientes

Las Lozas

Cazadero

del Viento

Tres Quebradas

Aguas Calientes

Valle de Chaschuil

Nacimiento

Rio Cazadero

Cazadero Grande

Quemadito

To Fiambala

0   5   10   15km

To Lag. Azul   68°30'W

Nevado OJOS DEL SALADO 6893m   4 days   F/PD

Ojos del Salado is the highest mountain in Chile, the second highest peak in the Andes, and also the highest active volcano in the world. There are active fumaroles in the crater SW of the summit. The 1st and 2nd editions of this guidebook listed Pissis as the second highest peak in the Andes with Ojos at 6864m and Pissis at 6882m. However recent satellite surveys indicate that Pissis is much closer to 6793m and Ojos close to the Chilean IGM height of 6893m. Both peaks have also occasionally been surveyed higher than Aconcagua but these figures are now completely discredited.

The name is often wrongly translated as 'Eyes of the Salt Plain'. However Ojo is Spanish for 'source' as well as eye, and Salado is the name given to numerous salt rivers in the area so a better translation is 'Source of the Salt River'.

Ojos del Salado is logistically easier from the Chilean side because you can drive much nearer to the peak and there are also a couple of small refugios. The climb itself is technically easier and more interesting from the Argentine side. There are two tops with less than a metre difference in height between them. The E or "Argentine" summit is the main mass of the mountain and contains the highest bedrock, the 54cm higher W or "Chilean" summit is a detached pinnacle topped by loose blocks.

The time of 4 days given above is only realistic for those climbing on the Chilean side and already well acclimatised to the base height of 5000m.

CHILEAN ACCESS Access to the Chilean side is reasonably easy for a Puna peak. A permit is required to climb the peak and can be organised in advance on the web through www.difrol.cl Permission can also usually be obtained in a few days through the tourist office in Copiapó. In the past a permit also had to be purchased from a private logistics company in Copiapó, but this does not seem to be in force any more (at 2014).

The road from Copiapó to Fiambalá over the Paso San Francisco (4720m) passes about 20km N of Ojos del Salado and is now asphalted. At the E end of Lag. Verde (4300m) is the Arroyo Agua Dulce which is the only source of drinkable water for many miles. A base camp can be made here or at the thermal springs on the S side of the loch (now with some facilities and a charge). There is a serious 4x4 track up the N side of Ojos del Salado, starting about 15km W of the Lag. Verde at km246 and passing a partly ruined hosteria. Well acclimatised parties can drive all the way to the lower Refugio Atacama (no facilities) at 5250m and with very good 4x4 skills it is possible to drive to the higher refugio (no facilities, space for 7-8 people) at 5800m.

ARGENTINE ACCESS Access to the Argentine side of the mountain starts from the village of Fiambalá (see below) in the province of Catamarca. The approach is much longer than from the Chilean side but there is more fresh water and it is possible to arrange mules in advance in Fiambalá. The trailhead is at the refugio Quemadito near Cazadero Grande (3600m) in the Valle de Chaschuil. From here follow the Rio Cazadero W, staying high above the N bank for the first 2h., to reach a major junction of streams, 4h. total. Turn N here and follow this river for 1-2h. to its source at Aguas Calientes (4200m), various campsites possible. Then another 6-7h. on faint trails up dry quebradas gets you to Agua del Vicuña at 4950m - no water. This is sometimes as far as mules can go. Allow 3-4 hours more to reach a base camp between Medusa and Volcan del Viento at 5500m.

Some parties continue down to a large sandy plain known as El Arenal (5400m) a bit closer to Ojos, and it is also now possible to drive to this spot as well, via Coipa, Lag. de los Aparejos and the Rio Cazadero. This is an extremely long and complex 4x4 drive and should only be attempted by experts, over 8h.of driving at little more than walking speed. End of 4x4 drive 27°10'38" 68°29'46"

CHILEAN CLIMB The grade of PD is justified only by the summit rock tower, c. 30m, III. From the lower refugio the track to the higher hut is wide and obvious, 3-4h. From here climb a path up steep screes then make a rising traverse above a snow patch and around a shoulder to the right to reach the crater, 4-5h. The route then crosses the LHS of the crater on blocks and boulders to the bottom of a gully/chimney. Climb the chimney for 15m (III) then the ridge for 20m to reach the Chilean summit, 2-3h. more, some fixed ropes in place.

Ojos del Salado
from the N
Chilean side

ARGENTINE CLIMB From the sandy plain of El Arenal on the Argentine side some variation is possible but climb up the valley to the NW. A high camp at the stream junction at 5750m or a bit higher on the slopes at 6000m is usual, 2-3h. From here climb the steep snow slopes above to the wide bowl at 6400m SE of the summit, passing the worlds highest lake, then finally easy boulder slopes to the summit, 6-8h. The ascent is technically easier than the Chilean ascent.

OTHER PEAKS The western top about 2km away is 6720m.

KEY WAYPOINTS – CHILEAN SIDE Refugio at 5250m 27°00'33" 68°32'51" Refugio at 5800m 27°05'14" 68°32'20" 6500m 27°06'14" 68°32'35" Crater Edge 27°06'24" 68°32'39" Chilean summit 27°06'34" 68°32'24"

KEY WAYPOINTS – ARGENTINE SIDE Quemadito 27°22'15" 68°13'28" River junction 27°20'45" 68°20'21" Aguas Calientes 27°18'54" 68°20'15" Agua del Vicuña 27°11'52" 68°25'49" Camp at 5500m 27°09'38" 68°28'06" High Camp at 5750m 27°07'56" 68°31'09" Argentine summit 27°06'35" 68°32'30"

BEST MAPS Sheet 2700-6830, 'Nevado Ojos del Salado' 1:50,000 for the Chilean side. For Argentine side AIGM 1:250,000 sheet 2769-IV y III 'Fiambala'. Watch out for 200m contours!

Ojos del Salado
from the E

Argentine side

high camp

The summit pitch at 6800m on Ojos del Salado

FIAMBALÁ Base town for the Argentine Puna   1500m

This small Argentine town has basic facilities for organising an expedition into the Argentine Puna and is the best place to start if you're heading for Ojos, Cazadero, Pissis or Incahuasi. There are daily buses here from the provincial capital of Catamarca. Food and fuel can be bought and mules and mountain transport can be arranged through Jonson Reynoso, who knows the Puna very well. He can be contacted through the DirectTV offices on the NW corner of the plaza, or through his daughter Ruth who runs a climbers hostal. In the past permission was sometimes necessary for climbing peaks in the nearby Argentine Puna and this was obtained, quite quickly and free, from the Tourist Office in the Hotel Municipal and a separate permit from the Gendarmeria on the Tinogasta road. However in 2013 this was no longer required.

Nevado de SAN FRANCISCO 6018m   1 day   F

San Francisco lies immediately S of the main asphalted road at the Paso San Francisco (4720m) and can be climbed from there in one day making it probably the easiest and most accessible 6000m peak in the world.

ACCESS See map on page 225. Drive to Paso San Francisco from either Copiapó in Chile or Fiambala in Argentina.

CLIMB By the N slopes from the pass. Hard work up a steep path, then some loose scree for the final 100m or so, 5-6h. There is normally no snow.

OTHER PEAKS On the N side of the pass is the more attractive **dos Conos 5880m F,** which can also be climbed in one day. Drive up an old mine road to about 5200m then straight up over scree and snow to the summit.

SUMMIT WAYPOINT 26°55'10" 68°15'44"

BEST MAP ChIGM sheet 2645-6815 'Paso de San Francisco', 1:50,000.

San Francisco from the E

San Francisco from the N

Nevado de INCAHUASI 6621m 3 days F
Cerro el FRAILE 6061m 4 days F

Incahuasi is one of the highest peaks in the Andes, named after the Inca ruin discovered on the summit in 1913. There is a large snow filled crater to the S of the summit. Logistically Incahuasi is much easier to climb from the Argentine side. El Fraile is Spanish for friar. There is very little snow on either peak.

CHILEAN ACCESS See map on page 225. As for Ojos del Salado along the Paso San Francisco road to a base camp at the Lag. Verde. Both peaks can be climbed from here - allow about 2-3 days each. It may be possible to get closer in a 4x4.

ARGENTINE ACCESS For the Argentine side of Incahuasi drive SW from the border post at Las Grutas to reach about 5000m on the N side of the mountain. It's also possible to walk up the Rio de Las Lozas to the S side of mountains, no water after first 10km, 2d.

INCAHUASI CLIMBS The easiest and most popular route is by the NE slopes from Las Grutas in Argentina. From the end of the track climb to a high camp at 5700m in the col with a subsidiary peak, 4-5h. There is usually snow here. From this camp climb by steep paths to the summit in 6-8h. Incahuasi can also be climbed easily by the NW ridge from Chile or by the S slopes from the Las Lozas valley.

EL FRAILE CLIMB El Fraile is an easy climb too, better done from the NW in Chile.

INCAHUASI WAYPOINTS NE base camp 26°59'11" 68°16'16" NE high camp 27°02'04" 68°16'18"

Plateau edge 27°01'56" 68°16'56" Summit 27°02'02" 68°17'46"

BEST MAP ChIGM sheet 2700-6815 'Cerro El Fraile' 1:50,000. ChIGM sheet 2645-6815, 'Paso de San Francisco' 1:50,000 shows the Lag. Verde and would be useful for the approaches. For the Argentine side, AIGM 1:250,000 sheet as for Ojos.

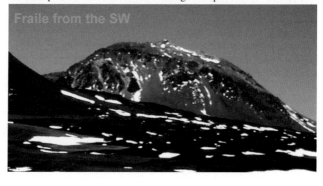

Fraile from the SW

Incahuasi from the NE

NE route

NW ridge

Cerro CAZADERO 6670m   7 days   F
Cerro NACIMIENTO 6470m   5 days   F

Cazadero is a huge, remote and little known peak lying about 10km S of Ojos del Salado. It is also known as Walter Penck after an early Puna explorer, and is shown as Nacimiento on the AIGM map. The real Nacimiento is S of Cazadero and marked incorrectly as Co. Bayo on the Argentine map! Cazadero means the hunter, Nacimiento means birth (i.e. source of a river). The slower, scenic access is given below, but both Nacimiento and Cazadero can also be approached in a 4x4 by driving N from Lag. de los Aparejos or Lag. Azul on the road to Pissis, saving a day or two. See the map on page 225 for access.

CAZADERO ACCESS Cazadero can be reached by following the Argentine Ojos access from the road head at Quemadito to a base camp at El Arenal (5400m), 3d., or by driving to the same point (long, difficult and complex).

NACIMIENTO ACCESS Easiest by driving N from Lag. Azul, relatively straightforward 4x4 terrain, to a camp at 5100m on the E side of the peak. On foot you can approach as for the Argentine side of Ojos del Salado to the river junction then follow the main valley W towards the Campo Negro pass. Before reaching this turn N to establish a base camp on the NE side of the peak at c.5000m, 3d.

CAZADERO CLIMB From El Arenal an easy ascent over two days with a higher camp at 5800m or 5900m on the E slopes. Several routes are possible on the N, NE, or E slopes. Very little snow. The summit is a confusing area of lava pinnacles. A GPS is useful to locate the highest of these, which is at 27°11'47" 68°33'39".

NACIMIENTO CLIMB From the 5100m vehicle camp Nacimiento is a long but easy climb by the E slopes over a subsidiary top, on a mixture of scree and snow, 7-9h. The highest summit is the one at the NW corner of the summit plateau, and may be as much as 6475m high. The 6436m spot height on the AIGM map belongs to the lower NE summit (actually about 6460m!).

OTHER PEAKS The subsidiary 6000m peak of **Volcan Olmedo 6240m,** is a striking cone on the SE flank of Cazadero. It can be climbed easily from El Arenal in one day, via the col with Cazadero, about 5-6h.

CAZADERO WAYPOINTS See under Ojos for waypoints on the Rio Cazadero approach trek. End of 4x4 drive 27°10'38" 68°29'46" High camp 27°11'33" 68°31'46" Start of valley 27°11'19" 68°32'29" Summit pinnacle 27°11'47" 68°33'39"

NACIMIENTO WAYPOINTS 4x4 camp at 5100m 27°17'32" 68°28'33" NE Summit 27°16'50" 68°30'47" NW, highest, summit 27°16'52" 68°31'28"

BEST MAP AIGM 1:250,000 sheets as for Ojos.

Cazadero from the E

summit

camp

Base camp at El Arenal

Olmedo

Nacimiento

Nacimiento from the E

Monte **PISSIS** 6793m   4 days   F

Pissis is the third highest summit in the Andes. There are several big summits on the extensive summit ridge, which runs roughly W to E. The highest is the W summit, but the two central summits are only just lower at 6785m and 6780m. Although it has more snow and ice than other peaks in the area Pissis is still an easy ascent. It is one of the few peaks in the Puna that makes a good, but challenging, ski-mountaineering ascent. The mountain is named after a French scientist.

ACCESS Drive by 4x4 from Fiambalá and the Valle de Chaschuil, turning off the main road at Coipa and passing Lag. de Los Aparejos, Lag. Azul and the S end of the Salina de la Laguna Verde, then finally off-road to a base camp (4600m - no water, but usually snow) in the valley below the main glacier on the N side of Pissis. Total drive about 80km from Coipa, first by a bulldozed track, then poor tracks in quebradas. Access is also possible from Jagüe to the S although this will be very long (see under Bonete).

CLIMB One or two higher camps will be necessary; there are good sites at 5400m and 5900m. The most attractive route is on the N glacier. Follow scree slopes to the E of the large glacier then traverse

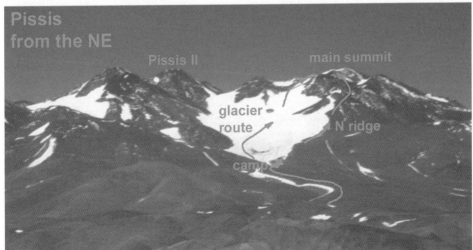

Pissis from the NE

Pissis II

main summit

glacier route

N ridge

camp

the glacier (some small crevasses) to climb direct to the main W peak. If snow conditions are bad on the glacier it can be avoided by climbing the N ridge on the RHS of the glacier all the way to the summit, some variation is possible higher up.

If approaching from the S side establish a camp by lakes at 5250m, then climb the steep S slopes directly.

OTHER PEAKS The central summit **Pissis II, 6785m,** also known as UPAME can be climbed from the same high camp at 5900m by its NE ridge or by climbing the glacier to the col with the main summit at 6400m then up the NW slopes. **Nacimiento del Jague 5829m,** F is a fine viewpoint climbed in one day from camps to the NW.

KEY WAYPOINTS Base camp 27°42'50" 68°42'38" Camp one 27°44'25" 68°45'32" Camp two 27°45'21" 68°46'03" Summit 27°45'20" 68°47'54" Summit of Pissis II 27°46'10" 68°46'54"

BEST MAP AIGM sheet 2769-34, 'Monte Pissis' 1:100,000 and the larger scale sheet 2769-IV y III, 'Fiambalá' 1:250,000.

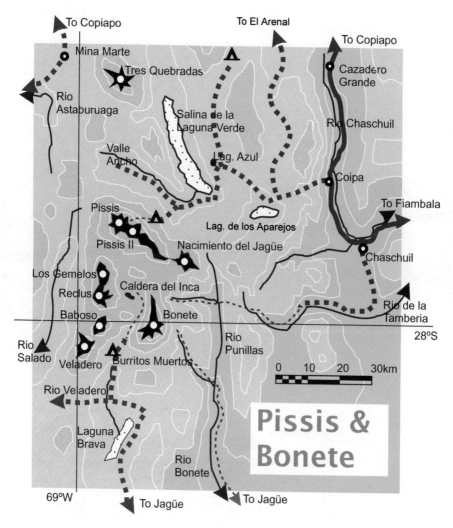

Cerro BONETE 6759m
4 days   F

Bonete is probably the 4th highest peaks in the Andes. The peak is a very easy ascent normally with very little snow lying. The summit massif is complex with two main tops, the S top is the highest.

This peak was for many years (and still is) marked as Bonete Chico (Little Bonete) on Argentine maps, giving rise to much confusion because a much smaller peak to the N is labelled Bonete Grande. To eliminate further confusion the simple name Bonete is used here.

ACCESS Bonete is best approached from the S via Laguna Brava and the village of Jagüe as described here. In the past expeditions approached Bonete from the N, E and even W from Chile, but all of these are no longer sensible options.

From Jagüe follow the new asphalt road past the Refugio del Peñon to the Lag. Brava. Then drive N past Lag. Brava to near the Ref. del Veladero and finally up the Veladero valley towards Lag. Caldera del Inca. With good conditions and 4x4 it is possible to reach dry or snow-patch base camps as high as the Campo de los Burritos Muertos at 5000m. This valley can also be used to give access to the peaks of Reclus, Gemelos and Veladero and the S side of Pissis. For the SW route described here a detour off this track to reach a base camp (known as Penitentes B.C.) at 5000m is recommended.

Bonete from the SW

Cordon de los Pioneros from the W

CLIMB By the SW slopes. From the Penitentes base camp at 5000m climb easily up a series of ramps and plateaus over small snow patches, with one or two higher camps possible, then more steeply up the final pyramid.

OTHER ROUTES It is also possible to climb the W side of Bonete from the Veladero valley starting up by a small valley at the extreme E end of the Campo de los Burritos Muertos and joining the route above from about 6000m.

OTHER PEAKS The Cordon de los Pioneros is a range of 6000m peaks to the N of Bonete, which includes four subsidiary 6000m peaks (with more than 200m prominence). The highest peak is known as **Pioneros, 6240m, F**. All four 6000m summits can be climbed from one high camp at about 5250m on the W flank of the range, reached in 4-5h. walk from the Burritos Muertos base camp.

BONETE KEY WAYPOINTS Penitentes base camp 28°04'01" 68°49'16" Start of steep climb 28°02'10" 68°47'44" Bonete high camp 28°01'46" 68°47'03" Pass cliffs 28°01'29" 68°46'18" Summit 28°01'07" 68°45'21"

PIONEROS WAYPOINTS Burritos Muertos base camp 28°02'12" 68°51'39" Cordon de los Pioneros high camp 27°58'21" 68°47'06" Pioneros summit 27°56'23" 68°44'51"

BEST MAPS AIGM sheets 2969-4 "Cerro Bonete Chico" and 2769-34, 'Monte Pissis' both at 1:100,000.

At 6600m on Bonete

Wading the Burritos Muertos river beneath Los Gemelos

RECLUS 6275m
LOS GEMELOS 6196m

4 days   F
5 days   F

These peaks lie W of Bonete in the Sierra del Veladero. There are extensive ruins on the summit of Reclus, including fireplaces, foundations, cairns and walls. Los Gemelos is Spanish for the twins; not surprisingly there are two summits. If you are in the area the spectacular Lag. Caldera del Inca is well worth a visit. It lies at 5100m in the bottom of a 300m deep volcanic explosion crater.

ACCESS See map on page 233. The best way into this area is from the S and Jagüe, with a 4x4 by the route described under Bonete to reach the Campo de los Burritos Muertos. These peaks have also been approached from Chile via the Rio Astaburuaga. For both peaks a base camp at about 5200m to the E or SE will be most suitable, reached in one days walk from the Campo de los Burritos Muertos.

RECLUS CLIMB An easy ascent by the S or SE slopes, with just a few false summits.

LOS GEMELOS CLIMB Easily by the S or SE slopes from the area around the Caldera del Inca.

BEST MAP AIGM 1:250,000 sheet 2769-III y IV 'Fiambala'. AIGM sheet 2769-34, and 'Monte Pissis' 1:100,000.

Reclus from the S

Cerro VELADERO 6436m
Cerro BABOSO 6070m

5 days   F
3 days   F

These two peaks lie SW of Bonete in the Sierra del Veladero. Baboso was named Veladero NE in the 2nd edition of this book. There is still some confusion about names and heights in this area and in particular the name Veladero seems to have been used for other peaks in the area. Baboso has a surprisingly large glacier high up on the S side, the peak was probably climbed for the first time as late as 2000.

ACCESS See map on page 233. The only realistic way into this area is from Jagüe, with a 4x4 by the route described under Bonete to reach the Veladero valley. From S of the Campo de los Burritos Muertos head W to high camps at 5000-5200m under the peaks, the terrain is generally all easy, 1d.

VELADERO CLIMB The easiest route is up the slopes of the S side, but with a bit of effort Veladero can be climbed from almost any direction. The NE ridge is also a good route.

BABOSO CLIMB The easiest route is by the SW ridge, an easy angled but narrow and scenic ridge.

BEST MAP AIGM 1:250,000 sheet 2969-II 'Tinogasta' and sheet 2969-4 "Cerro Bonete Chico" 1:100,000.

Veladero from the NE

NE ridge

camp

Baboso from the SW

Steak and salad in Fiambala

Nevado de FAMATINA 6097m   3 days   F

Nevado de Famatina, also known as La Mejicana or by the very cumbersome name of Cerro General M. Belgrano, is the highest point of the Sierra de Famatina range, an isolated spur of the southern Puna. The alternative name is that of a famous Argentine general. A ruined aerial cableway runs from the town of Chilecito to the old mine at 4380m on the peak.

ACCESS From La Rioja by bus to the town of Chilecito (1100m, all services). Then through the small village of Famatina (PT) via Corralles to a base camp (no water) at the abandoned Mejicana mine at 4380m on the E slopes of the mountain range. 4x4 necessary.

CLIMB From the abandoned Mejicana mine climb the hillside to the W on zig-zag tracks to reach the ridge at 4800m. Go towards the summit on the ridge, turning a knoll on the R, still on abandoned vehicle tracks. Behind the knoll stay on the ridge to reach the Lagunita camp (5050m) on a small plateau, usually with snow patches or a lagoon, 4h. From camp climb the RHS of the steep hillside behind on scree to a small saddle "La Montura" at 5500m, then continue up the ridge to reach a large plateau under the summit. Cross the plateau passing the beautiful Lag. Turquesa, and climb directly to the summit, easy, some small snowfields, 6h.

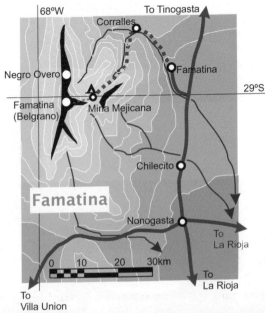

OTHER PEAKS To the north **Co. Negro Overo 6000m, F** has Inca ruins on the summit.

FAMATINA WAYPOINTS   Mina Mejicana   29°00'46"   67°46'29" Lagunita camp 29°00'57" 67°47'32" La Montura 29°01'09" 67°48'02" Lag. Turquesa 29°00'59" 67°49'00" Summit 29°00'51" 67°49'35"

BEST MAP AIGM 1:100,000 sheets 2969-24 'Sañogasta' and 2969-18 'Famatina'.

Famatina from the NE

THE HIGH ANDES

INTRODUCTION

This chapter covers the Andes from 29°S to 35°S and includes the highest peak in the Andes, Aconcagua as well as several other giants. South of 35°S the Andes make a sharp transition to lower peaks. This high part of the Andean chain is much narrower than the Andes further north and the mountains in many places form a single distinct range. Although there are a few volcanoes in the area most of the mountains are of folded origin.

In general the area is one of the best known in the Andes, though it is very little explored by European and North American mountaineers. Several of the lower and more accessible ranges, notably the Loma Larga and Vallecitos groups offer numerous alpine peaks with classic ridges and ice-faces. These ranges have been well explored by local Chilean and Argentine mountaineers, although many good unclimbed lines will still be found. Away from these areas are many unspoilt and rarely climbed peaks and probably still some unclimbed 5000m peaks. Aconcagua is the only really busy peak in the area, and it is extremely busy!

Despite being near some of the biggest Andean cities the highest peaks are relatively remote and all have long approach walks of several days. The low altitude of the base cities can lead to acclimatisation difficulties.

The area is probably the poorest in the Andes for seeing wildlife and traditional culture. It is on the other hand one of the easiest from which to organise an expedition as both Chile and Argentina are modern, well organised and relaxing countries in which to travel.

GETTING THERE

The two main options for most of this area are to fly to the Argentine capital Buenos Aires and then make a connection to Mendoza or to take an international flight direct to Santiago, the capital of Chile. There are direct flights to both Buenos Aires and Santiago from most European capitals, including London, Paris and Madrid, with flights from Rome and Frankfurt to Buenos Aires as well. Aerolineas Argentinas can offer good deals on internal flights if you fly into Argentina with them.

From North America there are daily flights from Miami, New York, Atlanta, Dallas Toronto and Los Angeles to both Santiago and Buenos Aires.

There are also flights from Sydney and Auckland direct to Santiago with Qantas and LAN-Chile.

For the northernmost peaks of the Agua Negra either fly to San Juan or travel via Santiago by bus or plane to the city of La Serena in Chile. Flying to San Juan from Buenos Aires is the best option if you are climbing Mercedario.

SEASON AND WEATHER CONDITIONS

The summer season of December to March is the climbing season in this part of the Andes. At this time of year the climate is in general very dry and stable - particularly so in the far N of this area, bordering the Puna. However storms lasting a few days occur several times a month even in summer and these can bring heavy snowfalls as low as 4000m. Strong winds are common all year at altitude and Aconcagua has a particularly bad reputation, with perhaps half of all days being affected by strong winds. Mountains on the Argentine side are drier than those in Chile but obtaining water is not normally a problem as there are plenty of large rivers.

CLIMBING CONDITIONS

In the far N expect conditions resembling those found in the Puna de Atacama - dry approaches and very high snowlines. Around Santiago and Mendoza climbing is about as similar to the Alps as it gets in the Andes, although snowlines in summer are much higher. There are large exposed rock faces (as opposed to snow and ice faces) and long sunny days can lead to soft snow in the afternoons. The nights are usually cold enough to produce a re-freeze. Penitentes are common, especially on N facing slopes. Snow lines are about 5500m in the N of the area, dropping to about 4500m in the mountains around Santiago, with some bigger glaciers on Aconcagua and Juncal as low as 4000m. Glaciers tend to be biggest on the S and E slopes. Because of the frequency of strong westerly winds many N and W slopes, such as the normal route on Aconcagua, are normally free of snow. River crossings can be a major hazard on the approaches to many peaks in this area - using mules may be necessary for this reason alone. On all but the most popular approaches it will be hard to find mules, and they certainly won't be available on demand, because there are far fewer people living off the land here than there are in the Andes of Peru and Bolivia.

OTHER GUIDEBOOKS
Aconcagua, R. J. Secor, The Mountaineers.
Guia de Excursiones a la Cordillera, pub. Turiscom. A recent Spanish language guide with some useful information on the bigger peaks and descriptions of many lower peaks around Santiago.
Montañas de Luz, Alejandro Geras, A nice climbing guide to the Cordon del Plata, with some information on Aconcagua too.
Adventure Handbook Central Chile by Franz Schubert. A good varied guidebook in English to all sorts of outdoor activities.

SAN JUAN A large and pleasant city north of Mendoza   650m
San Juan has all the services of a large city including supermarkets, good shops etc. There are two camping shops on the corner of San Luis and Tucuman. Mountain info can possibly be obtained from the Club Andino in a hut on a small un-named spur off Urquiza, 100m S of San Martin. The museum at La Laja in the northern suburbs has some interesting information on high-altitude archaeology and the mummy that was found frozen on the slopes of El Toro in January 1964.

RODEO A convenient base for the Agua Negra range   1600m
A small and friendly town 4h. by (daily) bus N of San Juan and the best base for trips to the Agua Negra mountains and Colangüil and del Toro. There are small shops, cafes and basic accommodation.

Cerro El TORO 6168m   6 days   F
Toro lies in a transitional area between the Puna and the High Andes of the Santiago-Mendoza area. A mummified corpse, with only the top of the skull showing, was found on the first modern ascent of Toro in 1964 and can be seen in the museum at La Laja near San Juan. The corpse was of a young man, wearing grey trousers, red cap and poncho. There was a wound to the back of his neck, so he was probably a sacrifice victim. Co. El Toro is Spanish for 'peak of the bull'.
CHILEAN ACCESS From the Chilean city of Vallenar (1d on bus from Santiago) through Alto del Carmen (PT) then up the river which becomes the Rio del Transito then the Rio Conay on tracks for a further 60km to the place called Conay, (1600m) (facilities n/k). From here follow the Rio Valeriano to a base camp at c.4000m on the NW side of the mountain. Much of this may be driveable in a 4x4.
ARGENTINE ACCESS Access was possible from Rodeo by various routes to reach the Baños de San Crispin SE of the summit, probably best to go via the Portezuelo de Conconta and the Valle del Cura. However there is a large new gold mine in this area and access may now be heavily restricted.
CLIMB Normally from Chile by the W side. Routes on the Argentine side are easy too.
BEST MAP ChIGM sheet SH-19-6 'Guanta' or AIGM sheet 2969-III 'Maliman' both 1:250,000.

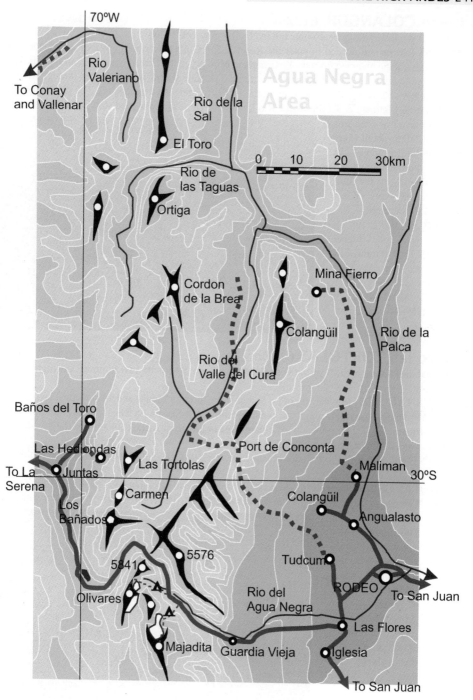

70°W

Rio
Valeriano

To Conay
and Vallenar

Rio de la
Sal

El Toro

Rio de
las Taguas

Ortiga

Agua Negra
Area

0   10   20   30km

Cordon
de la Brea

Mina Fierro

Colangüil

Rio de la
Palca

Rio del
Valle del Cura

Port de Conconta

Baños del Toro

Las Hediondas

Las Tortolas

Maliman

To La
Serena

Juntas

Carmen

30°S

Colangüil

Angualasto

Los
Bañados

5576

Tudcum

5841

RODEO

To San Juan

Olivares

Rio del
Agua Negra

Majadita

Guardia Vieja

Las Flores

Iglesia

To San Juan

Cerro COLANGÜIL 6122m   6 days   F

Colanguil is a little known peak some 60km N of the town of Rodeo.

ACCESS Permits are needed to enter the Reserva San Guillermo which covers the NE side of the peak. These can be obtained from the Environment Ministry in the Centro Civico in San Juan. It should be possible to climb the peak form the SE without a permit. Access is from Rodeo through Maliman (PT) and then the track on the R leading to the El Fierro mine (4x4 necessary). The reserve entrance is 50km from Maliman at 3200m by the Rio Lavadero. There are two good start points for the ascent

1. The Arroyo Los Ocucaros stream at 3400m about 15km N of the Ref. Lavadero. 2. A smaller un-named stream about 5km S of the Ref. Lavadero and more or less due E of the summit.

CLIMB By the E or NE slopes, with one higher camp, all easy terrain. The summit lies some way back across the plateau.

BEST MAP AIGM sheet 2969-III 'Maliman' 1:250,000.

Colangüil from the NE

Cerro las TORTOLAS 6160m   5 days   F

This peak lies about 30km N of the Paso del Agua Negra. There are two summits, the highest is the W summit.

CHILEAN ACCESS From the city of La Serena drive through Vicuña and towards the Paso del Agua Negra. Infrequent buses go through this pass in summer (La Serena-La Rioja service). Turn off up the Rio del Toro and drive to the abandoned mining area of Las Hediondas (c.3600m) on the W side of the mountain (condition of track n/k).

ARGENTINE ACCESS From Rodeo via the Portezuelo de Conconta to the upper reaches of the Valle del Cura.

TORTOLAS CLIMB From Las Hediondas the mountain can be climbed via the Paso de los Tortolas and the N slopes. A high camp at 4800m in the pass is usual. The climb is mostly scree but with some

small snowfields near the summit. The climb will also be relatively straightforward by the E slopes from the Valle del Cura in Argentina.

BEST MAP ChIGM 1:250,000 sheet SH-19-6 'Guanta' covers both sides of the peak in enough detail. AIGM sheet 2969-III 'Maliman' shows only the Argentine side of the mountain.

Tortolas from the S

Cerro de OLIVARES 6216m   3 days   F

This is the second highest peak of the group around the Agua Negra pass. Olivares lies on the border and is a 10km long N-S ridge. Access is very easy from either the coastal resort city of La Serena in Chile, or from Argentina via San Juan and Rodeo. It is probably easier to climb Olivares from the Argentine side due to the altitude advantage. There is a large glacier on the E flank. In Spanish 'olivares' are olive groves.

ARGENTINE ACCESS From San Juan to Rodeo by bus daily, then hire transport or hitch up the valley towards the Agua Negra pass. About 10-20 vehicles a day use this pass in summer. Leave the road at the Arroyo San Lorenzo (4100m) where the road turns sharp R. Walk up this valley to good camps at 4500m. There is now a mine road in this valley that may restrict access.

CHILEAN ACCESS From La Serena via Vicuña (PT) then on towards the Agua Negra pass. A base camp can be established in the main valley W of the peak (3400m)

OLIVARES CLIMBS From a base camp in the Arroyo San Lorenzo (c.4500m) two routes are possible. The first goes W up beside a small icefall to a plateau at 5100m N of the peak (camps possible). From here traverse S over two tops to the summit in one long day, F. The other route goes via the Port. de Olivares then the E slopes, glaciated but probably possible to find a route at F/PD. The mountain has also been climbed by the W slopes from the Chilean side on scree.

OTHER PEAKS The unnamed Olivares NE **5841m** which lies immediately N of the Arroyo San Lorenzo can be climbed by several routes on the S face on scree.

BEST MAP ChIGM 1:250,000 sheet SH-19-10 'Pisco Elqui' covers both sides of the peak in enough detail. AIGM sheet 3169-I 'Rodeo' shows only the Argentine side of Olivares.

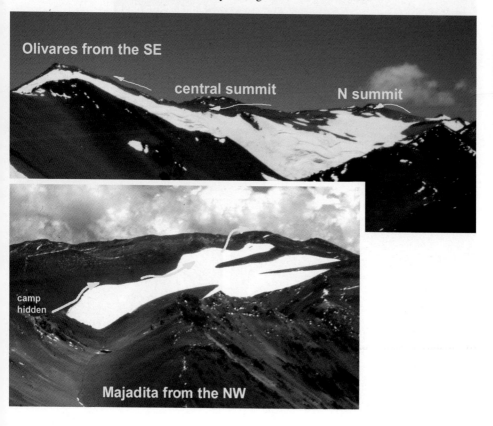

Olivares from the SE

central summit   N summit

camp hidden

Majadita from the NW

Cordon de la MAJADITA 6266m   3 days   F

This is the highest peak of the group around the Agua Negra pass. Access is very easy from either the coastal resort city of La Serena in Chile, or from Argentina via San Juan and Rodeo. On Majadita there is a large glacier on the N side.

ACCESS See map on page 241. As for Olivares but leave the main road at the Arroyo de la Pirca (3900m) a few kn below the Arroyo San Lorenzo. This can be difficult to find. It is a small stream coming down a steep slope at the W end of a flat sandy area. From Chile cross the Paso de Agua Negra and descend the Argentine side of the pass as far as the Arroyo de la Pirca.

MAJADITA CLIMB The best route is by walking up the hanging valley of the Arroyo de la Pirca, which usually contains water. Camps are possible at a flat area at 4600m. From here continue to the LH glacier tongue at 4900m and then up the LHS of the N glacier, either on the glacier or on scree beside it with a higher camp possible at 5200-5300m. Above this camp the summit becomes visible. The glacier is quite crevassed in the centre but these can usually be avoided, 8h. from 4600m camp.

BEST MAP AIGM sheet 3169-I 'Rodeo'.

Skiing down from Majadita, Agua Négra pass

Guanacos

Cerro MERCEDARIO c.6710m
8 days   F

Mercedario, the eighth highest peak in the Andes, is another of the high peaks which was probably climbed by the Incas. There are ruins at 5100m and at 6400m on the normal route up the NE ridge. With La Ramada and La Mesa the peak forms a huge glaciated cirque, nearly 15km across and facing NE. The native name for Mercedario is Lihue. The mapping in this area is very poor but recent satellite surveys suggest Mercedario is about 6700m high rather than the 6770m as often quoted.

ACCESS From the Argentine city of San Juan travel via the pleasant wee town of Barreal (PT) then on up the Rio de los Patos and Rio Blanco valleys to an abandoned mining camp at Los Molles (2300m). A 4x4 willl be needed beyond Casa Amarilla. The state of this road can vary from year to year due to snowfall, washout and mining company activity and permission is normally required to drive beyond the bridge over the Rio de los Patos. About 1km beyond Los Molles head L up the side valley of the Arroyo de la Laguna Blanca. Walk on the LHS, very rough at first, then steeply up to the scenic Laguna Blanca (camp possible - 3000m). From here easier walking leads to a ruined building at 3200m, 4-5h. Continue on an old track to the Guanaquitos base camp at 3700m, 2h.

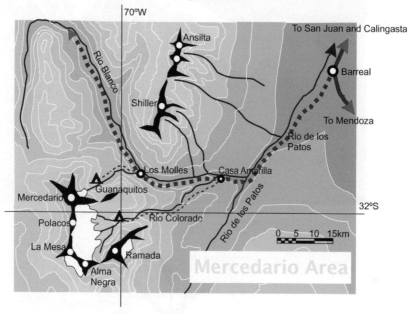

MERCEDARIO CLIMB From the Guanaquitos camp head up the Arroyo del Pilar on the RHS, passing a camp at 4100m to reach the Cuesta Blanca camp at 4500m under a steep slope, normally with many penitentes on it, 3-4h. Mules can then go no further. Continue up the dry hanging valley above then turn L and climb 100m to reach the camp known as Pircas Indias (Inca walls) at 5200m, 3-4h. From here climb steeply S on an obvious path to the high camp at 5800m at the edge of the La Ollada glacier, 3-4h. From this high camp climb steeply up to the NE ridge, via some black rocks called El Diente (possible high camp but not recommended), joining the NE ridge at about 6400m. Just beyond is a small wall, presumably of Inca origin. Go easily along the NE ridge, with great views of Ramada, Aconcagua and the Caballito glacier, to the summit, 6-8h. from the Ollada high camp.

OTHER ROUTES From the Guanaquitos base camp the **E face** can be climbed directly via the Caballito glacier (to 50°). One day up the main valley from Guanaquitos to reach the foot of the glacier. Climb initially by steep snow and rock slopes on the LHS, then up the glacier to a high camp on a glacial shelve at 6000m. From here easily to the summit.

The 2000m **S face** of ice and snow can be climbed (in 2-3d.) from a camp in the upper Colorado valley at Pirca de los Polacos. (See below under Ramada for access). It is quite hard, 40-60°, but both easier and much less serious than Aconcaguas S face.

OTHER PEAKS The highest point in the Cordon Ansilta to the N, **Co. Ansilta 5887m, F** is approached from Calingasta by the W bank of the Rio de los Patos.

KEY WAYPOINTS Los Molles 31°53'58" 69°56'25" Laguna Blanca 31°53'34" 69°58'51" Guanaquitos camp 31°55'42" 70°01'16" Pircas Indias camp 31°56'20" 70°05'25" High camp 31°57'28" 70°05'25" Summit 31°58'45" 70°06'45"

BEST MAP AIGM 1:250,000 sheets 3169-III y 3172-IV, 'Barreal' cover the northern approaches and the Cordon del Ansilta.

Mercedario from the NE

6400m, summit lies behind

El Diente

La Ollada

Caballito Glacier

camp

to Cuesta Blanca

Guanaquitos

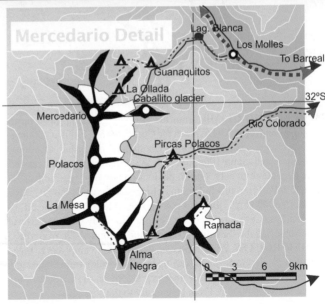

Mercedario Detail

Cerro la RAMADA 6384m
Cerro de la MESA 6180m
Cerro de los POLACOS c.5935m

7 days	F
7 days	F/PD
7 days	N/K

These three high summits lie S and E of Mercedario and form a massive and heavily glaciated cirque. Each of them can be climbed in 2-3 days from a base camp at the head of the Colorado valley, in an area known as Pirca de los Polacos. The heights quoted above are based on the latest satellite data, since no accurate mapping of this area is available.

ACCESS From Casa Amarillo walk with mules SW up the Rio Colorado (some big river crossings make mules essential) to a base camp beneath the N slopes of the peaks, 2d.

RAMADA CLIMB From near the base camp climb up steeply to the SE on a reddish coloured ridge to reach a high camp at the foot of the NE ridge c.5800m, depending on snow availability. Follow the NE ridge or glacier slopes on the L of the ridge to the summit.

LA MESA CLIMBS From the Pircas base camp follow the valley S between Ramada and Mesa to a high camp just under the col at about 5000m, 1d. From here climb the E ridge of the subsidiary peak **Alma Negra c.6120m, F** then continue up the SE ridge of La Mesa. the highest point is at the northern end of the long summit ridge. A shorter but slightly more difficult route is via the NE glacier, grade n/k, but probably PD/AD.

POLACOS CLIMB The steepest and most technical of the peaks in the cirque can be climbed from the Pirca base camp as well, by the NE slopes with a camp at about 4500m. Grade n/k but about AD.

BEST MAP AIGM 1:250,000 sheets 3169-III y 3172-IV, 'Barreal' covers the northern approaches. Sheet 3369-I, 'Cerro Aconcagua' covers the summits but is pretty much useless. A satellite photo at 1:250,000 is also available and a bit more useful.

Aconcagua

La Mesa from the N

Juncal

Mesa summit

Alma Negra

NE glacier route

high camp

NE ridge route

Ramada from the NW

MENDOZA A big city in Argentina near Aconcagua 750m

Mendoza is one of the biggest and most prosperous cities in Argentina and the normal base for climbing Aconcagua. Permits need to be obtained here in person. It is a very pleasant, clean and modern city with many tree lined avenues and pavement cafes. In the climbing season it is normally very hot and dry, though big thunderstorms are common.

SIGHTS There is not much to see in Mendoza but tours to the vinyards can be enjoyable. A walk round Parque San Martin to the W of the centre, with good views of the city from **Co. La Gloria** is a good half day trip. Otherwise hang out in the pavement cafes on Sarmiento or San Martin.

FOOD There are many supermarkets in the centre of town. Most convenient is probably the very large "Carrefour" on the corner of Las Heras and Belgrano.

FUEL Bencina blanca (white gas/Coleman fuel) is available in the camping shops on Las Heras or from Orviz (address below). Camping Gas can also be bought at the many general outdoor shops on Las Heras and on the pedestrian Paseo Sarmiento.

ROCK CLIMBING There is good rock climbing in an extensively developed area at Arenales near Tunuyan and a smaller area at Salto near Potrerillos.

MOUNTAIN TRANSPORT AND INFO Try El Refugio or some of the other outdoor shops on Paseo Sarmiento, or Turismo Aymara at 9 de Julio 983 or the Orviz shop at J.B. Justo 550. For information on Aconcagua go to the tourist office on San Martin (also where you currently buy the necessary permits).

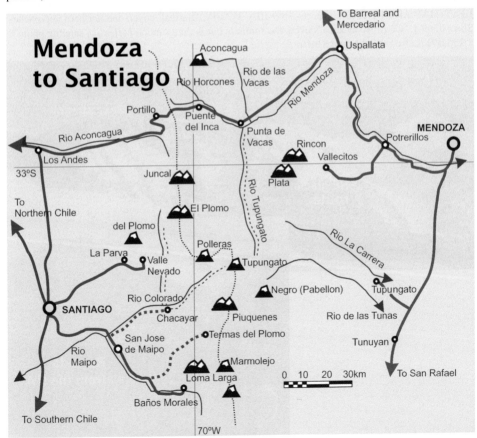

MOUNTAIN EQUIPMENT The best mountaineering shop is called Orviz, located at Juan B. Justo 532, but it is a bit out of town. In the centre of town there are several smaller shops on Paseo Sarmiento near the main square, but they tend to change owner and exact location every year or two!. These generally sell and hire ropes, plastic boots, axes and karabiners. Several shops on Las Heras sell camping and outdoor equipment and also do ski-hire.

Cerro ACONCAGUA 6959m   8 days   F

Aconcagua is the highest peak in Argentina, the highest in the Andes and in both the Western and Southern Hemispheres, and finally the highest in the world outside the Central Asian ranges. It also has a reputation as the highest peak in the world which is just a walk (i.e. no mountaineering skills are needed) but it should not be underestimated. The weather can be appalling, there are loose boulder fields at over 6500m and there is sometimes snow and ice requiring the use of an ice-axe and crampons. More people die on this mountain than any other mountain in South America, usually from altitude illness, exposure or both. While this is no doubt partly due to the large numbers attempting the mountain the lack of experience of many also leads to what is one of the highest death rates on any of the major Andean peaks.

The body of a guanaco was found high on Aconcagua in 1947 giving rise to speculation that the Incas may have climbed the mountain and giving the Cresta del Guanaco, which connects the N and S summits, its name. More recently the body of a pre-Columbian boy was discovered on the flanks of the mountain by Argentine archaeologists. The name Aconcagua means 'stone sentinel' or 'white sentinel'.

Aconcagua has attracted a lot of stunt ascents. Bikes have been ridden on the summit, and bears, cats and dogs have all been up to the top and motor bikes have been driven to 6500m. Fortunately the provincial park authorities do not allow such stunts any more.

Two routes are described in detail here **1.** the normal route up the Horcones valley and the NW flank of the mountain and **2.** the Polish glacier route up the Vacas valley and then the Polish glacier on the NE side of the mountain. Traverses are possible between these two routes once high on the mountain (5900-6300m) so in fact either approach can be used for either route. There is generally more water on the Vacas (E) side of the mountain.

Although ascents have been made in only a few days, the above time of 8 days should be regarded as a minimum safe time to attempt the normal route by a very fit party already acclimatised to c.4000m. There is a long approach walk and days will be needed for acclimatisation higher on the mountain. The Polish glacier route will need a minimum of 10 days. Average times for most parties are 14 days for the normal route and 16 days for the Polish glacier. If you can allow more time for bad weather you should.

REGULATIONS The regulations change regularly, and the price of permits keeps rising! At present they are very simple. A permit needs to be obtained for each member of the expedition from the tourist office on San Martin in Mendoza (normally open all week and Saturday and Sunday mornings). This requires basic personal details and a fee of many hundreds of US$, more in high season from Christmas to late January. You must attend in person with your passport and Argentine cash. The process takes only an hour at the most. The fee is supposed to include helicopter evacuation from base camps but they aren't always available. It also includes basic medical service at base camps, which are staffed by friendly and helpful rangers with radio communications and doctors.

HORCONES ACCESS Go from Mendoza to the village of Puente del Inca (2720m) (PT). Mules to carry gear to base camp can be arranged quite quickly here. The natural bridge nearby is worth a look. There are cafes, hotels, bunkhouse and camping at Puente del Inca. The 30km walk to the Plaza de Mulas base camp usually takes two days with a camp at Confluencia (3400m). The trail actually starts at the ranger station at Lag. Horcones (4km W along the main road then 2km N on a track). The trail is very easy to follow. Start on the L side of the Rio Horcones but cross by a bridge and go up the RHS. Cross the Lower Horcones river, which comes from the S face, by the bridge at Confluencia (3400m). This campsite, 3-4h. from the ranger station has good facilities in season. About 3-4h. from Confluencia you pass the distinctive Piedra Ibañez (3800m) rock. 1-1½h. walk beyond this rock a steep climb leads to the Plaza de Mulas (4250m) base camp, 6-8h. in total from Confluencia. There is a hotel, restaurants and organised camping here. Porters, mules, satellite phones, hamburgers, cokes and beers are always available in season, although everything costs lots of US$.

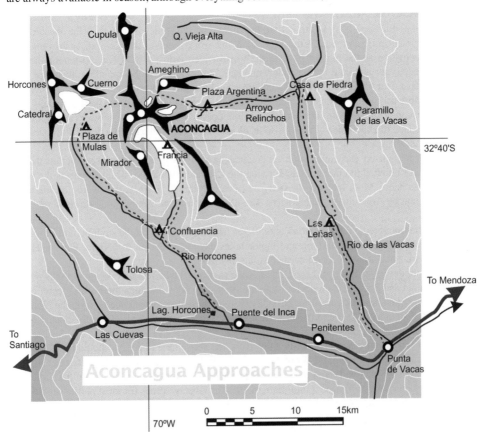

VACAS ACCESS The Vacas valley is a much more scenic and quieter approach to the mountain, but it is longer and therefore more expensive to hire mules. It is better to arrange mules in advance in Mendoza or Puente del Inca as far fewer climbers use the Vacas approach. The route starts at Punta de Vacas (2400m) where there are a couple of cafes. The village of Penitentes a few km further up the main road is a better place to arrange mules if you didn't do this in Mendoza. A good path starts on the W side of the river. It is 4-5h. to the first camp, ranger station and river crossing at Las Leñas. There is a bridge over the Vacas river here, about 1km upstream from the camp. Once across the river the second day is normally up the E side of the valley (no water) to Casa de Piedra, where the Relinchos valley joins the main valley, 4-5h. The third day is then usually up the Relinchos valley to base camp. The braided Vacas river is easy to cross at Casa de Piedra to gain the N bank of the Relinchos. Follow the Relinchos on a good but steep path above the river. After a steep climb of c.100m to reach a hanging valley cross the Relinchos river to the LHS and follow the wide flat valley to the Plaza Argentina base camp in the moraines (4200m), 5-6h.

Crossing the Rio Relinchos on the way to base camp, Aconcagua

NORMAL ROUTE Although there is no permanent snow and the route can be entirely over scree, an ice-axe and crampons may be needed and they should be taken at least to base camp. All refugios are in a very poor state. From Plaza de Mulas follow the wide and clear trail N for a short way and then E up vast scree slopes to Nido de Condores at 5550m, 8-10h. There are also poor campsites at 4900m (Camp Canada) and 5200m. From the Nido camp the summit and Canaleta can be seen at the top of the huge scree slope known as the Gran Acarreo. The route however continues E to gain the poorly defined NNW rib at 5950m - Berlin camp, 4-5h. Continue up the LHS of the ridge to the White Rocks camp at 6000m. Most parties go to the summit from either here or Berlin in one long day but higher camps are possible. From White Rocks weave up the ridge to the Independencia ruin at 6400m. From here to the summit hard snow and ice may be encountered in some years. Continue over the Cresta del Viento and then on a path across the top of the Gran Acarreo past a prominent vertical rock to the foot of the Canaleta. The Canaleta is a notorious unstable boulder slope which leads to the summit ridge at 6900m, best routes are on the RHS of the slope. Just below the summit ridge turn L and climb along just under the ridge to reach the summit, 7-10h. from Berlin.

POLISH GLACIER ROUTE, PD Two or three higher camps are usually made. From Plaza Argentina base camp follow a good path up moraines and through penitentes onto the rubble strewn glacier. Cross this (the route varies each year) and climb a steep penitente slope to the first good camp at c.4900m, 4-5h. This camp usually has running water (afternoons only). From here the route follows scree to gain the NE rib just L of the 5350m Ameghino col. Poor and exposed camp sites here at about 5600m. Follow the general line of the rib up towards the glacier, passing through or to the right of the rock teeth (several routes are possible here) to reach the high camps at the foot of the Polish Glacier, 5-6h. from the 4900m camp (several possible camps at between 5800m and 5900m).

The Polish glacier is usually climbed in one day from these high camps by the LHS passing close to the prominent banded rock face. This is called Piedra Bandera (6400m) because it looks like the Argentine flag (campsites possible here). The glacier reaches about 40° just R of Piedra Bandera. A variation weaves its way up the right and centre and may be easier in icy conditions (40°) and a harder (50°) direct variation takes the extreme RHS. All finish by the E ridge with many false summits and one short exposed section (this will be dangerous in high winds), 7-10h. to the summit. Descent is often made by the normal route.

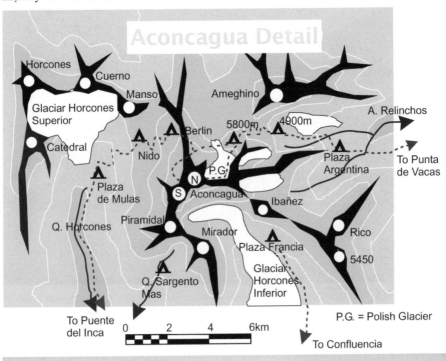

Aconcagua
from the W

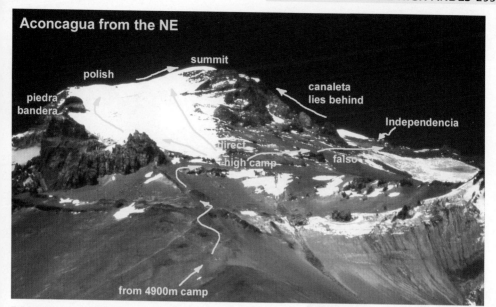

Aconcagua from the NE

polish
summit
piedra bandera
canaleta lies behind
Independencia
direct
high camp
falso
from 4900m camp

POLISH GLACIER TO NORMAL ROUTE AND VICE VERSA To gain the normal route from the Polish glacier high camp (5800m) make a rising traverse on a good path across the scree and snow slopes of the N face to reach the NW rib at 6300m (camps possible), just below Independencia. This route is known as the 'Falso de los Polacos'.

From the normal route the Polish glacier high camps (5800m) can be reached by making a rising traverse eastwards from Nido de Condores (5550m) across the scree and snow slopes of the N face.

OTHER ROUTES The **Ibañez-Marmillod route** makes a rising traverse of the SW face from Plaza de Mulas to gain the SW ridge by a huge 45° couloir. The **E glacier** route starts from 4900m above Plaza Argentina. There is a 60° section between the middle and upper glaciers. The route then climbs a 200m rock wall (to VI) then mixed ground to gain the E ridge at the top of the Polish glacier. The huge 3000m **S face** has seen many different lines and variations climbed. Most routes are very dangerous. Approach up the E side of the Lower Horcones valley from Confluencia to Plaza Francia at 4500m (this is worth the walk for a look at this impressive face). The French Route climbs the central buttress direct to the N summit (VI, 55°). The even more desperate Slovene route takes a direct line to the S summit (VI, 90°, A3). See Secor's guide for a description of these and other routes.

OTHER PEAKS From Casa de Piedra peaks in the **Cordon del Tigre** such as **Paramillo de las Vacas 5215m, F** provide good views of Aconcagua.

HORCONES ROUTE KEY WAYPOINTS Confluencia camp 32°45'26" 69°57'53" Piedra Grande 32°44'08" 70°00'03" Plaza de Mulas camp 32°38'50" 70°03'29" Camp Canada 32°38'38" 70°02'36" Nido de Condores camp 32°38'13" 70°01'47" Berlin camp 32°38'17" 70°01'18" White Rocks camp 32°38'16" 70°01'06" Independencia 32°38'46" 70°00'56" Summit 32°39'11" 70°00'43"

VACAS ROUTE KEY WAYPOINTS Casa de Piedra 32°38'04" 69°50'19" Plaza Argentina 32°38'46" 69°56'36" Camp one 32°38'18" 69°58'39" High camp 32°38'30" 69°59'51" Falso route meets Normal route 32°38'39" 70°00'55"

BEST MAP The 1:50,000 map published by Meridies and usually available in Mendoza is by far the best. Also in circulation is a useful sketch map published in 1987 by the American Alpine Club. The AIGM maps are dated, very inaccurate and are of absolutely no use.

Aconcagua and Ameghino from the E

Aconcagua S summit

Polish glacier

Ameghino

4900m camp

Ameghino from the SW

Plaza Argentina (hidden)

Cerro AMEGHINO c.5940m   8 days   PD/AD

Dwarfed by Aconcagua, Ameghino is nevertheless an impressive summit, with dramatic icefalls on the S face clearly seen from the Plaza Argentina base camp on Aconcagua.

ACCESS As for Aconcagua by the Vacas valley to Plaza Argentina base camp (4200m) and then the 4900m high camp.

CLIMB From the 4900m camp Ameghino can be done in one long day. Climb easily to the col at 5350m and then up the SW ridge. Follow this easy ridge on very loose scree, with one short section of about III, to the summit.

BEST MAP As for Aconcagua.

Cerro CUERNO 5400m   5 days   PD/AD
Cerro de los HORCONES 5383m   5 days   F/PD

These two peaks could be combined with an ascent of the normal route of Aconcagua and make excellent training peaks.

ACCESS Follow the Horcones access description for Aconcagua to the Plaza de Mulas base camp.

CUERNO CLIMB From Plaza de Mulas this snow and ice peak can be climbed by the S ridge.

LOS HORCONES CLIMB An easy ascent to the foresummit in one day from Plaza de Mulas by the SE glacier, some seracs and slopes to 40°. The traverse to the main summit is very loose and probably dangerous.

BEST MAP As for Aconcagua.

Cerro MIRADOR 5511m   4 days   N/K

The peak of Mirador lies S of Aconcagua and provides superb views of the S face. Mirador is Spanish for viewpoint.

ACCESS Follow the Horcones access described above for Aconcagua to the Confluencia camp.

MIRADOR CLIMB Climb by the Q. Sargento Mas, which ascends R from the Horcones valley about 2h. above Confluencia. A high camp can be made at about 4500m where this valley is a bit flatter. From here ascend steep screes to the Puerto Sargento Mas, then follow the NW ridge to the summit. Grade n/k but not too difficult.

BEST MAP As for Aconcagua.

Cerro PLATA 5955m   4 days   F
Pico VALLECITOS 5470m   3 days   F
Cerro RINCON c.5420m   3 days   F

These three peaks are in the range known as the Cordon del Plata. They lie S of the Mendoza to Santiago road only 50km from Mendoza. The range is quiet compared to Aconcagua although local Argentine climbers are quite a common sight. There are a few small glaciers but most of the peaks are rock scrambles.

ACCESS From Mendoza drive via the Potrerillos Hotel to the ski resort of Vallecitos (2900m) where there is a bunkhouse and mules can be hired to get to the Salto camp. From here walk up the hairpin bends of the service road to a prominent orange hut. Drop down to the small stream on the L, cross it and ascend the Vallecitos valley SW over pleasant alpine pastures to the Piedra Grande camp at c.3500m, 3h. From here a good path over moraines continues to the high camp (Salto camp) near the tongue of the Vallecitos glacier at about 4300m, 2h. There is often a tent at this high camp serving food and beer. Other camp sites, higher and lower, are possible

PLATA CLIMB From the Salto camp climb to the L of the glacier to gain a higher bowl (4600m), possible camps. Climb up the S slopes of the bowl to reach a col at c.4850m between Lomas Amarillas and Co. Vallecitos, turn R and continue up the ridge then continue over easy ground S and SW to the summit, traversing around the lower sub-summit of Pico Plata, 6-8h. from the Salto camp.

VALLECITOS CLIMB An easy scramble, grade probably about PD. Follow the Plata directions as far as La Ollada then climb the S ridge of Pico Vallecitos. Follow this to the summit, some scrambling.

RINCON CLIMB From the Salto camp go up moraines on the S side of a brown peak (point 4520m). Climb easily northwards on to the ridge (4700m) and follow this W to a snow bowl (5000m). Climb the easy and very prominent snow couloir on the RHS of the headwall then walk S to the summit across a broad plateau, 6h.

OTHER ROUTES The 'Supercanaleta' on Rincon is the obvious ice couloir splitting the E face. Many harder routes have also been climbed on the E face of Co. Vallecitos.

OTHER PEAKS From a camp at Piedra Grande **Pico Franke 4850m, F** can be climbed easily by a path on the N ridge, 6-8h. **Lomas Amarillas c.5050m,** can be climbed by the easy E ridge from Pico Franke or by the harder SW ridge from the 4850m col above the Salto camp. The guidebook Montañas de Luz, available in Mendoza, has details of ascents in other parts of the range.

Co. PLATA KEY WAYPOINTS Vallecitos ski resort 32°58'25" 69°21'31" Piedra Grande 32°58'50" 69°23'11" Salto camp 32°58'46" 69°24'52" Plata summit 33°00'57" 69°27'18"

BEST MAP There is a good 1:50,000 map published by Meridies and usually available in Mendoza.

Vallecitos and Rincon from the E

Vallecitos

Rincon

to La Ollada Vallecitos and Plata

to Rincon

to Pico Franke

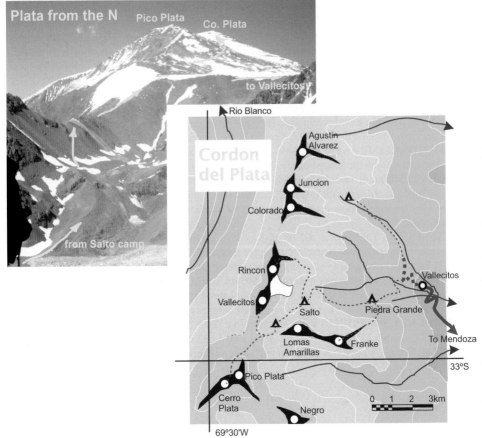

Plata from the N

Pico Plata

Co. Plata

to Vallecitos

from Salto camp

Rio Blanco

Cordon del Plata

Agustin Alvarez

Juncion

Colorado

Rincon

Vallecitos

Salto

Piedra Grande

Vallecitos

Lomas Amarillas

Franke

To Mendoza

33°S

Pico Plata

Cerro Plata

Negro

0   1   2   3km

69°30'W

SANTIAGO The capital city of Chile

600m

Santiago the capital of Chile, is a bustling city which lies at the foot of the Andes. On clear days (most common in spring and summer) it is possible to see the great humpbacked peak of Co. del Plomo 5424m, from the city centre. Access to the mountains around Co. del Plomo and the Maipu valley is very easy but the low altitude of Santiago can lead to acclimatisation problems.

The city is built along an E-W axis road, known as the Alameda (or O'Higgins) under which runs the main metro line. The smart suburbs and shopping areas are nearest to the mountains and the poorest areas are in the W near Estacion Central.

SIGHTS There is some nice architecture around the older part of town near the Plaza de Armas and Presidential Palace. Near the centre of the old town **Co. Sta. Lucia 634m**, makes a worthy ascent for a view of the city and surrounding mountains, ½h. The hill is a maze of pathways and bizarre architecture that is a delight to explore on your first day of 35°C, January weather! **Co. San Cristobal 880m**, with its funicular, gondola and huge statue of the virgin is another pleasant escape from the city fumes.

ROCK CLIMBING Several areas near the city have good rock climbing, and most are now well equipped with bolts. The most popular areas are about 1h. N of Santiago near the Panamerican highway. They include Las Chilcas, conglomerate rock and a lot of road noise, and the Torrecillas de Manzano nearby which are reported to be better. In the Cajon del Maipo to the S of the city there is more rock climbing around San Gabriel, mostly on granite and at Punta Zanza above Baños Morales. In the Yerba Loca valley E of the city there is more traditional rock and in winter some good ice routes. See the Adventure Handbook Central Chile for details and also a locally produced topo guidebook to the Las Chilcas area.

FOOD There are plenty of big supermarkets in Santiago selling a good range of food. Near the centre try those on San Diego, or near Estacion Central, or several in Providencia called Santa Isabel.

FUEL White gas (bencina blanca) can be bought from some farmacias. Camping Gas is available in most camping shops, e.g Casa Italiana at Prat 169 or the mountain equipment shops below.

MOUNTAIN TRANSPORT AND INFO Casa del Andinista at Almirante Simpson 77 or La Cumbre details below.

MOUNTAIN EQUIPMENT By far the best climbing and camping shop is called La Cumbre and is at Av. Apoquindo 5258, tel. 220 9907. Also try Patagonia Sport at Almirante Simpson 77 or at Santa Victoria 0220.

Santiago

Cerro JUNCAL 5953m   6 days   PD

Juncal is a high peak with the most extensive glaciers in the High Andes, the Glaciar Juncal Sur being 15km long. The highest summit is the NE peak, certainly over 5950m but with no accurate survey height. Juncal is often quoted at a height of 6110m, but it is almost certainly under 6000m high. It is quite a popular peak with Santiago climbers. In Spanish juncal is a reed bed.

ACCESS There may now be problems with this access due to a private landowner. From just below the hairpin bends on the main Mendoza-Santiago road at Estacion Juncal (PT)(2200m) you can drive about 5km on a track, then walk SE up the Rio Juncal. Take the RH valley after 8km and continue to a base camp at Vega Nacimiento (2900m), about 4h.

JUNCAL CLIMB The Italian route is described here. From Vega Nacimiento follow moraines on the LHS of the Glaciar Juncal Norte until at about 3500m, camps possible, 5-6h. Leave the glacier here and climb by a wide couloir parallel to, and east of, the glacier Juncal Norte to reach a high camp at 4600m on the RHS, 5-6h. From here climb a second higher glacier to the summit, finishing up the N ridge, 7-8h.

OTHER ROUTES Juncal can also be climbed by the 'Glaciar Colgante' route. From Vega Nacimiento follow the Est. Monos de Agua to the end of the valley (4000m) then climb the small glacier on the W side of the valley and the ridge above to join the Italian route at 5400m. Juncal has also been climbed from Argentina via the Rio Tupungato and Valle del Rio Plomo, finishing up the NE glacier.

BEST MAP ChIGM sheet 3300-7000 'Cord. de los Piuquenes' 1:50,000.

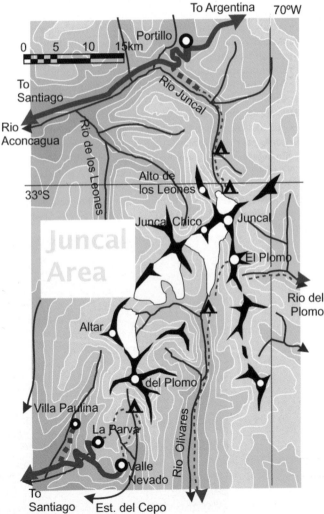

Juncal from the N — main summit — high camp

Nevado El PLOMO 6070m   10 days   F

El Plomo is the high border peak about 5km S of Juncal, and confusingly marked on the ChIGM map as Co. Juncal. To add to the problems there is a Co. del Plomo 5424m, much nearer to Santiago. There are Inca ruins near the summit.

ACCESS As for Tupungato up the Rio Colorado valley, then take the Rio Olivares to the N. There will be big river crossings on this route, 3-4d. to a camp beneath the SW slopes of the mountain.

EL PLOMO Plomo is climbed easily by the Chilean side from the Olivares valley. The normal route on the mountain is a walk up the W slopes. From the Argentine side climb by the N or NE ridge, technically difficult - approach via Rio de los Taguas.

BEST MAP ChIGM sheet 3300-7000 'Cord. de los Piuquenes' 1:50,000.

Cerro del PLOMO 5424m   3 days   F

Not to be confused with No. El Plomo 6070m, which lies on the border about 20km to the NE. This is the peak seen prominently from Santiago as a curving ice-cap. It makes a fine acclimatisation ascent with easy access and is one of the easiest big peaks of the High Andes to ski in winter. The summit was reached by the Incas. A mummy was found buried near the summit in 1954, the first such discovery. This body proved that warts existed in the New World before Columbus arrived!

ACCESS Drive from Santiago to the Valle Nevado ski resort (no facilities in summer). From here follow tracks to the hill at the top of the 4 person chair (3322m) or traverse slightly R of this to reach the Estero las Bayas valley behind. Climb up the far side of this valley keeping W of Co. Tres Puntas then descend Estero Las Yaretas to reach the main valley of the Estero Cepo. Follow this upstream past a camp by the large boulder at Piedra Numerada (3400m) and a very small hut at 3900m to the base of the SW glaciers, known as La Olla. Various camps here at 4000-4200m, 6-8h. from Valle Nevado. The Estero Cepo can also be reached from the La Parva ski centre but this is longer and involves a fair bit of ascent and descent.

CLIMB From a high camp at the foot of the glaciers climb the RH and broader of two ribs on rock and scree (or the snowfield immediately L of this if conditions are good). Move L at the top and go back over less steep ground to summit.

OTHER PEAKS About 5km N of del Plomo is **Co. Altar 5180m, F** which can be climbed by its W ridge in 4 days from the road end at Villa Paulina (to reach Villa Paulina turn L before the hairpin bends up to La Parva).

BEST MAP ChIGM sheet 3300-7000 'Cord. de los Piuquenes' 1:50,000. Sheet 3315-7000 'Rio Olivares' for access.

del Plomo
from the SW

summit
lies behind

high
camp

Cerro de las POLLERAS 5993m   8 days   N/K

Polleras is another high peak in the area and is one of the highest peak in the Andes not to reach 6000m! It lies on the border NW of Tupungato.

ACCESS A base camp at c.4200m below the SW face of the mountain in the Estero de Morado can be reached in 2-3 days from Punta de Vacas by the Rio Tupungato and Rio del Plomo. There will be some big river crossings. The Morado valley can probably also be gained from the Colorado river valley in Chile through the Portezuelo del Morado.

CLIMB Polleras is usually climbed by the glacier on the W-SW slopes from the upper reaches of the Estero del Morado in Argentina. Grade probably about PD, 2d.

BEST MAP ChIGM sheet 3300-6900 'San Jose de Maipo' 1:250,000

Polleras from the high
camp on Tupungato

Cerro TUPUNGATO 6570m

8 days F

Tupungato is one of the highest peaks in the Andes and the third of the big peaks in the Santiago to Mendoza area. Old Argentine surveys putting the mountain at 6800m are definitely erroneous. The peak is much quieter than Aconcagua but a very similar climb. Access is currently much shorter and easier from the Chilean side.

ACCESS From Santiago drive as far as possible up the Colorado river valley, via Alfalfal, where mules can sometimes be hired. A vehicle track goes for about 20km beyond Alfalfal to a place known as Chacayar, 2100m, roughly where the Estero Parrraguirre comes in from N. To enter the Rio Colorado valley permission is needed from the Chilean army, there are details of how to obtain this on the website www.difrol.cl. From the end of the road walk along the S side of the valley to a high camp at the Paso Tupungato, 4800m, or at about 5000m on the NW flanks of the mountain, 3-4d. There are some big river crossings, but they can usually be done without mules.

CLIMB An easy ascent by the very broad N ridge. About 5-6h. above the pass a high camp is often made on scree terraces at about 5600m. The whole route is open to variation and not complicated but involves a steep snow gully on the LHS at about 5900m, to gain the summit block.

OTHER ROUTES The N ridge of Tupungato can also be reached from Punta de Vacas or from the village of Tupungato in Argentina. Both routes involve 3-4 days walking and very serious river crossings which will need mules. The S glacier from near Tupungatito is also straightforward, the E glacier gives more difficult alpine routes.

OTHER PEAKS To the S lies **Tupungatito 5682m, F,** an active volcano and an easy ascent by the N slopes from the Chilean side (upper Rio Colorado).

BEST MAP ChIGM sheet 3300-6900 'San Jose de Maipo' 1:250,000

summit lies behind

Tupungato summit from the N

Cerro NEGRO 6070m

8 days N/K

Cerro ALTO 6148m

7 days N/K

Nevado de los PIUQUENES 6019m

7 days PD

These rarely visited peaks are outliers of the Tupungato massif. Piuquenes and Alto are on the border to the S of Tupungato and Negro lies entirely within Argentina to the SE of Tupungato. There is little information about these peaks. Negro is also known as Co. Pabellon, Piuquenes is also known as Meson San Juan.

NEGRO ACCESS The best route appears to be as follows. Follow the Rio de las Tunas from the village of Tunuyan in Argentina to get to the NE slopes of the mountain.

PIUQUENES AND ALTO ACCESS For Piuquenes and Alto approach from Santiago by the Rio Colorado (as for Tupungato - permission needed) to the Rio Museo, then follow this river up to a base camp at Vegas del Zinc (3100m), 1d.

ALTO CLIMB No definite details but the easiest route appears to be the NW glacier. Grade n/k but not desperately hard, 2-3d. from Vegas del Zinc.

PIUQUENES CLIMB From Vegas del Zinc follow the valley S to a camp at 4100m at the first moraine covered glacier. Climb the glacier E to a high camp on a large plateau at 4800m. From this high camp climb Piuquenes by the SW ridge on rock, scree and snow, 6-8h. Piuquenes could also be climbed from the Argentine side from the town of Tunuyan via the refugio Real de la Cruz (3000m)

NEGRO CLIMB Negro can be climbed from the NE. It can also be climbed from the Refugio Real de la Cruz by the Rio Negro valley. No details of difficulty, but not thought to be hard.

BEST MAP ChIGM sheet 3300-6900 'San Jose de Maipo' 1:250,000

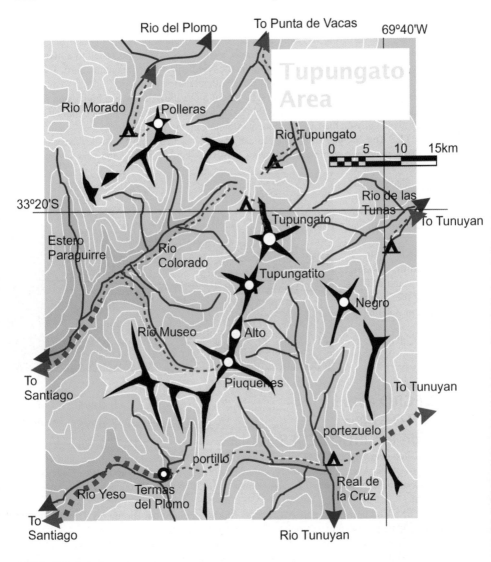

Cerro MARMOLEJO 6108m   5 days   F
Volcan SAN JOSE 5856m   5 days   F

Marmolejo is the southernmost 6000m peak in the Andes and, indeed, in the world. It has impressive faces on many sides but the W ridge provides an easy route to the summit. San Jose is an active volcano. The two peaks can easily be combined in one expedition with a base camp at La Engorda. Marmolejo is named after a Chilean general.

ACCESS From Santiago to the village of Baños Morales (PT) (1900m). There are a few basic shops, cafes and accommodation in this small mountain resort. Buses are very busy in summer. From Baños Morales follow the vehicle track up the main valley for about 5km and cross the river on a vehicle bridge (2300m), then follow a path N around a prominent ridge (El Morro) into the flat grassy area known as La Engorda (2600m), 2h. For San Jose follow the Est. de la Engorda for another hour, then cross it and climb up a small subsidiary valley to the refugio Plantat at 3200m (condition n/k), 3h.

For Marmolejo follow the Estero Marmolejo (Estero Colina on ChIGM map) N for about 10km (several river crossings may be necessary) to reach the head of the valley. Climb the slightly higher RHS of the col by steep snow slopes to reach point 4138m (erroneously marked 138 on ChIGM). There is good camping on the N side of the ridge here. An alternative approach for Marmolejo is from the Rio Yeso to the N. A bad 4x4 road from San Gabriel goes up the Rio Yeso to Termas del Plomo. Make a serious river crossing here and then an easy walk S up the Estero del Plomo valley to point 4138.

MARMOLEJO CLIMB From the col at 4138m follow the broad W ridge sometimes on scree and rock and sometimes on glacier (few crevasses) to reach the easy final summit cone of screes. A higher camp will probably be necessary near the glacier edge, 8-10h. in total from the col.

SAN JOSE CLIMB Climb easily from the refugio Plantat on a zig-zag path past the source of the Q. de la Engorda at 3800m, then up a snow couloir for several hours, exiting L to reach the normal high camp at 4500m, 6h. Continue climbing between two large snowfields to reach the W side of the crater rim, mostly on scree but with some snow. Follow the crater rim to the R to reach the highest SE summit, 8-10h. A higher camp at 5200m may be necessary.

BEST MAP For Marmolejo ChIGM sheet 3330-6945 'Rio Yeso' 1:50,000. For San Jose ChIGM sheet 3345-6945 'Volcan San Jose' 1:50,000.

San Jose in winter from the W

N summit   main summit

La Engorda

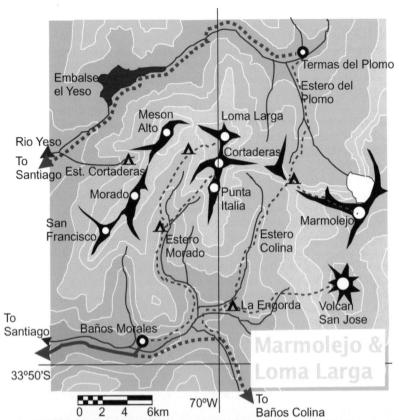

Embalse el Yeso

Termas del Plomo

Estero del Plomo

Rio Yeso

To Santiago

Meson Alto

Loma Larga

Est. Cortaderas

Cortaderas

Morado

Punta Italia

San Francisco

Estero Morado

Estero Colina

Marmolejo

La Engorda

Volcan San Jose

To Santiago

Baños Morales

33º50'S

70ºW

Marmolejo & Loma Larga

0 2 4 6km

To Baños Colina

Marmolejo and San Jose from the SW in winter

LOMA LARGA 5404m
MESÓN ALTO 5257m

4 days   PD

4 days   PD

These peaks are the two highest points of a compact group of peaks which give some of the best and most accessible 'alpine' climbing in this part of the Andes. They lie immediately W of Marmolejo. From a high base camp at about 4000m in the Morado valley a number of good days out can be enjoyed. The Estero Cortaderas to the W of the group should not be confused with the peak known as Cortaderas in the E. Loma Larga is Spanish for the big hill and Mesón Alto translates as the high table.

ACCESS For the majority of the routes go from Santiago to the village of Baños Morales (see Marmolejo above). From Baños Morales (1900m) follow a path on the N side of the main valley E then go N up the Estero Morado to a base camp on the glacier moraines at about 4000m, 1-2d.

Other routes can be reached from the Rio Yeso valley. From Santiago drive towards Baños Morales but turn off the road (to the N) just after San Gabriel and follow the track up the Rio Yeso to km17.

LOMA LARGA CLIMBS The Loma Larga is an E-W ridge with 3 summits of nearly equal height, but with the highest at the W end. This summit is climbed easily (PD) by the S glacier. For the Central summit (PD/AD) climb the same glacier but turn towards the Loma Larga - Cortaderas col then follow the S ridge. Similarly to reach the E peak (AD).

MESON ALTO CLIMB Meson Alto is a N-S ridge of 3 peaks, the N being the highest. The normal route is from the Rio Yeso valley to the W. From km17 (2100m) climb the Estero Cortaderas to the base of the glacier at over 4000m, 8h. Climb the lower glacier turning seracs to a camp at about 4500m under the prominent rock peak of Punta Saavedra. Cross the glacier to the N and climb up to the L of the summit by a couloir (PD) to reach the W ridge and then the summit. There are very difficult routes on the S face from the Morado valley (TD, 60°, IV)

OTHER PEAKS From a high camp in the Morado valley many other climbs can be done besides Loma Larga. These include **Cortaderas 5197m, PD** climbed from the Cortaderas - Loma Larga col (see above) by the rocky N ridge. **Punta Italia 4863m, AD** is normally climbed from the W from a camp at the tongue of the glacier. Climb by the RHS of the glacier to gain an easy couloir which leads

Punta Italia   Cortaderas   Meson Alto   Loma Larga

Loma Larga group from the E

to the Punta Italia-Cortaderas ridge. From here climb to summit by the N ridge (III). The N summit of **Morado 4490m PD** is the highest. It is normally climbed from the Morado valley by the SE glacier. From a camp in the valley climb an easy rock wall to reach a high camp by the glacier. From this camp cross the glacier to the N and climb the final cone by any of a variety of routes.

From a camp in the Estero Cortaderas (see under Meson Alto above) **San Francisco 4345m**, **F** can be climbed easily by the N slopes. The 1400m S face has a number of difficult routes.

BEST MAP ChIGM sheet 3330-7000 'Embalse El Yeso' 1:50,000.

Skiing into the hills above Santiago, with the Loma Larga in the background

Volcan MAIPO 5264m   3 days   F

An extinct volcano in a remote part of the frontier. Access is quicker and easier from Argentina.

ARGENTINE ACCESS From RN40 a good track leads to the Lag. Diamante E of the peak (3300m). Turn R here to reach the northern slopes of the mountain (4x4).

CHILEAN ACCESS From El Volcan on the road to Baños Morales a track leads up the Maipo valley for 20km to the Fundo Cruz de Piedra. Beyond this it is necessary to walk and permission is required from the owners of the ranch (Gasco). Mules can be hired here. From the Fundo Cruz de Piedra it is 30km to the Refugio Cruz de Piedra (2600m) W of the mountain, 2d, then a further day to reach a high camp at the Paso Alvarado N of Volcan Maipo (3800m).

CLIMB The ascent is easy, from either Paso Alvarado by the NW slopes in 6-8h. or from above Lag. Diamante in 1-2d.

BEST MAP ChIGM sheet 3400-6900 'Volcan Maipo' shows the peak and access on the Chilean side. The AIGM map is very poor.

Maipo from the E, in winter

Sunset over Tinguiririca

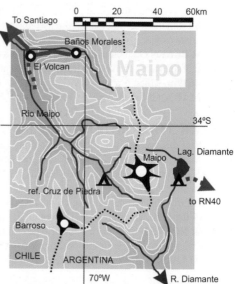

0   20   40   60km

To Santiago

Baños Morales

El Volcan

Maipo

Rio Maipo

34°S

Maipo

Lag. Diamante

ref. Cruz de Piedra

to RN40

Barroso

CHILE   ARGENTINA

70°W   R. Diamante

CHILE ARGENTINA

0   10 / 20   30km

V. Overo

Sosneado

Tinguiririca   4670m

4699m

To San
Fernando

Risco Plateado

Termas del Flaco

Rio Atuel

35°S

Sosneado Area

To San Rafael

El Sosneado

70°W   To Malargue

Cerro SOSNEADO 5189m   5 days   N/K

Sosneado is the most southerly 5000m peak in the Andes. It lies east of the main crest, entirely in Argentina. There is an imposing rocky E face.

ACCESS From El Sosneado north of Malargue drive up the Rio Atuel on a track (4x4 not really necessary). This is a beautiful valley and a great place to see wildlife. A good base camp can be made near the thermal springs at Termas el Sosneado, where there is a ruined hotel. A few km further up the valley there is a small refugio at 2200m, this is sometimes locked.

CLIMB From the Ref. Soler at 2200m ascents can be made by the NW ridge mostly on rock, with two intermediate camps.

OTHER PEAKS On the opposite side of the Rio Atuel from Sosneado is **Risco Plateado 4999m**. At the head of the valley the vehicle track climbs to an abandoned sulfur mine at about 4500m on **Volcan Overo 4619m,** which is a very easy ascent

BEST MAP AIGM sheet 3569-I 'Volcan Maipu' 1:250,000 is a very old survey but all there is!

Volcan TINGUIRIRICA 4280m   4 days   F

It was near this volcano that a Uruguayan plane crashed into the hills in 1972 and the survivors were forced to resort to cannibalism to stay alive, as famously recounted in the book and film 'Alive'.

ACCESS From San Fernando to the Termas del Flaco at 1800m on the Rio Tinguiririca, where there is a hotel and campsite.

CLIMB From the Termas del Flaco by the Rio de Las Damas to reach a camp at about 3000m on the S side of the peak. Then easily to the summit in one day.

OTHER ROUTES Tinguiririca can also be climbed from Los Maitenes (1350m) to the W. The climb is easy, via the Est. de los Humos and the Arroyo Fray Carlos and takes 4d.

BEST MAP ChIGM 3400-6900 'Volcan Maipo' 1:250,000

Ski Mountaineering by Sosneado

MAULE & THE LAKES DISTRICT

INTRODUCTION

If you like your mountaineering to be easy with mellow forest and field scenery, long warm days and cosy tea-rooms to relax in, then the Maule region and the Lakes District is definitely the place to go in the Andes. The peaks described here are mostly very accessible and can often be climbed in a day from a hotel in the valley.

This section covers the area between Volcan Peteroa and Puerto Montt i.e between latitudes 35°S and 42°S. The peaks described here are very much a selection of the most frequently climbed and more accessible summits as large parts of this region are well hidden by forests and have yet to be properly explored by mountaineers. The peaks in the south around Bariloche and the Lakes District are climbed very frequently, but some of those in the remote areas of the Maule district receive very few ascents. The most prominent peaks are almost all volcanoes with a modest amount of glaciation. They are generally very easy ascents, and make great ski descents, the main exceptions being the eroded volcanoes of Campanario, Velluda, Tronador and Puntiagudo. Some of the volcanoes are spectacularly active. Most notable in recent years for activity have been Llaima and Villarrica.

Few areas of good rock or challenging Alpine climbing have been discovered in this area, although there is some good scrambling and climbing in the Cordillera Catedral above Bariloche.

GETTING THERE

Access to the majority of the peaks is simpler from the Chilean side, and travelling north-south to climb in a variety of different areas is certainly easier on this side, with the Panamerican now being a modern freeway all the way from Santiago to Puerto Montt. For the Chilean side of the mountains the best way to get to the area is an international flight to Santiago and then by car or bus south, although for the southernmost peaks it may be worth saving time with an internal flight to either Temuco or Puerto Montt. For the Argentine side of the mountains fly to either Mendoza or Bariloche via Buenos Aires then travel overland.

See 'The High Andes' chapter for details of international flights to Santiago and Buenos Aires.

SEASON AND WEATHER CONDITIONS

The whole area is far enough south to experience quite noticeable temperate summers and winters, so December to March is the best time to climb in the area and August to October the best time to ski. The Chilean side of the mountains are much wetter than the Argentine side and even in summer it can rain for several days at a time. There is also a big difference in the amount of rainfall between north and south, with the south, especially beyond Pucon, being considerably wetter. Because of the lower altitude of the peaks the weather is rarely very extreme, but winters can be windy.

CLIMBING & SKIING CONDITIONS

The majority of the higher mountains are glaciated but crevasses are often not a big problem, indeed only Tronador and Osorno have major crevasse zones on their normal routes. Glaciers are larger on the south slopes of all the peaks. The snow cover is generally fairly soft and wet during the summer months and it will soften noticeably on hot sunny days. Summer snowlines vary from 3500m in the north of the region to just 2000m around Osorno. The upper sections of some of the highest peaks e.g. Lanin and Tronador can be quite icy at any time of year.

Ski-mountaineering conditions are generally at their best from mid-September to mid-October, when spring snow is likely to be encountered and day length is reasonable. In July and August the snow tends to be much more "wintry" with wind slab, rain crust and icy conditions common. Powder snow is extremely rare. Compared to the European Alps the snow tends to arrive in fewer, heavier storms, especially in the more northern part of the region.

OTHER GUIDEBOOKS

A good general Spanish guide to the Catedral range is available in Bariloche, 'Las Montañas de Bariloche' by Toncek Arko and Raul Izaguirre. 7th edition 1993. Also available in Bariloche is the walking guide 'Guia de Sendas y Picadas' published by the Club Andino Bariloche.

Guia de escaladas - Cerro Catedral by R. Garibotti has details of rock climbs in this range.

Handbook of Ski Mountaineering in the Andes, Frederic Lana, 2007, Belupress.

Guia de Excursiones a la Cordillera, pub. Turiscom. A recent Spanish language guide with some useful information on the Maule and Lake District peaks.

Adventure Handbook Central Chile, Franz Schubert, 2002, TrekkingChile.com. They also produce a nice series of topographic maps.

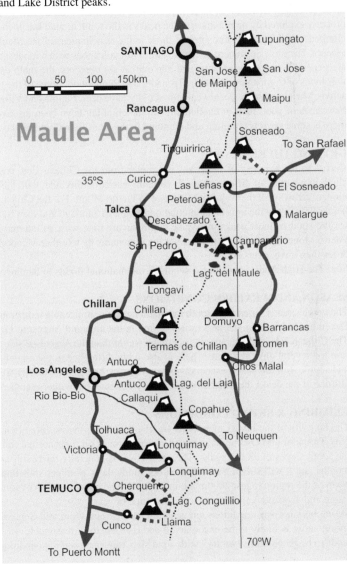

Volcan PETEROA 4101m

4 days   F

Peteroa is a highly active volcano, located in a beautiful and very quiet part of the Andes famous for its hot springs.

ACCESS From Curico by 4x4 up the Rio Colorado to the Baños de Llolli (1800m). From here a high camp will probably be necessary on the S slopes of the mountain at 3000m. Peteroa can also be approached by 4x4 via the Paso Vergara (2500m - also known as Planchon) to the N by climbing around or over

Volcan Planchon 3920m, F. From Argentina by 4x4 from Las Leñas to the Termas del Azufre which lie SE of the mountain.

CLIMB By the S slopes from Baños de Llolli, no details of exact route.

BEST MAP ChIGM sheet 3500-7015 'Talca' 1:250,000.

Peteroa and Planchon from the N in winter

Volcan DESCABEZADO GRANDE 3830m

4 days   F

Descabezado Grande is a very flat-topped volcanic cone. 'Descabezado' means headless in Spanish. It is the highest point on a very active volcanic plateau which includes the volcano Quizapu 2928m, on the slope of Co. Azul, 3788m.

ACCESS From Talca via San Clemente to the small settlement and summer recreation area of Vilches (PT - 1200m) and Vilches Alto. From here follow the marked trail to the Valle del Venado, crossing the Rio Lircay valley to the ruins of a refugio at 1800m, 4h. From here drop down W on a good path into the Rio Claro valley, 2h. Follow this valley SE until it is possible to follow the Rio Blanquillo E and then NE around a large lava field, passing the Lag. del Blanquillo to reach a base camp at the Vegas del Blanquillo (2000m, hot spring) in 5-6h.

CLIMB From the Vegas del Blanquillo climb by the W or SW slopes on snow and scree to the summit, 7-8h. Lots of bizarre white pumice makes this a very interesting ascent.

OTHER PEAKS The nearby **Co. Azul 3788m** could also be climbed from the same high camp. It will be an easy ascent by the N or NW slopes.

BEST MAP ChIGM sheet 3500-7015 'Talca' 1:250,000.

Cerro CAMPANARIO 3942m

3 days   N/K

Campanario is a steep and dramatic peak rising above the N shores of the Laguna del Maule. Access to this peak is relatively easy but the ascent of the final rock tower (c.200m) will be very dangerous and difficult. The rock has been described as 'solidified mud'. The peak is sometimes given a height of over 4000m.

ACCESS From either Talca in Chile or Malargue in Argentina to the Paso del Maule (2500m) where the road passes a few km S of the peak.

CLIMB No details known. It is not known if the highest point has even been reached yet, the steep remains of the volcanic plug will certainly be a challenging rock climb, probably grade D or higher. The N tower has been climbed by the NW spur. **BEST MAP** ChIGM sheet 3500-7015 'Talca' 1:250,000.

Volcan SAN PEDRO 3621m   4 days   F

Despite its apparent proximity to the central valley San Pedro is a remote peak that is only rarely climbed.

ACCESS From Talca by road up the Rio Maule to a few km beyond Las Garzas where there is a bridge over the Rio Maule (PT). Cross the bridge and turn R and drive a short way back W to the bridge over the Rio Colorado. Walk up the track on the RHS of the Rio Colorado to the Estero San Pedro, then follow a faint trail on the RHS of this river, crossing at about 1800m to the other side. The trail disappears as you leave the forest, 6-8h. from the Rio Colorado bridge. There are many places to camp, both higher and lower.

CLIMB From a high camp climb the NE slopes and ridge of the volcano, several routes possible, 5-6h.

BEST MAP ChIGM sheet 3600-7015 'San Carlos' 1:250,000 is adequate.

Nevado LONGAVI 3242m   5 days   F

Like San Pedro, Longavi is another remarkably remote peak that is only rarely climbed.

ACCESS From Linares to Pejerrrey (40km) where there are campsites and small shops. Then about 20km further to where the road (4x4) ends at about 700m. Continue up the Rio Archibueno and cross this (mules recommended) to reach the Estero Los Patos. Follow this river upstream, taking the R branch at the major fork at about 1200m, then bypassing a cliff with waterfall on the L to a high camp at 1800m beneath the NE slopes of Longavi, 2d.

CLIMB Easily by the NE slopes, 4-5h.

BEST MAP ChIGM sheet 3600-7015 'San Carlos' 1:250,000 is adequate

Volcan DOMUYO 4709m   4 days   F

This isolated and dormant volcano on the Argentine side of the Andes dominates the view to the E from many peaks. Domuyo is sometimes reported as the highest peak in Patagonia because it lies in the political province of Neuquen, but topographically this is not such an accurate claim.

DOMUYO ACCESS From the town of Chos Malal via Andacollo to Varvarco (PT, small shop and camping) then on a rough road to Aguas Calientes. A track continues about 10km further E to a parking area at approx. 2500m by the Rio Covunco.

DOMUYO CLIMB Follow the Rio Covunco valley, first on the N side then on the S side, up to the regular base camp at the third lagoon, c.3000m, 4-5h. Climb steep slopes on a good path then the E side of a ridge to reach a high camp by rock pinnacles at 3700m, 4-5h, great fossils in the rocks here! From here traverse up and over scree to a small col at 4250m, then climb the steep, usually snowy, slope behind to reach the crater with a small lake and cross this to the summit, 4-5h. from high camp.

KEY WAYPOINTS Aguas Calientes 36°40'36" 70°36'18" Parking 36°40'49" 70°30'52" River crossing 36°41'01" 70°30'04" Base camp 36°40'38" 70°26'45" High camp 36°39'42" 70°26'01" Col 36°38'54" 70°26'01" Crater edge 36°38'32" 70°26'04"

BEST MAP AIGM sheet 3772-II 'Las Ovejas' and sheet 3769-I "Barrancas", both at 1:250,000.

Domuyo from the SW

summit lies behind

high camp (hidden)

base camp

Skiing from the summit
of Volcan Domuyo

Volcan TROMEN 3978m   2 days   F

Tromen is sometimes quoted with a height of over 4000m.

ACCESS From Chos Malal to Lag. Tromen (2100m), NW of the volcano. There is a small refugio and ski resort on the W side of the lake, possibly only open in winter.

CLIMB From a camp at the SE corner of the lake climb on a path that keeps L of a dark lava flow. Above about 3000m the route becomes a rough scramble over rocks and scree in a gully to reach the summit plateau at 3800m, then more easily to the high point, 5-7h. from the camp.

OTHER PEAKS Behind the wee ski centre, **Co. Wayle 3296m, F** makes a pleasant ascent and a good winter ski ascent by the S slopes if there is enough snow.

KEY WAYPOINTS Camp 37°06'19" 70°05'31" Summit 37°08'26" 70°02'57"

BEST MAP AIGM sheet 3769-III "Chos Malal", 1:250,000.

Tromen from the NW in winter

Nevados de CHILLAN 3212m   2 days   F
Volcan CHILLAN NUEVO 3186m   1 day   F

The twin peaks of Volcan Chillan Viejo and Volcan Chillan Nuevo and the neighbouring summit of the Nevados de Chillan lie inland from the city of the same name. A ski resort on the S slopes makes for very easy access all year round. The peaks make interesting ski ascents in good snow conditions, although the chairlift company can be a bit obstinate about access.

ACCESS A good road now leads from Chillan to the ski and thermal resort of Termas de Chillan at 1750m, from where any of the peaks can be climbed easily in a day.

Nos. de CHILLAN CLIMB If the 'Don Otto' chair is running then this will save considerable time as it reaches 2500m. If it is not running then walk up the service roads. From the top of the ski resort head over lava flows straight towards the peak, dropping approximately 100m to a col, the Portezuelo de los Baños (aka Barros). From the col climb over a low foresummit (3000m) on the edge of a subsidiary crater before the final steep climb to the summit, 5-6h with chairlift, 7-8h without. There is a small glacier on the S side of the peak. The Nevados de Chillan summit can also be climbed more directly from Las Trancas by the SW slopes in 2d.

VOLCAN CHILLAN CLIMB Volcan Chillan is actually two peaks. The old 'Viejo' crater 3122m lies to the SE and the steeper 'Nuevo' new crater, 3186m to the NW. Both can be climbed easily by the SW slopes from the top of the Don Otto chairlift, 2-3h from the chairlift, 5-6h from the valley at Termas de Chillan.

VOLCAN CHILLAN WAYPOINTS Parking 36°54'11" 71°24'36" Top of Don Otto chairlift 36°55'16" 71°23'40" Col 36°52'18" 71°22'30" Crater Edge 36°52'08" 71°22'38"

BEST MAP TrekkingChile.com "Nevados de Chillan" at 1:50,000. The ChIGM sheet 3600-7015 'San Carlos' 1:250,000 is adequate

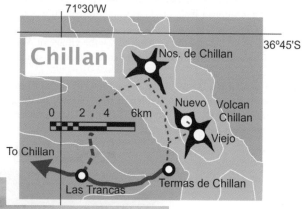

Nevados de Chillan from the S in winter

Volcan Chillan from the SW in spring

Volcan ANTUCO 2979m   1 day   F
Sierra VELLUDA 3585m   2 days   N/K

Antuco is a recent volcano whose last eruption formed a 200m high lava dam creating the beautiful blue Laguna del Laja. Velluda is an old eroded volcano with two rocky summits separated by a glacier saddle and is one of the most difficult climbs in the area. Antuco makes a fine ski ascent, and indeed the rough lava in summer makes a ski ascent preferable. It was first climbed in 1828, the earliest recorded ascent in Chile.

ACCESS From the city of Los Angeles via the village of Antuco (PT) to the camping area and forest park at Chacay (1100m). The road continues 4km to the small ski resort at 1450m, just before the Lag. de la Laja.

ANTUCO CLIMB Easily by the N and then NE slopes from the ski station, 5-6h. There is normally no snow on this route in summer, but there is a glacier on the SE slopes.

VELLUDA CLIMB The E summit is higher. The ascent is probably easiest by the N slopes from Chacay to reach the glacier saddle between the summits. Then by the W ridge, exact route n/k, 2d.

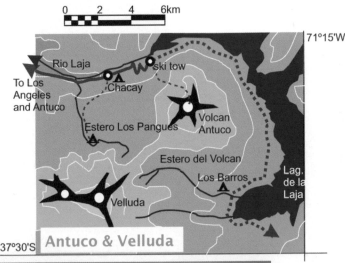

Antuco & Velluda

Antuco from the W in winter

Mixed snow, ice and rock, grade probably PD or AD.
ANTUCO WAYPOINTS Parking 37°23'17" 71°22'32" Top of ski-tow 37°23'37" 71°22'02" 2500m 37°24'03" 71°21'00" Summit 37°24'35" 71°21'06"
BEST MAP For Antuco and Velluda use ChIGM sheet 3715-7115 'Laguna de la Laja' 1:50,000. Also TrekkingChile.com "Antuco" at 1:30,000.

E summit

Sierra Velluda from the NW in spring

Skiing Volcan Antuco

Volcan CALLAQUI 3164m   3 days   F

A remote volcano rising above the upper Bio Bio valley. There are large glaciers on the N side.
ACCESS Travel from Los Angeles via Ralco (PT) to the Vegas de Ralco campsite. 2km N of the

campsite follow a path up the Rio Quillaicahue valley to a high camp at 1500m (or another higher camp at 1800m).
CLIMB From the high camp in one day by the E or NE slopes, exact details not known.
BEST MAP ChIGM sheet 3700-7030 'Laguna de la Laja' 1:250,000.

Callaqui from the E

Volcan COPAHUE 3001m   1 day   F

A volcano on the border with an absolutely spectacular crater lake at 2750m on the E slopes, flanked by an overhanging 100m high wall of glacier ice. Copahue is an easy one day ascent by the Argentine side. There are two summits, the W summit, entirely in Chile, is slightly higher.
ACCESS From the town of Zapala in Argentina by a good road to Caviahue where a large ski resort has recently been developed, continue to the small thermal resort of Copahue (2000m) (hotel, cafes, shops).
CLIMB Easily by the NE slopes from Copahue. Follow a track to a col on the Chilean border, 1½h. From the col climb the N or NE ridge directly to the 2965m Argentine summit, 3h. The impressive crater lake lies E of here and should not be missed. Then allow 1h to cross the other, snow filled, crater to the higher S summit, 5-6h. in total.
BEST MAP ChIGM sheet 3745-7100 'Volcan Copahue' 1:50,000 or AIGM sheet 3772-IV 'Andacollo' 1:250,000.

Copahue crater

Volcan TOLHUACA 2806m   1 day   F
Volcan LONQUIMAY 2865m   1 day   F

Two active volcanoes at the northern end of the Lake District. A subsidiary crater on the NE slopes of Lonquimay erupted on Christmas day in 1988. Tolhuaca is often spelt Tolguaca. Both peaks have partial craters blown out to the N.

LONQUIMAY ACCESS From Victoria on the Panamerican to Curacautin or Malalcahuello (PT) on the road to Lonquimay. Take the minor road 4km E of Malalcahuello and follow this for 7-8km past the old Ref. Puelche and on to the base of the new Corralco ski centre at 1500m. In summer it is usually possible to drive further up the track to a col at 1850m that lies E of the mountain.

LONQUIMAY CLIMB Lonquimay can be climbed by the E ridge in 4-5h. from the col. No difficulties and normally very little snow in summer. The highest point is on the SE side of the snow filled crater.

LONQUIMAY SKI Unfortunately the new higher ski-lifts have now made this a very short excursion. In winter the peak can be climbed from the top lifts (2400m) of the Corralco ski resort in just 2-3h., finishing by the summer route on the E ridge. The top section of the ridge is often too narrow and rocky to ski.

Lonquimay from the S in winter

TOLHUACA ACCESS AND CLIMB Access problems have been reported on this route in recent years due to new geothermal power exploration. From Curacautin follow the road to Lonquimay for 6km then turn off on a minor road which leads past a fish farm in about 15km to a fork in the road. Take the (4x4) road on the R which goes NE to the Laguna Blanca (1450m, good campsite). Climb up and round the RHS of the lagoon to gain the SE ridge of Tolhuaca, then continue easily to the summit crater. Lonquimay can also be climbed from the Laguna Blanca.

OTHER PEAKS Across the valley from Lonquimay the small peak of **Cautin 1975m, F** makes a good short ski-mountaineering ascent in winter by the SW slopes. 2-3h. ascent from the Corralco ski centre car park.

LONQUIMAY SUMMER ROUTE WAYPOINTS 1850m col 38°22'54" 71°33'23" 2400m 38°22'59" 71°34'34" 2500m 38°22'56" 71°34'48" Summit 38°22'47" 71°35'09"

LONQUIMAY SKI WAYPOINTS Parking 38°24'30" 71°33'02" Top of 2nd chairlift 38°23'23" 71°33'50" Top of top ski-tow 38°23'00" 71°34'34" Summit as above.

BEST MAP ChIGM sheet 3815-7130 'Malalcahuello', 1:50,000 ot TrekkingChile.com "Lonquimay" at 1:100,000.

Tolhuaca from the
E in summer

Volcan Lonquimay
from the E

Volcan LLAIMA 3125m 1 day F
Sierra NEVADA 2554m 1 day F

A very active volcano, Llaima was erupting through much of the 1990's and most recently in 2008. The name is Mapuche for 're-born'. The volcano is surrounded by beautiful monkey puzzle forests. The peak of Sierra Nevada is an extinct volcano that makes for one of the best and most interesting ski ascents in the Andes.

LLAIMA ACCESS From Temuco via the village of Cherquenco (PT) to the refugios on the W slopes of the mountain. The road splits at the national park entrance, from where the R fork leads to the old refugios and the L fork leads to the ski centre 'Las Araucarias' at 1500m.

LLAIMA CLIMB A one day climb up the W slopes, normally requiring ice-axe and crampons. The ascent is quickest from the ski resort but can also be made from the old refugios, about 6-7h. This is the best route for ski-mountaineering ascents in winter since the top ski-lift will get you to about 1900m, from where it will be just 4-5h. to the summit.

OTHER ROUTES Llaima can also be climbed from two places on the very scenic road which passes around the E side of the mountain through the Conguillio national park. This road also gives access to the peak of Sierra Nevada. Llaima can be climbed by the N slopes and NW ridge from at or near the Laguna Captren ranger station at 1300m, 6-7h. Also by the E slopes starting from the road just S of Laguna Verde, where faint 4x4 vehicle tracks head across the lava towards the volcano going as high as 1400m, 6-7h. Both these routes can be skiied in winter too.

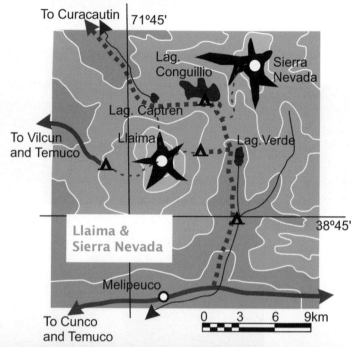

Llaima from the N in summer

Llaima from the E in winter

summit

Sierra Nevada from the W in winter

SIERRA NEVADA CLIMB Sierra Nevada can be climbed easily by the W slopes from the parking area at Playa Linda on the S shore of Laguna Conguillio at 1150m. From the car park walk a few minutes towards Playa Linda, then turn R and follow the well marked trail up through bamboo forest and along a ridge for about 2h. to reach the base of the mountain. From here climb a broad valley, overshadowed by big cliffs on the R, which curves up and R to reach the south end of the broad summit ridge. Follow the ridge N over a minor summit (2520m) to the main summit, 4-5h. total from the road. Follow the same route in winter, a beautiful and entertaining ski tour that always seems to have good snow.

LLAIMA WEST ROUTE WAYPOINTS Ski base station 38°41'08" 71°48'03" Top of tow 38°41'21" 71°46'52" 2300m 38°41'13" 71°44'44" 2600m 38°41'31" 71°44'16" Summit 38°41'46" 71°43'52"

LLAIMA NORTH ROUTE WAYPOINTS Parking 38°39'54" 71°42'41" Snowline 1800m 38°40'19" 71°42'50" 2300m 38°41'01" 71°43'40" Join ridge at 2800m 38°41'32" 71°43'57" Summit as above.

SIERRA NEVADA WAYPOINTS Parking 38°39'02" 71°37'10" Viewpoint 38°38'26" 71°36'16" On ridge 38°37'24" 71°36'01" At 2000m 38°36'20" 71°36'06" Plateau Edge 38°35'48" 71°35'35" S summit 38°35'27" 71°35'19"

BEST MAP Volcan Llaima 3830-7130 1:50,000, also TrekkingChile.com "Conguillio" at 1:100,000.

"Combat" skiing on the
ascent of Sierra Nevada

Fuchsia

PUCON A busy wee tourist town at the foot of Volcan Villarrica

Pucon is probably the most booming outdoor tourism centre in South America. Every summer thousands of Argentine students and Chilean families seem to descend on this tiny lakeside town to experience the great outdoors. In winter Brazilians now come in their hundreds with their snowboards. One day it will probably all be horribly commercial and tacky, but at the moment it is still quite a small and pleasant place.

SIGHTS The big tourist attraction of Pucon is Volcan Villarrica's spectacular crater, but there are also lots of opportunities for enjoying yourself rafting, biking, windsurfing or just sunbathing on the black volcanic sands of Lago Villarrica.

FOOD There is a big well-stocked supermarket on the main street.

FUEL Camping gas and white gas are readily available.

MOUNTAIN TRANSPORT AND INFO There are numerous agencies on the main street offering ascents of Villarrica. They don't know much about any other peaks in the area, but you might be lucky and find someone who does know something!.

MOUNTAIN EQUIPMENT Due to the large numbers of tour groups climbing Villarrica mountaineering equipment is relatively easy to buy and rent in Pucon, although as always in South America the quality is a bit suspect. Shops on the main street sell and rent ropes, karabiners, plastic boots and even some ski-mountaineering kit.

Volcan VILLARRICA 2847m   1 day   F

A spectacularly active and very accessible mountain. Villarrica is one of the most interesting ascents in the whole of the Andes and should not be missed if you are anywhere in southern Chile. Though the state of the crater varies from one year to the next you will almost certainly see red-hot lava. The crater is reported to be more active in the summer months. Standing on the crater rim is a powerful experience, with steam and sulphurous fumes belching out of the 200m deep crater, lava boiling and spuming in the lake below and a tremendous view out over Lago Villarrica and the surrounding peaks. There is a ski-resort on the northern slopes of the peak and the peak makes a fine and popular ski-mountaineering objective.

Due to large numbers of tourists climbing the peak and several fatal accidents in the 1990's the authorities sometimes control the mountain and for a while insisted on all parties being guided. The cost of joining a guided group in Pucon is approximately $80 but you'll be climbing at a very slow pace. The authorities are now more relaxed and it is possible to climb without hiring a local guide if you can "prove" that you have some experience e.g. Alpine club card and an ice-axe and crampons. Flashing a few bits of shiny climbing gear around at the entrance station may also help convince the park wardens. There are rarely any problems in winter as they will just assume you are piste skiing.

ACCESS From Pucon by a good road to the National Park entrance station. This is manned and access is restricted during summer (see above). There is a barrier to prevent vehicle access at night. Continue to the main ski resort complex above the forest at 1400m on the northern slopes. In winter the parking is usually lower and a chairlift takes you to this complex.

CLIMB Follow the chairlift that starts about 400m to the E of the ski complex to the highest lift station at 1850m. From here go up and leftwards for a short way, then take a more or less direct line to the summit. There are sometimes very small crevasses, easily avoided and not normally requiring the use of a rope. The top 100m can be icy and crampons and an ice-axe may be needed, 4-5h. This same route is the best option for a ski ascent in winter.

OTHER ROUTES Other routes are feasible on all sides of the mountain, although the S side is quite badly crevassed. The second easiest ascent option is probably by the SE slopes from the pass at Chinay (1264m) on the minor track above the Termas de Palguin.

OTHER PEAKS The next volcano east, **Volcan Quetrupillan, 2382m, F** can be climbed by the E slopes from Chinay above the Termas de Palguin, in one long day. Follow signs for the Laguna Azul along a well kept trail that follows a narrow ridge, until beneath the E slopes. Climb these easily. Quetrupillan can also be climbed from the Mocho valley to the N, but there may be access problems on this route.

KEY WAYPOINTS
Ski complex 39°23'30"
71°57'34"   Top   of
chairlift   39°24'10"
71°56'50"   Top   of
steep slope at 2400m
39°24'39"   71°56'29"
2650m   39°25'00"
71°56'24"   Summit
39°25'11" 71°56'30"
BEST MAP ChIGM
sheet   3915-7145
'Pucon' 1:50,000.

Villarrica from the N

top of chairlift

Volcan LANIN 3717m

2 days   F

The highest peak in the Andean Lakes District and a magnificent viewpoint. Relatively easy to access and climb. Lanin is an extinct volcano, the name is Mapuche for 'dead'. The normal route is up the NE slopes just inside Argentina. An ice-axe and crampons are usually necessary but there are no serious crevasses.

CHILEAN ACCESS From the town of Pucon on the shores of Lag. Villarrica by private vehicle or daily bus to the border, 2-3h. You need to pass through the Chilean border post but shouldn't need to officially enter Argentina. There are good campsites in monkey puzzle forest in the area of the beautiful Lag. Neltume but water can be scarce. The climb can then be joined (unofficially) without entering Argentina by cutting through the monkey puzzle forest from immediately before the border.

ARGENTINE ACCESS From Junin to the customs post at Guarderia Tromen (PT). There is an organised campsite here. The park wardens may ask to check your equipment and get you to complete some paperwork here. They have been known in the past to insist on groups having radios.

CLIMB The route is usually well marked and easy to follow. From the customs post at Guarderia Tromen (1200m) (or just before the Argentine border if coming from Chile) walk S through mixed scrub and forest heading for an obvious moraine with a crest-top path. This is the Loma Espina. Follow this path on increasingly steep ground to reach the very basic Ref. RIM at 2300m, 5h. No facilities and can be crowded. Further up there is another smaller refugio at 2600m, in poor condition, called CAJA (1h.).

From the refugio RIM go up and R over snow patches on the W side of the ridge above. At about 3000m traverse up and R to join the RH rib of a shallow couloir (rockfall). Climb the rib on good rock then pass through a shallow notch and continue directly to the summit over ice, 6h.

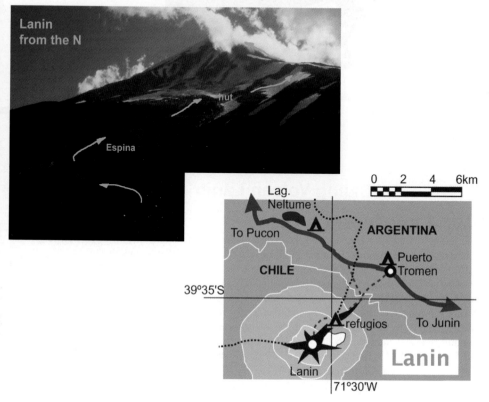

Lanin
from the N

hut

Espina

0   2   4   6km

Lag.
Neltume

To Pucon   ARGENTINA

CHILE   Puerto
Tromen

39°35'S

refugios   To Junin

To Junin

Lanin

Lanin

71°30'W

KEY WAYPOINTS Loma
Espina at 1500m 39°36'33"
71°27'47" Refugio RIM
39°37'00" 71°28'49" Refugio
CAJA 39°37'17" 71°29'19"
Summit 39°38'15" 71°30'10"
BEST MAP ChIGM
sheet 3930-7125 'Paimun'
1:50,000.

Skiing Volcan Lanin

Volcan CHOSHUENCO 2422m   1 day   F

The highest summit, a lava cone in the centre of the massif, is also known as El Macho. Volcan Choshuenco sometimes applies more specifically to the lower 2415m N summit.

ACCESS From the village of Panguipulli drive via the village of Choshuenco and Enco then on a 4x4 track to the Club Andino Refugio at 1000m on the W slopes. In 2008 the last section of the road above 600m was impassable except on foot, but rumours are it will be remade.

CLIMB From the refugio follow the old road SE for 1h. to the base of an old ski centre, then follow ski lift pylons to a moraine crest and up this to the glacier at 1950m. Cross the glacier NE to the final summit cone and climb this by the W or NW slopes, 5h. from the refugio.

KEY WAYPOINTS Refugio 39°56'13" 72°05'47" Old ski station 39°56'42" 72°04'36" 1720m 39°56'39" 72°03'00" Glacier edge 39°56'41" 72°02'34" Summit 39°55'56" 72°01'44"

BEST MAP ChIGM sheet G-122 'Choshuenco' 1:50,000.

Choshuenco
Macho
Tarantula
Volcan Choshuenco

Volcan PUYEHUE 2236m   2 days   F

An active volcano with a very large crater and some steaming fumaroles on the extensive summit plateau. There were some major eruptions in 2011 so conditions may have changed.

ACCESS Easiest via Osorno and Entre Lagos and then the good road up to the Paso Puyehue. Leave the road at the Guarderia Anticura (400m) (PT) border post. Walk to the settlement of El Caulle then take a new track rising NE up the lower slopes. Then follow a good path up to the ruined Ref. Volcan Puyehue at 1600m, 5h.

CLIMB From the Refugio the volcano is best climbed by making a rising traverse on to the W slopes, then cutting directly up to the summit, 2-3h. Normally no snow.

OTHER ROUTES Puyehue can also be climbed from Riñinahue on the shores of Lago Rupanco by the valley of the Rio Nilahue in about 4 or 5 days. The two routes can be combined to give the Puyehue Traverse as described in the Lonely Planet guide.

OTHER PEAKS Just S of Puyehue, **Volcan Casablanca 1990m,** can be climbed or skiied easily in a short day from the Antillanca ski resort at 1050m.

BEST MAP ChIGM sheet 4030-7200 'Volcan Puyehue' 1:50,000.

Puyehue from the S

Cerro PUNTIAGUDO 2493m　　　　　　1 day　　　N/K

A dramatic eroded volcanic plug and one of the most difficult ascents in the Lake District.
ACCESS Easiest from Puerto Rico on the S shores of Lago Rupanco.
CLIMB No details, but will be quite difficult.
BEST MAP ChIGM sheet 4045-7215, 'Co. Puntiagudo' 1:50,000.

Puntiagudo from the N

Volcan OSORNO 2652m　　　　　　1 day　　　F

One of the most beautiful peaks in South America and often likened to Fujiyama. Osorno rises above the SE corner of the beautiful Lago Llanquihue. Osorno is a much more serious climb than most of the other volcanoes in this area due to the presence of some large crevasses. A rope, ice-axe and crampons are essential. Permission is normally required to climb, obtained from the CONAF office near the Ref. Teski Club. Look for an interesting ice-cave on the N side of the summit.

ACCESS From 2km N of Ensenada a road runs up to the friendly and well equipped Ref. Teski Club at 1150m.

CLIMB From the refugio climb NNE beside a ski lift to reach point 1634. From here continue up a shoulder to the NE to reach the top of a scree cone at 2100m. Climb the glacier, crossing several large crevasses. Climb steeply up then trend gradually R beneath the plateau edge to find a way through the bergschrund to reach the summit plateau, 5-6h.

OTHER ROUTES Osorno can also be climbed by the NE slopes from the Ref de las Curas in 1d.

BEST MAP ChIGM sheet 4100-7230 'Las Cascadas', 1:50,000 shows the refugio and western slopes.

Osorno from the E

Volcan CALBUCO 2003m

1 day   PD

Calbuco lies only 25km NE of Puerto Montt. The summit has a small glacier. There have been some spectacular eruptions in the last century.

ACCESS From Puerto Montt via Chamiza and Correntoso towards Lago Chapo. About 6km beyond Correntoso take a L to Rio Blanco then go 2km to park at a fish farm at 350m altitude.

CLIMB Walk to the CONAF hut and cross the Rio Blanco on a bridge. Climb steeply to a small refugio at 1100m, 3h., then a further 1½h. to reach the tree-line at 1600m. From here cross open slopes and a ridge with a short steep rock step in it at 1800m, which often has a rope in place.

OTHER ROUTES Calbuco can also be climbed by the NE slopes from the El Ventisquero roadhead just outside Ensenada in 2-3d. There are sections of good trail and places where it is hard to follow and the route includes a scramble up a slab 200m R of a waterfall.

KEY WAYPOINTS Refugio 41°20'43" 72°38'07" Rock step 41°20'02" 72°37'22" Summit 41°19'47" 72°37'06"

BEST MAP ChIGM sheet 4100-7145 'Puerto Montt' 1:250,000

Chilean Plover

BARILOCHE A small city in the Argentine Lakes

750m

San Carlos de Bariloche is the undisputed capital of the Argentine Lakes. It is an affluent and bustling tourist city on the S shores of Lago Nahuel Huapi, full of skiers in winter and families and picnickers in the summer.

SIGHTS An evening stroll along the lake shore is about as good as it gets in the immediate vicinity. For a short day trip climb **Co. Otto 1405m** by a track up the E ridge, starting 1km W of the town.

ROCK CLIMBING There is some bolted rock climbing near the town at Cerro Otto in an area known as Piedras Blancas, a small guidebook is available in Bariloche. Around the Refugio Frey in the Catedral range (see below) there are a large number of routes and a good rock climbing scene. See the guidebook, available in Bariloche, 'Guia de escaladas - Cerro Catedral 'by Rolando Garibotti.

FOOD There is a good supermarket on Moreno. Bariloche is also famous for its chocolate!

FUEL Camping gas can be bought from outdoor stores and bencina blanca from ferreterias.

MOUNTAIN TRANSPORT AND INFO The best place to go is the Club Andino Bariloche (CAB) at 20 de febrero 30. A small cabin here is open every day selling maps and local guidebooks. They can also organise transport to the Catedral and Tronador areas. It may also worth trying some of the other tour agencies around town.

MOUNTAIN EQUIPMENT There are several good shops in town catering for climbers as well as skiers. Try 'Patagonia Outdoors' at Eleflein 27 or 'Outside' at Pasaje Juramento 184 or Scandinavian at San Martin 130. There are several poorer shops on Mitre and Moreno.

Monte TRONADOR 3491m   3 days   AD/D

Tronador is justifiably the most famous mountain in the Lakes District. A massive eroded volcano with some huge glaciers and ice falls it is the only truly Alpine peak in the area and attracts considerable numbers of climbers from Bariloche and all over Argentina. Tronador means thunderer.

There are three peaks, the Pico Internacional on the border is the highest, the Pico Chileno summit is fairly minor and the Pico Argentino is the easiest to climb and most frequently ascended. The Internacional summit is also called Principal or Anon and is sometimes given a height of 3554m.

ACCESS The main summits are much easier to reach from Argentina. From Bariloche drive via Lago Mascardi to Pampa Linda (PT - bus from Club Andino office daily in summer). There is a hostal and good organised campsite here, but no shops. Follow a vehicle track N up the valley for 2½km to the Rio Castaño Overo. Cross this river and take a left fork onto a trail which climbs the N side of the Castaño Overo valley in a long series of zig-zags and leads on to a ridge at 1450m. The trail then follows the ridge past some camping areas at 1700m to the large Refugio Otto Meiling, (1850m), 3-4h. The refugio has 60 beds, meals and cooking facilities.

PICO INTERNACIONAL CLIMB From the hut traverse the glacier towards the Ref. Viejo until the S ridge (known as the Filo La Vieja) can be climbed towards a plateau beneath the col between the Internacional and Argentino summits (c.3000m). It may be best to stay on the E side of the ridge beneath the crest. From the plateau cross the bergschrund and climb a ridge on 40° ice to beneath the 'Promontorio' a notable rock prow a few hundred metres S of the Pico Internacional summit. Climb the Promontorio on mixed grade III rock and ice then continue along the ridge to the col with the main summit. This col can also be reached directly from the plateau at 3000m by climbing the 200m E face on ice/mixed ground of 55° (rockfall). From the col climb to the base of the summit block, then a 40m pitch of grade III leads to a ledge, then two more pitches on loose rock lead to the summit. Grade approximately AD/D, 8h.

Tronador from the SE

International

Argentine

E face

OTHER ROUTES The Internacional summit can also be climbed by the W ridge, from the Col Reichert (3171m) which separates it from the Pico Chileno. Make a traverse from the ridge onto the N face to finish up two pitches of 50°/grade III+.

The much easier **Pico Argentino c.3300m, PD/AD** is often climbed from the Ref. Otto Meiling. From the hut climb as for the Pico Internacional to the plateau at 3000m, then continue to the col above which separates the Argentine and Internacional summits. From the base of the rocky Argentine summit go R then ascend the S face and zigzag up to the summit. Poor rock, to grade II and a short ice-pitch, 5-6h.

Pico Chileno 3320m, PD is best climbed from the Ref. Viejo. Start up the S ridge (Filo La Vieja) until it is possible to make a high traverse NW over the Glaciar Rio Blanco to reach the SSW ridge. From here traverse to the Col Reichert then climb the SE ridge, 6h.

See the Toncek guide for details of more technical routes on Tronador.

The main peaks can also be climbed from the old Ref. Viejo (also known as Refugio Tronador) at 2270m on the S slopes. This is reached from Pampa Linda by following the Rio Manso and Rio Cauquenes to reach the Paso de Vuriloche. Go round the S and W sides of a bog on the Chilean side of the pass then pick up a trail leading N up the long SSW ridge to the refugio, 8-10h. A traverse can be made across the W glaciers between the two refugios.

KEY WAYPOINTS
Pampa   Linda
41°13'51" 71°46'17"
Onto   the   ridge
41°11'25" 71°47'33"
Campsites 41°10'52"
71°48'35"   Ref.
Meiling   41°10'33"
71°48'05"   Glacier
edge   41°10'21"
71°49'34"   2400m
4 1 ° 1 0 ' 0 8 "
71°51'02"   Pico
Argentino 41°09'35"
71°52'41"

BEST MAP ChIGM
sheet   4100-7145,
'Monte   Tronador'
1:50,000   or   JLM
mapas sheet 11

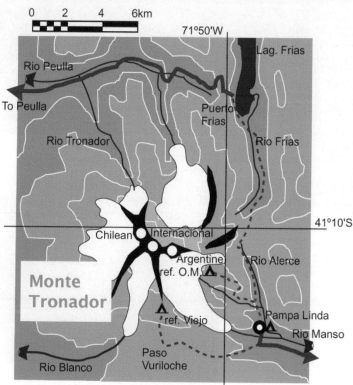

Cerro CATEDRAL 2409m   2 days   TD
Cerro CATEDRAL SUR 2388m   2 days   F
CAMPANILE ESLOVENO c.2300m   2 days   TD

These are the highest peaks in a range of dramatic granite peaks lying between Tronador and Bariloche. The range, sometimes called the Cordillera Catedral, is very well-developed for walkers with good paths, many refugios and lots of people hiking in summer. There are many rock pinnacles and needles amongst the peaks but only a few very small glaciers left.

The range is very popular with Argentine climbers and probably contains many of the hardest rock routes in South America. A climbing topo guidebook, by R. Garibotti, published in 1998 has topos for over 300 rock routes, from grade IV to French 7a+/7b on many of the pinnacles and towers in the area around Cerro Catedral and the Refugio Frey. The guide is for sale in Bariloche.

Catedral
route ascends
behind, IV

VI

V

IV

V 6a

V+ V

Campanile
Esloveno

summit

Campanile
Esloveno

Catedral Sur
from the N

CATEDRAL ACCESS By using ski-lifts the peaks could be climbed in one day, but it is more common to stay overnight in the Ref. Frey. Drive from Bariloche to the ski resort of Villa Catedral 1050m (PT). In winter this is a busy ski resort. From here there are two main routes to reach the Refugio Frey which sits by the small Lag. Toncek under the E side of Co. Catedral. The Ref. Frey is at 1700m and has 40 beds. There are camp sites nearby. **1.** Take the Lynch skilift out of Villa Catedral to the Ref. Lynch at 2042m. A well signposted trail follows the ridge S, (mostly on the W side) with a short difficult section around a boulder before finally crossing back over the ridge and descending E down the valley N of Co. Catedral to the Ref. Frey, 4h. **2.** A well marked trail heads S from the W side of the car park at Villa Catedral, rising gradually to reach the Arroyo Van Titter. Climb up the valley crossing the stream and passing the Ref. Piedrita to reach the refugio Frey, 3-4h.

The refugio Frey can also be reached by walking in from several other roadheads. The other most commonly used access points to the range include the Ref. Lopez above Colonia Suiza (N side), the Hotel Tronador on the road to Pampa Linda (W side) and the north end of Lago Mascardi (S side). From all of these points the Ref Frey can be reached in 1-2d.

CATEDRAL CLIMB The highest peak at 2409m is known as the Torre Principal. It is a distinctive 100m high double pinnacle. The normal route is on the LHS of the N face, on good rock and was first climbed in 1943, mostly grade III or IV but with a final short pitch of VI. To reach the tower from the Refugio Frey go around the RHS of the Lag. Toncek, then follow the stream uphill to a large boulder. Take the smaller stream coming in from the L here and climb to the col on the N side of the Torre Principal, 1-2h from Ref Frey to the base of the tower.

CAMPANILE ESLOVENO CLIMB The wafer thin 100m high needle of the Campanile Esloveno is also a difficult ascent on good rock. There are several routes of grade VI- on the E face, generally following prominent crack lines on the LHS to a shoulder, then finishing up the S face. To reach the Campanile from the Refugio Frey, cross the Col Parotida which lies S of Lag. Toncek, then head up the rocky N slopes to the prominent needle, 2h. from Ref Frey to the base of the pinnacle.

CATEDRAL SUR CLIMB The peak is an easy ascent from the Ref. Frey. Climb over the low ridge to the S of Lag. Toncek (Col Parotida). Then descend to the R beneath a big rock slab. Traverse around the head of the valley on a terrace to two small streams. Climb beside these on a faint path to a flat area beneath the Campanile Esloveno. From the far end of this flat area climb a scree gully directly towards the summit. There are a few final moves of grade II rock, 3h. The NE ridge (III-IV) makes a good scramble, reached by climbing directly up from the flat area beneath Esloveno.

BEST MAP Several reasonable sketch maps of the range are available in Bariloche, including one by the Club Andino Bariloche and the ones in the Spanish Language guide 'Las Montañas de Bariloche' (Arko/Izaguirre). Also JLM mapas sheet 11. The AIGM sheet 4172-IV 'San Carlos de Bariloche' 1:250,000 is also useful.

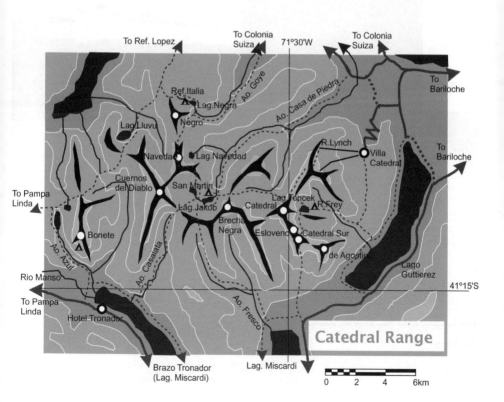

Catedral Range

Cerro BONETE 2257m   2 days   PD

Bonete is a fairly popular peak at the W end of the Catedral range.

ACCESS From the Hotel Tronador on Lag. Mascardi (800m), cross the Rio Manso by a bridge and follow poor paths up through the forest on the W bank of the Arroyo Azul (or Callvuco) to a stream junction. Cross the Azul here and follow the stream up NW through thick vegetation and boulders to a camp under the S face at c.1500m, 4-5h.

CLIMB The normal route is by the S face. From the camp climb towards the glacier but before reaching it go R to reach the corner formed by the S face and a ridge. Climb from here by a system of chimneys and ledges, on the S face and the ridge at up to grade II, 600m, 3h.

BEST MAP As for Catedral.

Refugio Meiling, Monte Tronador

Barbecue, Choshuenco base camp

PATAGONIA & TIERRA DEL FUEGO

INTRODUCTION

Perhaps the greatest variety of mountain scenery in the world is to be found at the southern end of the Andes. There are snow covered volcanoes, the huge granite towers of Paine and Fitzroy, the vast ice fields of the Northern and Southern Patagonian ice-caps and the forest choked and perpetually wet islands of the archipelago of Tierra del Fuego. Although the highest peaks reach only 3000-4000m, the glaciers descend to sea-level. Without a doubt this is the least explored and wildest part of the Andes. It is also the only region where a yacht and a machete can be the most useful items of equipment for a mountaineering expedition!

This chapter covers the vast area from 42°S all the way south to Tierra del Fuego. Most of the peaks in this area have never, or only rarely, been climbed. Almost all are very inaccessible, due to sheer remoteness, thick forests, poor weather and few roads. All the major and more accessible summits south of Puerto Montt are described. In Patagonia, more than in any other area of the Andes, the information about climbing routes and conditions is very poor, except for the towers and peaks of Fitzroy and Paine. This chapter of the book is as much a work of reference to point those who are planning an expedition in the right direction as a practical guide.

GETTING THERE

For the majority of the peaks on the Chilean side of the Andes the best way to get to the area is an international flight to Santiago and then an internal flight south to either Puerto Montt (for the most northerly peaks around Chaiten), Balmaceda (for peaks near Coihaique) or Punta Arenas (for Paine and Tierra del Fuego). Puerto Natales near the Paine national park can also be reached by ferry from Puerto Montt, a beautiful three day voyage if the weather is good. For the peaks of Tierra del Fuego fly to Punta Arenas, then charter a boat ....

The only significant Argentine peaks in this chapter are the Fitzroy/Cerro Torre group, which can be reached most easily by flying to Calafate from Buenos Aires. See 'The High Andes' chapter for details of international flights to Santiago and Buenos Aires.

SEASON AND WEATHER CONDITIONS

The region has a reputation for poor weather and the weather is generally unpredictable even in summer. The area has a climate similar to western Europe, although the climate in Patagonia is colder and windier for any given latitude and the mountains are more exposed to westerly storms than European ranges such as the Alps are. The austral summer from December to March is generally the best season to climb. However winter temperatures are not very low and the persistent winds are usually less strong at that time of year, so winter ascents are relatively popular.

Generally speaking as you head south or west the weather becomes worse. The western Chilean fjords are one of the wettest places on the planet, with the average rainfall at Laguna San Rafael recorded as over 5000mm. By contrast on the Argentine side of the mountains there are semi-desert conditions. The whole of southern Patagonia from about latitude 45° to Cape Horn suffers from seriously strong winds and these give rise to the biggest problems when climbing. Expect gale or storm force winds on up to five days per week, and rain or cloud on roughly half of the days.

CLIMBING CONDITIONS

There is such a mixture of peaks that it is difficult to give an overall description of the climbing conditions on peaks in this area. The 500m vertical granite faces of Paine can never be compared to a remote ice cap peak requiring a three day ski approach. In between these extremes are the volcanoes of Chaiten and Aisen and the alpine peaks of Tierra del Fuego, which generally have very difficult access up remote fjords and/or through thick forest. Once reached these peaks do give easy or moderate climbs on glaciated summits.

Times given for ascents in this section are very much a best possible time. It is likely that for the majority of difficult peaks several weeks of waiting for good weather may be required.

PERMISSIONS
All the peaks in the Torres del Paine national park currently require a permit which can be arranged through the Chilean forestry and park administration authority, CONAF.

OTHER GUIDE BOOKS
The beautifully produced "Patagonia Vertical: Chalten Massif", by Garibotti & Pietron, published by Sidarta in 2012 has many useful topos and photo-diagrams.

Patagonia: terra magica per alpinisti, Buscaini & Metzeltin, Dall'Oglio Ed., 1998 in Italian (also an earlier German edition, 1990 and a Spanish edition published by Desnivel in 2000), is a useful book with first ascent details, topos and maps for many peaks.

Mountaineering in Patagonia by Alan Kearney, Cloudcap, 1993. Describes ascents of Fitzroy/Chalten, Cerro Torre and the Torre Central del Paine. There are topos for three routes only.

Both the American Alpine Journal and Mountain Info online have an extensive list of expedition reports, particularly useful for researching big rock routes in Patagonia

Volcan YATE 2111m   5 days   N/K

Yate is a steep glaciated volcanic peak which lies across the Seno de Reloncavi only 50km from Puerto Montt. The highest summit is Pico Sur, at the S end of a long ridge. Incorrectly given 1408m on the 1:250,000 ChIGM map, a height which is in fact for a small volcanic crater on the S side.

ACCESS From Puerto Montt by road to the town of Puelo which lies 15km NE of the peak.
CLIMB No details known. Grade probably F/PD
BEST MAP ChIGM sheet 4145-7215 'Volcan Hornopiren' 1:50,000.

CHAITEN A small port at the north end of the Carreterra Austral

Chaiten is a small village with hotels, shops etc. It is easily reached by ferry from Puerto Montt or the island of Chiloe and suitable as a base for Minchinmahuida and Corcovado. Nicolas La Penna at Chaitur in the old bus station is a useful source of information on the mountains and can arrange boats and horses for access. The CONAF office may also be able to give some information on access to these peaks.

Volcan MINCHINMAHUIDA 2450m+   5 days   F/PD

Minchinmahuida is a massive glaciated volcano 20km NE of the town of Chaiten. The peak is sometimes given a height of 3120m, the above height is from satellite topography data. The name means 'young mountain'

ACCESS Access is easiest from the small village of Amarillo 30km from Chaiten. Horses can be arranged here with the Hosteria Marcelo. Drive up a side road to the Termas and continue for about another 3km to where the track deteriorates. From here it is two days on horseback to a lagoon at 600m at the base of the glaciers. Horses are more or less essential due to the deep mud on the trail.

Access is also reported to be possible by the NW slopes via the Rio Rayas o Blanco.

CLIMBS No details are known but Minchinmahuida is a relatively easy angled peak with very large and quite badly crevassed glaciers. Several ways onto the S slopes look feasible from the lagoon at 600m.

BEST MAP ChIGM sheet 4245-7215 'Volcan Minchinmahuida' 1:50,000.

Minchinmahuida
from the S

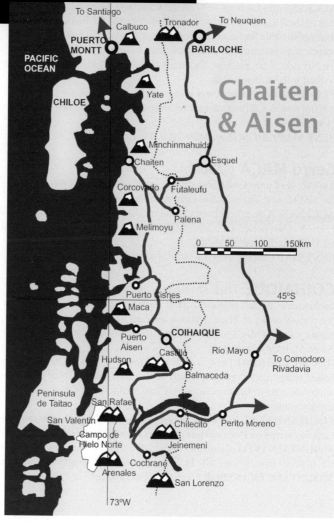

Volcan CORCOVADO c.2100m   3 days   AD?

A beautiful volcano with a very steep N face, rising almost straight from the sea 20km S of Chaiten.
ACCESS Easiest by boat from Chaiten, 3-4h. The summit is less than 10km inland.
CLIMB From the coast by an old lava flow which provides an easy way through the thick forest. The top 100m or 200m are very poor rock and it is possible the summit has not yet been reached. A winter ascent when the rocks are still held together by ice may be more secure.
BEST MAP ChIGM sheet 4300-7120 'Palena' 1:250,000.

Monte MELIMOYU 2420m   6 days   D?

A very remote volcanic peak at 44°S. Also known as Volcan Nevado. There are several unpleasant rocky summit blocks on a large summit plateau. It is possible the highest point was not climbed until January 2000. Combined with almost continuous rain, thick forest and numerous leeches this is an impressively unpleasant ascent.
ACCESS From La Junta (PT) on the Carreterra Austral 120km S of Chaiten a road leads down the S side of the Rio Palena. Just before the bridge over the Rio Correntoso look for a faint path cut through the impenetrable forest, now probably overgrown. This leads up the LHS of the river twice taking a left branch at prominent forks, and sometimes following the bed of the river to reach a camp at c..900m on the NE side of the glaciers. This track took the first ascenscionists 15 days to cut but can probably be walked in 2-3d. if still clear.
CLIMB Easily over the lower glaciers to the summit plateau and rock towers. The highest point is on a 100m tower, a difficult ascent on steep and unconsolidated mud and rocks. A winter ascent may be more secure.
BEST MAP ChIGM sheet 4400-7100 'Puerto Cisnes' 1:250,000.

Cerro MACA c.2300m   4 days   F

Another very remote volcano, often quoted as high as 3078m, the above height was determined from the SRTM data. The peak has large glaciers and is partially eroded.
ACCESS Will be easiest from Coihaique via Puerto Aisen and then a boat to the Termas de Chitconal, 15km S of the peak.
CLIMB No details
BEST MAP ChIGM sheet 4500-7100 'Coihaique' 1:250,000.

COIHAIQUE This small city is a regional capital

Coihaique is a small regional capital at 45°S and makes a good base for a trip to the Castillo range or the remote peaks of Maca, Hudson and San Valentin on the Hielo Patagonico Norte. There are daily flights from Santiago to the nearby airport of Balmaceda and daily buses north on the Carreterra Austral towards Chaiten.
ROCK CLIMBING There is some good rock climbing at Cerro Mackay, immediately SE of the town, bolted routes, up to 5 pitches mostly at V and 6a grades. There is also some climbing a few km further out on the road to Balmaceda at Rio Claro on the RHS of the road and on the opposite side of the river, similar grades.
FOOD AND FUEL There are good supermarkets in town e.g. at the corner of Lautaro and Prat and the camping shops on Horn sell gas canisters. The Sodimac DIY centre sells bencina blanca.
MOUNTAIN INFO A number of adventure travel companies have opened offices in recent years, try the El Ricer cafe bar on Calle Horn for expedition transport and information.
MOUNTAIN TRANSPORT Try asking at El Ricer.

Volcan HUDSON c.1800m   10 days   N/K

A remote active volcano which erupted in 1991 and threw huge clouds of ash into the Southern Hemisphere. The height used here is from satellite topography data.

ACCESS A very remote peak, the nearest road is the Coihaique to Cochrane road over 40km away to the S. Access may be easier up the Rio Ibañez from Villa Cerro Castillo

CLIMB No details.

BEST MAP ChIGM sheet 4500-7100 'Coihaique' 1:250,000.

Cerro CASTILLO 2675m   3 days   AD

Co. Castillo is the highest point of an easily accessible range of steep and rugged peaks lying only 60km S of the town of Coihaique. Sometimes given a height of only 2318m, which may be the height of a subsidiary summit. The area around Castillo is a beautifully scenic area.

ACCESS From Coihaique by the Carreterra Austral to the village of Villa Cerro Castillo (PT). Opposite the square take the dirt road passing a house on the L (mules can be hired here) then along N shore of Rio Ibañez. The road deteriorates to a 4x4 track then a path before reaching a house below the Estero Parada, good views of Cerro Palo, 1h. Cross the stream below the house and go round stock fences to the L, then follow the path easily up the RHS of the valley, past a camp at 900m, to the NZ base camp at approx. 1200m near the tree line, 4-5h.

CLIMB From the NZ camp climb a steep boulder (or snow) slope to the E and enter the very long LH couloir, running up to a col just R of the main summit. From this col c.2400m, go onto the S face and traverse a wide ledge for about 10m, exposed. Climb a snow gully, steep at first then easier, to the foresummit. Continue up rocks and mixed ground to the main summit, the last 5m at grade III-IV are the hardest, 7-8h. Unstable rock reported.

OTHER PEAKS The impressive **Co. Palo 2320m** is very difficult and has only rarely been climbed. Easier is **Co. Puntudo 2061m, F**. It can be climbed from the major river confluence ½h. below the NZ camp. Climb easily up the other fork of the river to a hanging valley and lagoon beneath the peak.

summit

Castillo
from the W

This would make a good campsite from which Puntudo and several other easy peaks could be climbed.

BEST MAP ChIGM sheet 4600-7100 'Chile Chico' 1:250,000.

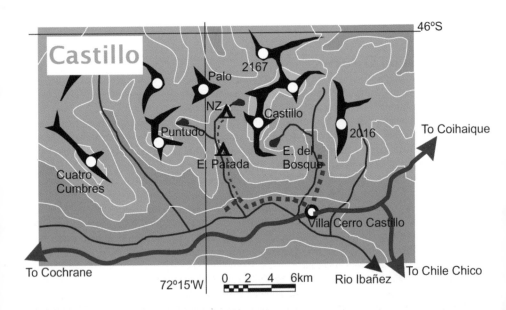

Cerro Castillo from the E

Cerro JEINIMENI 2600m   5 Days ˙   N/K

Jeinimeni is a high peak lying near the Argentine frontier and is much drier and less glaciated than other peaks in this area.

ACCESS From the village of Chile Chico follow a track for 50km S to the Lago Jeinimeni where there is a basic campground run by the national park.

CLIMB No details known.

BEST MAP ChIGM sheet 4600-7100 'Chile Chico' 1:250,000.

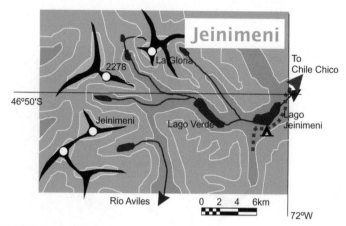

Monte SAN VALENTIN 4058m   12 days   AD

Also known as San Clemente, this is the highest peak in southern Patagonia. On the Chilean 1:50,000 map it is given a height of 3910m, but satellite data indicate that it is certainly over 4000m high. San Valentin lies at the extreme north end of the Hielo Patagonico Norte, the smaller of the two Patagonian ice-caps, which is still 100km long by 45km wide. The grade of AD reflects the very serious nature of the weather on this ascent. There have been many accidents and fatalities in recent years, mainly due to inexperienced parties struggling to cope in the predictably atrocious weather conditions.

There are two commonly used access point nowadays, the E route from Lago Leones, is a little bit longer and more difficult logistically, but possibly less exposed to bad weather. The traditional W route from Laguna San Rafael is quite a bit more straightforward but gets the worst of the weather. Many parties elect to combine an ascent of San Valentin with a traverse of the ice-cap, and for this the W to E direction is probably sensible given the prevailing wind direction.

SAN RAFAEL ACCESS From Coihaique arrange a boat or plane to the San Rafael glacier tongue where there is a hostel and airfield but no other facilities. These can be arranged easily, though not cheaply, in Coihaique. The cheapest option is to try your luck with one of the many tour agencies for a place on one of their scheduled tourist services.

SAN RAFAEL CLIMB The first ascent and many subsequent ascents have been from the W at Lag. San Rafael. On most ascents five or six intermediate camps are needed to reach the peak.

Access starts right behind the hostel on a boardwalk, followed for 1h. to the glacier viewpoint. From here descend scree, then re-ascend to the top of a short but steep 5m rock step. Continue up the edge of the glacier for ½h. to the next rock promontory, which is climbed by a series of short pitches (grade III-IV) and a path well marked with cairns. Just past the highpoint is the usual first camp, 3h.

From this camp descend to the glacier and follow the edge E for 1km to the next 150m high promontory, which is again climbed with a few short rock pitches and cairns, mostly following a small stream which cuts slightly back L. Traverse to near the nose of this promontory and then descend to the glacier bay behind. Go onto the glacier here and continue E along the edge of the glacier for 2km, then out along a moraine arm. From here ski more or less directly E to the S end of a nunatak where camp II is situated at about 600m, 5-6h. from camp I.

From camp II follow the ice around the S side of this nunatak, then slightly down to a basin and steeply up to a crevasse zone. Now the route is much more obvious and (if you're lucky) you can see San

Valentin ahead of you. From here it is about 10km in a straight line ESE to camp III on another nunatak at 1400m, 4-6h. Then about 10km NE to a camp at 1700-1800m below the icefall guarding the E basin of San Valentin, 3-4h. Climb through this serious icefall on the LHS to a fifth and final camp at 2700-2800m underneath the peak, 3-4h.

The peak itself has usually been climbed from this camp by either the SE ridge or S face in 6-8h.

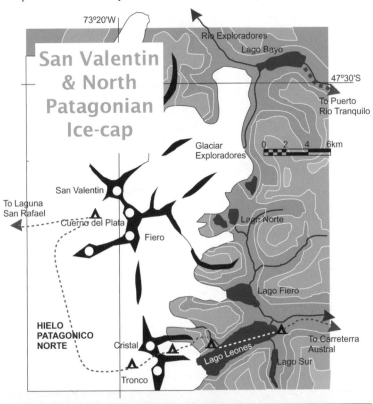

San Valentin from the N

Tronco

Cristal

pass

Ice-cap approach
from Lago Leones

LAGO LEONES ACCESS Access to San Valentin is also possible from the E from Puerto Tranquilo via Lago Leones (350m). You can drive some of the way towards the lake then use horses for the last day up to the lake. You'll need a zodiac boat or similar to cross the lake to a base camp by an unnamed river on the N shore two thirds of the way down the lake. Climb from here up slopes to the W to a camp on the edge of a plateau at the glacier edge, 1100m. Cross the Glaciar Leon Poniente to a camp under the col which lies N of Tronco. Another day will get you established on the ice-cap, then a further 2d. will be needed to reach the high camp at 2700m on San Valentin as above.

The author heading for San Valentin, north Patagonian Ice-cap

OTHER PEAKS A few km further S is **Cuerno del Plata 3680m**, (sometimes called Tararua or Silberhorn) first ascended by the easy S ridge from the 2700m high camp.

OTHER ROUTES The Glaciar Soler is another possible entry and exit point to the ice-cap.

BEST MAP ChIGM sheet 4630-7320 'Monte San Valentin' at 1:50,000 covers the summit but has many blank areas. Sheet 4630-7300 'Lago Fiero' covers the approach via Lago Leones. The difficult to find Andes Patagonicos sheet 5, 1:250,000 pub. 1976 'Iwa to Yuki' no. 49 is also very useful.

Cerro ARENALES 3365m   12-15 days N/K

The highest point in the S part of the Hielo Patagonico Norte, an extremely remote peak.

ACCESS The southern part of the ice cap can be gained most easily by the long Glaciar Colonia which flows into Lag. Colonia, 40km W of Cochrane. This gives access to the E side of the peak.

CLIMB No details known.

OTHER PEAKS 10km further S, **Co. Arco 2992m** has been climbed by several parties. Most other peaks in the area are unclimbed.

BEST MAP ChIGM sheet 4700-7140 'Cochrane' at 1:250,000 has quite good detail. Andes Patagonicos sheet 5, 1:250,000 pub. 1976 'Iwa to Yuki' no. 49 is also good.

Monte SAN LORENZO 3706m   5 days   AD

A high and impressive peak on the frontier 200km N of the Chalten/Fitzroy massif. San Lorenzo is known as Cochrane on the Chilean side of the border. There is a huge, 2000m high, 5km long ice and rock wall to the E and a large easier angled glacier basin to the W. There is a very good map of the massif in Buscaini's book.

ACCESS From Coihaique by plane or bus to Cochrane (PT). Follow a track from Cochrane up the Rio Tranquilo then walk 2h. to reach the Fundo San Lorenzo 10km N of the mountain, where there is a small climbers hostal. The Fundo is owned by Lucy and Luis Soto, who can be contacted in Cochrane at Merino #750 and will help with transport and horses. From the Fundo walk up the Arroyo San Lorenzo on a good path on the S bank to the old base camp just below a small lagoon at 1000m, 3h. There is now a climbers hut here run by the Soto's. This camp can also be reached by ascending the Rio Oro from the Estancia Los Ñires on the Argentine side of the peak.

CLIMB From the hut follow the river upstream until 200m past the end of the forest then follow a small stream up and R until behind the moraine. Climb steep snow/scree slopes SW to the edge of the glacier at 1700m. Follow the LHS of the glacier to reach the Paso del Comedor at 1950m, 4-5h. Cross this pass and traverse the glacier basin to the S to cross a second pass. This pass, known as the Brecha de la Cornisa (2250m) can have a 20m rock pitch in lean snow years. Drop down onto the Glaciar Calluqueo on the other side of this pass to establish a high camp at 2050m below a shoulder, 3h. From the high camp cross the glacier S until it is possible to climb up onto the N shoulder of San Lorenzo (3250m) through seracs. From here follow the NW ridge over a forepeak 3567m, to the main summit, 7-8h. The summit ice mushroom is often unclimbable.

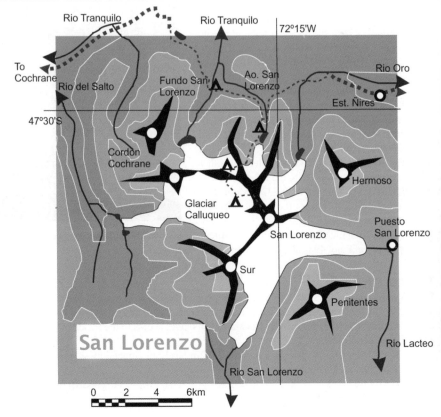

OTHER ROUTES The mixed **E ridge** has also been climbed at about TD from the Lacteo glacier on the E side of the peak. It lies directly above the Puesto San Lorenzo.

OTHER PEAKS The **South peak, D** has been climbed by the S face and W ridge. To the SE of San Lorenzo **Co. Penitentes 2943m, AD** can be climbed by the N side in 2d. from Puesto San Lorenzo.

KEY WAYPOINTS Refugio 47°31'06" 72°18'57" 1700m 47°32'01" 72°20'12" Paso del Comedor 47°32'32" 72°20'56" Brecha de la Cornisa 47°33'20" 72°20'53" High camp 47°33'50" 72°21'27" Shoulder 2250m 47°34'49" 72°21'31" Foot of icefall 47°34'40" 72°20'14" Top of icefall 3250m 47°34'29" 72°19'52" Forepeak 47°35'04" 72°19'30" Summit 47°35'24" 72°18'51"

BEST MAP The one in Buscaini's book is the most useful or ChIGM sheet 4700-7140 'Cochrane' 1:250,000.

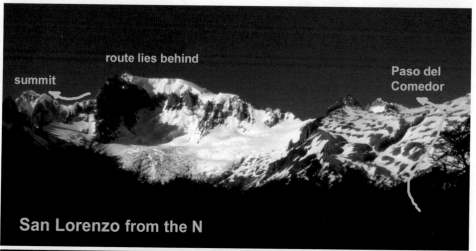

route lies behind

summit

Paso del Comedor

San Lorenzo from the N

Leaving high camp, San Lorenzo

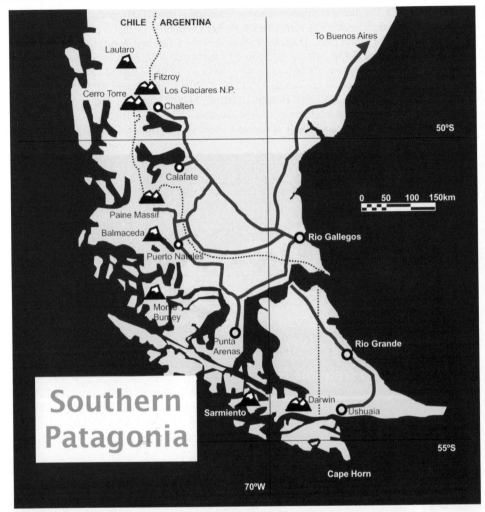

Southern Patagonia

EL CALAFATE The gateway town for the Los Glaciares park

A pleasant wee town on the shores of Lago Argentino which becomes very busy in summer with tourists from all over Argentina and indeed all over the world. Although rarely enforced, permission is officially required for all peaks in the Fitzroy/Cerro Torre massif and can be obtained from the Intendencia del Parque Nacional Los Glaciares in the town. There are direct flights to Calafate from Buenos Aires in the summer.

SIGHTS If you've time to spare the one day trip to the famous Perito Moreno glacier is worth doing. Also check out the flamingos down by the lake shore.

FOOD There are several good supermarkets in the town.

FUEL White gas is available from several chemists in the middle of town. Gas canisters are also available but they are expensive here.

MOUNTAIN TRANSPORT AND INFO There are numerous tour agencies in the middle of town who will provide private transport to El Chalten and Los Glaciares. They also run frequent and convenient public bus services in the summer months.

EL CHALTEN A town at the foot of Fitzroy 600m

El Chalten is a rapidly growing small town at the entrance to the Los Glaciares national park, now with many hotels, campsites and tour agencies. Several daily buses run to and from Calafate with connections to Rio Gallegos.

FOOD There are several supermarkets, but not much fresh food.

FUEL White gas is known locally as 'solvente' and can be bought in several shops as can gas canisters.

PERMITS The regulations have changed in the past and at times have included fees. A climbing permit is needed to do any of the climbing routes in the national park. It is currently free and relatively easy to obtain from the national park office in town. If you are crossing to Chile you will need your passport and you must register first with the gendarmeria in Chalten.

MOUNTAIN TRANSPORT AND INFO Several of the agencies are very helpful with arranging transport, mules to base camps and providing information on current conditions. There are plenty of cafes and bars where other climbers can be found and bought a beer in return for up to date information.

MOUNTAIN EQUIMENT It is possible to rent or buy a wide range of climbing and camping equipment but prices are very high.

GORRA BLANCA 2860m 4 days PD

This peak lies on the edge of the ice-cap only 15km N of Fitzroy and is one of the more accessible and easy peaks in this part of Patagonia. There are two summits joined by a N-S ridge, the N summit is higher. There are magnificent views from the summit towards Lago Viedma, Cerro Torre, Fitzroy and the ice-cap.

ACCESS See map on page 310. From the village of El Chalten drive to Puente Electrico then walk on a good path to Piedra del Fraile, 2h. There is a fee of about $30 to trek up this valley and there is now an organised camp and refugio at Piedra del Fraile. Then walk around the rough S shore of Lag. Electrico to a camp at the W end of the lake, 2h. Continue onto the glacier via steep moraine and rock slabs on the S side of an unnamed lake, then climb the middle of the glacier and then more steeply up to the wide glaciated Paso Marconi (1500m), the entrance to the ice-cap 5-7h.

Gorra Blanca
from the S

summit

CLIMB By the NW ridge from Paso Marconi (a higher camp is possible in the glacier basin W of the peak at about 1900m). Climb to the col at 2350m formed with a small peak to the W, then follow the ridge or slopes on the R before a few final steep sections (to 40°) to the summit. The **SW face, PD** is also climbed more directly quite frequently.

OTHER PEAKS The **S peak 2803m** is also reported to be an easy ascent.

BEST MAP The best map for access is a 1:50,000 sheet widely available in Calafate and Chalten and published by Zagier and Urruty, though it just misses the summit of the peak.

Cerro LAUTARO 3580m   10 days   F
Cerro MORENO 3505m   8 days   F/PD

Lautaro is an active volcano in the northern half of the Hielo Patagonico Sur approximately 40km NW of Fitzroy. Recent satellite topography surveys have shown that Lautaro is higher than previously thought and is also the highest point of the South Patagonian icecap an honour which Moreno used to hold. The Hielo Patagonico Sur is the larger of the two Patagonian ice-caps and is 330km long (N-S) and between 30 and 80km wide.

LAUTARO ACCESS Access is easiest across the ice-cap on skis from the Paso Marconi. Follow the Gorra Blanca access above to the Paso Marconi glacier camp, 2d. From here ski directly towards Lautaro taking 2d to reach a camp beneath the SE side at about 1700-1900m.

LAUTARO CLIMB There are two main summits either side of a partial crater. Climb the wide valley just S of the mountain to reach the S summit, then continue round the W side of the crater to the main N summit.

Moreno from the E

Lautaro from the SE

camp

MORENO ACCESS Access as above to Paso Marconi, 2d. Then ski to Paso Moreno to the N of the peak and climb the glacier leading SE to reach a high camp at c.2500m on the NW slopes of the peak, 2d. from Paso Marconi.

MORENO CLIMB Climb by the NE shoulder, 1d. This is not a difficult ascent.

OTHER PEAKS E of Lautaro, the beautiful wedge shaped **Co. Piramide c.2800m** has been climbed by the SE ridge in 6 days return from the Paso Marconi, grade about AD.

BEST MAP ChIGM sheet 4800-7140 'Villa O'Higgins' 1:250,000 may be useful for access. There is a sketch map in AJ 1970.

A bird nesting in the old climbing boots of Gino Buscaini, famous Patagonian climber and explorer

Skiing towards Lautaro, South Patagonian Ice-cap

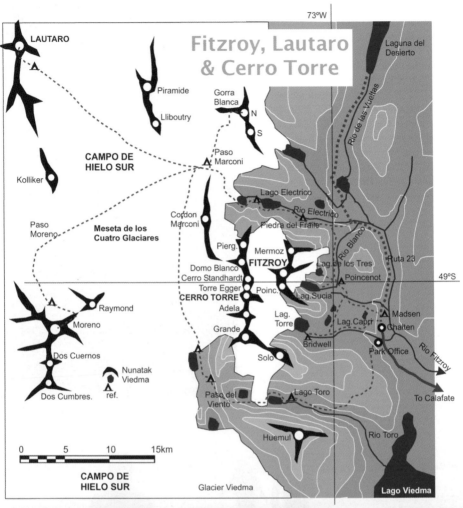

Fitzroy, Lautaro & Cerro Torre

LAUTARO

73°W

Laguna del Desierto

Piramide

Gorra Blanca

Lliboutry

N

S

Río de las Vueltas

CAMPO DE HIELO SUR

Paso Marconi

Kolliker

Lago Electrico

Río Electrico

Piedra del Fraile

Paso Moreno

Meseta de los Cuatro Glaciares

Cordon Marconi

Pierg.

Río Blanco

Mermoz

FITZROY

Lag. de los Tres

Ruta 23

49°S

Domo Blanco

Cerro Standhardt

Poincenot

Torre Egger

Poinc.

Lag. Sucia

CERRO TORRE

Adela

Lag. Torre

Lag. Capri

Madsen

Raymond

Chalten

Moreno

Grande

Bridwell

Park Office

Río Fitzroy

Dos Cuernos

Nunatak Viedma

Solo

Dos Cumbres.

ref.

Paso del Viento

Lago Toro

To Calafate

Río Toro

Huemul

0   5   10   15km

CAMPO DE HIELO SUR

Glacier Viedma

Lago Viedma

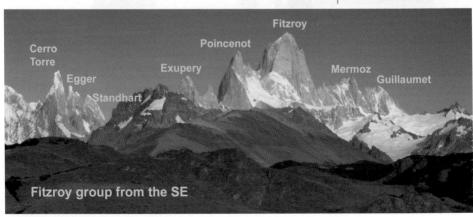

Fitzroy group from the SE

Cerro Torre

Egger

Standhart

Exupery

Poincenot

Fitzroy

Mermoz

Guillaumet

Aguja MERMOZ 2754m
4 days   TD

Aguja GUILLAUMET 2503m
4 days   D/TD

These two pinnacles lie N of Fitzroy. The Aguja Guillaumet is one of the most frequently ascended peaks in the area, if only because it is one of the easiest. Both peaks are named for South American aviation pioneers.

ACCESS For Mermoz drive and walk from El Chalten (PT) to the Piedra del Fraile camp, 2h. Continue by the S shore of Lago Electrico, then up the Rio Pollone and Glaciar Fitzroy Norte to a camp beneath the NW face at 1500-1600m.

For Guillaumet walk from El Chalten to the Paso Superior as for Fitzroy, then traverse the Glaciar Piedras Blancas to a camp near the col beneath the NE ridge.

MERMOZ CLIMB Mermoz was first climbed by an Argentinean party by the NW shoulder and N ridge. This is 600m of sustained climbing, mostly on rock, to grade VI.

GUILLAUMET CLIMB Most frequently climbed by the E face and NE ridge. Climb from the Glaciar Piedras Blancas by one of two prominent 350m couloirs. These have ice to 60° and the LH couloir has an awkward exit on rock (V+). The RH couloir is more frequently climbed and is known as the Amy route; it is a very similar but slightly easier route. Once at the top of the LH couloir follow a snowy ramp on the E face and a III chimney to the summit snowfield.

GUILLAUMET OTHER ROUTES The first ascent route (Argentine Route) via the **NW shoulder**, **TD** from the Glaciar Fitzroy Norte is a straightforward route that is also climbed fairly often. It is a 500m route with climbing to VI+, 40°. See either the Garibotti or Buscaini guidebooks for topos and further details.

OTHER PEAKS N of these two peaks **Co. Electrico 2270m** is a fine viewpoint for Fitzroy and is a fairly easy climb from a base at Piedra del Fraile by the NE slopes, 3h.

BEST MAP As for Fitzroy.

Mermoz

Guillaumet

NE ridge

Electrico

Paso Superior

Paso Inferior

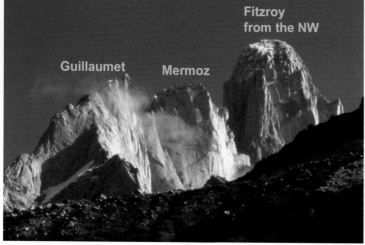

Fitzroy from the NW

Guillaumet   Mermoz

Cerro FITZROY (CHALTEN) 3441m   4 days   TD/ED

One of the worlds great mountains, Fitzroy is a granite monolith rising from the edge of the Southern Patagonian ice-cap, now often known by its native name of Chalten. It is sometimes given a height of 3375m or 3405m. The most commonly climbed 'normal' routes are the Argentine variation of the original French route on the SE face/S shoulder, the American (or Californian) route on the SW pillar and the Supercanaleta on the NW face. The peak was first climbed in 1952 by Terray's French expedition. The time of 4 days could only be achieved by an exceptionally competent party in perfect weather!

ACCESS From Chalten (PT) on good signposted paths to the Poincenot base camp by the Rio Blanco (800m) and on up to the Lag. de los Tres, 1160m, 1d. From here go round the LHS of the lake and climb the glacier to the Paso Superior (c.2000m) where a high camp or snow cave can be made.

CLIMB The most climbed route and the fastest way to the summit is the Franco-Argentine route on the **S shoulder, ED**. This is a more direct variant of the original 1952 route. From Paso Superior continue up the Glacier Piedras Blancas and climb up to the Brecha de los Italianos 2627m, (III/60°). Beware of rockfall on this section. From the Brecha, climb III rock on the W side of the ridge to reach the prominent snowy plateau beneath the SE face. The face above has c.600m of difficult climbing, mostly III/IV but with some VI+ and A2. It can be climbed free at about F6c. (See the Garibotti/Pietron guidebook or High #154, Sept. 1995 for a detailed topo).

Formerly climbed frequently and possibly the easiest way to the summit is the more devious American 1968 route on the **SW pillar ED**. It is easier than the original French 1952 line and is normally climbed from the Paso Superior via the Brecha de los Italianos with 1 bivouac. Reach the base of the S shoulder as for the normal route above then traverse L over glacier to the col known as La Silla (col with Aguja de la Silla). Above La Silla there are approximately 20 pitches on good rock, mostly V/V+ with a few sections of A1 and small amounts of snow/ice, several of the pitches are only grade I or II. See the Garibotti/Pietron guidebook for a detailed topo.

OTHER ROUTES The **Supercanaleta ED,** a 1500m route on the NW face, is probably the third most climbed route on Fitzroy, despite bad stonefall. It is a huge 1300m gully with sustained climbing to 60°/VI/A1 which joins the SW ridge high on the mountain. Access to the Supercanaleta is from a base

Fitzroy
SE face

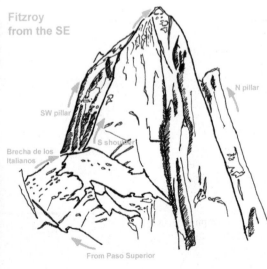

Fitzroy
from the SE

N pillar

SW pillar

S shoulder

Brecha de los
Italianos

From Paso Superior

camp at Piedra del Fraile by the Glaciar Fitzroy Norte, as for the Aguja Mermoz.
REFERENCES The Garibotti/Pietron guidebook is extremely useful. Buscaini's book also has details of a couple of these routes. High #203, October 1999, has photo diagrams of all 17 routes climbed to that date on Fitzroy.
BEST MAP The best map is a sheet widely available in Calafate published by Zagier and Urruty at a scale of 1:50,000.

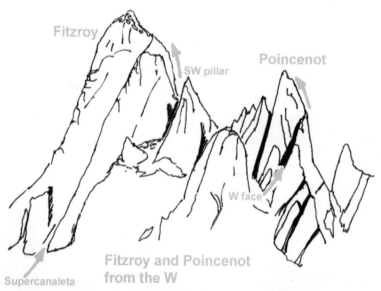

Fitzroy and Poincenot from the W

Aguja POINCENOT 3036m

4 days   TD/ED

The Aguja Poincenot was first climbed in 1962 by Don Whillans and an Irish expedition via the E face and SE ridge. It is named for a member of Terray's 1952 expedition who drowned crossing a river.
ACCESS As for Fitzroy to the Paso Superior camp or snow cave.
POINCENOT CLIMB The easiest and most popular route is the Irish route via the E face with one bivouac from the Paso Superior. The route takes the prominent diagonal ice ramp (50°) across the E face for 300m to reach the SE ridge, which is climbed on rock at grade IV/V for 300m. See the Garibotti guidebook or the Alpine Journal 1962 for details.
OTHER ROUTES The **W face, ED** of Poincenot was climbed in 1977 by a prominent R sloping ramp, grade VI.
BEST MAP As for Fitzroy.

Aguja Poincenot from the E

SE ridge

Aguja ST. EXUPERY 2680m   5 days   TD/ED

The Aguja St Exupery, named for an aviation pioneer in Patagonia was first climbed by an Italian expedition which included Gino Buscaini in 1968.

ACCESS From Lag. Torre (see Co. Torre) climb NE over four small cols on the E side of Co Techado Negro to reach the Glaciar Rio Blanco, then traverse W under the Aguja de la S. to a camp on the glacier under the SE side of the peak at about 2000m.

CLIMB The Aguja is climbed fairly often by the E shoulder from 1880m on the glacier, via two prominent snow patches. This gives an 800m, 30 pitch climb, mostly at III-IV but with some harder pitches at VI/A1 above the small snow patch. See Buscainis book for a detailed topo. This route can be climbed free at F7a.

OTHER PEAKS To the N, the lower **Aguja Rafael 2501m,** (also known as Innominata) was first climbed by the SE ridge reached from the W side by a couloir, at about VI/VI+.

BEST MAP As for Fitzroy.

E shoulder

Aguja de la S

Aguja St. Exupery from the E

Cerro TORRE 3128m   7 days   ED++

Cerro Torre is one of the worlds most famous mountains, partly because of the controversial history surrounding the first ascent of the peak and partly because it is such an outstanding and dramatic peak. Maestri claimed to have climbed the peak in 1959, but his companion Toni Egger and their camera were lost during the descent. Egger claimed to have climbed the N face from the inappropriately named Col de la Conquista (Col of Conquest) when it was unusually heavily rimed up. For many years there was considerable doubt about this claim due to the difficulties of the route under normal conditions and the fact that no evidence of their climb remained any higher than the prominent triangular snow-patch. Maestri then climbed Cerro Torre in 1970 by the SE ridge, but he used a gas compressor and rock drill and was widely criticised for his unsporting tactics. Also, he did not climb to the top of the ice-mushroom which forms the summit. His route became known as the Compressor Route and was climbed relatively frequently until the removal of the bolts in 2012. The SE ridge is now a considerably harder route.

The first true ascent was by another Italian party in 1974 on the W face above the ice-cap (see Garibotti AAJ 2004). Their line, known as the Ferrari or Ragni line is now effectively the mountains "normal" route although it has only ever seen 20 or so ascents.

ACCESS See map on page 310. From Chalten (PT) a 4h. signposted walk leads to a base camp in the trees at Lag. Torre (700m). From here it is a 5h. walk to a camp or bivvy on the Glacier Torre, N or NE of the peak, known as the Niponino camp. To reach the foot of the W face from here climb up and over the Col Standhart (2100m), 60° snow, then S to a camp or bivvy beneath the Col de la Esperanza (Col of Hope). Access to this bivvy is also possible by the ice-cap via Paso Marconi (as for Gorra Blanca p. 307) to the N, or via the Lago del Toro and Paso del Viento to the S of Cerro Torre. Either way 2-3d.

CERRO TORRE CLIMB The **W face**, route of the 1974 Italian ascent, and known as the Ferrari or Ragni route, is usually climbed from a base camp at 1600m on the ice-cap beneath the Col de la Esperanza. Climb to the col (c.1000m, M2, 50-60°). The route from here gives 600m of climbing at M4/90° mostly on heavily rimed up rock, which can be secure or can be entirely insecure and require much tunneling. See the detailed topo in Garibotti & Pietron's book.

SE RIDGE CLIMB The SE ridge was climbed frequently by the 'Compressor route' until the removal of the bolts after the first free ascent in 2012. The route starts from the col with El Mocho, known as the Col de la Paciencia (Col of Patience), which is reached by the N side from the Glaciar Torre. The

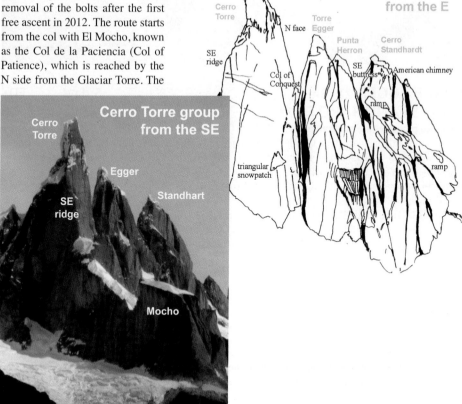

Cerro Torre group from the E

Cerro Torre group from the SE

climb is now approximately 27 pitches from the Col de la Paciencia, mostly F5+ to F6b but with obligatory F7a/A1 moves on the final headwall, and some sections of ice to 90°.
BEST MAP As for Fitzroy.

High on the historic (infamous) Compressor Route, SE face, Cerro Torre

| **TORRE EGGER** 2873m | 5 days | ED+ |
| **Cerro STANDHARDT** 2730m | 5 days | ED |

These two pinnacles are northern outliers of Cerro Torre and are just as impressive climbs. The summit of Co. Standhardt, named after a German photographer, was not reached until 1988, although a British party climbed all but the summit ice mushroom in 1977. Torre Egger, named after Maestri's unlucky companion, was first climbed in 1976.
ACCESS As for Co. Torre SE ridge, to the Lag. Torre base camp (700m) then up the Glaciar Torre to a camp under the E face.
TORRE EGGER CLIMB The line of the first ascent in 1976 (American) climbed the E face of Co. Torre past the triangular snow patch to the Col de la Conquista (Col of Conquest, 2400m) then climbed the S face of Torre Egger, VI, A4, 80°. Routes on the E face, such as Badlands and Titanic (VI, A2, 90°) are more frequently climbed now.
CERRO STANDHARDT CLIMB The first ascents were all on the E face, gained from the Standhardt-Bifida col by a rising snow ramp which cuts up and left across the face. The 1988 American line (known as Exocet) takes an icy chimney about halfway across the ramp, (250m, 6 pitches to VI+/A1 and ice from 70-95°). It is now a relatively popular climb and could be considered the "normal" route to the summit. The British 1977 line climbed the SE buttress, ED from the extreme L end of the ramp VI/A2, but did not reach the very summit.
BEST MAP As for Fitzroy.

PUERTO NATALES The gateway town to the Torres del Paine park

A pleasant wee town on the shores of the Seno Ultima Esperanza. Puerto Natales is the southern terminus for the famous ferry through the Chilean fjords from Puerto Montt. The town becomes quite busy in summer with tourists stopping off on the way to and from the Torres del Paine national park. There are regular buses from the airport at Punta Arenas in summer, and onward transport to the Torres del Paine park is easy to arrange.

SIGHTS If you've time to spare the one day boat cruise up the Seno to the foot of **Balmaceda 2035m** is very worthwhile.

FOOD There are a number of small grocery stores in the middle of town, but nothing great.

FUEL White gas is available from several chemists in the middle of town. Availability of gas canisters is n/k.

MOUNTAIN TRANSPORT AND INFO There are numerous tour agencies in the middle of town who will provide private transport to the Paine national park. They also run frequent and convenient bus services in the summer months

MOUNTAIN EQUIPMENT Basic equipment such as tents and gas stoves can be rented or bought, but no mountaineering equipment.

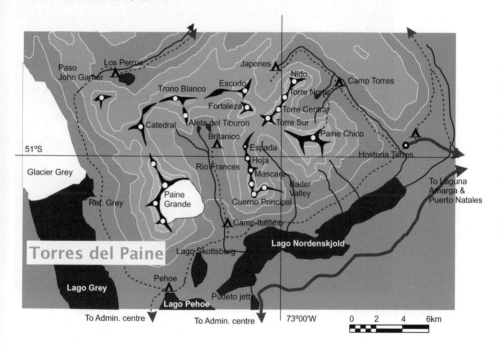

Cerro PAINE GRANDE c.2750m   4 days   TD/ED

Paine Grande is the highest peak in the Paine massif and the only one with a substantial glacier. Satellite topography data has shown the height of 3050m to be a gross exaggeration, the above estimate is nearer the truth. Because of its proximity to the ice cap and exposure to wet westerlies the highest point is a mass of unstable snow formations rising above the NE end of a large glacier plateau. This point was only climbed for the second time in 2001. The peak at the S end is known as Bariloche. Paine Grande is a big bulky mountain and quite different in character to the pinnacles of the Torres and Cuernos, but it is still a very difficult ascent.

ACCESS From Puerto Natales to the Hosteria Pehoe, then take a boat across Lago Pehoe to the Refugio Pehoe campground which lies S of the peak, walk NW for 2-3h. up Lago Grey to reach the foot of the enormous W face.

CLIMB The easiest ascents are from the W, up the huge broken 2000m face to reach the glaciated summit plateau via the col between the Central and S (Punta Bariloche) summits. The highest point, at the NE of the plateau has then been climbed by the NE ridge from this plateau, mainly ice to 80-90°. Once on the plateau the central and south peaks are considerably easier.

OTHER PEAKS To the N is **Co. Catedral 2200m.** The S face - W ridge, the line of the first ascent in 1971, can be climbed in 21 pitches (V+/A2) from above the Glaciar de los Perros. Also at the head of the Frances valley is **Aleta del Tiburon, 1850m,** the 'sharks fin'. It is a dramatic peak which has been climbed several times by routes on the W face and on the S ridge, TD/ED.

BEST MAP 'Patagonia - Torres del Paine' produced by Juan Luis Mattassi and readily available in Puerto Natales at approximately 1:50,000. Various similar trekking maps are also available.

summit

Paine Grande from the SE

Cerro FORTALEZA c.2500m   4 days   TD/ED

Co. Fortaleza (The Fortress) is a massive granite peak at the head of the Frances and Ascensio valleys, with steep walls, a huge E face and a cap of unstable black slate and rime and snow formations. The height used here is an estimate based on satellite topography data.

ACCESS As for Cuerno Principal to the Rio Frances.

CLIMB The first ascent was by the W face from the head of the Rio Frances valley. The climb started up a moderate snow gully at the S end of the face, followed by a steep ice runnel then a finish up a huge 300m rock corner. 1700m of climbing to VI/A2/70°. The first ascent took one month, recent ascents have taken as little as 8h.!

OTHER PEAKS The neighbouring peak of **Co. Escudo 2450m** can also be climbed from the Frances valley. Climb by a long ramp on the SW face which rises L to reach the summit ridge, grade n/k.

BEST MAP As for Paine Grande.

Fortaleza and Escudo from the NE

Escudo

Fortaleza

CUERNO PRINCIPAL 2100m   4 days   TD

Also known as the Cuerno Central. The only real difficulty is the final 90m tower of unstable black slate which caps this peak.

ACCESS As for Paine Grande to the Ref. Pehoe campground, then walk NE on a good path past Lago Skottsberg to the Campo Italiano in the Frances valley, 2h.

CLIMB The summit tower is reached up the S and W sides of the peak from Campo Italiano. This was the line of the first ascent by a Chilean expedition, climbing to VI/A1.

OTHER PEAKS The **Cuerno Norte, 2000m** has been climbed from the col to the S with Cuerno Principal, V/A2, 300m. **Co. Mascara 1850m,** (the Mummer) has been climbed by a 700m diedre on the SW face VI/A3 and **Co. Hoja 1950m,** (the Blade) has been climbed by the N ridge, 380m, TD.

BEST MAP As for Paine Grande.

Norte

Fortaleza

Este

Principal

Cuernos del Paine from the S

TORRE NORTE 2260m   4 days   D/TD
TORRE CENTRAL 2460m   4 days   TD
TORRE SUR 2500m   4 days   TD

The three peaks of the Torres del Paine are one of the landmarks of Patagonia and as with Co. Torre and Fitzroy they have a fascinating and well documented climbing history. All three towers are sometimes quoted as being 200-300m higher than the heights given here.

ACCESS See the map on page 317. From Puerto Natales to Hosteria Los Torres (PT) near the park entrance. There is a campsite here. Then walk up the valley of the Rio Ascensio by a path on the W side past Campo Torres then over increasingly rugged ground to Campo Japones (1100m) which lies NW of the peaks, 6-7h. All the towers were first climbed from this camp by routes starting on the N sides, and these form the easiest lines today. (See High #152 July 1995 for a good photo diagram of the N side of the Torres)

TORRE NORTE CLIMB Also known as Torre Manzino. The easiest of the Torres has two summits, the S summit is the higher. The first ascent was in 1957 by the **SW ridge**. This is now the standard route and is climbed quite frequently. From the Campo Japones climb by 300m of rock slabs and snow patches to the Col Bich, which joins the N and Central towers. Then climb by the SW ridge, the first two pitches are the hardest with easier ground above. The final 20m tower can be climbed on the SW face. Climbing to grade VI.

TORRE CENTRAL CLIMB Slightly smaller than the Torre Sur, but with a much more dramatic S face, 1200m of perfect looking and nearly vertical granite. The most commonly climbed line is the first ascent route (Bonington/Whillans) up the **N ridge**. From the Campo Japones climb to the Col Bich over mixed easy angled rock slabs and snow and then by the c.600m N ridge, grade VI/A2 or nearly free at French 6c. For a topo see Buscainis book.

The American route up the **S face**, may however be an easier line on the Central tower. This is also reached from Campo Japones via the col with the Torre Sur and involves 17 pitches of climbing up to grade VI and A2, but with a number of easier pitches. For a topo of this route see Kearneys book.

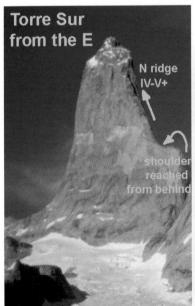

Torre Sur from the E

N ridge
IV-V+

shoulder reached from behind

Torre Central from the E

Torre Norte

Sur   Norte

N ridge

SW ridge

Col Bich
(reached from behind)

TORRE SUR CLIMB The highest of the three Torres is also known as Torre d'Agostini. Though no accurate surveys exist, heights of up to 2850m are probably exaggerated. The first ascent was by the Italians in 1963 up the **N ridge** in 21 pitches. Known as the Aste route, it starts from just below the col with the Torre Central on the N side, climbs steep rock to VI/A1 for 6 pitches, with some poor rock on pitches 3 and 4, then easy II-III slabs to the shoulder for 5 pitches, then 10 pitches of grade IV-V+ up the N ridge.
BEST MAP As for Paine Grande.

PAINE CHICO c.2640m   2 days   AD

There are two summits, the E summit is also known as Almirante Nieto. There is some confusion about which summit is higher, although most sources indicate the W summit is highest. The peak was first climbed in 1937, but only to the E summit.
ACCESS See the map on page 317. As for the Torres del Paine to the Campo Torres at 650m, 3h.
CLIMB The route to the E summit is described. From the Campo Torres follow the Mirador path. About halfway to the mirador aim left into a trough between moraine ridges located below and S of the Mirador. Head SW over scree to the obvious scree/snow filled gully. Climb the gully, mixed scree and snow/ice (300m, 40°) to reach the ridge at about 2100m, 5 hours. Follow the ridge SW over mixed ground then snow to the summit, 2-3 hours. There is some gear in situ on this route.
BEST MAP As for Paine Grande.

Paine Chico from the E

NE ridge

Cerro BALMACEDA 2035m   5 days   N/K

A remote snow and ice peak at the head of the Seno Ultima Esperanza, visible from the town of Puerto Natales. There are several summits, the S summit appears to be the highest.
ACCESS By boat from Puerto Natales (PT) up the Seno Ultima Esperanza to the Rio Serrano on the N side of the peak or Laguna Azul on the W side of the peak.
CLIMB The first ascent was from the N, another ascent has been made from the W at about AD/D.
BEST MAP None known.

Monte BURNEY 1768m   10 days   N/K

One of the most remote peaks in the Andes, with only one recorded ascent by Shipton in 1973. A volcanic peak with a crater.

ACCESS By boat from Puerto Natales (PT) to the coast on the W side of the peak.

CLIMB The first ascent was from the W, finishing by the W ridge, grade n/k, but not too difficult once you get here!

OTHER PEAKS Just to the north, the Cordillera Sarmiento have only very recently been explored, with the highest peak, **Dama Blanca 1925m** only receiving its first ascent in the year 2000.

BEST MAP None known.

USHUAIA The southernmost town in the world

At the southern end of Argentine Tierra del Fuego, lies Ushuaia, the southernmost town in the world. It is a scenic place with a Scandinavian or Icelandic feel which makes a good base for trips into the remote Cord. Darwin. Being almost 55°S Ushuaia enjoys long hours of daylight in December and January. There are regular flights from Rio Gallegos and Buenos Aires.

It can be hard to get into Chilean Tierra del Fuego from here, even by boat, and most expeditions to Chilean Tierra del Fuego travel out by Punta Arenas.

SIGHTS Boat trips down the Magellan straits are very worthwhile and there are some good day walks in the Lapataia park about 15km W of the town.

FOOD There are several very good supermarkets in the middle of town.

FUEL White gas may be available from several hardware shops (ferreterias) in the middle of town. Availability of gas canisters is n/k.

MOUNTAIN TRANSPORT AND INFO Hiring a boat is surprisingly easy, but not cheap. There are numerous tour agencies in the middle of town who will provide private road transport if necessary and may be able to help with yacht or boat charter to reach the more remote peaks in the area. The tourist office is also very helpful.

Monte SARMIENTO 2404m   8 days   N/K

A very remote peak lying in Chilean territory at the W end of the Isla Grande of Tierra del Fuego. Sometimes given a height of only 2184m. Given the difficulties of access and the appalling weather the eight days given as an ascent time should be seen as entirely theoretical.

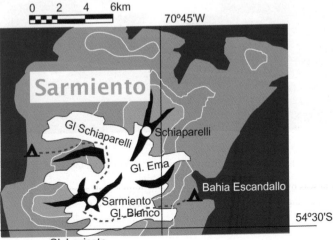

ACCESS Only by boat, probably quickest and easiest to arrange from Punta Arenas in Chile, which is 100km N of the mountain. Ascents have been made from landings on the E side of the peak at Bahia Escandollo on the Seno (Fiordo) Martinez and from the W on the Canal Magdalena.

CLIMB The main peak was first climbed from the E in 1955. Ascending the Glaciar Blanco to a camp SE of the summit

and climbing the higher E peak by the S (or SW?) ridge on ice-plastered rock. Grade about AD/D.
OTHER PEAKS An expedition in 1972 climbed the lower **W peak, 2350m** from the N approaching up the S side of Glaciar Schiaparelli and using three camps.
BEST MAP Andes Patagonicos sheet 2, 1:250,000 pub. 1975 'Iwa to Yuki' no. 45.

Sarmiento from the N

Cerro DARWIN 2562m   6 days   N/K
Darwin, also known as Mount Shipton, is the highest peak on the Isla Grande of Tierra del Fuego. It lies near the centre of a range also known as the Cordillera Darwin. Several sources give a height of 2488m but this may be for a lower peak. The Cordillera Darwin is a range that is largely unexplored though all of the main summits have been climbed. All the peaks lie in a remote part of Chilean Tierra del Fuego, but they are only 40-50km W of the Argentine town of Ushuaia. Climbs are generally easier from the W and the E faces are often very steep. All the mountains are very heavily glaciated and glaciers descend to sea level at many points. Access to all these mountains is difficult and only really possible by boat.
ACCESS By boat to Bahia Broken (also called Brookes or Brooker) then climb the E side of the fjord to reach a high camp on the Marinelli glacier, N of the peak (about 1400m).
CLIMB By the W side of the mountain, believed to be relatively easy. A partial description is given in the Alpine Journal, 1962, p.259
BEST MAP The best map is Andes Patagonicos sheet 2, 1:250,000 pub. 1975 'Iwa to Yuki' no. 45.

Cerro BOVE 2300m   4 days   N/K
Cerro RONCAGLI 2300m   4 days   N/K
Co. Bove and Co. Roncagli lie at the E end of the Cordillera Darwin and are about the only peaks in the range that can be approached by land. They are only 15km W of the Est. Yendegoia which lies on the bay of the same name in Chile but only 10km from the Argentine frontier.
ACCESS There is a 4x4 track into the Estancia Yendegoia from the Chilean part of Tierra del Fuego to the N. It may also be possible with the right permission to approach directly from Ushuaia in Argentina. The S side of Bove can also be accessed by boat, disembarking at the small bay known as Puerto Olla.
BOVE CLIMB The first ascent was by the S slopes from Puerto Olla, with a high camp on the Glacier Frances at 1600m, and finishing on the W ridge. Grade n/k but fairly easy PD/AD.
RONCAGLI CLIMB A very difficult ascent, finally ascended by the NW ridge on the 5th attempt in 1990. (AAJ 1991)

OTHER PEAKS   From the high camp for Bove **Pico Frances 2150m** can also be climbed without much difficulty, grade about F/PD.

BEST MAP   The best map is Andes Patagonicos sheet 2, 1:250,000 pub. 1975 'Iwa to Yuki' no. 45.

Cordillera Darwin from the S

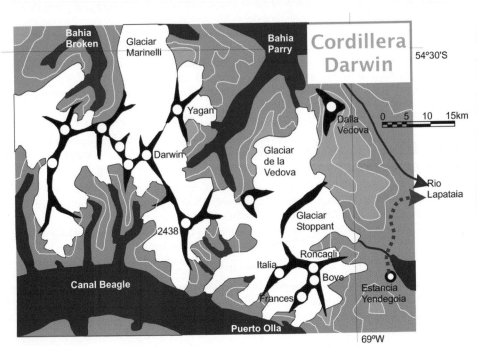

THE 6000M PEAKS OF THE ANDES

The criterion used to select this list is a prominence height (re-ascent from the lowest col) of at least 400m from any higher peak. This figure was chosen for several reasons. Without greatly affecting the overall number of peaks, any larger prominence requirement eliminates some of the most notable summits in the Andes such as Jirishanca and Illampu while any lesser prominence criterion includes minor summits such as both the N and E peaks of Coropuna and up to five more Pissis peaks. This criterion is also very close to the 7% rule as used in other studies of mountain topography.

By this criterion there are now exactly one hundred major 6000m peaks in the Andes. Of the total of 100 peaks, 15 are in the Cordillera Blanca of Peru and 39 are in the Puna de Atacama area of Chile and Argentina.

The peaks are arranged below in groups of ten. The grades given are for the easiest ascent route. An asterisk by the date of first ascent denotes a peak known to have had a Pre-Columbian ascent, or on which significant ruins have been found high up. Dates in brackets indicate a disputed or uncertain first ascent.

All heights are in metres

THE SECOND HIGHEST PEAK

Perhaps the biggest debate in recent years was whether Ojos del Salado or Pissis is the second highest summit in the Andes. Ojos del Salado has been nominated here after careful studying of the SRTM elevation data. While not producing exact summit heights for any mountains this data appears to confirm Pissis as being under 6800m and Ojos well over 6850m, with an accuracy of just +/-10m. The heights given here are also supported by handheld GPS readings from several sources, including the author.

PEAK	HEIGHT		AREA	COUNTRY	1st ASCENT
Aconcagua	6959	F	High Andes	Argentina	1897*
Ojos del Salado	6893	F/PD	Puna	Argentina-Chile	1937
Pissis	6793	F	Puna	Argentina	1937
Bonete	6759	F	Puna	Argentina	1970
Tres Cruces Sur	6748	F	Puna	Argentina-Chile	1937
Huascarán Sur	6746	PD/AD	Cord. Blanca	Peru	1932
Llullaillaco	6739	F	Puna	Argentina-Chile	1952*
Mercedario	6710	F	High Andes	Argentina	1934*
Cazadero (W.Penck)	6670	F	Puna	Argentina	1970
Huascarán Norte	6655	PD/AD	Cord. Blanca	Peru	1932 (1908)
Tres Cruces Cent.	6629	F	Puna	Chile	1937
Incahuasi	6621	F	Puna	Argentina-Chile	1913*
Yerupajá	6617	ED/ED+	Cord. Huayhuash	Peru	1950
Tupungato	6570	F	High Andes	Argentina-Chile	1897
Sajama	6550	PD	Cord. Occidental	Bolivia	1939
Muerto	6510	F	Puna	Argentina-Chile	1950
Nacimiento	6460	F	Puna	Argentina	1937
Antofalla	6440	F	Puna	Argentina	1954* (1904)
Illimani	6438	PD/AD	Cord. Real	Bolivia	1898
Veladero	6436	F	Puna	Argentina	1986

PEAK	HEIGHT		AREA	COUNTRY	1st ASCENT
Ancohuma	6427	PD/AD	Cord. Real	Bolivia	1919
Coropuna	6425	F	Cord. Occidental	Peru	1911*
Condor	6414	F	Puna	Argentina	1996
Huandoy	6395	AD/D	Cord. Blanca	Peru	1932
Ramada	6384	F	High Andes	Argentina	1934
Cachi (Libertador)	6380	F	Puna	Argentina	1950* (1904)
Ausangate	6372	AD	Cord. Vilcanota	Peru	1953
Huantsan	6369	TD	Cord. Blanca	Peru	1952
Illampu	6368	AD/D	Cord. Real	Bolivia	1928
Chopicalqui	6345	AD	Cord. Blanca	Peru	1932
Siula Grande	6344	D/TD	Cord. Huayhuash	Peru	1936
Parinacota	6342	F	Cord. Occidental	Chile-Bolivia	1928
Ampato	6288	F	Cord. Occidental	Peru	1966*
Pomerape	6282	F	Cord. Occidental	Chile-Bolivia	(1946)
Reclus	6275	F	Puna	Argentina	1986*
Salcantay	6271	AD	Cord. Vilcabamba	Peru	1952
Chimborazo	6270	PD/AD	Ecuador	Ecuador	1880
Majadita	6266	F	High Andes	Argentina	1996
Santa Cruz	6241	TD	Cord. Blanca	Peru	1948
Tres Quebradas	6239	F	Puna	Argentina-Chile	1937
Pular	6233	F	Puna	Chile	1960*
Chinchey	6222	AD	Cord. Blanca	Peru	1939
Olivares	6216	F	High Andes	Argentina-Chile	1964
Solo	6205	F	Puna	Argentina-Chile	(1949)
Palcaraju	c.6200	D	Cord. Blanca	Peru	1939
Copa	6188	PD/AD	Cord. Blanca	Peru	1932
Quemado	6184	F	Puna	Argentina	1979
Mesa	6180	F/PD	High Andes	Argentina	1934*
Aucanquilcha	6176	F	Cord. Occidental	Chile	1935*
Toro	6168	F	High Andes	Argentina-Chile	1964*
Ranrapalca	6162	D	Cord. Blanca	Peru	1939
Tortolas	6160	F	High Andes	Argentina-Chile	1924*
Hualcan	6160	AD/D	Cord. Blanca	Peru	1939
Pucaranra	6156	AD/D	Cord. Blanca	Peru	1948
Alto	6148	n/k	High Andes	Argentina-Chile	1944
Ermitaño	6146	F	Puna	Chile	1967
San Pedro	6145	F	Cord. Occidental	Chile	1903
Queva	6140	F	Puna	Argentina	1954*
Sierra Nevada	6140	F	Puna	Argentina-Chile	2000
Colangüil	6122	F	High Andes	Argentina	before 2010

PEAK	HEIGHT		AREA	COUNTRY	1st ASCENT
Medusa	6120	F	Puna	Argentina-Chile	1986
Vallecitos	6120	F	Puna	Argentina	1999
Barrancas Blancas	6119	F	Puna	Chile	prior to 2002
Callangate	6110	n/k	Cord. Vilcanota	Peru	1957
San Pablo	6110	F	Cord. Occidental	Chile	1910
Chacraraju	6108	ED+	Cord. Blanca	Peru	1956
Marmolejo	6108	F	High Andes	Argentina-Chile	1928
Jatunriti (Chumpe)	6106	AD	Cord. Vilcanota	Peru	1955
Chearoco	6104	AD/D	Cord. Real	Bolivia	1928
Famatina (Belgrano)	6097	F	Puna	Argentina	1895
Aracar	6095	F	Puna	Argentina	1958*
Jirishanca	6094	TD/ED	Cord. Huayhuash	Peru	1957
Jatunhuma	6093	AD/D	Cord. Vilcanota	Peru	1957
Solimana	6093	PD	Cord. Occidental	Peru	1970
Huayna Potosi	6088	PD	Cord. Real	Bolivia	1919
Colorados	6080	F	Puna	Argentina-Chile	1999*
Chachacomani	6074	AD	Cord. Real	Bolivia	1947
Baboso	6070	F	Puna	Argentina	2000
Negro (Pabellón)	6070	n/k	High Andes	Argentina	1969
Plomo	6070	F	High Andes	Argentina-Chile	1910
Vicuñas	6067	F	Puna	Chile	1969
Guallatiri	6063	F	Cord. Occidental	Chile	1926
Fraile	6061	F	Puna	Argentina-Chile	1956
Chachani	6057	F	Cord. Occidental	Peru	1889*
Acotango	6052	F	Cord. Occidental	Chile-Bolivia	1965
Copiapó	6052	F	Puna	Chile	1937*
Socompa	6051	F	Puna	Argentina-Chile	1905*
Yayamari	6049	PD/AD	Cord. Vilcanota	Peru	1957
Pili	6046	F	Puna	Chile	1939*
Pucajirca	6046	TD	Cord. Blanca	Peru	1961
Chaupi Orco	6044	PD	Cord. Apolobamba	Bolivia-Peru	1958
Quitaraju	6036	AD/D	Cord. Blanca	Peru	1936
Palpana	6035	F	Cord. Occidental	Chile	1977*
Peña Blanca	6030	F	Puna	Chile	1956*
San Francisco	6030	F	Puna	Argentina-Chile	1913
Salin	6029	F	Puna	Argentina-Chile	1960*
V. del Viento	6028	F	Puna	Argentina	1937
Hualca Hualca	6025	PD	Cord. Occidental	Peru	prior to 1990's*
Laguna Blanca	6012	F	Puna	Argentina	2006
Uturunco	6008	F	Cord. Lipez	Bolivia	1955

SOME NOTES

The Shuttle radar Topography Mission (SRTM) data have now shown that the peak of Cienaga in the Argentine Puna near Salta and the peak of Los Gemelos 6196m do not have sufficient prominence to count as major peaks.

The following peaks, all sometimes quoted higher than 6000m, have been omitted from the list after extensive studies of digital elevation data and the relevant IGM maps. Artesonraju 5999m, Pumasillo 5991m, Plata 5955m, Contrahierbas 5954m, Juncal 5953m, Caraz c.5980m, Tocllaraju c.5980m Ameghino c.5940m, Lasunayoc 5936m, Polacos c.5935m, Chañi c.5930m, Nuevo Mundo 5929m, Galan 5912m, Pilar de los Pailas (Luracatao) 5946m and Acay 5770m. Sabancaya 5976m is now possibly higher than 6000m as it was erupting for many years in the 1990's!!

SOURCES FOR HEIGHTS USED IN THIS GUIDEBOOK

In areas of South America the heights of some peaks are still subject to debate. The main areas for which no accurate survey maps exist are the Mercedario to Tupungato area of Argentina and the Patagonian ice-caps area. The heights given in this book are thought to be generally the most accurate figures taken from the following sources. In some areas Neate's book was used when no survey height was available. In other cases heights have been estimated from the SRTM or other digital elevation data.

Venezuela and Colombia - Neate, confirmed where possible in Colombia by CIGM 1:100,000

Ecuador - IGM 1:50,000 newest sheet available.

Peru - IGM 1:100,000 sheets. The AV surveys of the Cordillera Blanca have been used where the PIGM sheets do not give a height. There appears to be some doubt about many heights in the Cordillera Blanca, with digital elevation data indicating lower altitudes for some famous peaks. In this edition, the peaks of Tocllaraju and Caraz have been demoted below 6000m for this reason.

Artesonraju from Pisco,
Cordillera Blanca

Bolivia - The AV maps for the Illimani and Ancohuma areas, otherwise BIGM 1:50,000 sheets or 1:250,000 sheets.

Argentina - mostly Argentine IGM 1:250,000 sheets. SRTM data was used to confirm or change many heights in poorly surveyed areas. Extensive use has been made of digital elevation data in the Puna de Atacama area.

Chile and **Chile/Bolivia** and **Chile/Argentina** border peaks - Chilean IGM 1:50,000 or 1:250,000 sheets, which are generally much more modern than Argentine surveys in this area.

Patagonia - ChIGM 1:250,000 sheets where possible, Andes Patagonicos sheets for peaks on the icecaps, Fitzroy area and Cord. Darwin with some more important heights confirmed (where possible) by the SRTM data.

THE NEXT TEN

The ten peaks which don't quite make the 6000m peak list are
Artesonraju 5999, Alto Toroni 5995, Polleras 5993, Pumasillo 5991, Capurata 5990, El Muertito 5988, Tacora 5980, Sabancaya 5976, Sairecabur 5971m, Caquella 5960m.

THE TEN MOST PROMINENT PEAKS

The ten peaks of any height in the Andes in order of prominence are listed here. Thanks to Jonathan de Ferranti and Eberhard Jurgalski for help with this list and many other height questions. See www.peaklist.org for further information and prominence lists.

Mountain Name, Location, Height (Prominence)
Aconcagua, Argentina, 6959 (6959). Pico Bolivar, Colombia, c.5710 (5519). Chimborazo, Ecuador, 6270 (4125). Pico Bolivar, Venezuela, 4979 (3955). San Valentin, Chilean Patagonia, 4058 (3696). Ojos del Salado, Chile-Argentina 6893 (3688). Ritacuba Blanco, Colombia, 5410 (3645). Mercedario, Argentina, 6710 (3343). San Lorenzo, Chile-Argentina, 3706 (3319). Volcan Lautaro, Chilean Patagonia, 3580 (3302).

SUBSIDIARY 6000m PEAKS

The following is a list of the 34 6000m+ peaks with over or around 200m of prominence but without the 400m prominence needed to qualify for status as a major peak. The two peaks on this list which come closest to the 400m prominence required for full status are Cienaga and Tres Cruces Norte. The SRTM data show that the whole Pissis and Bonete area has been mapped c.100m too high by the AIGM - hence the disparity between some names (such as Bonete 6144) and heights.
The peaks are listed in order of height above sea level, not prominence.
The use of ???? indicates the peak is known for sure to have been climbed, just the date is unknown.

PEAK	HEIGHT		AREA	COUNTRY	PROM. (m)	F.A.
Pissis - Upame (II)	6790	F	Puna	Argentina	300	1986
Cazadero - Huayco	6475	F	Puna	Argentina	200	2012
Pissis - Hombro	6430	F	Puna	Argentina	220	1994
Illimani Norte	6403	D	Cord. Real	Bolivia	240	1950
Antofalla Central	6385	F	Puna	Argentina	345	-
Coropuna Casulla	6377	F	Cord. Occidental	Peru	350	1952
Nacimiento Sur	6345	F	Puna	Argentina	210	????
Huandoy Oeste	6342	AD/D	Cord Blanca	Peru	230	1954
Antofalla Oeste	6326	F	Puna	Argentina	265	-
Coropuna Este	6305	F	Cord. Occidental	Peru	365	1911
Bonete Norte I (Pioneros)	6240	F	Puna	Argentina	300	2011
V. Olmedo	6214	F	Puna	Argentina	225	19??
Bonete Norte II (Sargento Federico)	6185	F	Puna	Argentina	210	2011
Bonete 6144	6175	F	Puna	Argentina	200	1997
Huandoy Sur	6160	D	Cord. Blanca	Peru	350	1955
Pissis - Media	6140	F	Puna	Argentina	300	1992
Los Gemelos Norte	6135	F	Puna	Argentina	350	1986
Los Gemelos Sur	6130	F	Puna	Argentina	260	-
Pissis - Altar	6130	F	Puna	Argentina	280	2010
Sarapo	6127	TD	Cord. Huayhuash	Peru	210	1954

Cumbre del Laudo	6122	F	Puna	Argentina	290	????
Yerupaja Chico	6121	n/k	Cord. Huayhuash	Peru	370	1957
Alma Negra	6120	F	High Andes	Argentina	250	1934
Colquecruz	6102	n/k	Cord Vilcanota	Peru	340	1953
Bonete 6092	6092	F	Puna	Argentina	200	2011
Medusa N.E	6065	F	Puna	Argentina	220	2010
Cienaga	6050	n/k	Puna	Argentina	390	????
Pucajirca Oeste	6039	n/k	Cord. Blanca	Peru	360	1936
Tres Cruces Norte	6030	F	Puna	Chile	390	1973
Piuquenes	6019	PD	High Andes	Argentina-Chile	281	1933
Rasac	6017	AD/D	Cord. Huayhuash	Peru	320	1936
Pucajirca Central	6014	n/k	Cord. Blanca	Peru	340	1961
Callangate N.	6000	n/k	Cord. Vilcanota	Peru	280-310	1957
Marmolejo NE	6000	n/k	High Andes	Chile	240	-

The peak of El Muertito is about 5990-6005m high and has about 395-410m prominence. It is currently classed as a major 400m+ prominence peak but with its survey height of 5988m. It may well need to be re-classified in future.

A full list of 5000m peaks in the Andes can be found on the 'Andes' website at www.andes.org.uk, where there are also lists of less prominent 6000m peaks.

Camp at Aguas Calientes, Argentine Puna

A BRIEF MOUNTAINEERING HISTORY OF THE ANDES

1400-1500's   Repeated ascents of many peaks by native Indians at the time of the Inca Empire including Llullaillaco 6739m, Licancabur 5930m, El Toro 6168m, Queva 6140m and almost certainly Aconcagua 6959m.

1736   Chimborazo surveyed at 6270m and believed to be the world's highest mountain for the next 70 years. An early attempt to climb the peak fails.

1802   Humboldt reaches 5600-5800m on Chimborazo.

1872   Reiss and Escobar ascend Cotopaxi 5897m.

1880   Whymper and the Carrels ascend Chimborazo 6270m and Antisana and Cayambe in Ecuador.

1897   The Swiss guide Zurbriggen ascends Aconcagua 6959m alone. Vines and Zurbriggen also make the first ascent of Tupungato 6570m.

1898   Conway makes the first ascent of Illimani 6438m in Bolivia.

1908   Disputed first ascent of Huascaran Norte 6655m, by Annie Peck, an American schoolmistress.

1930's   German and Austrian expeditions led by Schneider ascend many peaks in the Peruvian Cordilleras Blanca and Huayhuash, including Huascaran Sur 6746m, Huandoy and Chopicalqui in 1932 and Siula Grande in 1936.

1937   Polish expedition makes first ascent of Ojos del Salado 6893m, Pissis 6793m and many other 6000m Puna peaks.

1939   First ascents of Colombia's two highest peaks, Colon and Bolivar by American and German expeditions.

1950's   Extensive exploration and many first ascents in the Peruvian Andes including Yerupaja in 1950 (American), Salcantay in 1952 (Anglo-French), Ausangate in 1953 (German) and Pumasillo in 1957 (British).

1952   Evidence of previous ascent found near the summit of Llullaillaco by the first modern ascensionists. Ruins, figurines, pottery etc. were later found.

1952   Terray and Magnone make the first ascent of Chalten (Fitzroy).

1954   French Andean Expedition climbs the huge and dangerous south face of Aconcagua.

1954   A mummy is discovered on Co. del Plomo near Santiago, the first complete mummy found and the first such discovery to be widely reported.

1956   A French expedition makes the first ascent of Chacraraju, the last and most difficult of the 6000m peaks in the Cordillera Blanca.

1957   First ascent of Alpamayo, by a German expedition.

1959   Maestri and Egger make an unproven first ascent of Cerro Torre

1963   First ascent of Altar, Ecuador's most difficult peak.

1963   British expedition make the first ascent of the Torre Central del Paine.

1966   Paragot route climbed, the first on the 1500m N face of Huascaran Norte.

1974   Italians make the first verified and ethical ascent of Cerro Torre

1970's-1980's   Climbing in the Cord. Blanca moves to exploration of the harder ice faces e.g. the S faces of Chacraraju and Ocshapalca and the needle of Cayesh.

1990's   Hard rock routes in Peru and Patagonia, the enchainment of the Torres del Paine in one day. Extreme routes on Peruvian south faces.

2000's   The last unclimbed, or at least unrecorded major 6000m peaks are climbed, almost all of them in the Puna de Atacama of Argentina.

2012   The first free ascent of the SE ridge of Co. Torre, bolts removed on descent.

THE INCA MOUNTAINEERS

Perhaps the most fascinating aspect of the history of climbing in the Andes is the large number of ascents which were made around the time of the Inca Empire (c. 1400-1530). The highest peak they are known for sure to have climbed is Llullaillaco 6739m on the Chile-Argentina border. A few metres below the summit are a couple of primitive huts, a sight which must have surprised the climbers who thought they were making the first ascent in 1952. Archaeological expeditions have since unearthed pieces of cloth, pottery, wooden utensils and statuettes and even the corpses of sacrifice victims on this and many other peaks. The indications are that considerable periods of time were spent at the summits of many of the peaks in the Cordillera Occidental, Cordillera Lipez, Puna de Atacama and High Andes.

The first discoveries were actually made as long ago as 1884 on Licancabur but it was only in the 1950's and 1960's when the first mummified corpses were discovered (on the summits of del Plomo 5424m and El Toro 6168m) that interest in high altitude archaeology really began. Burial sites have now been found on many peaks of over 5500m. Unfortunately many of these have been disturbed by grave robbers.

Ascents seem to have been made mostly for religious purposes, though it is possible that the peaks were also used as watchtowers or signal stations. Mountains are still worshipped in many parts of the Andes. Though there are many reasons for this mountain worship the main reason appears to be as a source of water and fertility. Johan Reinhard states that peaks with crater lakes (such as Licancabur) appear to have been especially important.

Human sacrifice victims have been found on many peaks including El Toro (neck wound), Pichu Pichu, Aconcagua (strangled) and most recently Ampato (sharp blow to skull) and Llullaillaco. The bodies, which are nearly always of adolescents or young adults, are commonly referred to as mummies. Technically however they are not mummies, because they have only been preserved accidentally by

Summit ruins, Volcan Llullaillaco

the very cold and dry conditions prevalent. Most remains have been dated to around the time of the Inca Empire, though the ascents were not necessarily all made by the Inca's themselves.

It now seems probable that the Incas or their subjects climbed Aconcagua. In 1947 a guanaco was discovered at over 6800m on the ridge connecting the N and S summits. More recently, in 1985 a grave containing a sacrifice victim was discovered lower on the mountain. Technically the summit is no more difficult than Llullaillaco. Due to the difficulties of investigation and the lack of written records from the time of the Incas (who had no written language) we may never know for sure.

There are still discoveries to be made. In September 2013 the author climbed Alto Toroni, a 5995m peak on the Chile-Bolivia border. On the summit was a large Inca platform, which has never been reported before. The peak has no recorded first ascent date, so the author's may have been the first modern ascent, although there was a cairn which looked to be of modern construction.

For more information on this fascinating subject see various books and articles by Johan Reinhard.

The platform on the summit of Alto Toroni, Cordillera Occidental

Machu Picchu

ABBREVIATIONS

ENGLISH ABBREVIATIONS

a.k.a	Also known as
N/K, n/k	Not known
N	North
S	South
E	East
W	West
R.	River
4x4	4 wheel drive
PT	Public Transport
L	Left
R	Right
LH	Left-hand
RH	Right-hand
LHS	Left-hand side
RHS	Right-hand side
d.	days
h.	hours
b.c.	base camp
SRTM	Shuttle Radar Topography Mission

SPANISH ABBREVIATIONS

Ref.	Refugio	Hut, refuge
Ao.	Arroyo	Stream
Co.	Cerro	Hill, mountain
No.	Nevado	Snow peak
Po.	Pico	Peak
Sra.	Sierra	Range
V.	Volcan	Volcano
Lag.	Lago	Lake
R.	Rio	River
Q.	Quebrada	Valley, ravine
Hac.	Hacienda	Farm
Ag.	Aguja	Needle
Cord.	Cordillera	Range
Est.	Estero	Stream
Mte.	Monte	Mount
Gl.	Glaciar	Glacier

IGM Instituto Geografico Militar, the national map and survey offices:- AIGM=Argentina, BIGM=Bolivia, CIGM=Colombia, ChIGM=Chile, EIGM=Ecuador, PIGM=Peru, VIGM=Venezuela.

Ojos del Salado and Medusa from El Arenal, Argentine Puna

GEOGRAPHICAL TERMS AND MOUNTAIN FEATURES

Most of the geographical terms are translated from Spanish (Español) but a few words are of native Indian language origin. The two main native languages are Q = Quechua and A = Aymará. Words relating more specifically to climbing and mountaineering appear in the mountaineers vocabulary on the following pages.

ESPAÑOL (Q,A)	ENGLISH	DEUTSCH	FRANCAIS	ITALIANO
abra	pass	pass, joch	col	passo
acequia	aqueduct, ditch	graben	rigole	fosso
aguja	needle, spire	spitze, turm	gendarme, pointe	campanile
altiplano	high plateau	plateau	plateau	altipiano
arista	ridge (arete)	grat, kamm	arete	cresta, spigolo
arroyo	stream	bach, strom	ruisseau	corso
baños	thermals		source chaude	
bofedal	bog, marsh	sumpf, moor	marecage	pantano
brecha	notch		breche	
caida de hielo	icefall	eisbruch	barre de seracs	seraccata
camino	path	fussweg	sentier	sentiero
campo de hielo	ice-cap	eiskappe	calotte glaciere	calotta di ghiacciaio
campo de nieve	snowfield	firnfield	neve	nevaio
canaleta	gully, couloir	rinne	couloir	canalone
cara	face	wand	face	parete
carreterra	road	strasse, weg	route	strada, via
casa	house	haus	maison	casa
cascada	waterfall	wasserfall	cascade	cascata
cerro	hill, mountain	hugel	colline	collina
circo	cirque	kar, mulde	cirque	circo
cocha, cota (Q, A)	loch, lake	see, lagune	lac	lago
collado	col	joch, scharte	col	forcella
contrafuerte	buttress	rippe, pfeiler	pilier	contrafforte
cordillera	mountain range	gebirge	chaine	
cresta	ridge	grat, kamm	arete	cresta, spigolo
cuerno	horn	horn	corne	corno
cueva	cave	hohle, grube	caverne	caverna
cumbre	summit	gipfel	sommet	cima
embalse, represa	reservoir		reservoir	
espolon	spur, buttress	rippe	eperon	spigolo
estancia	large farm / village	bauernhof	ferme grande	fattoria grande
este	east	ost	est	est
estero	stream	bach, strom	ruisseau	corso
filo	ridge	grat	arete	spigolo, cresta
glaciar	glacier	gletscher	glacier	ghiacciaio
glaciar suspendido	hanging glacier	hange-gletscher	glacier suspendu	ghiacciaio pensile
grande	big	gross	grand	grande
grieta	crevasse	gletscherspalte	crevasse	crepaccio

ESPAÑOL (Q, A)	ENGLISH	DEUTSCH	FRANCAIS	ITALIANO
hacienda	ranch, farm	ranch	ranch	ranch
hierba	pasture	weideland	pature	pastura
hito	cairn, marker post	steinhugel	cairn	
huanca (Q)	rock		rocher	
janka, hanca (Q)	snow peak	schneeberg	montagne de neige	montagna nevoso
jirka (Q)	mountain	berg	montagne	montagna
lago, laguna	lake, lagoon	see, lagune	lac, lagune	lago, laguna
lengua de glaciar	glacier tongue	gletscher-zunge	langue de glacier	lingua di ghiacciaio
loma	hill	hugel	colline	collina
macizo	massif	gebirgsmassiv	massif	massiccio
mina	mine	bergwerk	mine	mina
monte	mount		mont	monte
morrena	moraine	morane	moraine	morena
muro	wall	mauer	mur	muro
nevado	snow mountain	schneeberg	montagne de neige	montagna nevosa
norte	north	nord	nord	nord
nudo	group	gruppe	groupe	gruppo
occidental	western	westlich	occidentale	occidentale
oeste	west	west	ouest	ovest
oriental	eastern	ostlich	oriental	orientale
pampa (Q)	plateau, plain	ebene	plaine	altipiano
paramo	moorland	heidemoor	lande	landa
pared	wall	wand	paroi	parete
paso	pass	joch	defile	
pata (Q)	summit, hill	gipfel, hugel	sommet, colline	cima, collina
penitente	natural snow spikes	eiszapfen		
peña	boulder		rocher	masso
pico	peak	gipfel, berg	pic, cime	cima
piedra	rock, stone	stein	pierre	pietra
pirca	cairn	steinmann	cairn	ometto
portachuelo	pass	pass, sattel	col	passo
portezuelo	pass	pass, sattel	col	passo
puca (Q)	red	rot	rouge	rosso
puente	bridge	brucke	pont	ponte
puna (Q)	high plateau	plateau	plateau	plateau
punta	point	punkt	point	punta
quebrada	ravine-gorge-river	klamm	ravin, riviere	burrone
rampa	ramp			
razo, raju (Q)	snow summit	schneeberg	montagne de niege	montagna nevosa
refugio	mountain hut	hutte	cabane, refuge	rifugio
rio	river	fluss	riviere	fiume
riti (Q)	snow peak	schneeberg	montagne de niege	montagna nevosa
salar	salt lake		sale	
salto	waterfall	wasserfall	chute d'eau	cascata
sendero	path	fussweg	sentier	sentiero
sierra	mountain range	gebirge	chaine	

ESPAÑOL (Q,A)	ENGLISH	DEUTSCH	FRANCAIS	ITALIANO
sur	south	sud	sud	sud
talud	scree, talus	schutt, geroll	eboulis	ghiaione
termas	thermal springs			
torre	tower	spitze	aiguille	campanile
urcu, orco (Q)	mountain	berg	montagne	montagna
valle	valley	tal	vallee	valle
yana (Q)	black	schwarz	noir	nero
yurac (Q)	white	weiss	blanc	bianco

Trekking south of Yayamari, Cordillera Vilcanota

MOUNTAINEERS VOCABULARY

This vocabulary is intended primarily to help foreign language users of this guidebook to translate English language climbing terms into their own language. See also the geographical glossary above for more general mountain terms such as ridge, buttress, etc. In alphabetical order in English.

ENGLISH	ESPAÑOL	DEUTSCH	FRANCAIS	ITALIANO
above	arriba	über	au dessus de	sopra
abseil, rappel	rappel	abseilung	rappel	corda doppia
altitude	altura	hohe	altitude	altitudine
altitude sickness	soroche	hohenkrankheit	mal d'altitude	
anchor	ancla		attache	
ascender, jumar		steigbugel	jumar	jumar
ascent	subida, escalada	beisteigung	ascension	salita
avalanche	avalancha, alud	lawine	avalanche	valanga
belay (point)	reunion	sicherung	relais	assicurazione
bergschrund	rimaya	bergschrund	rimaye	creppacia terminale
to belay	asegurar	sichern	assurer	fissare?
below	abajo	unten	au dessous de	sotto
bivouac, bivvy	vivac	biwak	bivouac	bivacco
boots	botas, zapatos	stiefel	bottes	scarpone
(to) bypass	desviar	umgehen	devier	deviare
camp (base)	campamento base	basis lager	camp de base	campo base
carabiner, krab	mosqueton	karabiner	mousqueton	moschettone
climb	escalada	klettern	escalade	scalata
(to) climb	escalar	ansteigen	grimper	scalare
cornice	cornisa	wachte	corniche	cornice
crack	fisura, grieta		fissure	
crampons	grampones	steigeisen	crampons	rampone
(to) cross	atravesar	kreuzen	traverser	attraversare
degrees	grados		degres	grados
(to) descend	bajar	absteigen	descendre	scendere
dihedral	diedro	verschneidung	diedre	diedro
distant	lejos		lointain	distante
donkey	burro	esel	ane	asino
exposed	aereo, expuesto	ausgesetzt	expose	esposto
fluted	acanalado	rillenformig	flute	scannelato
frozen	congelado	gefroren	gele	gelata
(to) go down	bajar	absteigen	descendre	scendere
(to) go up s	ubir	hinaufgehen	monter	montare
guide	guia	bergfuhrer	guide	guida
hail	pedrisco	hagel	grele	grandine
hammer	martillo	hammer	marteau	martello
ice	hielo	eis	glace	ghiaccio
ice-axe	piolet	eispickel	piolet	piccoza
ice-screw	tornillo	eisschraube	piton a vis	vite de ghiaccio
kerosene, paraffin	kerosina	kerosin, paraffin	kerosene, petrole	cherosene
(to) leave	dejar	lassen	laisser	lasciare
ledge	cornisa, terraza	leiste	corniche	

ENGLISH	ESPAÑOL	DEUTSCH	FRANCAIS	ITALIANO
left	izquierda	linke	gauche	sinistro
lightning	relampago	blitz	eclairs	fulmine
loose	suelto, flojo	locker	friable	friabile
map	mapa	landkarte	carte	carta, mappa
mist, fog	neblina	nebel	brouillard	nebbia
mountaineer	andinista, alpinista	bergsteiger	alpiniste	alpinista
muleteer	arriero	eseltreiber	muletier	carrettiere
near	cerca	naher	pres de	vicino
normal route	ruta normal		voie normale	via normale
nut	empotrador	nute	picoin	dado
overhang	desplome	überhang	surplomb	strapiombo
pack animals	asemillas, pilcheros	saumtiere	animaux a charge	animale de soma
path	sendero	fussweg	sentier	sentiero
petrol, gas (Am.)	gasolina	benzin	essence	benzina
(to) pick up	recoger		ramasser	prendere
pick-up truck	camioneta		camionette	
pitch	largo	seillange	longueur	passaggio
piton, peg	clavo	hacken	piton	chiodo
porter	porteador	trager	porteur	portatore
rain	lluvia	regen	pluie	pioggia
right	derecha	recht	droit	destro
rock (substance)	roca	fels	rocher	roccia
rockfall	caida de piedra	steinschlag	chute de rochers	frana
roof	techo	dach	toit	tetto
rope	cuerda, soga	seil	corde	corda
(to) rope up	encordar	anseilen	s'encorder	mettersi in cordata
route	via, ruta	führe, weg	voie, route	via
rucksack	mochilla	rucksack	sac a dos	zaino
serac	serac	serac	serac	seracco
slab	placa	steinplatte	plaque, dalle	
sleeping bag	esleeping	schlafsack	sac de couchage	sacco a pelo
sleet	agua nieve	graupeln	pluie gelante	nevischio
snow	nieve	schnee	neige	neve
(to) snow	nevar	schneien	neiger	nevicare
snowshoes	raquetas	schneeschuh	raquettes	racchetta
solid, firm	solido	fest	solide	roccia solida
steep	pendiente	steilhang	raide, abrupt	ripido
stone	piedra	stein	pierre	pietra
storm	tormenta,tempuesto	sturm	tempete	temporale
stove	cocina, estufa		rechaud	cucina, stufa
straight on	derecho		tout droit	dirito
tent	carpa	zelt	tente	tenda
traverse	travesia	traverse	traverse	traversa
(to) traverse	atravesar	überschreitung	traverser	traversare
verglas		glasseis	verglas	vetrato
via	por la via	über	via	via
(to) walk	caminar	gehen	marcher	camminare
white gas	bencina blanca			
wind	viento	wind	vent	vento
wind slab	placa de nieve	scnee brett	plaque a vent	sventata

SELECTED BIBLIOGRAPHY

OOP = Out of Print

MOUNTAINEERING TECHNIQUE
The ABC's of Avalanche Safety, **Ferguson & La Chapelle,** The Mountaineers 2003.
The Complete Guide to Climbing and Mountaineering, **Hill,** David & Charles 2008.
Mountaineering - The Essential Skills, **Richardson,** A & C Black 2008.
Glacier Travel and Crevasse Rescue, **Selters,** The Mountaineers 1999.

MOUNTAINEERING MEDICINE
Altitude Illness: Prevention & Treatment, **Bezruchka,** The Mountaineers 2005.
Pocket First Aid and Wilderness Medicine, **Duff & Gormly,** Cicerone 2012.
Medicine for Mountaineering, **Wilkerson et al,** The Mountaineers 2010.

ENGLISH LANGUAGE CLIMBING & SKIING GUIDEBOOKS
Bolivia - A climbing guide, **Brain,** The Mountaineers 1999.
Ecuador - A climbing guide, **Brain,** Cordee 2000.
Climbs & Treks in the Cordillera Huayhuash of Peru, **Frimer,** Elaho 2005.
Patagonia Vertical: Chalten Massif, **Garibotti & Pietron,** Sidarta 2012.
Classic Climbs of the Cordillera Blanca, **Johnson,** Peaks & Places 2009.
Guide to the Worlds Mountains, **Kelsey,** Kelsey Publishing 2001.
Handbook of Ski Mountaineering in the Andes, **Lena,** Belupress 2007.
Mountaineering in the Andes, **Neate,** Expedition Advisory Centre, RGS 1994 (OOP).
Yuraq Janka, **Ricker,** American Alpine Club 1977.
Aconcagua, **Secor,** The Mountaineers 1999.

SPANISH LANGUAGE CLIMBING GUIDEBOOKS
+6500, **Dario Bracali,** Ediciones Vertical, 2012
Patagonia : Terra magica para Viajeros y Alpinistas, **Buscaini & Metzetlin,** Desnivel 2000
Guia de escaladas - Cerro Catedral, **Garibotti,** 1998.
Montañas de Luz, **Geras,** 2003.
Los Andes de Bolivia, **Mesili,** Ediciones Prod. Cima 2002.
Alta Colombia, **von Rothkirch,** Villegas 1998.
Ecuador - Montañas del Sol, **Serrano & Rojas & Landazuri,** Ediciones Campo Abierto 1994.
Escaladas en los Andes - Guia de la Cordillera Blanca, **Tome,** Ediciones Desnivel 2000.

ENGLISH LANGUAGE TREKKING GUIDEBOOKS
The Andes - A Trekking Guide, **Biggar & Biggar,** Andes 2001 (OOP) .
Trekking in Bolivia, **Brain, North & Stoddart,** Cordee 1997.
Peru's Cordillera Blanca & Huayhuash: the Hiking and Biking Guide, **Pike & Pike,** Trailblazer 2015.
Trekking in the Patagonian Andes, **various,** Lonely Planet 2009.
Trekking in the Central Andes, **various,** Lonely Planet 2003.

GENERAL TRAVEL GUIDEBOOKS
South American Handbook, **Footprint Handbooks.** A detailed travel guide to the whole continent, revised annually. Individual country travel guidebooks are now available as well.
Lonely Planet Publications - Good general guidebooks to the individual countries of South

America, revised every few years.
Insight guides - General guides to all the countries, less informative but with better pictures!

ANDEAN HISTORY & CULTURE
Ancient Kingdoms of Peru, **Davies**, Penguin 1997.
Conquest of the Incas, **Hemming**, Harvest Books 2003.
The Ice Maiden, **Reinhard,** National Geographic 2005.
Penguin History of Latin America, **Williamson**, Penguin Books 1993.

CLASSIC MOUNTAINEERING LITERATURE
The Conquest of Fitzroy, **Azema,** 1957 (OOP).
The Puma's Claw, **Clark,** Hutchinson, 1959 (OOP).
The Highest Andes, **FitzGerald**, Methuen, 1899 (OOP). Remarkably, ascents of Aconcagua are much the same now as they were 120 years ago, except nobody consumes raw onions and red wine on summit day anymore!
White Mountain and Tawny Plain, **Hauser,** Allen and Unwin, 1959 (OOP).
Ascent of Alpamayo, **Kogan & Leininger**, 1954 (OOP).
A search for the Apex of America, **Peck**, 1911 (OOP).
Aconcagua - South Face, **Poulet & Ferlet**, Constable, 1956 (OOP). An incredible story.
The Butcher: The ascent of Yerupajá, **Sack**, Rinehart and Co, 1952 (OOP). Possibly the funniest climbing book ever?
Touching the Void, **Simpson**, Cape, 1988 and numerous paperback editions, e.g. Vintage 2003.
Travels amongst the Great Andes of the Equator, **Whymper**, John Murray, 1891 or Charles Knight 1972 (OOP).

Climbing Volcan Llaima

JOURNAL REFERENCES

The following references are a selection of the most useful recent articles on mountaineering in major areas of the Andes published in English language journals. For a comprehensive list of older references to peaks throughout the Andes see Neates book 'Mountaineering in the Andes', RGS 1994. The Alpine Journal and American Alpine Journal throughout the 90's and 00's both have extensive expedition reports, particularly useful for researching big rock routes in Patagonia. 'Mountan INFO', published in magazines from 1969 until January 2005 is also a very useful source of information on new routes and other developments. Since 2005 Mountain INFO has been published online at www.climbmagazine.com/mountain-info

ALPINE JOURNAL (AJ) (UK)

1990/91	Santa Marta
1992/93	Paine
1998	Cerro Torre
2004	Cord. Darwin
2006	Quimsa Cruz, Co. Torre N face.
2008	Cord. Carabaya
2010/11	Central Andes of Chile

AMERICAN ALPINE JOURNAL (AAJ) (USA)

1994	Torres del Paine
1998	Cord. Blanca
1999	Central Tower of Paine
2001	Patagonia
2004	Jirishanca, Co. Torre controversy
2008	Torre Traverse, Siula Chico
2012	Co. Torre

ONLINE INFORMATION
The following are further sources of information available online.

EDITED
www.climbmagazine.com/mountain-info
www.andes.org.uk
www.peaklist.org
www.saeexplorers.org

USER SUBMITTED
www.summitpost.org
www.andeshandbook.org

Skiing Volcan Lanin

ACKNOWLEDGEMENTS

This fourth edition could not have been compiled without the help of many people. In particular the following deserve special mention:-
Guillermo Almaraz, Mar del Plata, Argentina information
Damian Aurelio Vargas, Huaraz, Peru, information
Linda Biggar, Castle Douglas, Scotland, help and advice, both on and off the mountains
Edward Earl, Washington, USA, peak heights
Jonathan de Ferranti, Fife, Scotland, peak heights
Javier Herrera, Quito, Ecuador, information and photos
Eberhard Jurgalski, Germany, peak heights, SRTM data
Maximo Kausch, Brazil & Argentina, digital elevation data & information
Paul-Erik Mondron, Brussels, Belgium, information
Neil and Harriet Pike, Oxfordshire, England, lots and lots of information, GPS co-ordinates
Jonson Reynoso, Fiambala, Argentina, information and logistics
Ruth Reynoso, Fiambala, Argentina, accommodation, information and logistics
David Roberts, Llwyngwril, Wales, information and ski coaching!
Ingo Roger, Chemnitz, Germany, information
Marcelo Scanu, Buenos Aires, Argentina, information
Carlos Zarate, Arequipa, Peru, information

In addition the following people helped extensively with the first three editions: -
Derek Bearhop, Denns Belillo, Cathy Biggar, Gordon Biggar, Bob Black, Dario Bracali, Evelio Echevarria, Marcos Frischknecht, Peter and Dominic Goodwin, Alexander von Gotz,, Gregory Horne, Ian Humberstone, Jeremy Ivens, Sergio Llano, Rick Marchant, Alfredo Martinez, Rodrigo Mujica, Andy and Luz Owen, Ric Potter, Steffen Salzmann, Richard Scroop, Matthew Shaw, Ken Vickers, Pere Vilarasau, Juan Villaroel

High camp at 6000m, Tres Cruces

PHOTO CREDITS

All 400 odd photos are by the author and are © John Biggar or © John Biggar Collection, except for the following 31:-

Damian Aurelio Vargas, Huaraz, Peru — Santa Cruz x2
Derek Bearhop, Edinburgh, Scotland — Salcantay NE ridge
David Breen, St. Helens, England — Queva
Dennis Chevallay, Punta Arenas, Chile — Bove, Sarmiento
Dave Galloway, Scotland — Cashan Este
Javier Herrera, Quito, Ecuador — Sangay, Carihuairazo
Ian Humberstone, Aberdeen, Scotland — Condoriri, Illampu, Ancohuma
Sergio Llano, Bogota, Colombia — Reina, Colon
Rick Marchant, Chamonix, France — Quitaraju, Alpamayo SW face
Jon Morgan, Chamonix, France — Palcaraju
Marcelo Parada, Buenos Aires, Argentina — Chañi
David Roberts, Llwyngwril, Wales — Author x2, Janco Huyo, Ice-cap in intro, Peligro
Ingo Roger, Chemnitz, Germany — Jallacate, Pariacaca, Ticlla, Tunshu
Steffen Salzmann, Erfurt, Germany — Condor
Mattt Shaw, Edinburgh, Scotland — Pequeño Alpamayo
Pere Vilarasau, Barcelona, Spain — Compressor route
Juan Villaroel, La Paz, Bolivia — Acamani

Traditional cardigans and alpaca fibre ropes on the Jatunriti glacier, Cordillera Vilcanota

GEOGRAPHICAL INDEX

All minor words such as del, el, los and all mountain descriptions such as Pico, Monte, Cerro etc. are ignored.
The Spanish alphabet is used. **K** and **W** aren't normally used - see **C/Q** or **HU** respectively. The letter **Ñ** follows the letter **N**.
All entries are mountain peaks unless stated.
Abbreviations used for other entries are -
Cord.   Cordillera
T   town or city

Where there are two or more identical names the country or region is indicated as follows -
Ar   Argentina
Bo   Bolivia
Co   Colombia
Ch   Chile
Ec   Ecuador
Pa   Patagonia
Pe   Peru
Ve   Venezuela

Ausangate

Chichicapac

Chimborazo

Coropuna

Janco Huyo

Moreno

Parinacota

Pisco

Ruiz

San Pedro

Toco

Villarrica

Tronador

Yerupaja